Chinese Economic Development

The book provides a meticulous analysis of economic development and concomitant problems in China since the late 1970s and advances suggestions on further economic modernisation and transition from both theoretical and practical angles.

Based on theories from development economics and solid empirical studies, the authors, two renowned Chinese economists, provide a perceptive analysis of the Chinese development model in the post-Mao era. They shed light on questions that have perplexed many: How can China sustain the rapid growth of the past 40 years? Is there a unique "China path" to economic progress? They argue compellingly that China's development model has to switch from a manufacturing-driven one to a brand-new approach, centring on scientific and technical innovation and the integration of its existing economic structure into an increasingly complex global economy. Such transformation will help overcome the "middle-income trap" while addressing other institutional and economic challenges.

The book will appeal to students, scholars and policymakers interested in the Chinese and global economies, as well as transnational studies in the post-COVID-19 world. General readers willing to obtain a grasp of Chinese economic development from the insider's perspective will also find it useful.

Yinxing Hong is Senior Professor in Humanities and Social Sciences at Nanjing University (China). He specialises in macroeconomic theory and policy.

Ninghua Sun is Professor of Economics at Nanjing University. He specialises in macroeconomics, as well as financial derivatives and financial risk management.

Xiao-huang Yin is Professor at Occidental College (USA) and Dean of the School of Foreign Studies at Northwestern Polytechnic University (China).

Xiaojia Zang is Associate Professor and Associate Dean of the School of Foreign Studies at Northwestern Polytechnic University.

China Perspectives

The *China Perspectives* series focuses on translating and publishing works by leading Chinese scholars, writing about both global topics and China-related themes. It covers Humanities & Social Sciences, Education, Media and Psychology, as well as many interdisciplinary themes.

This is the first time any of these books have been published in English for international readers. The series aims to put forward a Chinese perspective, give insights into cutting-edge academic thinking in China, and inspire researchers globally.

To submit proposals, please contact the Taylor & Francis Publisher for China Publishing Programme, Lian Sun (Lian.Sun@informa.com)
Titles in economics partly include:

Chinese Economic Development
Theories, Practices and Trends
Yinxing Hong and Ninghua Sun

Economics of the Pandemic
Weathering the Storm and Restoring Growth
Edited by Cai Fang

The Economics of Government Regulation
Fundamentals and Application in China
Wang Junhao

Macroeconomic Policy and Steady Growth in China
2020 Dancing with Black Swan
Edited by Zhang Xiaojing

Political and Economic Analysis of State-Owned Enterprise Reform
Huiming Zhang

Political Economy in the Evolution of China's Urban-Rural Economic Relations
Fan Gao

For more information, please visit https://www.routledge.com/China-Perspectives/book-series/CPH

Chinese Economic Development

Theories, Practices and Trends

Yinxing Hong and Ninghua Sun

Translated by Xiao-huang Yin and Xiaojia Zang

Routledge
Taylor & Francis Group

LONDON AND NEW YORK

Translation of this book is funded by the Humanities Grants of Northwestern Polytechnic University in China and the Faculty Enrichment Grants of Occidental College in the United States.

First published 2021
by Routledge
2 Park Square, Milton Park, Abingdon, Oxon OX14 4RN

and by Routledge
605 Third Avenue, New York, NY 10158

Routledge is an imprint of the Taylor & Francis Group, an informa business

© 2021 Yinxing Hong and Ninghua Sun

Translated by Xiao-huang Yin and Xiaojia Zang
The right of Yinxing Hong and Ninghua Sun to be identified as authors of this work has been asserted by them in accordance with sections 77 and 78 of the Copyright, Designs and Patents Act 1988.

English Version by permission of Nanjing University Press.

British Library Cataloguing-in-Publication Data
A catalogue record for this book is available from the British Library

Library of Congress Cataloging-in-Publication Data
Names: Hong, Yinxing, 1950- author. | Sun, Ninghua, author. | Yin, Xiao-huang, translator. | Zang, Xiaojia, 1980- translator.
Title: Chinese economic development : theories, practices and trends / Yinxing Hong and Ninghua Sun ; translated by Xiao-huang Yin and Xiaojia Zang.
Description: Abingdon, Oxon ; New York, NY : Routledge, 2021. | Series: China perspectives | Includes bibliographical references and index. |
Identifiers: LCCN 2020056756 (print) | LCCN 2020056757 (ebook) | ISBN 9781032016252 (hbk) | ISBN 9781032019123 (pbk) | ISBN 9781003179382 (ebook)
Subjects: LCSH: Economic development--China--History. | China--Economic conditions. | China--Economic policy.
Classification: LCC HC427 .H624 2021 (print) | LCC HC427 (ebook) | DDC 338.951--dc23
LC record available at https://lccn.loc.gov/2020056756
LC ebook record available at https://lccn.loc.gov/2020056757

ISBN: 978-1-032-01625-2 (hbk)
ISBN: 978-1-032-01912-3 (pbk)
ISBN: 978-1-003-17938-2 (ebk)

Typeset in Times New Roman
by SPi Global, India

Contents

Figures

Tables

Preface (Translators)

This carefully crafted monograph written by two renowned Chinese economists is a groundbreaking and thought-provoking study that explains the mainstream scholarship guiding China's search for a viable alternative route to economic development during the post-Mao era. Their argument, illuminated by comparative theoretical analyses and based on meticulously detailed empirical research, sheds light on a question that has perplexed many: Is there a "China path" to economic growth? Further, can China sustain its momentum and avoid "the middle-income trap" that has blocked the progress of many developing nations throughout the world?

The China case is unique because worldwide, there is simply no parallel model for China to reference in its economic reform and opening to the outside world. Under the circumstances of the world's largest population, the entrenched urban-rural dual household registration system in place since the 1950s and enormous gaps between wealthy coastal regions and the poverty-stricken interior, any economic development has to be "made in China." This is the case whether one is talking about how to satisfy the growing popular demand in China for a more affluent life, transform China's manufacturing-driven development model into one based on scientific and technological innovations, shift its growth to one of sustainable and intensive development featuring a sound ecosystem and further integrate its economic structure into the global community. By applying theories of development economics to Chinese realities, the authors demonstrate convincingly and compellingly, from a non-Western perspective, that China's rapid rise as an economic giant and its remarkable achievement in the global marketplace represents a distinctively different path of growth and an alternative model of development in modern history. Transcending the dichotomy of state socialism and prototypical capitalism, it is imbued with Chinese characteristics and rooted in Chinese realities. In this sense, China's rapid economic growth during the past 40 years is truly unparalleled and original, and its experience has significantly enriched the research and teaching of development economics.

There is no need to further elaborate on the profound implications of the authors' study for the global economy. Representing prevailing academic thought in China on development economics, it functions as a lens through which readers can better understand China's progress, as well as broader issues: What makes China's development a model? What is "socialism with Chinese characteristics"?

Can China redefine its niche in the changing global market and maintain its status as the world's second-largest economy? And, finally, what lessons can we draw from China's continuing progress in the post-COVID-19 world?

What we do want to emphasise, however, is that this volume provides a much-needed opportunity and insider's analysis for scholars and policymakers in the multilateral world to reach more nuanced understanding of critical issues in the English-language discourse on China's economic development. In reality, how to tell the "Chinese story" to overseas audiences today has become a challenge. This book provides some answers.

There are a few issues related to the English translation that need to be explained. As the principal translators and editors of the English version of the book, we have tried to avoid discrepancies and misunderstandings that sometimes appear in translation. To be faithful to the authors' meaning, however, we have kept the English translation of special terms in Chinese, such as "socialism with Chinese characteristics," throughout the volume, although doing so *may* sound redundant to native speakers. Translating Chinese usages such as *sannong* [三农] or "Three Rural Issues," we have placed *pinyin* in the notes with explanations of their Chinese originals. Readers who have questions about our translation can thus find answers themselves. Unless otherwise noted, we have traced the sources of English works quoted in the Chinese text and cited the titles of the English originals in the notes and bibliography. Because of limited space, the bibliography is highly selective, with the criteria for inclusion being those works that are particularly relevant to the authors' writing in Chinese.

Acknowledgements (Translators)

As the principal translators and editors of the volume, we are grateful to our friends, colleagues and students who have generously contributed their expertise to the successful completion of this significant yet rather challenging translation project. Translators of various drafts of the monograph include Li Limin (Chapter 2), Pu Dongmei (Chapter 3), Wang Xuelian (Chapter 4), Xiaojia Zang (Chapter 5), Kang Tan (Chapter 6), Gao Jie (Chapter 7), Wei Yanlong (Chapter 8), Li Yali (Chapter 9), Chen Jie (Chapter 10) and Wang Xiaotao (Chapter 11). Professors James Tranquada, Adrienne Tien, David Prestel, Peter Koehn and Zhang Liwei helped proofread the drafts at various points. Li Yali, Cui Xiaobin, Pan Yifei and Zhang Wentao provided assistance in editing the manuscript in one way or another. The Humanities Grants of Northwestern Polytechnic University in China and the Faculty Enrichment Grants of Occidental College in the United States generously provided support for the translation project.

Despite our best efforts, errors and inconsistencies undoubtedly remain in the English translation. We take full responsibility, but we hope that they are few and will not detract from this vitally important and timely study of the theories, practices and trends of China's development in today's increasingly complex global economy.

Xiao-huang Yin and **Xiaojia Zang** (Translators)
Los Angeles and Xi'an

Foreword
Development economics in China: A fresh start in a changed historical context

The theory of economic development in China set forth in this book is in essence about development economics at the middle-income development stage in China.

Development economics dates back to the 1940s when newly independent countries, which used to be colonies or semi-colonies, were faced with challenges of economic development. These countries were categorised as developing nations. Alleviating poverty, establishing an independent industrial system and achieving economic take-off became missions of these nations after they entered their growth phase. Development economics came into being in such a historical context. Taking the economic growth of developing nations as its research object, the field thus aims to investigate patterns of economic progress in nations developed from their backward stage to that of a modern state.

Development economics has emerged as an independent academic discipline because the existing economics, including both microeconomics and macroeconomics, was established fundamentally upon the mature and normative economics of developed countries. Its main purpose is to solve the problem of allocation of resources. Such a theory of economics, however, cannot encompass the special problems of developing nations, which have their unique features and development patterns. The most pressing problem these nations faced was the very issue of economic development. Thus there arises development economics, which takes developing nations as its research object and development as an end.

There were two categories of developing nations arising after World War II. One was socialist nations based on the state-ownership system, while the other was newly independent nation-states practicing capitalism. Although they had different social systems and chose different development paths, these nations experienced similar underdeveloped conditions and shared the same development problems. In terms of development, these nations had many common problems, lessons, goals and patterns. Therefore, it was possible to establish some general theories that could be applicable to many different categories of developing nations. When the development reality in these nations is considered, one observes that many developing nations have experienced the low-income development stage. In this sense, the economic development status of these nations can be divided into the low-income stage and the middle-income stage. Accordingly, while related, the development theories of the two stages must differ from each other.

Development economics at its inception took the low-income-stage developing nations as its object. It was, therefore, an economic theory that aimed to alleviate poverty, promote development and achieve economic take-off. The PRC was born out of a semi-colonial and semi-feudal society. Development economics thus played a positive guiding role in China's low-income development stage. For example, China took such measures as supporting its economic growth with a high accumulation and high investment rate, transferring the rural-surplus labour force to the industrial workforce and urbanising and industrialising the nation.

The reform and opening policy institutionalised in 1978 in China liberated the productive forces and promoted the process of industrialisation, urbanisation and economic internationalisation. After 30 years of reform and opening, China's economic development achieved a historic new high level. This is shown conspicuously in the following four aspects.

- First, the total gross domestic product (GDP) of China reached 40.1 trillion RMB (US$ 5.88 trillion) in 2010, making China the second-largest economy in the world. It is expected that China will overtake the United States to become the world's largest economy in the foreseeable future. Meanwhile, China has become the largest exporting, as well as the largest foreign exchange reserve country, and the second-largest manufacturing powerhouse. These changes indicate that China's economic status in the world has been enhanced significantly.
- Second, China's per capita GDP reached 35,083 RMB (5,432 US$) in 2011, reflecting China's successful transition from a low-income nation to a middle-income country. In 2016, the per capita GDP in China increased to 55,412 RMB (8,866 US$), matching the level of an upper-middle-income country. This economic-capacity expansion heralds China's entry into a new historical stage.
- Third, the agricultural sector percentage in China's GDP has dropped to 10.1%, while its industrial sector has risen to 46.8%. Furthermore, the urbanisation rate in China has grown to more than 50%. This means that China has been successfully transformed from an agricultural nation to an industrial one, thus earning the label "an emerging industrialised country."
- Fourth, China's economy experienced an annual average growth rate of 9.9% over the past 30 years. In recent years, China has taken the initiative to slow down its economic growth in order to push forward structural adjustment and shift its development paradigm. Sustaining a medium-to-high growth rate around 7% will become the new normal of China's economic development.

For this reason, countries throughout the world have focussed attention on the economic miracle created by China. In response to global interest, an important mission for Chinese development economics is to investigate, summarise and theorise the Chinese way of economic development.

"The middle-income trap" is the gravest risk China faces after entering the stage of a middle-income country. Latin American nations long ago entered the rank of middle-income countries. However, they have failed to ascend into the category of high-income countries with a threshold of US$ 10,000 per capita income. This situation is attributed to two factors. One centres on their development mode. Although these nations have reached the level of middle-income countries, they still follow the development pattern of low-income nations. The other is about the ultimate end of development. After entering the middle-income stage, the public's demand to share the fruits of development in these nations has not been satisfied, especially with regard to equitable distribution, medical care and education. Social contradictions brought by these inequities have further hindered economic development in these nations. Therefore, it is urgent to establish an innovative theory of development economics that can help to guide middle-income nations to rise into the ranks of developed countries.

At the new development stage, the mission of the times for development economics is highlighted in three aspects. First, and most importantly, the field should provide theoretical direction for the countries that are at the starting point of the middle-income stage to stride across the "middle-income trap." Second, it should provide theoretical direction for transforming the economic development mode. The development mode adopted when a country is moving from its low-income stage to the middle-income stage cannot be used again after it has entered into the middle-income level. Third, it should provide theoretical direction for the promotion of modernisation in developing nations, thereby facilitating their entrance into the high-income development stage and revealing the processes and regularities of how they develop from middle-income countries to high-income ones. Therefore, development economics, which guides economic development, changes from the economics of getting out of poverty to that of enriching the public, from guiding economic take-off to guiding modernisation.

Based on the previous analysis, the Chinese economic development theory illustrated in this book involves two objectives. One is to demonstrate the path of development that China has gone through from a low-income to a middle-income country – that is, the theoretical explanation of China's road to economic development. The other, which is more important, is to investigate and elaborate on the road of economic development (modernisation) after the starting point of the middle-income development stage. This requires the innovation of development theory, which, in turn, needs the guidance of a new development view.

One's view of development shapes development theory. To clarify the key point of theoretical innovation of economic development at the present stage, therefore, it is necessary to review the evolution of the economic development view of several generations of economists around the world.

The first generation of development economists originated in the early 1940s and 1950s. The theory of that period is represented by the Harrod-Domar model. This generation's view of development can be summarised as follows: (1) The focus of development is on the rapid growth of GDP. (2) The proposed model of economic growth specifies that economic growth is a function of labour, capital, land and other factors of production. It attaches great importance to the input effect of productive factors on economic growth. In particular, it takes the accumulation of capital as a necessary condition of development. (3) It emphasises the role of industrialisation in development. This development theory had a great influence on the formation of the development view in many developing nations.

The second generation of development economists generally was active from the late 1950s to the 1990s. Economists such as Simon Kuznets (1901–1985), Robert Solow (1924–), Theodore Schultz (1902–1998) and Paul Romer (1955–), who studied modern economic growth, and the Club of Rome's doomsday-scenario report are the representatives. The development view of this period can be summarised as follows: (1) realising that growth is not development, thus shifting the concern from the amount of economic growth to its long-term growth capability (especially the effect of structural adjustment and optimisation); (2) changing from merely pursuing the input of material factors to attaching emphasis on the roles of technological progress, institutional factors and human capital; (3) shifting from merely pursuing economic growth to paying attention to the environment and sustainable development; and (4) changing focus from industrialisation to agricultural and rural development.

A new generation of development economists from the beginning of the 21st century is represented by Amartya Sen, Joseph E. Stiglitz and the World Bank. Their concepts of development can be summarised as follows: (1) The growth rate is as important as growth quality. The sources and modes of growth affect the outcomes of development. (2) Development means growth and reform. Reform not only aims to increase the GDP but also involves other goals. (3) High-quality growth requires more broad development standards, such as poverty reduction, equitable distribution, environmental protection, empowerment of people and development of freedom. Successful development policies must, therefore, not only determine how real income can grow at a faster rate; they also must determine how real income can be used to achieve other values that are reflected in "development." (4) Freedom is the primary purpose of development and an indispensable and important means to promote development.

Gerald M. Meier summarises the evolution of thinking on development in the chart shown in Figure 0.1.

Drawing on the evolution of the aforementioned development thinking, we need to refine theories of development economics based on learning about China shaking off poverty and becoming a moderately prosperous society. Theories dealing with the development stage of low-income countries explain the past development process, but they cannot fully guide today's economic development. Moving from the development stage of a low-income country to that of a middle-income country should also be kept in mind.

The scientific outlook on development formulated during China's long-term economic development mainly includes the following aspects: (1) development as the top priority; (2) human orientation as the core position; (3) comprehensive, coordinated and sustainable development as the basic requirements; and (4) overall planning as the fundamental method of scientific development. After entering the new era, President Xi Jinping made a new generalisation regarding the scientific outlook on development, which states, "Development must be scientific and follow the law of economic development. It must be sustainable and follow the law of nature and must be inclusive and follow the law of society."[1] On this basis,

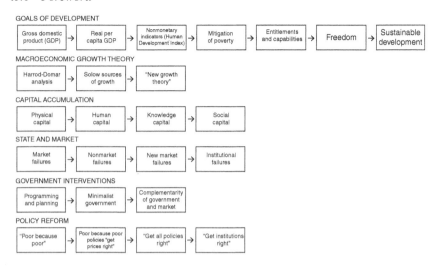

GOALS OF DEVELOPMENT

| Gross domestic product (GDP) | → | Real per capita GDP | → | Nonmonetary indicators (Human Development Index) | → | Mitigation of poverty | → | Entitlements and capabilities | → | Freedom | → | Sustainable development |

MACROECONOMIC GROWTH THEORY

| Harrod-Domar analysis | → | Solow sources of growth | → | "New growth theory" |

CAPITAL ACCUMULATION

| Physical capital | → | Human capital | → | Knowledge capital | → | Social capital |

STATE AND MARKET

| Market failures | → | Nonmarket failures | → | New market failures | → | Institutional failures |

GOVERNMENT INTERVENTIONS

| Programming and planning | → | Minimalist government | → | Complementarity of government and market |

POLICY REFORM

| "Poor because poor" | → | Poor because poor policies "get prices right" | → | "Get all policies right" | → | "Get institutions right" |

Figure 0.1 The Evolution of Development Thought

the new concepts of development should be characterised as innovative, coordinated, green and open. The new concepts of development are based on the basic conditions of the primary stage of socialism. It sums up China's development practice and learns from foreign development experience, meets the new development requirements and reflects the modernisation and localisation of economic development theory.

Although China is entering the stage of middle-income countries, we must be clear that our country is still in the primary stage of socialism. Development is the paramount principle, and economic construction is still the central task, but the idea of economic development needs to be changed. Four aspects should capture our attention: first, to shift to improving people's income levels from pursuing GDP growth and achieving the transition from "powerful country" to "prosperous people"; second, to guarantee that people fairly and reasonably share the fruits of economic growth by protecting and improving people's livelihoods and promoting social fairness and justice; third, to construct a resource-saving and environment-friendly mode of production and consumption and to achieve harmony between man and nature; and fourth, to think creatively like a world economic power, reposition the direction of China's economic development, grasp the new position of the global economic division of labour and realise the new advantages of participation in international economic cooperation and competition. Obviously, the basic path of implementing the scientific outlook on development is to change the mode of economic development and push society onto a path towards civilised development featuring "growing production, an affluent lifestyle and a sound ecosystem."

According to the evolution of the aforementioned development concepts and ideas, the basic framework of economic development theory to be elaborated on in this book is based on the reality of China. It mainly includes the following content:

1   **Studies on the goals of economic development.** According to the economic development goals set in view of the scientific outlook and the new concepts of development, development should first be human-oriented. Studies will focus on how to realise this development path. In the past, China as a developing nation implemented the catch-up strategy, which was mainly to realise GDP growth and depend on investment as the main pulling force. Now economic development tends to be human-oriented and aims to improve the income level of the people rather than only to realise GDP growth. It takes both doubling the total GDP and doubling per capita income into consideration, reflecting the transition of China's economic development goals from "powerful country" to "prosperous people." Studies must also focus on how to avoid the "middle-income trap" after entering the development stage of a middle-income country in terms of per capita income. Its basic path is to transform from efficiency growth to fairness growth. Correspondingly, income distribution policy selection needs to be transferred from efficiency first to fairness and justice first. The basic requirements are that fairness and efficiency should be coped with successfully during the initial distribution and redistribution processes, and fairness should be emphasised more during the redistribution process. Finally, it is time to shift our focus from allowing a portion of the people to get rich first to enriching the majority. Seeking people's affluence can be said to be the primary goal of economic development. In the modern stage, enriching the people not only involves accelerating economic growth but also relates to how to distribute the achievements of economic growth in order to enable people to secure the maximum benefits and the greatest social welfare. In terms of the relationship between enriching some people first and then enriching the majority, some people were allowed to get rich to promote GDP growth institutionally in the past. Now it is also necessary to enrich the majority to achieve the goal of sharing the growth achievements fairly and reasonably.

2   **Studies on the economic development pattern.** Growth is not necessarily equal to development. Economic development theory needs a scientific explanation of economic development patterns and the goals and path of economic transformation. Existing development theory illustrates the connection of the transition from an extensive economic growth pattern to an intensive economic growth pattern. Transformations of the economic development pattern of the present stage are wider in range and more demanding than the transformations of economic growth models. Here we are interested in four major transformations. (1) *Changing the engines of economic development from outside to inside.* Domestic demand expansion becomes a strategic point for economic growth. Correspondingly, studies will focus on the conditions and paths to position the overall scale of the domestic market in the forefront of the world. (2) *Changing the economic growth model.* Economic growth should not be driven exclusively by investment but by

consumption, investment and export simultaneously. It is necessary to high-light the driving role of consumption and, at the same time, pay attention to the mutual coordination of consumption, investment and exports in stimulating economic growth. (3) *Adjusting economic structure as the main direction of changing the economic development pattern.* We need to study the transformation and upgrading of the three industries according to our current development stage. Studies will be carried out on establishing the modern industrial system characterised by structural optimisation, advanced technology, clean and safe production, high value added and adequacy in absorbing labour to meet the requirements of industrial restructuring and upgrading. (4) *Changing economy development from reliance mainly on material production to innovation.* Studies will be conducted on how to lead rather than follow the trend of global science and technology.

3   **Studies on innovation-driven development strategy.** Scientific and technological progress and innovation are an important engine for accelerating the transformation of the economic development mode. For a long time, as a developing nation, China has been lagging behind the developed countries in science, technology and economy. The prevailing concept of technological innovation was to implement follow-up strategies and develop high-tech and new industries through learning and adapting from developed countries. Now China has become the world's second-largest economic entity; the world is flat, and globalisation of economy and science and technology are mutually synergistic. The prevailing conception of technological innovation needs to be changed from follow-up to lead; standing at the same starting line with the developed countries, China will leap forward in some key areas and occupy the high ground of the world's technology and industry in some areas. To achieve this goal, the main research should be divided into four aspects. First, it is significant to study concrete forms of innovation-driven development. Innovation-driven development not only improves efficiency; more importantly, it achieves a new combination of visible elements with invisible elements. It is the first application and spread of science and technology achievements in production and commerce, as well as the creation of new growth factors. Second, it is important to study the blueprint for technological innovation under the new technological revolution. In the past, the source of technological innovation lay in enterprises. Now it turns to breakthroughs in science and technology from universities and academies. Third, it is valuable to study the construction of national innovation systems, paying particular attention to the transformation of scientific and technological achievements. Such studies will focus on the cohesive integration of knowledge innovation, technological innovation and the incentive system of innovation institutions, and they will emphasise collaborative innovation research as well. Finally, it is necessary to study the decisive role of intellectual capital and workforce capital in innovation-driven and modern economic growth.

4   **Studies on dual economic structure.** As a large developing nation, an outstanding problem related to the economic imbalance China faces at present

is the uneven and uncoordinated development between various regions and disparities between urban and rural areas. Therefore, the modernisation of China's dual economic structure is the fundamental issue. The related research subjects in coordinated development thus should be mainly concerned with the following four aspects. The first one is the modernisation of the "Three Rural Issues."[2] China has made headway in the "Three Rural Issues" through interrelated problem solving, meaning that agricultural issues have been solved by the non-agriculture sector, rural issues have been dealt with by urbanisation and farmers' issues have been solved by granting them urban resident status. As the problem of the "Three Rural Issues" in China enters a new phase, China will confront it through promoting agricultural modernisation, enriching farmers, improving agricultural labour productivity and added value and revitalising socialism in the countryside. The second subject is to investigate urbanisation. China has created a pattern of urbanisation that differs from that in developed countries (i.e. local transfer).[3] Now what confronts urbanisation with its new components is the propelling of the integration of urban and rural areas, as well as urging farmers to urbanise so that they are able to enjoy equal rights along with townspeople. The third subject is to investigate simultaneous development between industrialisation, agricultural modernisation, urbanisation and challenges of the Information Age. The fourth subject calls for the investigation of imbalanced and uncoordinated regional development. Through an integrated policy dealing with the latter issue, we should reshape China's economic geography and achieve the much-sought resolution of the disparities.

5   **Studies on sustainable development.** Global climate change, energy and resource security, as well as food security, have gradually become an important global concern. It is a field that demands investigation. Sustainable development, which involves population, resources and environment, aims to address the problem that the development of the contemporary world will not harm the material benefits of future generations. Developed countries have put forward the requirement of sustainable development after the completion of their own industrialisation. In comparison, China's sustainable development has been put forward even as its industrialisation remains in progress, while some regions are still in the initial stages of development. It is thus not only urgent but also complicated to investigate sustainable development and establish a resource-conserving and environment-friendly society because, in many ways, China's development as a whole is incomplete. Of concern are issues of production, as well as types of development, such as spatial patterns, industrial structures, modes of production and the living of daily life. Another related issue needing investigation is the natural maximum capacity China can bear for economic growth. We should establish a mutually constraining system involving population, employment, resources, ecology, the environment and economic growth. Severely scarce natural resources of land have set a boundary for economic growth. The natural environment must be treated with reverence that begins with the study of energy-saving technology and the implementation at every turn of (carbon)

emission reduction. At the same time, we must also improve the use and efficiency of environmental resources, capitalising on them through various investments and maximum use of the latest technological advances. The third issue is to investigate ecology and civilisation, leading as much as possible to the harmonious coexistence between people and nature. To build a beautiful China and achieve the sustainable development of the Chinese nation, the ideal of an eco-conscious civilisation founded on respecting, conforming to and protecting nature should be integrated into all aspects and periods of economic, political, cultural and social development. The fourth issue is to develop models to evaluate systems of sustainable development. Resources consumption, environmental damage and ecological benefits should all be parts of an evaluation system of our economic and social development. The ultimate purpose of establishing an objective system for assessment, which includes rewards and penalties, is to increase the likelihood of a harmonious union between the demands of modern civilisation as it develops and the maintaining of a healthy ecology in China.

6 **Studies on socialist modernisation.** China's modernisation includes three developmental stages: (1) a comprehensive well-off society, (2) the basic realisation of modernisation and (3) the full realisation of modernisation. In accordance with the timing of modernisation, China will likely achieve a comprehensive well-off society in most sectors by 2020 and will enter the stage of modernisation. It will then make China a truly modern nation by the middle of the 21st century. Thus the task of theoretical research on economic development is to offer an updated modernisation theory. In comparison with the phase of a comprehensive well-off society, modernisation cannot be measured by a simple quantitative evaluation index but rather by a qualitative upgrade, which involves the setting of modernisation objectives and a frame of reference, as well as the determination of an evaluation index that measures basic modernisation. In addition, the road and choice that can propel modernisation are also crucial. The goal and connotative meaning of modernisation need to be studied first. The goal is to catch up with developed countries. This is a process and a standard to obtain. Modernisation refers to the economy entering the modern growth phase. It encompasses the modernisation of science and technology, economic structure and human daily life. The second issue on modernisation is the development of an evaluation index and analysis of the interconnection between a comprehensive well-off society and basic modernisation. They will play a guiding role in establishing a comprehensive well-off society in an all-round way, along with the state of modernisation. Socialist modernisation requires the modernisation in the thinking of a substantial number of the population, essentially achieving all-round development of the consciousness of the members of this modernised society. It is obvious that specific quality requirements on modernisation will play a guiding role in the quality of economic growth. Therefore, it is an important topic to research through an investigation of the level of growth reached by developed countries. It is also significant to explore the quality indicators of socialist modernisation in the context of China's development reality.

7 **Studies on the opening-type economy.** Similar to economic reform, opening to the outside world is a powerful driving force to speed up the transformation of China's economic development. In today's world, the economic development of any country has an international foundation. Thanks to economic globalisation and China's entry into the WTO, China's economic opening level has been greatly improved. China now has become the second-largest economy in the world, while the economic growth of Europe, the United States and other developed countries have slowed down. Consequently, there have emerged anti-globalisation reactions. In light of this new background, China should adopt a more comprehensive opening policy. It should combine the improvement of its economic growth with the enhancement of its international competitiveness and full participation in global economic governance. To this end, opening theory and policy need to be adjusted in the following aspects. First, it is important to lay equal emphases on import and export, absorbing foreign capital and investing overseas instead of merely an export-oriented opening strategy and absorption of foreign capital. The "two equal emphases"[4] should become a new research project in terms of the creation of an opening strategy. Second, with respect to participating in the global economy, China needs to turn its comparative advantages from resources and labour towards an emphasis on competitive advantage. The new opening strategy for China must shift to increasing opening efficiency by relying on and fostering international competitive advantages. Third, the emphasis on bringing in foreign elements should be shifted from material factors to innovation factors. The important characteristics of modern economic growth are the drawing on worldwide technology and information reserves. In the previous phase, China mainly acquired foreign advanced technology through bringing in foreign capital. China now has implemented the strategy of innovation-driven development, which means to stand at the same starting line of innovation with developed countries. At this special moment, the focus should veer to bringing in advanced foreign technologies, especially high-end innovative talents, in conjunction with international cooperation that emphasises scientific and technological cooperation. Fourth, we should combine the strategy of opening to the outside world with enlarging domestic demand. This means expanding China's domestic demand market to the outside world. As for the scope of foreign investment access, it can expand from the manufacturing industry to finance, education, culture and health care. Finally, as a global economic powerhouse, China should institutionalise this opening economy with a complete opening on all financial fronts: foreign trade, foreign exchange, marketisation of the RMB exchange rate, free convertibility of RMB, free capital flow, etc.

8 **Studies on economic reform.** The basis and impetus of development lie in a system. Economic development is always carried out under certain systems. For this reason, a system is always the decisive factor for promoting economic development. It is particularly important for developing nations to have an effective development system. In reality, each developing nation comes to the top in economic development by means of the market's effective

allocation of resources and the government's strong management. By allowing its economic policy to be more greatly determined by the market, China has laid a solid foundation in increasing resource allocation efficiency. In developing nations, however, promoting economic development needs the help of government. Development issues concerned with market and government include the following four aspects. First, we need to find an effective way to combine market forces with government policies to promote development. For example, adjustment of the economic structure relies on selection by the market and survival of the fittest. It also relies on transforming and upgrading the industrial structure, which will be guided by national industry policies. Another example is the drive for innovation. It needs both market orientation and pressure from market competition. In addition, the government needs to set up major scientific programmes to establish systems and mechanisms that can stimulate innovation. Second, we need to improve the national macroeconomic control system by determining the bottom line of economic growth, such as unemployment rate and income growth rates, and the ceiling of the inflation rate within the reasonable boundary of the macroeconomy. The government should implement a neutral monetary money policy without constantly launching monetary policies for stimulating or tightening and leave more room for the market to run its course. Third, we need to improve the management systems on specific projects. Developing nations have numerous development projects covering many different fields. Some of these major development projects, such as the construction of social infrastructure projects, projects related to people's livelihoods and those aimed at participating in international competition, are carried out by individual enterprises. However, they need the government's planning and management. To ensure that limited development funds can achieve maximum benefits, the government needs to look for scientific and rational methods for project evaluation.

Developing nations are in the process of development. Likewise, development economics is growing. It is a great and challenging mission to establish socialist development economics. For the moment, research on socialist development economics has just started; many development issues with socialist characteristics need to be explored further, and the system of socialist development economics needs to be carefully studied. The authors of this book are committed to contributing to the establishment of socialist development economics that is suitable for China's unique reality. Although socialist development economics in China has begun quite late, it has a higher starting point. We can use theoretical materials of Western development economics as reference. Further, we have the scientific theory of Marxist economics as guidance. Along with the experiences and lessons of China's development and its evolving course as background, we are confident that we can quickly establish and perfect socialist development economics with Chinese characteristics in a relatively short period.

Notes

1 Xi Jinping, "Speech at the Meeting of the Political Bureau of the Communist Party of China," Beijing, 29 July 2013.
2 The term "Three Rural Issues" [*sannong*] can also be translated as "Three Nong Issues." The term "three nong" in Chinese means "nongye" (agriculture/rural economy), "nongcun" (countryside/rural areas) and "nongmin" (farmers/rural residents).
3 Here the term "local transfer" refers to transferring the rural surplus labour force to working in local enterprises.
4 The term "two equal emphases" means to lay equal emphases on import and export businesses.

1 Phases and goals of economic development

China's economic development has entered a new historical phase. The future goals were set forth by President Xi Jinping in his keynote speech at the Fifth BRICS Summit in March 2013. President Xi stated,

> Looking ahead, China will work to realize two grand goals: First, we will double China's 2010 GDP and the per capita income of both urban and rural residents by 2020 and complete the process of building a well-off society in all aspects that benefits more than one billion Chinese people. Second, we will complete the process of building a modern socialist country that is prosperous, strong, democratic, culturally advanced and harmonious by 2049 when we celebrate the centenary of the founding of the People's Republic of China (PRC). To achieve these two goals, we will continue to make development our top priority and economic development our central task, and we will promote socio-economic development. We will put people first and strive to promote all-round progress in the economic, political, cultural, social and ecological spheres, and to ensure coordinated development in building a modern beautiful China.

1.1 Development goals in the new phase of economic development

1.1.1 New phase of economic development

To make a fair judgement regarding the economic status of a developing nation and identify its initial development characteristics is a precondition for mapping economic development goals and their corresponding development strategies and policies. Generally, development economics measures the economic status of a developing nation according to two basic criteria:

- First, the people's living standard and quality of life. On the one hand, developing nations generally face the pressure of a large population and a high population growth rate. Today, the developing world, which accounts for 75% of the world's population, enjoys only 15% of the world's income. Rapid population growth has brought about multiple social and economic problems, including low quality of life, severe unemployment, slow development of culture and education, and a heavy burden of social support. On the other hand, living standards in developing nations are low. Development economics usually measures the material and cultural life of the people by the number of calories and protein each person takes in per day, the birth rate, the infant mortality rate, the average life expectancy and the illiteracy rate. In developing nations, the total calories and protein each person takes per day, the average life expectancy and other indicators are much lower than those of developed countries, while the birth rate and illiteracy rate are far higher. With a low overall standard of living, the disparity between the haves and have-nots in developing nations is far wider.

- Second, there is the problematic economic structure. On the one hand, the level of industrialisation is low in developing nations, and their reliance on the agricultural sector is too high. More than 80% of the population in developing nations as a whole live in rural areas, while in developed countries, 35% or less are rural inhabitants. In terms of the labour force, 66% of the workers in developing nations are in the agricultural sector, compared with 21% in developed countries. Agricultural output makes up 32% of the gross national product (GNP) in developing nations and just 8% in developed countries. The agriculture sector's 66% of the total labour force only produces 32% of GNP. It shows clearly that agricultural productivity in developing nations is low. On the other hand, the import and export structure of developing nations reflects their dependence on developed countries. The export volume of developing nations as a whole accounts for no more than 30% of the world's overall volume, and these exports are mainly primary products (80% of total export volume). The production of the exports is owned or controlled by foreign capital. The volume of imports in developing nations, mainly manufactured goods, is especially large. Consequently, the export-oriented economy of developing nations becomes dependent on foreign capital.

At the founding of the PRC in 1949, China had its own unique challenges in addition to the general dependent conditions characteristic of developing nations. These included a poor economic foundation, a large population and limited arable land. The long-time destruction brought about by imperialism, bureaucratic capitalism and feudalism had turned China into a poor and underdeveloped nation. Since 1949, especially after more than 30 years of reform and opening to the outside world, China has made tremendous progress and is quickly moving beyond economic dependency. Now China's economy has reached a new historical starting point, as demonstrated by the following trends:

- China's gross domestic product (GDP) reached RMB 40.1 trillion (the equivalent of US$5.88 trillion) in 2010. Since then, China has become the second-largest economy in the world.
- China's per capita GDP reached RMB 35,083 (the equivalent of US$5,432) in 2011, marking China's entry into the ranks of middle-income countries.

- China's primary industry decreased to 10.1% of overall industrial production in 2011, while its secondary industries rose to 46.8%. This change indicates that China has successfully transitioned from a large agricultural-based economy to an industrial country.
- China's urbanisation rate reached 51.27% in 2011. Crossing the threshold of half of the country's population being urban residents marked China's entry into the intermediate phase of urbanisation.
- The living standard in China has passed the stage of simply having adequate food and shelter. Chinese people generally are better off. China will reach the ranks of a well-off society by 2020. In terms of quality of life, China's per capita caloric intake, infant mortality rate, adult literacy rate and life expectancy rate all have attained the level of a middle-income country.

However, what remains unchanged is that China is still in the primary stage of socialism and will be so for a long time to come. Moreover, China's international status remains unchanged as the world's largest developing nation. Faced with people's demands for a better life, China's economy has many problems. It is unbalanced, inadequate and unsustainable. Scientific innovation capacity is low. The industrial structure is unbalanced, and the agricultural foundation is weak. Environmental constraints are serious. Income disparities between rural and urban areas are wide. Social friction has increased significantly, and there are many problems regarding issues related to the vital interests of the people, including education, employment and social security. All these challenges can only be solved by development. Therefore, development is still China's top priority.

1.1.2 Overcome "the middle-income trap"

According to the World Bank's East Asia Development Report (2006), some emerging economies were caught in the so-called middle-income trap after entering the ranks of middle-income countries. In a typical case involving Latin American countries, per capita GDP fluctuates between US$3,000 and US$5,000, and there are no signs or hope of growth stimulation. The main cause of this phenomenon is that development promoted by the economic growth mechanism in the low-income phase frequently fluctuates and can become stagnant. After entering the middle-income stage, these countries continued the high-input and high-consumption development mode of the low-income stage. The result is that they cannot compete with low-income countries on wages, nor can they compete with developed countries in terms of cutting-edge technology development. Consequently, their international competitiveness decreases significantly. Meanwhile, many social conflicts built up during the time of rapid growth under the old model may begin to break out all at once after entering the middle-income stage. There are three primary social conflicts: (1) increased income disparities, (2) severe corruption on the part of some government officials and (3) insufficient resources and environmental deterioration. All these factors keep these nations at the middle-income stage. Since their per capita GDP does not exceed US$10,000, they do not qualify for entry into the rank of high-income countries.

However, the middle-income trap experienced by Latin American countries did not occur across the board. East Asian countries, such as Singapore and South Korea, escaped the trap by promoting a modernisation strategy. Nevertheless, the threat remains.

Although China has entered the ranks of middle-income countries, its mode of development remains unchanged. The main manifestations of this dilemma are as follows:

1   The development goal is a pure pursuit of GDP and ignores economic quality and social development.
2   The development strategy is export-oriented and does not attach importance to the expansion of domestic demand.
3   Development relies on the input of materials, and innovation is insufficient.
4   Development is dependent on high savings and low labour costs while consumption-driven growth is lacking.

Given that the supply of resources and the carrying capacity of the environment are not infinite, rising labour costs and declining savings rates drive development to its limits. In terms of social conflicts, there is no sign that the income gap will decrease when it reaches the highest point of the Kuznets inverted U-shaped curve, nor is there any sign that the index of corruption will decrease after reaching the highest point of the Kuznets curve. When economic development reaches the level of other middle-income countries, people's expectations regarding their living standards will enter a new stage. They are more concerned about education, health and environmental issues. Their awareness of rights is heightened, and their demand for equitable development increases. At the low-income stage, people may tolerate a widening income gap. But at the middle-income stage, people are far less tolerant, especially if the gap is caused by inequality. If we cannot solve these problems properly, China will inevitably fall into "the middle-income trap."

China cannot afford to fall into the trap; it has to overcome it. Development is the only way to do it successfully. The main path is threefold: shift the development paradigm, practice inclusive and equitable development and stress social development while continuing to promote economic development.

1.1.3 Development is a top priority

Economic development is the basic task for any developing nation. There are specific requirements to accelerate economic development under socialism. In the past, China pursued the upgrading of the means of production while neglecting the development of productivity. As a result, the socialist economy did not develop fully, and improvements in people's living were slow. People gradually realised that poverty is not socialism, neither is slow economic development. It is regarding this very issue that Deng Xiaoping raised the question of what should be called socialism. When he put forward the theory of building socialism with Chinese characteristics, he clearly linked the development of productivity with the nature of socialism.

On the one hand, developing nations seeking to build socialism now and for the future are handicapped by productivity levels that are lower than those of developed capitalist countries. They cannot eliminate poverty completely. Thus socialist countries must vigorously develop productivity, gradually eradicate poverty and constantly improve people's living standards. Otherwise, how can socialism prevail over capitalism? On the other hand, socialism is the primary stage of communism. Developing socialism into communism, which is character-ised by "doing one's best" and "on-demand distribution," requires a high degree of social productivity and great social wealth. The superiority of socialism man-ifests itself in higher and faster productivity and better and faster improvement of people's material and cultural life. This is how Deng Xiaoping explained the development of productivity as the height of socialism: "The nature of socialism is the liberation and development of the productivity, the end of exploitation and polarization, and the ultimate achievement of prosperity for all."[1]

The acceleration of development is determined by the historical mission of the primary stage of socialism in which the Chinese nation has found itself. In the-ory, the socialist revolution could achieve the ultimate victory in underdeveloped nations—but this is unlikely. Throughout human history, a key criterion upon which to judge the superiority of the socialist society over the capitalist one is that the former surpasses the latter in terms of all aspects of economic development. Just as Vladimir Lenin once said, the remarkable labour productivity created by socialism is amongst the key factors to transcend capitalism. A socialist society that is unable to meet this criterion must still be in the primary stage of socialism. Subjective and random elevation of socialism could only lead to the destruction of the productive forces and put off further improvement and development of the socialist economic system.

China has never experienced a capitalist period. Instead, it transformed its social system from a semi-colonial and semi-feudal one to a socialist one. The 1956 socialist transformation symbolised China's successful transition from a new democracy to the realisation of socialism. Nonetheless, what had been left behind by the semi-colonial, semi-feudal society was an underdeveloped social economy and outdated science and technology. National industrialisation was not achieved during the transition period in China. Even though China had already become a socialist country, a solid foundation of socialist materialistic technol-ogy had not been established and still does not exist. Evidence of this situation is obvious: the majority of the national population remains in the agricultural sector. These kinds of non-industrial activities continue to drive a proportion of the national economy. People's standards of living are comparatively low. The proportion of poverty-stricken people remains rather large. All of these factors indicate that – owing to the limited development level of productive forces – socialism has not yet been fully established in China. China's socialism, in other words, is still in a primary stage of development.

The previous analysis shows that the primary stage of socialism that China has been experiencing is not parallel to that experienced by other countries when they adopt the socialist system. Instead, China's primary stage is a special his-torical phase that the Chinese people have experienced under the condition of an immature market economy. Through this particular phase, China will achieve the industrialisation, socialisation, marketisation and modernisation of the national economy that quite a few countries achieved under the condition of capitalism. This phase commences with the formal establishment of the socialist system. It concludes with the realisation of socialist modernisation and a remarkable level of productive forces that can enable China to keep up with or even surpass developed capitalist countries.

To keep up with or surpass the developed capitalist countries in terms of the level of productive forces requires a dynamic transition. The current level of productive forces amongst the socialist countries has already reached the same productive level of Great Britain in the mid-1800s—the conditions that led Karl Marx to predict the realisation of socialism. However, this does not mean that socialism at present has its own foundation of materialistic technology. This is because from Marx's era to the present, capitalist countries have enjoyed rapid development once again. Although the economic growth rate of capitalist countries is comparatively low, their aggregate economy is tremendous. Therefore, socialist countries must further accelerate their economic growth. Only in this way will they catch up with or surpass capitalist countries in terms of the level of productive forces and ultimately rise out of the primary stage of socialism.

The previous discussion reveals one of the two features of the primary stage of socialism in terms of the level of productive forces. The other feature of the primary stage is people's increasing demand for better material and cultural lives. This feature reflects the essential demands arising from the socialist economic system. This is because people, under the socialist system, have already been playing the key roles in various economic activities. In general, people's increasing material and cultural demands will not be constrained by the economic system. After achieving an overall well-off society, people will inevitably want to enjoy a better life that features enhanced health-care, security and education services. The present level of economic development in China, however, cannot satisfy such a demand. This condition constitutes the principal contradiction of the primary stage of socialism. Such a contradiction will run through the entire primary stage and determine the characteristics of all economic relations during this stage.

As a result, the central task at this stage is to develop China's productive forces. Although the ultimate goal of socialism is to eliminate ownership, such a result is unlikely to be realised at the primary stage of socialism. The realistic goal of socialism at this stage is simply to develop the productive forces. During this stage, all efforts must be made to ensure that top priority is given to this goal.

In accordance with people's urgent need to develop the productive forces and establish the material basis of the socialist system, the primary stage of socialism should bid farewell to economic underdevelopment and strive to realise the socialist modernisation. This stage features a vital transition from an agricultural country, in which manual farm labour is still the dominant productive force, to an industrial one that enjoys a larger manufacturing labour pool and a prosperous modern agriculture and service industry. This stage is characterised by a gradual transition from a natural or semi-natural economy with a larger proportion of illiterate and semi-literate workers and a problematic educational system and culture to a more advanced market economy that enjoys advanced science, education and culture. This is also a stage that fulfils an ideal change from a country in which the poverty-stricken population is large and the standard of living low to one with a higher, widely shared standard of living that bridges regional gaps caused by imbalances in the economy and culture. The latter needs to be dealt with in a sequential manner.

Despite the emergence of the characteristics of a demand-restricted economy in some special industries, the economy of the primary stage of socialism is still supply restricted as a whole. The supply restricted economy is generally characterised by an imbalanced and inadequate supply. Sustainable economic growth plays an essential role in fulfilling the goals of a socialist economy. We should not blindly seek a rapid economic growth rate because growth should be in line with national conditions. On the other hand, we should not completely slow down the growth rate. Without a reasonable growth rate, there will predictably be more and more severe problems and contradictions in our economic life. Maintaining the sustainable growth of the national economy will realise the goal of economic development, as well as conform to the fundamental interests of the people.

Economic development is unlikely to be achieved without a certain minimum growth rate. In a socialist society, economic growth must meet people's constantly rising material and cultural needs. A substantial increase in population stemming from an enormous population base is inevitable even though the current population in China has been brought under control. In light of the increasing needs of such a huge number of people, the national economy of a socialist country that aims to satisfy people's needs must exceed the growth of the population. In short, the extended reproduction of a socialist country is unlikely to be achieved without a remarkable economic growth rate. In this sense, a low rate of development stands for nothing but stagnation or even recession.

During the period of improvement and rectification that started in 1989, some local governments attached too much importance to stability, slowing down the development rate. As a result, they missed plenty of opportunities to develop. Such a situation led Deng Xiaoping to issue a significant statement, stressing that development was of overriding importance. In this connection, a correct understanding of the relationship between stability and development is needed. In Deng Xiaoping's view, for a major developing nation such as China, rapid economic development is unlikely to be accomplished in a solely stable situation. Although the stable and coordinated development of the economy is necessary, it should be understood in a relative way, instead of an absolute one. If one is unable to emancipate one's mind and look boldly upon reform, one will definitely lose the golden opportunities to develop. Just as a famous Chinese saying goes, "A boat sailing against the current must forge ahead or it will be driven back." Therefore, as Deng Xiaoping once said,

> Those areas that are in a position to develop should not be obstructed. Where local conditions permit, development should proceed as fast as possible. There is nothing to worry about so long as we stress efficiency and quality and develop an export-oriented economy. The low rate of development stands for nothing but stagnation or even recession.[2]

1.1.4 A People-centred development objective

The goals of economic development are diverse. They can be demonstrated by a table in Charles Kindleberger's book *Economic Development* (Table 1.1). The diversity of goals clearly reflects a multifaceted process of economic development. Economic growth rate, production capacity, social welfare and efficiency of development constitute the goal system of economic development. There is likely to be more than one process to realise different goals. These processes are likely to collide with each other. For example, there may be a substitution relationship between the growth of productive forces and the increase of people's standards of consumption. The goal of economic growth and the goal of equitable income distribution may be contradictory. High-speed economic development may collide with price stability. All these indicate that the design of a reasonable development plan should take all the relevant factors into account. In the process of economic development, if only one or just a couple of goals are excessively stressed, the overall goal system of economic development will be in a state of imbalance. Therefore, adjustment of the process of economic development is essential, and the relevant mechanisms need to be optimised.

When a country is still at the low-income development stage, the major goal of development is to pursue GDP growth. Moreover, its economic growth is mainly dependent on investment. When the country achieves middle-income status, the major goal of development should be shifted to continue in a people-centred direction. People-centred development is not only the goal of development but also a means of development. A people-centred approach aims to realise people's all-round development, as well as to pursue and promote development that will secure their ultimate interests by satisfying increasing material and cultural needs. This form of development strives to enable people to obtain tangible benefits,

Table 1.1 Various Goals of Economic Development Pursued by All Countries

Economic Goals*	Statistical Target
1. High-level gross output and income	1. GNP and GDP
2. Rapid growth of total income	2. GNP and the average GDP growth rate per year
3. Greater equality of income distribution	3. Gini coefficient
4. More opportunities for productive employment	4. The labour force distribution that is distinguished by industries, categories of employment and income
5. Less dependence on the international community	5. The proportion of foreign trade and international payments in the total value of output
6. Stable price	6. Price index
7. Wider balance amongst different areas	7. Regional per capita output

* Charles Kindleberger, *Economic Development* (Shanghai: Shanghai Translation Press, 1993), 375.

share the achievements equally and, ultimately, to invite the entire population to share in the dividends of China's prosperity and development.

People-centred development must balance the increase of residents' income and economic development. All development economists propose that the goal of economic development is to alleviate both absolute and relative poverty. So far, tens of millions of Chinese are still living under the poverty line. Thanks to poverty-reduction programmes sponsored by Chinese governments at all levels, the number of poor will be gradually reduced. Economic development in China will be significantly upgraded from simply helping people alleviate poverty to making people wealthy. In 2012, the 18th National Congress of the Communist Party of China (CPC) set the goal to double both the GDP growth rate and per capita income levels, which reflects this upgrading process. It is unlikely that China will be transformed into a welfare state. The goal to double per capita income does not mean that the central government should simply double the income of the people. Limited national revenues cannot afford this. The true purpose of the goal of economic development lies in the creation of more employment and income-earning opportunities for citizens, as well as increased prospects that the benefit of economic development will be broadly shared.

Income increases play a key role in the process of wealth generation. However, what should be increased to make people wealthy is not only income but also property ownership—a category that includes real estate, stock shares and intellectual property. Citizens can obtain legitimate income not only through work but also from their property ownership.

The goal of people-centred development demands that economic growth shift from an investment-driven model to a consumption-driven model. Economics researchers in China used to focus on studying production rather than consumption. The previous theories of economic development mainly originated from supply-side economics. China cannot stay at the stage of leading manufacturer. It should become a leading consumer as well. After consumer demand becomes the main driving force, consumption force, consumption demand and consumption format will appear on the radar of economic development theorists.

People-centred development involves the issue of equitable development. Over the past 30 years, the focus on China's reform efforts has been improving efficiency. Emphasising efficiency was a top priority while taking equity into account. The policy was to allow some regions and some people to get rich first. As a result, China has become the world's second-largest economy and reached the level of middle-income countries. But now China is faced with the pressure of "the middle-income trap"; eliminating relative poverty is becoming a pressing task. It is important to emphasise inclusive economic growth. National policy needs to shift from allowing a small number of people to get rich first to making the majority of the population rich. The emphasis, which used to be on economic efficiency, should now be turned to economic equity.

People's yearning for a better life is not only reflected in their income level but also in being spiritually and culturally enriched. The more developed and more open the economy is, the higher people's happiness demands will be. In particular, people's demands for health care, human development, social security and a clean and healthy environment will become more and more prominent after they have reached the overall well-off level. All these demands need to be included in the people-centred modernisation goals.

Common prosperity is the essential requirement of socialism in the first place, and it should naturally be the main feature of socialist modernisation with Chinese characteristics. Some countries, after entering the ranks of middle-income countries, were caught in "the middle-income trap." Now when China is shifting from a comprehensive well-off society to modernisation, it is necessary to make clear the goal of common prosperity – that is, to transition from allowing a minority of people to get rich first to making a majority of people wealthy. China needs to raise the income level of the low-income group across the board, expand the proportion of the middle-income group and then gradually make it reach a majority of people. When the income levels of a majority of people reach the average level, the social gap is diminished.

1.2 The stage of economic growth and economic take-off

1.2.1 The stage of economic growth

A country that elevates itself from poor to wealthy needs to experience a stage of development from the traditional to the modern, from the lower stage to the advanced one. It is particularly important to define the characteristics of each stage of development.

According to Rostow's analysis, economic growth is divided into six stages:

1   Traditional society: The basic feature of such a society is that there is no modern science and technology, and the level of productivity is very low. More than 75% of the population is engaged in agriculture. Family and clan relations play a leading role in social organisation.
2   Creating conditions for take-off: This is a transitional period from the traditional society to the take-off stage.
3   Take-off: This is a fundamental transformation of the society from a traditional type to a modern one.
4   Propulsion maturity: At this stage, people in the society can effectively apply modern technology to various economic fields.
5   High mass consumption: At this time, the society enters the highly developed industrial period. The automobile and consumer durables are widely promoted for use.
6   The pursuit of quality of life: At this time, the relevant sectors (i.e. culture, education, health) are established to improve citizens' life quality and take on a leading role.

In these six stages, the third and sixth are of revolutionary significance in the process of social development. Many developed countries in the West are now in the fifth or sixth stage, respectively, while developing nations are mostly in the second or third stage.

1.2.2 The stage of economic take-off

Take-off is an important concept of economic development. In economic terms, modernisation is defined as the stage of modern economic growth after take-off. According to the Rostow theory, a country must go through the take-off stage to realise modernisation. In China, take-off is the equivalent of building a well-off society in an all-around way. Therefore, it is necessary to study the connotation and the role of take-off.

For underdeveloped nations, the main problem of economic development is the initial step of development; once begun, development towards modern industrial countries becomes a natural trend. Just like a plane once airborne, without special circumstances, it will fly straight ahead to its destination. Therefore, take-off can be said to be a clear dividing line in the history of a society. After entering this stage, the innovation process is no longer haphazard; it becomes a regular, institutionalised part of life. The resistance that constrained economic growth is eventually overcome, and growth becomes a normal condition, with the economy entering a stage of self-sustained growth. The reason that the economies of many developing nations are resistant and fluctuating is because their economies have not yet entered the take-off stage.

To break through all kinds of resistance, the aircraft will need to have enough power and a good engine when it begins to take off. Likewise, the economic take-off of a country requires the following three conditions:

1 The take-off thrust: The ratio of productive investment in GNP is at a high level. Rostow's empirical figure is that the investment rate is up to 10%. Of course, the investment rate is based on a certain rate of population growth and capital output ratio.
2 The take-off engine: The powerful core engine of take-off is one or several new manufacturing sectors rapidly coalescing into the leading sector. These sectors, with a high growth rate, exert a significant diffusion effect on the economy as a whole through forward and backward linkages. The society is ready to respond positively to the effect in terms of system, structure and culture, making full use of the potential of the leading sector.
3 The take-off runway: There exists or emerges a political, social and institutional system that is able to promote the growth of the modern sector, to bring about the external economic effects from take-off and to make the growth continuous. The socialist market economy system that China has been establishing is this kind of system.

The practice of economic development in various countries shows that take-off is an inevitable and insurmountable stage of economic growth. The stage of economic take-off will not come out of the blue – it is necessary to create the appropriate conditions. According to Rostow's analysis, these include having a minimum of construction as social infrastructure capital (such as transportation and power resources), increasing agricultural production, expanding domestic and foreign trade, training the labour force and facilitating the emergence of a critical mass of entrepreneurs. Amongst these, basic capital construction and entrepreneurs are the key factors for take-off, as they can prepare technical conditions and conduct rules for the diffusion effect of the leading sector.

Rostow once cited China's "Great Leap Forward" as an example, pointing out that for countries trying to take off without the preparation of corresponding prerequisite capital, their structural deficiencies could lead to serious problems.

For China, creating conditions for take-off also means abandoning the pillars that have long underpinned the traditional social structure. The natural economy and the centralisation based on it and the "closed-door policy" that once supported pre-modern Chinese society become cultural barriers to modernisation. Although China is currently advancing to opening further to the outside world and developing a market economy, the natural economy still accounts for a large proportion of production and employment. China's market economy is still in the immature stage, and openness to the outside world is still not high. With all these conditions unchanged, China's economy will find it difficult to take off, and modernisation will become empty talk.

How long will it take to achieve take-off? In Rostow's view, it will take a long time (his estimate is 20 years) for a society to show that it has the ability to overcome the structural crisis that may arise from the initial growth boom and generate the continuous introduction of new technologies on which sustained growth depends. This conclusion is based on the experience of advanced developed countries, so it cannot be fully applied to contemporary developing nations. In terms of the relationship between capital formation and take-off, the capital needed for take-off by late-mover nations does not rely entirely on domestic savings. They can make use of foreign technology, experts, capital and equipment that are not available in advanced industrialised countries. Of course, late-mover nations also have difficulties that advanced countries have not had in the first place; specifically, the occupation of overseas markets by advanced countries greatly restricts the opening of the international market. Moreover, the relationship between the savings rate and take-off cannot be absolutised. Today, many developing nations have savings rates that exceed the standard set by Rostow, but few have dared to claim that the "central problem" of their economic development has been resolved. The reason is that in developing nations, the rise in savings rates is accompanied by a huge waste of money, such as poor investment choices, low efficiency in implementation and management and the adoption of misguided price policies.

If the late-mover developing nations seize certain opportunities, they can shorten the process of creating the necessary conditions for take-off. For example, the sudden discovery of some kind of resources which can be exported in large quantities can work well in the international market. Or because export products sell well in the international market and the profits are high, foreign exchange income increases rapidly, and the country has the ability to import significant amounts of machinery and equipment from abroad. Therefore, many domestic industries can be established quickly. China lost the opportunity for development many times and thus lost its status at the forefront of the world's nations. Today, in the process of globalisation, we must seize the opportunity offered by the international and domestic markets to realise take-off as soon as possible.

Apart from benefits, growth also brings about a price to pay, as well as social friction. There is a need to seek the road to modernisation at the lowest cost and, meanwhile, to make the corresponding institutional arrangements. First, there is the depletion of natural resources for economic growth. The process of modernisation needs to solve the problem of sustainable development. Only when resources are fully and effectively used, environmental pollution is effectively controlled and workers' leisure time is increased is the growth achieved valuable. Second, there is the social cost of modernisation. Kuznets once pointed out that certain manifestations, such as changes in the living conditions caused by urbanisation, contain a variety of losses and benefits. To move from the countryside to the city, people have to bear great losses. To them, learning new skills while losing the value of their old skills is a kind of waste. Structural adjustment will reduce the status of farmers, small producers and landowners. Modernisation will lead to adjustments in the interest structure. If the long-existing vested interests and status of some groups continue to be in turmoil, they will breed conflict. Based on these considerations, Kuznets concludes,

Because we have to resolve the burgeoning conflict arising from the rapid changes in economic and social structures, in the early stages of modern economic growth, this modern economic growth can be said to be a controlled revolutionary process.[3]

1.3 Building a moderately well-off society in all aspects and bringing about modernisation

When it was first established, the theory of development economies aimed to eliminate poverty. China has now entered into the middle-income phase and faces the realisation of the "Two Centenary Goals" – i.e. to build a comprehensive, well-off society by the 100th anniversary of the founding of the CPC and to build a prosperous, democratic, civilised and harmonious socialist modern country by the 100th anniversary of the founding of the PRC. The Chinese Dream cannot be realised without the scientific development theory which guides development practice.

1.3.1 The modernisation of developing nations

For developing nations, modernisation is the goal of economic development – namely, catching up with the developed countries by improving the quality of life, economic modernisation, scientific and technological modernisation and social development modernisation. In terms of specific catching-up goals, the choice of the reference system should be phased in. It means that the basic aim of modernisation is to catch up with moderately developed countries, such as South Korea, while comprehensive modernisation means to catch up with developed countries, such as the United States. Modernisation has two aspects. The first involves clarification of the target (i.e. to achieve the goal of modernisation). The second is clarification of the process (i.e. to regard modernisation as a process).

In terms of the goal of modernisation, the level achieved by the catching-up countries involves improving the level of science and technology, economic structure and quality of population. This level is dynamic, not static. For example, Deng Xiaoping proposed in 1987 that the basic realisation of modernisation is to catch up with moderately developed countries. Since these countries' economies are also developing, the modernisation target and the reference system of the developing nations should be dynamic. Therefore, the catching-up goal of modernisation in China cannot be fixed at the level of modernisation reached by the developed countries in 1987, nor can it be fixed at the level of modernisation of these countries when they entered the ranks of the moderately developed countries. The latest level of modernisation in these countries should be regarded as the frame of reference.

The process of modernisation begins in the West and starts from industriali-sation. But modernisation is by no means Westernisation for developing nations. The universal rules of industrialisation and modernisation must be obeyed by countries in both East and West. So, modernisation cannot be attributed to Westernisation. Modernisation includes not only industrialisation but also the modernisation of agriculture and other sectors. For many developing nations, the transformation of traditional agriculture is an important part of modernisation. Classical modernisation theory has regarded industrialisation and urbanisation as the main paths of modernisation. Modernisation should now have a higher frame of reference, which involves not only industrialisation and urbanisation but also informatisation and greenisation. In particular, it is necessary to make clear that the developing nations should follow the general rules of modernisation and go through the basic path adopted by the modernised countries. They must combine their national conditions and the new international and domestic economic and social-political environments to find the modernisation road with their own characteristics. The leading example is industrialisation and urbanisation with Chinese characteristics.

The catching-up goal of modernisation involves not only the target but also the specific reference indicators. We can then identify the gap and have a clear idea of the modernisation goal. Kuznets's so-called indicators of economically developed countries which have already entered the modern economic growth stage are

- sustained and stable growth in per capita output,
- industrial structural changes driven by technological progress,
- income growth that almost parallels the increase in GNP,
- narrowing of the income gap,
- consumption expenditure growth that outpaces the growth of savings and
- shifts in consumption to the consumer items required by education and higher living standards.

The Human Development Index, compiled by the United Nations Development Program, measures the level of economic and social development according to the following factors:

- Health and life expectancy (life expectancy index): measured by the percentage of people who die before the age of 40,
- Education level (years of schooling): measured by the percentage of adults with literacy,
- Standard of living (income index): measured by the percentage of people with access to health-care services and safe drinking water, as well as the percentage of malnourished children under five.

As measured by the Human Development Index, the national economies can be divided into four categories: (1) highest, (2) high, (3) medium and (4) low.

1.3.2 The cohesive connection between building a well-off society and the basic realisation of modernisation

The modernisation of developing nations is a long-term process that cannot be achieved overnight. It needs to be phased in and have clear development goals at each phase. According to the three-step modernisation strategy designed by Deng Xiaoping, China's modernisation needs a well-off society construction phase. This is an important feature of socialist modernisation with Chinese characteristics. The report of the 16th CPC National Congress in 2002 put forward the goal of building a comprehensive, well-off society in the first 20 years of this century. Ten years later, the 18th CPC National Congress made it clear that China would achieve a comprehensive well-off society by 2020 and a modernised country by the middle of the century. Of course, this level of modernisation is the level of moderately developed countries (i.e. the basic realisation of modernisation). It is clear that modernisation in China has specific short-term goals and long-term goals – namely, each phase of the modernisation has calculated achievable goals.

The process of modernisation with Chinese characteristics includes the construction of a comprehensive well-off society phase and the basic and then full realisation of the modernisation phase. A comprehensive well-off society and the basic realisation of modernisation are two different development phases in the process of socialist modernisation with Chinese characteristics. They are mutually connected and form a cohesive whole as society moves from the lower to higher form of development.

A comprehensive well-off society is an important development phase in the process of modernisation in China. According to the report of the 18th CPC National Congress, the goal of a comprehensive well-off society in terms of economic and social development is mainly dependent on sustained and sound economic development. Major progress should be made in changing the economic growth model. On the basis of making China's development much more balanced, coordinated and sustainable, we should double GDP and per capita income for both urban and rural residents. The contribution of scientific and technological progress to economic growth should increase considerably, and China should become an innovative country. At this point, industrialisation should be basically accomplished. The application of information technology should be significantly expanded. The quality of urbanisation should improve significantly. Notable progress should be made in modernising agriculture and building new socialist rural areas. The basic mechanism for promoting balanced development between regions should be in place. China should be opened further, and China's international competitiveness should be increased significantly. Living standards have to be fully raised. Equal access to basic public services should be generally achieved. The educational level of the entire population should be raised significantly and training of innovative professionals markedly improved. China should have a large pool of competent professionals and be rich in human resources; to achieve this, it should modernise education in the country. There should be more employment opportunities. Income gaps should be narrowed, and middle-income groups should keep growing. The number of people living below the poverty line should drop by a large margin. Social security should cover all the people. Everyone should have access to basic medical and public health services. The system of housing for low-income groups should take shape, and there should be social harmony and stability. Major progress should be made in building a resource-conserving and environmentally friendly society. The establishment of functional zones should be basically completed, and a system for recycling resources should begin to take shape. Energy consumption and carbon dioxide emissions per unit of GDP, as well as the discharge of major pollutants, should decrease sharply. Forest coverage should increase, and the ecosystem should become more stable. The living environment should improve markedly.

In 2020, when China fully achieves a comprehensive well-off society, the country will enter the stage of basic realisation of modernisation. From the study of Rostow's stages of economic growth theory noted earlier, we find that the take-off stage is the equivalent of our well-off society construction stage. The three stages after the take-off stage classified by Rostow can be seen as three aspects or characteristics of a modern society. For example, the drive to the maturity stage refers to the widespread use of modern technology in various fields to achieve sustained economic growth over the long term. The high mass consumption stage refers to the increasing tendency of resources to be directed to the production of durable goods and the popularisation of services. The beyond consumption stage involves the natural (beautification and purification of living environment) and the social (education, health care, transportation, life services, social trends and social order). On the one hand, the development of medical, educational, cultural, recreational and tourism services sectors needs to be accelerated so that they can become the leading sectors. On the other hand, we should seriously deal with and solve the problems of environmental pollution, urban traffic congestion and overpopulation.

The basic realisation of modernisation is the consolidation, promotion and transcendence of an overall well-off society. It is not a simple expansion of quantity on the basis of building a comprehensive well-off society, but the promotion of quality in building momentum for development and growth. By comparing indicators of modernisation and comprehensive well-off society construction, it is worth noting that in the process of the shift from the construction of an overall well-off society to modernisation, some indices are the extension and expansion of well-off indicators. These include per capita GDP and per capita income.

Others are qualitative changes, such as the fundamental transformation of industrial structure and environmental quality requirements. Some others are not mentioned in a well-off society but are put forward in the modernisation stage, such as the requirements of human modernisation. A comprehensive well-off society has its Chinese characteristics, and modernisation has not only Chinese but also international standards. The core indicators of the so-called international standards of modernisation relate to

- the reach of per capita GDP to the level of moderately developed countries,
- high technology,
- overcoming the urban and rural dual structure,
- popularisation of higher education,
- strong science and technology innovation ability and
- good ecological environment.

Here, although the basic realisation of modernisation still has a per capita GDP level requirement, it is not a fundamental indicator. For socialist modernisation, whatever the modernisation indicators are, people's wealth and happiness should be the starting point. In comparison to a comprehensive well-off society, basic modernisation is not only the promotion of the level of economic development but also an emphasis on the people-oriented concept and people's happiness. It emphasises the coordinated development of economy and society and the overall coordination of material, spiritual, political, ecological and social civilisation.

Modernisation ultimately comes down to human modernisation, just as the core of urbanisation is the urbanisation of people. Human modernisation is not only the goal of modernisation but also its driving force. Man is the subject of modernisation. Promotion of the overall development of people, improvement of their material and cultural lives and promotion of the development of economy and culture are inseparable. Modernisation is ultimately driven by people. Therefore, if the quality of people does not reach the modern level, there can be no modernisation. In this way, the corresponding development is not only economic development but also social development. Overall, human development needs all aspects of modernisation, such as the modernisation of science, education, health and so on.

The pursuit of freedom is also an element of human modernisation. Marx named the future society "Free Man Union" in his classic *On Capital*, indicating that freedom is the basic goal of social development.[4] In 1999, more than 100 years after the publication of *On Capital*, Amartya Sen, the Nobel Prize-winning Indian economist, published his book *Development as Freedom*. He again linked freedom with the goals and means of development. In his view, the fact that the concept of development has long been defined as an increase in GDP or per capita income is incomplete. He uses ample evidence to show how freedom promotes development while the lack of and repression of freedom can hinder development. Therefore, freedom is the primary purpose of development. It is also an indispensable and vitally important means to promote development. In Marx's view, of course, freedom should be separate from personal attachment, and it is established on the basis of the overall development of individuals.

Notes

1 Deng Xiaoping, *Selected Works of Deng Xiaoping*, vol. 3 (Beijing: People's Press, 1993), 373.
2 Deng, *Selected Works*, 413.
3 Simon S. Kuznets, "Modern Economic Growth," in *Comparative Modernization*, ed. Cyril E. Black, trans. Yang Yu et al. (Shanghai: Shanghai Translation Press, 1996), 280.
4 Karl Marx, *On Capital*, vol.1, trans. Central Compilation and Translation Bureau (Beijing: People's Press, 2004), 96.

2 The rate and quality of economic development

The growth of GDP is the principal goal of economic development in the low-income stage. The pursuit of the growth rate is its chief focus, while the primary economic development mode is heavily dependent on material and environmental resources. China's economic development has now entered a new era, characterised by its shift from high-speed to high-quality development. Accordingly, the development mode has to undergo a fundamental shift (i.e. from simply pursuing GDP growth to the pursuit of quality and efficiency and from relying heavily on material and environmental resources to an innovation-driven mode).

2.1 Economic development and total factor productivity

Economic growth usually refers to a country or region during a certain period of time. Its economic scale at that time expands in quantity (i.e. there is a growth in the output of goods and labour services) because of an increase in the input of production factors or the improvement of efficiency. Its measurement indicators are those total quantity indices, including GNP and GDP. The economic growth rate refers to the GDP growth rate during a certain period of time.

2.1.1 The economic growth model

The economic growth model mainly shows the role of various economic growth factors. The earliest economic growth model is the production function model expressed as $Y = f(K, L, R)$.

In this formula, "Y" is the output increment, "K" is the capital increment, "L" is the labour increment and "R" is the increase of arable land and natural resources.

The economic growth model shows that the growth rate depends on the growth of capital, labour and natural resource input.

Robert Solow, Nobel Prize laureate in economics, studied the effects of other factors in economic growth except the capital factor, focussing especially on the contribution of technological advancement to the growth. The economic growth model he described is expressed as $Y = f(K, L, R, A)$.

In addition to those letters defined in the preceding formula, "A" means a technological advancement. Solow's formula shows that the contribution of technological advancement to economic growth is the "remainder value" minus the contribution of material resources input into the growth. The contribution rate of technological advancement is increasing, reaching 80% in some developed countries.

In the production function model, it takes effect if various factors can act as independent variables. In reality, no single factor is homogeneous. Different material capitals have different technological contents and efficiencies, while different kinds of labour draw on different stocks of human capital. Furthermore, natural resources are also heterogeneous – land fertility has advantages and disadvantages, while minerals have different grades. Clearly, the inputs of different quality factors into economic growth are also unequal. Therefore, examining the effects of various factors on economic growth requires attention not only to their input but also to the quality of their input.

2.1.2 *Total factor productivity*

Economic growth depends not only on the input of each factor but also on the total factor productivity generated by the combination of different productivity factors. Because the core elements of economic growth that economists are concerned with are beginning to shift to the quality and technological advancement of various inputs, the concept of total factor productivity is proposed. The sum of the productivity produced by the various factors is greater than that of every single input. Its difference is expressed as total factor productivity. The total factor productivity indicator can be regarded as an important review indicator for evaluating growth patterns.

Solow, who originated this concept, pointed out the role of other factors apart from capital in economic growth. The production function he and his colleagues use contains more factors of production and, in particular, highlights the contribution of increased efficiency of input factors to economic growth. They also converted the production function into a form that could measure the contribution of each input into economic growth. As a result of their measurement of the causes of growth, the increase in the quality of input factors plays a growing role in the growth rate. This means that on the applicable measurement model, the change in total factor productivity is reflected in the total output growth minus the surplus after the input change. This surplus is generally understood as a general technological advancement. In the 1950s, Solow proposed a method of total factor productivity analysis to distinguish individual factors affecting it. They include the impact of economies of scale, the impact of education and training and the organisational structure of a company. The validated result of this method is that the main factors driving per capita income growth are capital investment and technological advancement, and the impact of the latter is even more pronounced. According to Solow's statistical analysis, about 80% of U.S. economic growth is due to technological innovation, while only 20% comes from capital accumulation. This means that the reason for more output is "technological advancement and improved worker skills."

Denison summarised the factors contributing to economic growth in five categories:

1 Increase in the quantity and quality of labour input,
2 Increase in the quantity and quality of capital and land inputs,
3 Resources improvements in configuration,
4 Economies of scale and
5 Progress in knowledge and its due application to production.

In his view, the quality of input factors such as capital, labour and land belong to the category of total factor productivity. To get more income from the same input of production factors, it is necessary to use the growth in total factor productivity to illustrate. In Denison's analytical framework, the factors of economic growth are divided into transitional factors and persistent factors. Improvements in resource allocation and economies of scale are transitional factors. Only advances in knowledge and technology can contribute to persistent economic growth. It means that as the economy grows, technological advancement factors will increasingly become the main explanatory factors for intensive growth.

To sum up the aforementioned analysis, the maximum output of a society depends not only on the number of material elements that are put into production but also on whether these elements are effectively allocated and whether technological development is present. In other words, environmental factors, such as social, cultural and institutional progress, are the decisive factors affecting economic growth. Undoubtedly, such environmental factors are difficult to quantify, but they must not be ignored in the empirical theoretical analysis. Taking into account the factors of total factor productivity that affect output levels, the aforementioned economic growth model can be improved as $Y = f(K, L, R, A, E)$.

In this formula, "Y" still represents output increment, "K" means total social capital, "N" indicates natural resource utilisation and "L" is labour use. Because factor productivity depends on technological innovation and the improvement of labour proficiency, it is necessary to introduce technological advancement factor "S" in the production function, indicating the progress of knowledge and the level of technological development. Similarly, social, cultural and institutional innovations have a major impact on factor productivity across society, while environmental factors that reflect the social, cultural and institutional characteristics of economic operations are also included in the production function denoted by "E." This function combines the output level of national wealth over a certain period with the number of various input factors and the conditions and factors that affect the productivity of these areas.

In terms of quantity, the technological advancement factor "S" is equivalent to the total amount of applied science, technology and organisational social knowledge. As with material input elements, technological advancement is also a multidimensional vector. Each parameter of the technical, organisational or scientific skill level used in the production process is part of it. By introducing technological advances into production functions, it is possible to analyse changes in factor productivity caused by capital, natural resources and labour resulting from these advances. Through these variables, we can consider the changes in production technology, the improvement of labour proficiency and health levels and the role of economic growth.

The environmental variable "E" is a complex synthesis of social, cultural and institutional factors. In terms of economics, environmental factors can mean a kind of competition rules in economic order. It can also be an institutional innovation used indirectly to represent entrepreneurship. A reasonable and normal economic order has contributed to the effective allocation of factor resources. A good market and legal environment are conducive to the birth and growth of entrepreneurs, leading to an increase in output. Any change in environmental factors would affect the output alone, even if the total input of material elements and technological advancement remains unchanged.

In summary, the growth of national wealth is not only a function of the input of material elements, such as capital, natural resources and labour, but it is also a function of technological advancement factors in the production process and environmental factors on which the economy depends. All of these variables are functions of time. There are also costs to improve total factor productivity, including research costs, development costs, education and training costs, technological innovations and promotion costs, etc., but its input has higher output efficiency.

There are costs to improve total factor productivity, including research, development and education and training costs; technological innovation costs; and the cost of promotion. The output benefits are higher, however. According to the empirical research by some economists, the total factor productivity in developed countries is generally higher, and the general economic growth rate of these countries is generally explained by total factor productivity. For example, according to Denison, the annual average economic growth rate in the United States between 1929 and 1969 was 3.41%, of which 1.82% can be explained by total factor productivity.

2.1.3 Changes in the potential economic growth rate

The so-called potential economic growth rate refers to the maximum economic growth rate that a country can achieve under the conditions of optimal and adequate allocation of various resources. Specifically, a country's economic growth rate depends on the following factors:

- the increase in the quantity and quality of labour (through population growth and education),
- the growth of capital (through savings and investment) and
- technological advancement.

In addition, changes in economic structure, sustainable resource supply and market demand capacity will also affect potential economic growth rates. Therefore, to understand China's economic development in a new era, we need to fully understand the changes in the potential economic growth rate that will occur

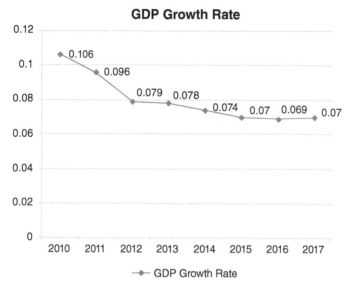

Figure 2.1 GDP Growth Rate, 2010–2017

after entering a new era. The key factors at this stage are mainly the economic structure, the technical basis and the sustainable supply of resources.

China's GDP had a sustained high growth rate averaging 9.9% in the 31 years during the period of reform and opening up between 1971 and 2010. Since 2012, however, China's economic growth has officially bid farewell to such a rapid rate of growth. Its GDP grew at a rate of 10.6% in 2010 but declined to 9.6% in 2011, 7.9% in 2012, 7.8% in 2013, 7.4% in 2014, 7% in 2015, 6.9% in 2016 and 7% in 2017 (see Figure 2.1).

Unlike the rapid growth in the past, the rate in recent years has been medium to high. Such a growth rate has become the new normal in China's new stage, reflecting inevitable changes in the potential economic growth rate.

The main reason for China's high growth rate over the past 30 years is that reform and opening liberated potential production factors, thus supporting a relatively long-term potential economic growth rate. After such a long period of rapid development, the potential growth factors have been fully released. Without the mobilisation of new elements, the potential economic growth rate will decline, as shown by the following factors:

• First, the supply of low-cost labour – chiefly agricultural surplus labour – has been on significant decline. The rapid economic growth of the past 30 years, especially the rapid advancement of industrialisation, is largely a result of the shift of agricultural surplus labour to the non-agricultural sector. Although rural industrialisation and urbanisation continue, the urbanisation rate has passed 50%, and the transfer rate of surplus labour has slowed down markedly. A shortage of migrant workers in coastal areas has begun to appear.

Another relevant problem is that the low wages of migrant workers are difficult to sustain because of the diminishing supply of surplus agricultural labour. In addition, as migrant workers have entered the second generation, living standards have been growing accordingly, as shown in their increased wages. In 2009, their average wage was RMB 1,783, twice that of 2001. The low-cost labour supply in general is gone.

- Second, the demographic dividend that supports high investment and high savings has been decreased significantly. Over the past 30 years, the implementation of the one-child family planning policy has resulted in a demographic dividend effect with fewer workers supporting a small population and maintaining a high savings rate. An ageing society has arrived, however. The population over 65 has risen from 4.9% in 1982 to 8.87% in 2010. In 2016, China's population aged 65 and over was 150,030,003, accounting for 10.8% of the total population. In addition, since the implementation of the one-child policy in the late 1970s, the population under 14 years old decreased from 33.59% in 1982 to 16.67% in 2016. Although it means the number of children raised by the labour force is smaller, it reveals that people spend more years in school. It should also be noted that the number of people entering working age has been significantly reduced. According to the National Bureau of Statistics, in 2012, the absolute number of working-age people ages 15 to 60 in China decreased by 3.45 million. In 2013, although the working age was raised from 15 to 16, the number still decreased by 2.44 million. The number saw a further net decrease of 3.71 million in 2014. From 2015 to 2016, there was another decrease of 3.49 million. Totalling 907 million, this group accounted for only 65.6% of the total population. Consequently, the number of people raised by the labour force is on the rise, with three to four labourers raising one person. As the working-age population continues to decrease in the near future, the increase in the support population will inevitably lead to a reduction in the demographic dividend that supports high savings and high investment.

- Third, with consumer goods such as housing and automobiles entering ordinary households, China's high consumption stage is coming, and the residents' marginal propensity to consume will tend to increase. The consumption level of the Chinese has increased significantly, shifting from meeting subsistence needs to mid- to high-end consumption. The middle-income population has reached 300 million. Even amongst the low-income groups, there is increased consumption. As a result, China's national savings rate reached a maximum of 51.5% in 2010. Since then, the savings rate has declined gradually, with an average annual decline of 0.5%. The national savings rate in 2015 was 48.4%, although it was still higher than that in other countries (19.2% in the United States, 27.0% in Japan, 12.9% in the United Kingdom, 27.7% in Germany and 32.5% in India).

- Fourth, the problem of the unsustainable supply of material elements has become more and more prominent. Limits on energy, resources and environment are constraining economic growth. Taking energy as an example, the China Energy Development Report (2014) shows that China's energy consumption in 2013 totalled 3.75 billion tonnes of standard coal, an increase of 3.7% over the same period of 2012. It accounted for 22% of the world's total while China's GDP only accounted for 12.3% of the world's output during the same period. This high-energy consumption was unable to support sustained economic growth. Whether it is worldwide or in China, the institutional constraints of energy conservation and emission reduction are increasingly rigid. To ensure China's food supply, the amount of land devoted to capital construction has fallen, causing a significant rise in land prices. All these resources and environmental constraints are increasingly becoming the natural limits of growth. If we want to break through these boundaries, we need to change how development occurs.

Developing nations face not only supply problems of the aforementioned factors that affect the potential economic growth rate. There are also structural problems. As modern development economics explains:

> A country needs to transform from a traditional economic system to a modern one. In addition to the need for capital accumulation, including physical capital and human capital, it requires a series of interrelated economic structural changes. These changes cover almost all economic functions, including changes in production patterns and the composition of consumer demand, changes in international trade and resource utilization, and changes in socio-economic factors such as urbanization, growth and distribution of national population, etc.[1]

This means that for developing nations, development is not only a matter of the growth rate but also an important issue of structural change. It is not only the industrial structure in the middle and low end but also the imbalance between supply and demand. Structural optimisation and upgrading can support long-term development, while slow change may reduce potential economic growth rates.

The previous analysis shows that in the new era, China's potential growth rate can only be medium to high. Analysis of the potential growth rate demonstrates that one should not blindly pursue the highest possible growth rate and that the real growth rate should fully release the potential rate. In reality, an overheated or overcooled economy has a real economic growth rate that is higher or lower than the potential rate.

2.2 The quality of economic growth

There are two kinds of economic growth: quantity and quality. The amount of growth generally includes an increase in nominal GDP over a given period of time, an increase in the absorption of labour by the three industries and an increase in the nominal income of residents. For economic growth in a country with a low starting point, increasing the amount of growth is a simple, quick and effective strategy because of the low requirements for various growth conditions, such as the type and composition of input elements, the system and mechanism of economic operation.

The quality of economic growth requires the optimisation of economic structure and technological advancement. It means a simultaneous increase in people's income and their happiness. It also requires implementation of environmental protection measures and sustainable development. Further, the economic growth should be coordinated with the development level of society, culture, value system, etc. Today, quality economic growth is generally called "economic development," while economic growth in the traditional sense that refers only to quantitative expansion is called "economic growth."

2.2.1 Growth does not equal development

Conventional thinking treats economic growth and economic development as similar concepts. People also often understand and explain economic development in terms of growth. In reality, however, the pursuit of output value and speed regardless of costs is a manifestation of mixing growth with development. As early as the mid and late 20th century, development economics already put forth a clear proposition that growth did not equal development based on the observation that developing nations went after economic growth alone and appeared to have "growth without development."

Growth does not equal development. Apart from the products of economic growth, economic development also includes changes in the industrial structure, technological conditions and systems on which growth depends. The difference between growth and development can be easily illustrated in human terms: growth means increases in physical height and weight, while development focusses on improvement of function and quality. Moreover, economic growth focusses on the short term. In the short term, an increase or decrease of a country's GDP is greatly affected by natural factors. It may increase with favourable weather conditions or shrink in the event of a natural disaster. In comparison, economic development is concerned with long-term sustainable growth, which involves the issue of increasing output capacity. Simon Kuznets (1901–1985), a Nobel Prize laureate in economics, once gave a relatively complete definition of modern economic growth:

> A country's economic growth may be defined as a long-term rise in capacity to supply increasingly diverse economic goods to its population. This growing capacity is based on advancing technology and the institutional and ideological adjustments that it demands.[2]

The three components in this definition include not only an increase in the number and scale but also the advancement of technology, the optimisation of institutions and the adjustment of ideology in order to achieve sustained economic growth.

Economic development thus covers the output of more goods and labour services, as well as broader goals. The first is the optimisation of the industrial structure, technological structure and economic system on which economic growth depends. It is a development goal that involves long-term economic growth. The second is poverty alleviation, equitable distribution and improvement of social welfare. The growth is meaningless if it cannot maximise the benefits to the people. The third is the minimum cost target for economic growth. Economic growth yields not only benefits but also exacts a price for growth, such as resource input and environmental pollution. Only when resources are fully and effectively used, environmental pollution is successfully controlled and the leisure time of the labour force is increased can the growth be valuable.

It should be clear, however, that the fact that growth does not equal development does not mean that the two act in opposition. In fact, growth is closely related to other development goals. Economic growth is the basic driving force for development and the primary material condition on which all economic progress is based. It provides a material basis to realise other development goals, which is also an important condition for balanced development of the economic development target system. It does not mean, however, that simple growth can reach a balanced development goal. Over a relatively long period of time, China's growth has not been able to take advantage of the optimisation of the industrial structure and economic system. Despite the high economic growth rate, there has been little improvement in the social production capacity and the ability to increase output. Therefore, the basis of economic growth is very fragile because a slightly higher speed might lead to a fall. In particular, when accelerating the growth rate, environmental protections and ecological balance are neglected. The conditions for maintaining natural resources are severely damaged. Thus a high price is paid for seeking speed. These aforementioned "growth without development" conditions provided a different perspective of what development really means. For a developing nation like China, development is the absolute principle, and its necessity is clear. The establishment of a material foundation in the initial stage of socialism requires development. Poverty alleviation and the promotion of people's welfare also needs development. From the development perspective, economic growth raises the level of the sustainable long-term economic growth while avoiding fluctuation. To achieve sustainable economic growth, it is necessary to change the mode of growth from relying solely on the input of tangible elements to a reliance on technological advancement, structure and optimisation and efficiency improvement.

2.2.2 Economic growth mode

The mode of economic growth is generally differentiated by its sources. There are two: the growth of factor input and the improvement of the efficiency of factors. If economic growth is mainly driven by the growth of factor inputs, it can be called extensive economic growth mode. If it is mainly driven by the growth of factor efficiency, it can be called intensive growth mode. If measured by total factor productivity, economic growth with a lower proportion of total factor productivity is the extensive growth, and vice versa for intensive economic growth.

According to the requirement for total factor productivity, the economic growth rate is not the sum of physical capital, labour and natural resources, but the result of the effective combination of various factors of different kinds of productivity.

A common problem that occurs in developing nations is the excessive favouring of material capital investment to spur economic growth, ignoring human capital investment and investments that improve the supply of natural resources. Even in physical capital investment they often focus on machinery and equipment, neglecting social infrastructure. They tend to believe that the economic backwardness is mainly the lack of advanced machinery and equipment. Therefore, investment typically focusses on fixed assets, while foreign capital is always spent on construction and purchases of equipment and inventory. The fatal problem here is that because human capital investment is not seriously valued, it is seriously inadequate, which results in the reduced absorption rate of physical capital. In modern economic growth, however, human capital plays an irreplaceable role in economic growth, which has been and is receiving great attention from developing nations. They have realised that human capital in the form of knowledge and technology is the most valuable resource.

The demand for land and other natural resources for developing nations is also very large, but investment in them is seriously deficient. In the view of development economics, the only economic measure of land scarcity and other natural resources is the cost. In general, at the time when developed countries promoted economic growth, natural resources were not as scarce as today. Now developed countries can rely on their abundant capital and advanced technologies to overcome the parsimony of nature, discover new resources, change the performance of existing resources and increase their productivity. For them, natural resources are relatively less important. In developing nations, where the mitigation of the scarcity of natural resources is limited by capital and technology, the supply is more important. Severe shortages of land, mineral resources and environmental resources impose very strict natural limits on economic growth. Therefore, developing nations must pay attention to factor input efficiency from the outset to promote development. They must seek an optimal combination of various productivity factors based on their contribution to economic growth (output elasticity) and pursue total factor productivity that reflects the function of organisational and technological advancement.

The differences in total factor productivity amongst countries reflect different institutional backgrounds and varying opportunities for economic systems to absorb technological innovation and increase efficiency. Differences in the rate of economic growth and efficiency of countries with different systems should be mainly explained by the differences in their total factor productivity. In general, the proportion of total factor productivity in the growth rate of countries that implement the market economy system is relatively higher. The growth here is an intensive growth. The countries that implement the planned economy system, however, prefer to continue to increase the input of factors. They do not pay attention to improving the efficiency of the use of factors, so their total factor productivity is not high. As China turns to a market economy, it should change its economic growth strategy from extensive growth to intensive growth and increase total factor productivity.

There is a close relationship between the economic growth rate and economic development stage. At the primary stage of economic development, it is inevitable that large-scale investment in production resources will drive growth. This is characterised by the obvious extensive growth mode owing to the comparative advantages of cheap labour, land and other production factors. The previous economic growth stage in China generally had such characteristics, relying mainly on high input to expand production by investing in human, material and financial resources but neglecting the possible expanded production based on technological advancement.

2.2.3 The rate and quality of economic growth

At the primary stage of socialism, sustained and stable economic growth is crucial to the realisation of economic development goals. If there is not a higher rate of economic growth, the development goals will become empty talk. We cannot pursue a higher rate blindly because economic growth should be compatible with our national strength. We cannot intentionally suppress the rate either, however. Without a certain rate of economic growth, more contradictions and problems in economic life will arise and become more acute. By focussing on efficiency, stability and coordination, we can ensure sustained growth of the national economy and meet the need to achieve economic development goals and the fundamental interest of the people.

There are two foundations for the economic growth rate: input and efficiency. To emphasise development is to highlight the benefits of economic growth in a certain sense. Economic efficiency is the relationship between resources, labour occupation and consumption in social production activities and the extent to which their achievements (outputs) and social needs are satisfied.

It is true that in order to ensure economic growth, it is possible to adopt high investment methods, which require raising and maintaining a higher accumulation rate and mobilising more resources into the economic process. There is a limit, however. The maximum limit of the accumulation rate is the need to raise the material and cultural living standards of not only the original but also the newly added population. Otherwise, we cannot reach socialist production and economic development goals. In the past, China had pursued high accumulation and a high rate of development through direct reduction of people's consumption. Such a practice could achieve rapid economic growth in the short term, but it is not likely to maintain sustained economic growth.

Today, we have entered the middle-income country category and can no longer continue a development strategy that relies on high accumulation to achieve high input. Our high investment strategy is actually implemented at a time when per capita resources are very scarce, and the level of resource consumption is much higher than other countries. The existing resources can no longer support such an investment strategy. The limited supply of land and mineral resources, the limited capacity of environmental resources and the limited stock of knowledge and technology amongst labourers have posed a "bottleneck" to further economic growth. The economic fluctuations that have frequently occurred in China can also be explained by this high investment. Reliance on high investment means the rate will only go up temporarily. The "bottleneck" of resources cannot support a high rate for a long time. The rate will inevitably decline, and large numbers of construction projects will subsequently grind to a halt, resulting in a waste of human, financial and material resources. This shows that the strategy of high input economic growth has come to an end in China. Highlighting benefits is not simply a matter of adjusting the rate. The most important thing is to shift the foundation of economic growth to improving input efficiency.

The pursuit of an efficiency-based rate should be the goal of transforming economic development mechanisms. Nonetheless, we must also note during the transition of the mechanism that rate-based benefits remain effective. This means the benefits of economic growth still lie greatly in the growth rate. The reason is that the operating rate, the market purchasing power and other factors that directly affecting profits are relevant to the rate. Therefore, we cannot simply place efficiency and the rate in competition and assume that a high rate is bound to correspond to low efficiency. This puts forward two requirements for the economic growth at the present stage. First, it is necessary to maintain a higher rate when the benefit is associated with the rate, but efforts must be made to seek a mechanism to promote both efficiency and rate. Second, the rate must be controlled in the field of one-sided pursuit of GDP indicators. Simply relying on increasing the rate of investment will not produce rate-type benefits. The expected speed of economic growth in China at present has been adjusted greatly from the past 10% of high growth rates to the middle- to high-speed growth of 7.5%. The aim is to make greater space for the transformation of the economic growth mode and improve the quality of economic growth.

In some people's view, increasing input is the characteristic of extensive growth mode. Therefore, increasing input is closely related to intensive growth mode. However, a careful examination of the basic connotation of the growth pattern reveals that this judgement is one-sided. The premise for making a correct judgement is to confirm that China's current economic development stage is still a transition period in which investment drives consumption. The role played by investment remains great.

In terms of increasing investment, intensive growth does not exclude the necessary investment in essential factors. From an economic point of view, existing resources should be fully used and contribute to economic growth. Economic growth needs to mobilise existing available resources to secure full employment in the context of ensuring sustainable development. Intensive growth does not mean that these factors are not "employed" but that these "employment" resources must be used in the most effective manner and that these elements must be fully effective under conditions of economical use.

In the market economy, various factors, including tangible elements such as capital and labour, as well as intangible elements such as technology and organisation, are integrated into the production process through capital input. The improvement of the quality of various factors also depends on capital input. It means that the increase in capital investment is not exactly the characteristic of extensive growth; capital investment also can serve the intensive growth approach.

In modern times, the share of efficiency increase in the economic growth rate is clearly higher than the contribution of capital stock growth. However, as Roemer and Gillies point out, the reality of developing countries is that while capital is not as big as the early growth model, it does play a large role in developing nations today.

In any case, although capital accumulation is no longer regarded as a panacea for poor countries to get out of their plight, it is very clear that only if society sustains a considerable scale of investment in gross national product, can it maintain an appropriate and also a strong income growth rate in the long run.

Obviously, the purpose of the intensive growth mode is not to exclude capital investment but to attach importance to the efficiency and quality of capital input.

Roemer and other scholars listed a number of ways to increase the efficiency of capital investment. In countries with capital shortage, labour-intensive investment is more efficient than capital-intensive investment because a small amount of capital can promote a large number of abundant labour in developing nations. As some of the technological advances that lead to efficiency are reflected in capital equipment, capital flows (importing foreign capital) remain the focus of policymakers in developing nations. In addition, investment in human capital will also increase the efficiency of capital investment. After entering the new economic era, the decisive factor of economic growth turned to knowledge, technology and human capital. Although both intellectual capital and human capital are considered "capital," their formation and accumulation still require investment. Unlike other types of capital, investments in intellectual and human capital are more valuable and efficient.

In the report *The Quality of Growth* issued by the World Bank in 2000, President James D. Wolfensohn points out that the core of economic growth is not only the growth rate but also the quality of growth. The sources and patterns of growth affect the effectiveness of development. The report questions the mere reliance on GDP growth as a measure of progress. The specific requirements for highlighting the quality of growth are the following: combining policies of promoting economic growth with universal education, strengthening environmental protection, increasing civil liberties and strengthening anti-corruption measures so that people's living standards can be significantly improved. The report emphasises that we need more and better "high-quality" growth. This is not a luxury product but an outcome of decisive significance for a nation to seize opportunities to improve the lives of this generation of its people and their descendants. Obviously, all these quality requirements are included in the definition of development.

The quality of economic growth is also reflected in sustained and steady economic growth. Fluctuations in the economic growth rate are normal. The stability of economic growth refers to the fact that fluctuations will not be far away from the equilibrium point without drastic ups and downs. What shall we take to measure this stability? The most intuitive and representative measure is to use the annual GDP growth rate as an indicator. If the GDP growth rate varies slightly between different years, it shows that the stability of economic growth is good. If it varies greatly between different years, the stability of economic operation is poor.

It is unavoidable that economic operation and development have their cycles. The stability of economic growth cannot overcome the cycles, but it can iron out the ups and downs in a certain range and reduce any abnormal fluctuation.

From the perspective of economic development, the promotion of stable growth depends on a variety of conditions. First, the population must grow steadily. Only in this way can the per capita gross output value be steadily increased. Second, technological advances in agriculture will reduce the possibility of crop failures. Third, improvements in transportation will expand the scope of resource supply. Fourth, the decline in agriculture's share of total output value and the rise in the share of other industries will raise the level of controlled ability of technology. Fifth, and finally, the stability of the system and policies will provide a system guarantee for the steady growth of the economy. In addition, the stability of economic growth has a lot to do with the mode of the growth. The extensive mode of economic growth means a one-sided emphasis on the increase in economic values or indicators, ignoring related superstructure factors such as population, society, culture, legal systems and natural environment. Over time, this type of economic growth is bound to be unstable.

2.3 The intensive economic growth mode

The intensive growth mode focusses on the quality of input factors, the efficiency of organisational allocation factors and the progress of knowledge and technology. According to total factor productivity, the economic growth rate is not the simple addition of physical capital, labour and natural resources but the result of the effective combination of various factors of different kinds of productivity.

2.3.1 Replacement and supplement of elements

The intensive growth method includes the effective configuration and organisation of economic elements as well as improvement of the efficiency of resource allocation.

In economic growth, capital, labour and natural resources form basic alternative relationships. There are two bases for the substitution of factors: one is the output elasticity of various factors (the contribution to growth). In general, those factors that have greater elasticity of output should be used more frequently. The other is based on the degree of scarcity of domestic resources. We must use more of those relatively abundant resources. There may be contradictions between these two aspects, which put forward the equilibrium problem in factor substitution.

Judging from the current situation in China, capital output elasticity is undoubtedly greater than other factors. There is a great shortage of capital, which raises the question of how to make full use of domestic labour resources. Facing the scarcity of natural resources, especially non-renewable resources, we have to seek alternatives to deal with the need for sustainable development. It means we have to use the relatively abundant resources to replace the non-renewable, scarce resources and to replace the consumed natural capital with acquired capital.

In a market economy, an important mechanism for the market to determine the allocation of resources is the recognition that there are many different elements entering the market, and the prices of these factors are regulated by the supply and demand of each factor market. The mechanism of mutual replacement of regulatory elements is the price ratio of various elements. For example, the interest rate below the wage rate should encourage the use of more funds and less labour, which may lead to economic growth under the constraints of insufficient funds. Unless labour resources are used fully and effectively, there will not be appropriate economic growth. The key to solving the problem of substitution of non-renewable resources is to raise the price of using these resources.

Amongst the elements of economic growth, technology and organisation are complementary elements of others. Although technological progress may save money and labour and play an alternative role in the specific process of production, for the development of the entire national economy, all kinds of existing resources should play a full role in economic growth. The role of technological advancement is to overcome the "bottleneck" of insufficient supply of funds and improve the quality of labour and the supply conditions of natural resources. Technology clearly plays a complementary role here. As for the organisation, its supplementary role is beyond doubt. The larger the input scale is, the more important the organisation becomes.

In the economic growth process, the key to the allocation of technology and organisational elements is to actively promote technological innovation and organisational innovation and to strengthen the diffusion of technology and the improvement of organisational systems. The combined function of various factors – namely, total factor productivity – is thus fully released.

The price mechanism can be used to solve the problem of resource shortages. Raising the price of natural resources that may be exhausted can drive competing producers to replace them with more abundant and less expensive resources. If there are no other resources to be replaced, the price of commodities that use expensive resources, such as raw materials, is relatively higher than those of other commodities. Consumers will buy fewer of these commodities and turn to other commodities, which will ultimately serve to reduce the demand for resources.

2.3.2 Endogenous growth

Different factors invested in the economic growth model, such as capital, labour and natural resources, are all qualitatively different. Different quality input factors differ in their effects on economic growth, which means that economic growth is not in proportion to the increase in the input of these material resources. High-tech equipment, high-quality labour and high-quality natural resources will yield higher productivity than the general increase in material resources. The improvement of the quality of these material elements, as well as efficiency, depends on technological advancement, which does not take effect only as residual value and exogenous factors, but is inherent in the improvement of the quality and efficiency of various material elements, which leads to endogenous growth.

Endogenous growth theory is a new theory that emerged in the 1980s with the rise of the information technology revolution. The economists who contribute to this theory are Paul Michael Roemer and Robert Emerson Lucas Jr.

According to Roemer, knowledge accumulation is an important factor in modern economic growth. Knowledge is divided into general knowledge and specialised knowledge. The former is used to increase economies of scale, while the latter can increase the incremental benefits of factors of production. Combining the two functions generates incremental gains and increases the returns of other inputs, such as capital and labour. The virtuous cycle has thus formed: investment promotes knowledge innovation, while knowledge innovation promotes the increase of returns to scale and further expands the scale of knowledge investment, enabling long-term economic growth.

Knowledge not only has its own incremental effect but also can impact production factors, such as capital and labour. It makes capital, labour and other production factors generate incremental returns, thus increasing the scale of the economy as a whole. This is endogenous growth. Investment in knowledge innovation is more valuable than that in production. The total expenditure on research and development and their proportion in total GDP have a significant impact on long-term economic growth. Hence the differences between enterprises and countries in the investment of knowledge innovation ultimately manifest themselves in the differences in the rate and quality of economic growth.

Lucas holds that human capital accumulation is the source of economic growth. Specialised knowledge and skills and human capital accumulation can yield incremental gains in production and increase other input earnings and total-scale returns. Human capital is the determinant and permanent driving force of modern economic growth. Investment in manpower is the most valuable. The accumulation of human capital also has endogenous characteristics for economic growth. It is reflected in the improvement of people's ability to innovate and workforce quality, turning enterprisers into entrepreneurs. The differences in various economic growth can thus be explained by the difference in the level of human capital accumulation and the comparative advantages of the various countries in international trade.

Therefore, the effect of technological advancement on economic growth cannot be understood as an exogenous variable. Technological advancement is also a multidimensional vector. Each parameter used at the technical, organisational or scientific skill level in the production process is an integral part of this multidimensional vector. By introducing technological advancement to the production function, we can analyse the changes in capital, natural resources and labour productivity that it causes. Through these variables, we can take into account changes in production technology, the increase in the proficiency of the workforce, the improvement of health care and their roles in economic growth.

Economic growth is the increase in the amount of goods and labour produced by a country, which may result from an increase in the input of production factors or an increase in the efficiency of inputs. The general economic growth model is concerned with the role of factor inputs in economic growth, both tangible and intangible. Tangible elements include capital, labour and natural resources; intangible elements include technology, knowledge, organisation and systems. At different stages of economic development, the influence of various factors differs. Correspondingly, according to the main factors of economic growth, we can divide economic development into five stages: (1) resource economy, (2) labour economy, (3) capital economy, (4) technology economy and (5) knowledge economy. At present, the five kinds of economies coexist in China. The dominant one, however, is still the economy with the tangible elements of resources, labour, capital, etc. Therefore, when studying economic development, we must pay attention to the availability of these limited tangible elements and the efficiency of their allocation. We should also focus on the intergenerational allocation of exhaustible resources and the related sustainable development issues.

In their book titled *Economics of Development*, Malcolm Gillis and Roemer divide capital into three types, based on economic growth models that include only capital and labour elements. The capital stock of machinery, construction and infrastructure is considered acquired capital. The knowledge and technology labour force is human capital. They believe that natural resources should be included in the economic growth model. Corresponding to acquired capital, they formulated the concept of natural capital, which refers to the value of a country's existing natural resources. Like acquired capital, natural capital is usually consumed in the production process and can also be increased through the natural growth of renewable resources and investment in discovering new resources.

The efficiency of capital investment in terms of intensive growth is mainly related to the efficiency of capital allocation amongst various elements. Capital investment can be used to promote a greater amount of capital stock and labour, but intensive growth emphasises the importance of the quality of these elements. The quality of China's current factors is too low, including the lack of modern skills amongst the labour force, the backward machinery and equipment, the inadequate grade of mineral resources and poor land. Relying on such low-quality elements for the growth process cannot contribute much to economic growth. Therefore, in considering an increase in intensive growth, the key to enhance the contribution of factor inputs into economic growth is to improve the quality of inputs. Specifically, we must pay attention to human capital investment and improvement of the quality of workers, technological innovation and technological development investment, investment in the adoption of new technologies in production and, finally, improvement in land fertility and investment in various natural resources. Correspondingly, the chief focus of capital investment should be on research and development, education, technological innovation and promotion.

The input factor in China with the lowest quality is probably human capital—that is, the stock of human knowledge and technological skills. Labour is an element of economic growth, but labour elements are neither homogeneous nor irrelevant. In different countries and different periods, the physical quality, educational levels and skills of workers have varied widely. These variations – the differences in human capital – produce different levels of productivity and correspondingly different contributions to the input of labour factors. Clearly, at this development stage, the labour that can play a role in economic growth is no longer unskilled labour but workers with a greater level of knowledge and technological skills. The contribution of labour input into economic growth means the quality of input labour, not quantity, is the key. Obviously, investing in human capital and improving the quality of workers are important aspects of intensive economic growth.

Scientific and technological advancement, which is the basis of modern economic growth, involves not only cutting-edge machinery but also an increase in the stock of knowledge and technological skills of workers. At this stage, knowledge and technological skills have to be compatible with advanced machinery and equipment. Faced with the huge gap between China's current stock of human capital and the stock of physical capital, the focus of the current mode of economic growth should be to increase investment in human capital and improve the quality of workers.

The main aspect of human capital investment is investing in education. The new growth theory argues that the scale of benefits generated by improved education is increasing, which is reflected in the increased productivity of scientists and managers who make personal investments in their education. This sets a positive example for others. Such a mutual influence can create external effects. It means investments in human capital will make investments more profitable.

Therefore, when China is experiencing a shift in its economic growth mode, it is critical to offer the current working population improved education and technical training with an eye towards both supply and demand. In terms of supply, we must increase funding for education and training and establish a wide range of different professional and technical training schools or programmes. In terms of demand, we must establish a corresponding system to require labourers to undergo training, including the creation of employment and recruitment criteria based on professional knowledge and technical skills using such criteria to establish a standard wage level.

2.3.3 Economies of scale

Some scholars differentiate the mode of extensive growth from that of intensive growth based on the difference between extension-type and intensive-type reproduction. Consequently, they view the expansion of production scale as extensive growth but the increase in the efficiency of the original scale production as intensive growth. The fundamental error in this view is they confuse the difference between economies of scale and diseconomies of scale.

The role of economies of scale in the total factor productivity analysed by Solow and Denison posits that a considerable portion of income growth is attributed to the expansion of the scale of operation in the economy. This is based on the fact that when the scale of economic operations is expanded, the investment per unit of production is reduced. The reason is that the use of technology at a small scale is economically inefficient, but it produces savings at a larger scale of production and brings economies of scale.

Scale expansion is the inevitable result of economic growth. An important way to differentiate intensive from extensive economic growth is that the former is not keen to invest limited funds in new businesses but in the technological transformation of existing companies. The technological transformation of existing enterprise equipment will inevitably be accompanied by an increase in scale, which is not part of extensive growth. Moreover, according to the requirements of total factor productivity, intensive growth places special emphasis on economies of scale. Expanding the size of advantageous industries and enterprises is an important way to promote intensive growth.

What scale does an enterprise need to achieve to be considered economical? This involves a scientific understanding of the definition of economies of scale. In general, economies of scale are characterised by a reduction in the unit cost of products or services over time as the scale increases. As far as the relationship between scale and economic efficiency is concerned, there is a difference between economies of scale and diseconomies of scale. Economies of scale primarily mean that an enterprise must meet the minimum scale specified by a particular industry. For example, the minimum scale of an automobile factory is an annual output of X 10,000 cars, and the minimum size of a petrochemical enterprise is Y 10,000 tonnes of petrochemicals annually. Those companies that fail to reach this minimum size are illustrations of diseconomies of scale.

The size of a business can be expressed as the size of the input or the output. In a planned economic system, the scale basically refers to the scale of investment: how many employees are in the company, how large-scale the machinery and equipment are and what level the company reaches. Under this system, enterprises with small investment are not taken into consideration. The scale of the market economy system generally refers to the scale of output. In this scenario, a company may have several thousand employees and an annual operating income of tens of millions of RMB, while in another company, the operating income is equivalent to the previous one, but it may only have 100 or 200 employees. Which of the two companies has achieved economies of scale? Obviously, the latter. China's current failure to reach the main crux of economies of scale is precisely the scale of output. Because of repeated misjudgements in construction and investment, many companies produce the same product for the same limited market, and no one can reach the minimum scale. Therefore, the goal of achieving economies of scale is not to expand the investment scale of enterprises but to increase the output scale of enterprises.[3]

The term economies of scale does not mean that the larger the scale, the more economical it is. Whether the scale is economical depends on costs, as well as on the market. It is particularly important to point out that the size of the economy will change with its industrial base. Large-scale economies based on large-scale machines often require larger scales. After entering the information economy, however, economies of scale are not necessarily that big.

We have to solve the problem of how to ensure that enterprises reach the minimum scale, but this does not mean the enterprises have to do so. In addition to the grouping approach, there is another way, which has yet to be fully studied, for China to adjust its corporate structure (i.e. to establish a corporate team). If the former approach is to build an "aircraft carrier," the latter one is to form a "fleet."

The formation of a corporate team is a challenge for a large number of small- and medium-sized enterprises. In some industries, small businesses can also reach the minimum scale. Exceeding a certain scale may result in diseconomies of scale. For a large number of small- and medium-sized enterprises that are independent of the large-scale enterprises, organising a corporate team to enter the market can reduce competitive costs. This type of team cooperation may also form economies of scale.

2.3.4 Technological advancement

The depletion of natural resources can lead to a natural limitation of economic growth. Nicholas Gregory Mankiw proposed in his book *Principles of Economics* that "technological advancement will provide a way to avoid these restrictions." Comparing the modern economy with those of the past, the consumption of natural resources has been improved in many ways: fuel-efficient automobiles, newly built houses with better insulation, recycling of non-renewable resources and replacement of non-renewable resources with renewable ones. For example, tin and copper were key commodities 50 years ago. The former was used to make containers, while the latter was used to make wires. Environmentalists worried about overuse of tin and copper. As technology advanced, alternatives to tin and copper emerged: plastic has replaced tin to make containers, and telecommunications now use optical fibres made from sand instead of copper. Therefore, "technological advancement has made some once-vital natural resources less necessary."[4]

According to Roemer's growth theory, production in the information stage is composed of more than capital and labour. Knowledge has become an independent factor for growth, and knowledge accumulation is a decisive factor in promoting modern economic growth. If economic growth so far has relied heavily on the availability of natural resources, after entering the Information Age it will depend mainly on knowledge and information in the future. The significance of the knowledge economy for sustainable development lies in the following three aspects:

1   Substituting knowledge and information for material consumption leads to a reduction of material consumption and environmental pollution.
2   Natural substances can be used repeatedly.
3   Natural substances can be turned into available resources after use through recycling.

In general, technological advancement requires the formation of those technologies which can save energy and raw material consumption in the production sector, improve the efficiency of resource use, replace non-renewable resources, reduce and control environmental pollution, etc.

According to the theory that has been popular for a long time, owing to the obvious labour savings that result from advanced technology and the pressure of employment, China should choose intermediate technology or applicable technology. Such a theory now appears misleading, however. China's expanding employment comes at the expense of the adoption of new technologies in the economy, which is typical of extensive economic growth. This technology choice seems to have survived in the closed economy of the past. Now, with the deepening of reform and the opening of the domestic market, Chinese products have encountered international competition not only abroad but also at home. Our products based on intermediate technologies are clearly lacking in competitiveness. This explains the decline in the efficiency of many companies in recent years because of poor product sales. In reality, products made by some Chinese companies can compete for a larger share of the overseas market if they adopt the latest and most advanced technologies. In addition, those products favoured by Chinese consumers are also high-tech products. It proves that at present, we need to select the newest and most advanced technology in the world to make Chinese products fully competitive in global markets.

Solow uses historical facts to prove that promoting technological advancement and increasing productivity will not necessarily result in unemployment.

From a historical point of view, the situation that the workers worry about is obviously not happening. The current productivity is ten to twenty times that of the industrial revolution in the 18th century, but the unemployment rate is not higher than that time.[5]

Therefore, the fear that the improvement of technology and productivity will bring unemployment is overstated. In reality, technological advancement itself can create new jobs.

China must also take into consideration the challenges posed by some developed countries entering the era of knowledge economy while we promote technology advancement. The economies of developed countries such as the United States have entered the era of the knowledge economy. Obviously, the direct integration of the knowledge economy will lead to a new revolution in the mode of production and inevitably bring about tremendous impact and profound changes in the development of human society. Despite unprecedentedly fierce international competition, China's economic development has yet to enter the era of the knowledge economy. This is a challenge, but it also represents an opportunity for China.

We have now employed the concept of transforming the economic development mode because the development mode carries more meaning than the growth mode. It includes the optimisation and upgrading of industrial structure, innovation-driven economic development, etc. The shift to an intensive growth mode is an important aspect of the aforementioned transformation of the development mode.

Notes

1 Michael P. Todaro and Stephen C. Smith, *Development Economics* (New Jersey: Pearson Education, Inc., 2005), 81.
2 Simon Kuznets, "Modern Economic Growth: Findings and Reflections," in *Selected Lectures of Nobel Prize Laureates in Economics, 1969–1981*, ed. and trans. Wang Hongchang (Beijing: China Social Sciences Press, 1986), 97.
3 Carl Shapiro and Hal Varian use the concept of producer economies of scale and demand-side economies of scale in their book *Information Rules* to explain the external effects of network. In their view, under the information economy, economies of scale refer more to demand-side economies of scale. See Carl Shapiro and Hal Varian, *Information Rules*, trans. Zhang Fan (Beijing: China Renmin University Press, 2000), 12.
4 Nicholas Gregory Mankiw, *Principles of Economics*, tran. Liao Xiaomin (Beijing: Joint Publishing Company, 1999), 148.
5 Robert Solow, "Economic Growth," in *Exploring the Journey of Wisdom: Interviews with Famous Economists from Harvard and MIT*, eds. Liao Li et al. (Beijing: Peking University Press, 2000), 195–212.

3 The consumption drive of expanding domestic demand and economic growth

Having entered the development stage of middle-income countries, an important aspect of transforming China's economic development is a change from the original investment-driven mode in the low-income phase to the coordination of consumption, investment and export to boost growth. This is especially true regarding the consumption-driven impact on economic development. Increasing consumption's contribution to economic growth will play a key role in improving the efficiency and quality of that growth.

3.1 The driving force of economic growth

3.1.1 The basic balance of macroeconomics

The driving force of economic growth can be understood through the basic equilibrium of macroeconomics. According to Keynes, the total output of a country over a certain period will reflect both aggregate supply and demand:

$$Aggregate\ supply = consumption + savings + imports$$

$$Aggregate\ demand = consumption + investment + exports$$

$$Consumption + savings + imports = consumption + investment + exports$$

The previous equilibrium can be reduced further to a basic equilibrium:

$$savings = investment.$$

According to the general macroeconomic theory, economic growth is driven by demand. It is composed of investment, consumption and export—three fundamental factors known collectively as "the troika." In general, the troika should be coordinated, but it can play different roles in different stages of development—sometimes powerful and sometimes small in other circumstances.

When economic growth is driven mainly by investment demand, it suggests that the investment demand is stronger than consumption and export, and the driving force for growth is even greater. On the other hand, the importance of balancing aggregate supply and demand makes it necessary to convert the savings supply into investment demand to achieve economic growth. If savings are less than investment, it is essential to reduce consumption and increase savings to meet the demand for investment.

In a situation where economic growth is driven mainly by consumer demand, it means that consumption demand is stronger compared with investment and export, which contributes even more to growth. From the perspective of a balanced analysis of aggregate supply and demand, however, we need to convert consumption income into consumption demand to achieve economic growth. If consumption is less than consumption demand, we must reduce savings to increase consumption so as to meet the demand of consumption for that of supply.

3.1.2 Changes in the main driving force for economic growth

In the case of demand-driven economic growth, investment, consumption and export are likely to be the main driving forces for different periods in different countries. If some countries implement an export-oriented strategy at certain stages of their development, the main driving force for economic growth is export demand. The focus here is to conduct research on the driving force of investment and consumption.

In the initial growth stage of the economy, growth is mainly driven by the supply factor. At the same time, the level of per capita income is low, unable to produce a high level of consumption. Under these conditions, the main driving force of economic growth is investment demand. The so-called investment-driven mode involves the use of investment to drive supply growth. To achieve economic take-off, large-scale investment is needed. It includes government investment, infrastructure construction and investment in fixed assets to create basic conditions for economic growth. The effect of this investment on the low-income development stage is evident, with a large investment and output effect. The main driving force of China's long-term economic growth has been investment. For example, the contribution rate of the three major drivers of demand to GDP growth in 2010 was 54% investment, 36.8% consumption and 9.2% export, respectively.

When the economy emerges from the low-income development stage and enters that of middle income, the basic conditions for sustained growth have been met. The demand for fixed asset investment is no longer as strong as that of the low-income stage. Meanwhile, consumption by residents is steadily on the increase. In this context, the main driving force of economic growth has gradually shifted to consumption. To meet the needs of people for various products and services has become the driving force behind economic growth. This is particularly true in developed countries. At this stage, the contribution rate of consumption to economic growth is generally more than 70%.

The main driving force for China's long-term economic growth used to be investment; consumption played little role in this growth. However, the report of the 17th CPC National Congress in 2007 made clear that the promotion of economic growth should be shifted from an emphasis on investment and export to a coordinated focus on consumption, investment and export. This clearly gives consumption an impetus in economic growth. It also reflects the fact that Chinese consumption was on the rise in the period of transition between a low-income and middle-income development stage. In 2012, the report of the 18th CPC National Congress further indicated that economic development should be driven more by consumption. It clarifies the main driving force of China's economic growth after entering the middle-income stage. Of course, in the next period, shifting to a new drive of economic growth needs to follow a developmental process. Because of the lack of investment momentum, the power of consumption needs to be nurtured.

3.2 Domestic demand expansion becomes the strategic basis for economic development

The report of the 18th CPC National Congress clearly stated, "We should firmly grasp the strategic basis of expanding domestic demand, and accelerate the establishment of a long-term mechanism for expanding consumer demand." This makes clear that expanding domestic demand is not a quick fix, but a long-term strategic economic development strategy.

3.2.1 The adjustment of the strategic basis for economic development

In general, the driving force of a country's economic development is composed of supply impetus and demand pull. It can be further divided into overseas demand and domestic demand. The driving force of China's economic development has been shifting from supply to demand, and a growing percentage of the demand is domestic.

China's economic development used to be supply-driven, reflecting the characteristics of the low-income development stage of the country. The most salient were, first, the process of rural reform and the development of township enterprises that resulted in a large agricultural surplus labour transfer, thus forming an unlimited low-cost labour supply. Second, the implementation of the strict one-child policy in the late 1980s freed more people from housework to participate in the labour market. Prior to that, there was little family planning. Consequently, the next 30 years saw a very large working-age population in China. This led to a demographic dividend that generated a high savings rate to support high investment and economic growth. Coupled with the relatively abundant supply of land and environmental resources in the early stage of development, these factors supported China's rapid growth over the past three decades.

At present, the factors that have driven this rapid economic growth have begun to decline. First, with the increase in urbanisation (more than 50% nationwide in 2011), the surplus of agricultural labour has decreased significantly, and the supply of surplus labour has entered the "Lewisian turning point." A shortage of migrant workers in south-east coastal areas has begun to appear with a corresponding increase in migrant worker wage and welfare costs. This turns out to be a marked drop in the supply capacity of low-cost labour. Second, with the one-child generation becoming the majority of the working-age population, China has become an ageing society, and the supply of high savings has become unsustainable. This means that the demographic dividend for economic growth has entered a period of decline. In addition, with an increasingly significant bottleneck of energy, resources and environment, competition for buildable land is getting tough, and the price of land is soaring. China's supply-driven economic development has obviously declined. As a result, the engine of economy needs to shift from supply-driven to demand-driven.

The driving force of demand can be divided into overseas demand and domestic demand. Since the reform and opening policy was institutionalised, China's economic development has been stimulated by overseas demand, except for the promotion of supply. The first approach is export-oriented, and the second is the introduction and utilisation of foreign capital. According to the theory of comparative advantage, the expansion of overseas demand in China came from two factors. On the one hand, export and industrial structures are arranged on the basis of comparative advantage and committed to the production and export of labour-intensive, resource-intensive, high-energy consumption and high-emission products. On the other hand, with the introduction of foreign investment, international resources are best used with the availability of cheap labour, inexpensive land and loose environmental constraints. The ability of foreign enterprises to enter China is due to the labour- and resource-intensive link in the industrial chain, as well as production in need of environmental resources. It should be said that the open strategy based on comparative advantage was successful in the early stages of development. The introduction of elements such as foreign investment, technology and management combined with labour force and land elements in China promoted rapid economic growth. However, the development of an open economy driven by overseas demand, which served once as the primary engine, has now begun to decline.

• First, in terms of the international economic environment, the world economy decreased after the outbreak of the global financial crisis in 2008, followed by the sovereign debt crisis in Europe and America. In Europe, the sovereign debt crisis is still spreading, which will inevitably lead to tightening demand. Even if the economies of these countries gradually recover, they have moved slowly as the locomotive of the world economy. The shrinking overseas demand will inevitably strike a blow to China's real economy. Meanwhile, the industrial base of Western developed countries has started to undergo a restructuring process. For instance, the United States has proposed to double its export volume in five years and implemented a re-industrialisation strategy. Developed countries have begun to use their capital and technology advantages to enhance the competitiveness of labour-intensive export industries. To protect their markets, they have adopted various protectionist means to continuously set up import barriers in the name of anti-dumping and countervailing duties. It has inevitably resulted in over-competition and overcapacity in the global market.

• Second, China's labour force and natural resources, which once supported the expansion of external demand, have been losing their comparative advantage. The advantages of cheap labour and abundant natural and
environmental resources that have attracted foreign investment are disap-
pearing. Meanwhile, developed countries with comparative advantages
in technology and capital have entered labour-intensive manufacturing in
China with a real cost advantage. Further, foreign investments entering
high-tech industries in China are mainly labour- and resource-intensive
links. They have not relocated core and key technologies, even the brands,
to China. Therefore, although the volume of export products in China is
large, the added value is not high. In addition, along with the improvement
of China's economic development, the prices of labour and land have also
risen sharply. Although the prices of these elements may not seem high
compared with those of the developed countries, the corresponding productivity advantage is obviously no longer there. This means that in relation to
labour costs, labour productivity has no advantage, and land productivity
has no advantage either.

Therefore, the existing development effect of the overseas demand-oriented economic model, based on the use of our natural resources and labour force, has
obviously diminished. The economic growth achieved by foreign trade and the
utilisation of foreign capital based on this comparative advantage is only increasing in quantity with no improvement in quality and benefit. The disappearance
of this comparative advantage determines the objective necessity of China's economic development shifting to rely mainly on expanding domestic demand. It is
the basic explanatory factor for expanding domestic demand on a strategic basis.

Given that domestic supply capacity and the driving force of foreign demand
are simultaneously diminished, China's economic development engine needs to
shift from relying on foreign demand to domestic. As Stiglitz puts it,

> First, as its economy grows and as the global economic environment changes,
> China will no longer be able to rely as fully on the export- and FDI-ori-
> ented model that has so far driven its reform-era growth. At the same time,
> China faces the challenge of continuing to improve resource allocation and
> productivity.

The response to this challenge is "making the domestic economy the engine of
growth and equality."[1]

3.2.2 Expanding domestic demand

To stimulate economic growth by means of expanding domestic demand reflects
the need to transform China's economic system into a market economy.

Domestic demand refers to the investment demand and consumption arising from domestic development. When the domestic demand-driven impact on
economic development is clear, it is necessary to further study the extent of

China's capacity for domestic demand. A positive answer is that the overall size of China's domestic market will be at the forefront of the world. More specifically, China's 1.3 billion people mean an unmatched domestic demand market. China's regionally imbalanced development has also formed a diversified and multi-level market demand. In addition, the Chinese consumer culture is a potentially lucrative market. Chinese consumers may spend above their income level. Finally, China has one of the emerging market economies, which has two advantages. On the one hand, when China enters the stage of economic growth, all elements, such as industrialisation, urbanisation or information system construction, will produce strong investment demand and an increase in consumption. On the other hand, much market demand in China is in the process of developing from nothing. Such commodities as automobiles, housing, subways and other infrastructure are different from those in developed countries in which the demand is building on previous levels. In comparison, the demand in China is growing from scratch.

Economic development relies on expanding domestic demand; however, the emphasis is on "expanding," not just "demand." Moreover, the huge space for expanding domestic demand does not mean that it is a real domestic demand. Therefore, expanding domestic demand market needs not only to discover but also to blaze new trails. The main approaches include establishing a long-term mechanism for expanding consumer demand, maintaining a reasonable growth of investment, and expanding the size of the domestic market. If the mode of development driven by consumption demand is not yet fully in place, maintaining reasonable investment growth by initiating new investment projects can effectively promote the expansion of domestic demand. Of course, shifting to expanding domestic demand does not exclude continuing to open up to the outside world, accessing the overseas market and participating in an international division of labour with the goal of nurturing China's competitive advantages.

International experience demonstrates that economic development in large countries depends mainly on domestic demand regardless of their status as developed or developing nations. Only by strategically expanding domestic demand can we truly enhance the endogenous driving force of economic development and make it a complete success. In reality, China is the largest developing nation in the world, with a large population and a vast territory. We are now standing at the dawn of a development stage that represents an enormous strategic opportunity. We have entered a crucial stage in adjusting and upgrading our consumption and industrial structures. China has a huge market and ample room for development. Whether it is improving the living standards of urban and rural residents or strengthening the weak links in economic and social development, there is a huge demand for consumption and investment everywhere. We should firmly grasp the strategic basis of expanding domestic demand by seizing these favourable conditions. It means improving the consumption capacity of residents and the environment, upgrading the consumption structure, adjusting and optimising industrial structures in line with the new industrialisation, information system construction and urbanisation, as well as agricultural modernisation, and continuously improving the social security system. We should actively promote the consumption of green products and services and expand effective investment while optimising our investment structure.

Investment and consumption are the two primary engines for producing GDP. In other words, the driving force behind economic growth actually has two systems that promote GDP. The investment-driven chain works as follows: expanding investment demand (investment) – promoting economic growth (GDP growth) – further expanding investment demand (investment). The consumption-driven chain works in a similar manner: expanding consumption demand – promoting economic growth (GDP growth) – further expanding consumption demand. Both chains play a common role in expanding production. The former directly increases production capacity and thus creates more GDP, while the latter imposes needs on production and increases GDP by generating additional consumption. (Of course, consumption is not equal to wasting.)

Expanding domestic demand cannot rely solely on the chain of investment. Special attention should be paid to consumption. Although both consumption and investment fall within the scope of aggregate demand in the macroeconomy, consumption demand has more distinctive significance for a shift in economic growth mode. Compared with the investment demand, consumption demand belongs to the final phase of demand, and the products fuelling investment demand are only in intermediate demand. The effect of economic growth depends on the final demand. In contrast, the production of products and services increased by expanding investment demand cannot become a realistic and useful GDP without consumption. In reality, the investment-driven mode has led to overcapacity in many fields. This problem does not lie in producing too many commodities but in a lack of consumer demand. It is in this sense that consumption-driven GDP growth is more reliable.

In social reproduction, including production, exchange, distribution and consumption, production, as well as consumption, can be the starting point. There should be consumption before someone produces, and a product can complete the production process only when it enters the consumption process. Thus

> consumption posits the object of production as a concept, an internal image, a need, a motive, a purpose. Consumption furnishes the object of production in a form that is still subjective. There is no production without a need, but consumption re-creates the need.[2]

This clearly points out how consumption drives production and thus in turn economic growth. The shift to a consumption-driven economy is not only about the expansion of consumption but also the development of a consumer economy. The basic consideration for developing a consumer economy is that China is not only a big producer but also a big consumer. After China's total production becomes the second-largest economy in the world, the overall size of the domestic market will also be amongst the highest in the world. Faced with ever-increasing consumer demand, the point of new economic growth is to develop the consumption economy so as to promote China's economy to a new level with the goal of satisfying and guiding consumer demand. This is also the basis for China to become a consumer power.

3.3 Developing consuming power and increasing residents' income

The most important factor for expanding domestic demand is to expand consumption demand. Robert Solow has a well-known conclusion: the ultimate goal of economic growth is consumption. No country should be required to go after growth for the sake of growth.[3] The consumption growth rate depends not only on the growth of production but also on factors such as the size of the population, the employment opportunities, the growth rate of workers' income and the prices of consumer goods. Increasing the level of people's consumption itself is also a driving force for economic growth. Economic growth driven by consumer demand is reliable because of market assurance.

3.3.1 To develop and improve consuming power

Economic development in low-income countries generally emphasises the development of productive forces. After entering the stage of middle-income development, it is necessary to clearly identify the requirements for developing and increasing consumption capacity. In fact, the concepts of productivity and consumption capacity were put forward by Karl Marx. Developing productivity and consumption capacity are equally important.

So-called consumer spending power refers to a consumer's ability to consume within a certain period of time. Marx's concept of developing productive forces includes increasing consuming power. He said,

> It is by no means abstinence…but the improvement of productivity, to develop the capability to consume, and to develop the material of consumption. Consuming power is the prerequisite for consumption, and thus is the primary means of consumption. Developing one's consuming power also means to develop one's capability, thereby developing productivity.[4]

Here, Marx regards the development of consuming power as inextricable from that of productive forces. The development of productive forces is in synchronicity with the development of consuming ability and data. The development of that ability is equivalent to that of personal talents. Marx put forward the concept of social consuming power when analysing the contradiction of reproduction in capitalist society. He pointed out,

> [Consuming power] depends neither on absolute productivity nor on absolute consuming power, but on the consuming power based on adversarial distribution. The distribution of power that narrows the consumption of the majority of society to a minimum that can only be changed within a rather narrow boundary, which is also limited by the desire to seek accumulation.[5]

On the one hand, this illustrates the influence of social consumption on the macroeconomy; on the other hand, it also points out the distributional relationship that affects consuming power and the proportional relationship between accumulation and consumption.

The concept of consuming power can be used to perfect the aggregate supply and demand of the Keynesian macroeconomic equilibrium, which can be expressed as "consumption + savings = consumption + investment." It can be further reduced to "S = I" (i.e. "savings equals investment"). The disequilibrium between savings and investment, or how much savings can be transferred into investment, becomes the primary factor accounting for overall disequilibrium. The same logic can be applied to the relationship between investment on the left side of the equation and consumption on the right side. Investment is part of the total supply. It refers to the post-distribution income to be used for consumption (the consumption pool). Consumption, on the right side of the equation, refers to the demand for final consumption. At a certain stage, the disequilibrium between the two creates two possibilities: (1). Real consumption is less than the demand for consumption. Consumer demand is met through credit because it exceeds the supply of the consumption pool. (2). Real consumption exceeds consumer demand because the consumption pool resulting from the distribution of income is not fully used by consumer demand. The lack of consumer demand in China has long been attributed to the fact that the consumption share of the distribution of national income remains low. In addition, despite the presence of a consumption pool, people remain reluctant to spend in the current income stage. Both aspects have much to do with consuming power.

The consuming power of an entire society is determined by its social distribution. The immediate cause of the economic crisis arising from overproduction is confrontational distribution relationships. They "reduce the consumption of the bulk of society to a minimum varying within more or less narrow limits. It is furthermore restricted by the tendency to accumulate, the drive to expand capital and produce surplus-value on an extended scale."[6] From this analysis by Marx, we learn the important lesson that the ratio of accumulation (savings) to consumption is important to a nation. Consuming power, therefore, exerts a direct impact on macroeconomic equilibrium. Suppressing the consumption rate while allowing the investment rate to go too high will inevitably lead to an economic crisis. This fact indicates that it is not wise to attempt to achieve rapid growth through high investment alone. To maximise the driving power of consumption on economic growth, China must increase the ratio of its citizens' individual income in the distribution of national income, thereby proportionally increasing the consumption rate.

In addressing the consuming power of China's population, the most basic issue is whether people have money to spend. Individual consuming power is determined by a person's income. Raising the income of both urban and rural residents could enhance their overall consuming power. We should thus strive to increase the proportion of individual income to national income. Different income groups, however, will exhibit different consumption elasticity with increased income. Consumers can be categorised into low-, middle- and high-income groups. Studies find that the consumption elasticity of the low-income group is the greatest. Specifically, an increase of one dollar in income for the low-income group would be spent immediately. With the middle-income population, for every one-dollar increase in income, about half would be spent, and the rest would be saved. For the high-income group, however, the entire one-dollar increase would be saved, making their consumption elasticity the lowest. To increase consuming power in China, the priority should, therefore, be placed on the low- and middle-income populations. Increasing the income of the poor has a greater impact than poverty reduction. More importantly, it will enhance the driving force of consumption on the economy. The basic approach is to strive to achieve the synchronisation of residents' income growth and economic development with the increase of labour remuneration and labour productivity. The goal is also to increase the proportion of residents' income in the distribution of national income and the proportion of labour remuneration in primary distribution. We also need to protect the labour income and, meanwhile, increase residents' property income through multiple channels.

In addition to wage levels, employment and market prices are the most important of the many factors affecting the disposable average income. Employment is the basis of people's livelihood, and a stable employment environment is crucial to maintaining consumer demand. Unemployment cuts back people's income and reduces consumption. In addition, consuming power is also determined by market prices. With high inflation, people's real wages will decrease. In reality, the various income groups have different Engel coefficients, with that of the low-income population being the highest. In some cases, it reaches 50%, meaning the low-income group is the most sensitive to price increases. Inflation affects this group's consuming power the most. In a consumption-driven economy, the government should manage the macroeconomy better by curtailing inflation and managing unemployment to safeguard the consuming power of the low-income population in particular.

Another significant issue in the development of consuming power is the willingness of people to spend the money they have. The key here is consumer expectations. With good consumer expectations, increased individual income can be transformed into real consuming power and generate immediate consumption. Basic institutional arrangements must thus be established to foster such expectations on the part of the average Chinese. The public and social welfare expenditures of the government play a guiding role in this regard.

- First, China's social security system must be improved. In the past, the pensions and health-care benefits of urban residents were provided by the enterprises for which they worked. Rural residents depended on the land for their livelihood. China's ongoing urban reform has broken down the enterprise-based social security system, while the industrialisation and urbanisation processes are taking away the land-based guarantees in rural areas. The construction of a social security system in China cannot keep up with the country's fast development, which makes people hesitant to spend money, even with increased income. Establishing and improving the social safety net will assuage people's concerns. Their increased income will then be more likely to be spent in the market. At present, low-income groups with the least coverage under China's current social welfare programmes, especially farmers and migrant workers, have the highest consumption elasticity. Therefore, such groups should become the focus of expanding social security coverage.

• Second, the public service infrastructure must be improved. The government should provide people with equal access to compulsory education, basic medical care, public transportation and other public services to increase their consuming power. The government can also provide the average Chinese with better expectations. These basic public services are essentially quasi-public goods. Although paid for by the government, consumers are required to share a portion of the costs. The proportion of such costs borne by individuals has a direct impact on their capacity for consumption. At present in China, the supply of high-quality education and health-care resources cannot meet demand. In the meantime, the income gap between different groups results in the variable affordability of such quasi-public services. In this context, China's market-oriented reforms have penetrated the field of basic public services. In some regions, hospitals, schools and other public services have become completely privatised. Even without such full privatisation, the market's "invisible hand" is at work. Consequently, a few people profit through arbitrary fees and price hikes, leading to problems such as unaffordable schooling and health care. As a result, even people in the middle-income range have to save for a rainy day. Given these circumstances, basic public services should be provided by the public sector (state-owned enterprises or institutions). The private sector should play only a supplementary role in case of insufficient supply by the government. Meanwhile, the government should increase its investment in education, health care and other services to increase the supply of premium services and mitigate the financial pressures on service providers. The goal is to ensure the accessibility of public services to low-income groups so that they can develop positive consumer expectations and expand their consumption of commercial products and services.

At present, people are most concerned that, with an increasing living standard, China will lose its comparative advantage, which was built on low labour costs, thereby reducing its international competitiveness. We must note that, in the current global economic context, comparative advantage based on low labour costs has a diminishing return as a competitive advantage. In addition, whether and by how much to raise workers' wages is not arbitrary. It is decided by labour productivity and synchronised with its improvement. Finally, increasing labour costs will force China's enterprises to transform from labour-intensive to technology-intensive industries and explore new business models to compensate for increasing labour costs.

3.3.2 Full employment and employment efficiency enhancement

Because employment is the source of income, only when it expands and the income of labourers increases will there be a basis for expanding consumption.

In general, the labour and employment situation reflect the living standards of the people. Once employee income levels are set, the employment range will be wider, and the employment rate will be higher, leading naturally to a higher living standard for the people. At present, all governments should make full employment and achieving a high and stable level of employment major goals of the macro-control. This is even more so in the socialist countries where working people are the masters of their own lives. Under socialism, the right to work is a fundamental civil right. Labourers as owners of the society participate in the socialist construction, which is an institutional guarantee for full employment.

Full employment means that every labourer who has the ability to work and is willing to work can find employment opportunities. In the past, China adopted the "iron rice bowl (meaning a life-long job) employment system." Once a person is employed, the worker would have the job forever. In reality, however, there are a large number of on-the-job unemployed workers within any given enterprise. Now that China is entering a market economy system, the employment system has undergone tremendous changes. For example, if an enterprise abandons the "iron rice bowl" labour and employment system, some employees will flow out of the enterprise. The bankruptcy of enterprises will also make the workers lose their jobs. When the economy is in a downturn, employees will also be forced to stay home with discounted wages when the enterprises are stopped or half shut down. This will make the unemployment problem in China overt. Once the workers lose their jobs, they become "proletarians," and their livelihoods cannot be guaranteed. This brings us to the real challenge of the issue of full employment. As a government for the people, China has the responsibility to take effective measures to ensure full employment, which must rely on economic development. The economic development of the socialist countries must aim at establishing full employment.

Labour is an essential element of economic growth. The employment situation is linked to the level of economic growth. In general, the expansion of employment – i.e. an increase in labour input, can promote economic growth to a certain extent. Employment's role in labour-intensive sectors is particularly evident at the stage of economic growth that mainly relies on labour inputs. The employment rate is particularly high when the economy grows at full speed. In contrast, when growth slows down or stagnates, the employment rate decreases correspondingly. Economic growth itself also has the role of absorbing the expansion of the labour force. To maintain a certain rate of growth, it is necessary to maintain a certain rate of investment, which will always promote a certain amount of employment, although the two may not necessarily be in the same proportion. Implementing scale economy and developing new areas of production can provide more employment opportunities.

Although the socialist system has created sufficient employment opportunities for labourers, the imbalance of the total labour supply and demand remains a serious problem in China. The pressure of employment is very heavy. In terms of labour supply, urban employment is not only pressured by the additional working-age population but also the surplus agricultural labour force. With the improvement of agricultural labour productivity and the development of rural commercialisation, more surplus agricultural labour will have to leave the land to find new employment opportunities.

In terms of labour demand, employment opportunities provided by economic growth are limited. As far as the material conditions of labour are concerned, an average of RMB10,000 in fixed asset investment is required for each additional job position in the 1980s. With the improvement of reasonable sources of funds, more investment in fixed assets will be needed. This means that the expansion of employment scale is limited by the accumulation capacity of China. In terms of exploiting new fields of production, it is restricted not only by the limits of the technical level that has been reached at that time but also by the willingness of the workers to choose their jobs. Because of these restrictions, on the one hand, economic growth tends to reduce labour demand relatively. On the other hand, the increase of labour employment to a certain extent cannot play a role in promoting economic growth. Its marginal productivity may tend to be zero or negative.

Employment pressure is also reflected in a conflict of economic development goals. With a certain level of national income and share of consumption, an excessive increase in the employed population will reduce the income level of the working population to a considerable extent. To create jobs, labour-intensive technologies have to be used in many areas while giving up opportunities to adopt capital-intensive technologies. The pace of technological advancement is thus delayed, sacrificing many opportunities for development. All these analyses show that the so-called employment pressure is ultimately the pressure on China's long-term economic development.

Under the conditions of socialism and facing heavy employment pressure, China has not only expanded employment by widening production fields but also by developing various economic sectors. However, it should be made clear that the employment system which suits long-term development cannot only solve the problem of full employment but also must improve employment efficiency.

The improvement of employment efficiency means that the labour force is fully used, effectively allocated and labour provided by employees during working hours is effective. There is neither underemployment nor on-the-job unemployment. However, in reality, the contradiction that cannot be ignored is that increasing employment efficiency may reduce the demand for labour. The reason is that there are two conditions for improving labour efficiency. One is employment competition amongst workers, while the other is to determine the scale of labour demand based on the marginal productivity of labour.

In the past, China has tried to guarantee high employment with a low-wage policy. The practice of economic development shows that this does not overcome the objective contradiction between labour supply and demand. It only masks the unemployment phenomenon. On the surface, the unemployment rate is very low. All workers have jobs, but several people share a job requiring only one person's labour. The crowding of a surplus labour force in agriculture is also a hidden form of unemployment. All this hidden unemployment and underemployment reflect a huge waste of labour resources and a major cause for inefficient labour.

Addressing structural unemployment also requires efficiency. The pressure of structural unemployment mainly refers to the unemployment caused by the workers' lack of training, which cannot meet the needs of jobs. The structural contradiction will become increasingly acute as economic growth gradually shifts to a track that relies on scientific and technological progress. The willingness of workers to choose their jobs will also result in structural unemployment. Because of the large gap in different industries in terms of working conditions and income, the unemployed in cities with relatively developed economies are more likely to find a job with a desirable environment, light work and high pay. This makes it more difficult for labour-intensive industries, such as textiles, construction and mining, to recruit workers. Thus they have to recruit a large number of migrant workers from rural areas and out of town. As a result, the difficulty coexists in both recruitment and employment. On the one hand, the urban unemployment rate is high. On the other hand, the recruitment is difficult. This structural unemployment has made it difficult for economic growth to reduce the unemployment rate.

The fundamental way to solve the inefficient employment issue is to reform the employment system with the goal of developing a socialist market economy. The key to reform is to truly establish an enterprise's main position as an employer and a labourer's main position as a worker. Enterprises have the autonomy to employ their staff and workers, while employees have the right to choose their own jobs. Enterprises and labour are then in a position to sign labour contracts on this basis.

Increasing employment efficiency will inevitably further aggravate existing employment contradictions. The shift of unemployment from the hidden form to the overt one is a painful change. There will inevitably be frictions and shocks. As a socialist government which is responsible for its people, China needs to adopt a series of reform measures to reduce the possible frictions and shocks that may arise so as to achieve a balance between full employment and the ratio of employment. To this end, China needs to establish a sound social security system, including providing unemployment insurance, establishing and improving the labour reemployment mechanism and facilitating job creation by adjusting and optimising industrial structure. In addition, in the process of structural adjustment and technological progress, we should not exclude the use of labour-intensive technologies and the development of some labour-intensive industries so as to retain the necessary jobs in the process of economic growth and make full use of our abundant labour resources.

3.4 Medium- and high-end consumption and narrowing the income gap

Under socialism, consumption is not only a condition of social reproduction but also becomes its overarching goal. Production is no longer simply for the sake of itself but also for consumer demand, which truly becomes its starting point and destination. Consumption demand can be met to the maximum based on production development, with which its level has also been increasingly improved. When economic development relies more on expanding domestic demand, especially on consumer demand, achieving a better and faster economic development will depend on the growth and upgrade of consumer demand.

3.4.1 The trend of consumer demand growth

China is about to build an overall well-off society, which requires consumption with modern characteristics. The perfection of living services and facilities, as well as higher levels of health and nutrition, for people is characteristic of consumption at the well-off stage. This means the selectivity of people's new spending is gradually increasing; the proportion of household income used for food consumption is gradually decreasing as that of non-food consumption gradually rises; the proportion of service consumption is gradually increasing and so on. The growth of consumption in all these areas depends on the development of production and its structural adjustment. In general, as the goal and motivating force of production, consumption will play a leading role in the development of production, especially in the adjustment of product and industrial structure if consumption advances moderately. Stimulating consumption means stimulating production.

According to the Marxist theory, production determines consumption, but in turn, consumption also determines production. Consumption creates new needs for production, providing motivation and purpose for production. Marx concluded,

> If it is obvious that production provides the object of consumption externally, then it is equally obvious that consumption conceptually proposes the object of production, and presents it as an inner image, as a need, as a motivation and purpose. Consumption creates a production object that is still in subjective form. If there is no demand, there will be no production. Consumption reproduces the demand.[7]

Especially in the market economy, consumption plays a more significant role in promoting and stimulating supply. After entering the middle-income stage, the so-called consumption pull relies more on medium- and high-end consumption.

Medium- and high-end consumption reflects people's need for a better life after entering a new era, which is an important symbol of high-quality development. The report of the 19th CPC National Congress views medium- and high-end consumption as a new growth point and new momentum that needs to be cultivated. Improving the supply system is not only meant to enhance the supply capacity in quantity but also, more importantly, to keep up with the increase of consumption demand for quality so as to meet people's needs for a better life.

What is medium- and high-end consumption? It involves two levels: first, it means the consumption of medium- and high-end people, especially middle-income people with the strongest consumer desire and the highest consumption capacity. At present, China has the world's largest number of middle-income people, amounting to 300 million. Even the consumption level of low-income groups is escalating, especially because of the impact of comparison culture, which will also stimulate demand for medium- and high-end consumption. Second, compared with the low-end consumption aimed at solving the problem of food and clothing, medium and high-end consumption chiefly seeks to satisfy the development and enjoyment level of consumers. More attention is paid to the brand, quality, grade, environmental protection, safety, taste and so on.

The key to the growth of consumer demand is to mobilise people's consumption. For a long time, there has been an obvious imbalance in the growth of consumer demand in China, as shown by the relatively weak growth of household consumption. This is due in large part to institutional causes. In the traditional system, the main drawback of the consumption mechanism is that the market adjustment range of consumer demand is too small, subject to rigid budget constraints. The conspicuous feature is that on the one hand, the proportion of self-sufficient consumption is too large in the vast rural areas; on the other hand, the proportion of welfare and public welfare consumption is too high in urban areas. This kind of welfare-free consumption is conspicuously manifested by taking advantage of free medical services, using public funds for eating and drinking, as well as other recreational activities, sightseeing at public expense and so on. The institutional disadvantage of such consumption is that it resists market regulation and exerts strong pressure on the market. First, the consumer demand for income is inflexible. Second, the consumer demand is inelastic regarding prices. Third, the consumer demand lacks a meaningful hierarchy. Correspondingly, the growth of residents' consumption demand is based on the public expense and welfare expenditure, which is not regulated by the market. Until the consumption of public expense and welfare expenditure is restricted, the consumer demand will be weak.

In a developing market economy, the primary reform is to increase the proportion of commodity consumption and expand the scope of consumer demand previously restricted by rigid budgets. The specific measures needed are to narrow the scope of state-provided welfare expenditures and change the implementation of welfare policies so that people's income can cover all kinds of consumption. It means, through the reform of the housing, medical and public welfare systems, that the "hidden subsidy" in the form of low-cost consumption is transformed to the "public subsidy," which provides subsidies directly to consumers. Strict control is exercised until enterprises and institutions stop distributing physical consumer goods to their employees. This way, the price of consumer goods and consumer services can follow market laws, and the market will be able to play an automatic regulatory role in consumption. Based on this, we can afford to broaden income distribution so that we can place people at different income levels in terms of consumption structure. This includes allowing some high-income groups to carry out high consumption and creating products that satisfy the requirements of consumers at various income levels.

According to the National Bureau of Statistics, in 2017, China's consumption expenditure per capita was RMB18,322, of which urban residents accounted for RMB24,445 and rural residents RMB10,955. The consumption structure of urban and rural residents was ranked according to the proportion of consumption expenditure per capita. This was reflected in the following data: food and tobacco consumption expenditure per capita was RMB5,374 (accounting for 29.3%); residential consumption expenditure was RMB4,107 (22.4%); transportation and communication consumption expenditure was RMB2,499 (13.6%); education, culture and entertainment consumption expenditure was RMB2,086 (11.4%); medical and health-care consumption expenditure was RMB1,451 (7.9%); clothing consumption expenditure was RMB1,238 (6.8%); daily necessities and services consumption expenditure was RMB1,121 (6.1%); and other consumption expenditure was RMB447 (2.4%).

To narrow the income gap, we need to expand the middle-income group. According to income level, people can be divided into three classes: high-, middle- and low-income. The sign of poor countries is that the proportion of low-income groups is too large. To make people rich means not only allowing some people to get rich first but also, ultimately, requires the majority of the people to get rich. China is already the country with the largest number of middle incomers in the world. There are already 300 million people in the group, and the proportion of middle incomers continuous to grow. The middle-income group has the strongest consumer demand, which is the main force for medium- and high-end consumption. Meanwhile, they are the main force of China's "overseas shoppers" in Europe, America, Japan and South Korea, most notably in consumption of high-tech products.

For developing nations, the key to reducing low-income groups and making people rich is to increase the proportion of middle-income people. This is a direct manifestation of enriching the people. Because an increase in the proportion of middle-income people is an inevitable outcome of a decrease of low-income groups, their growth will bring the income level of most people close to the average income level. This is the driving force to overcome existing barriers on the path of building a well-off society. The middle-income class in developed countries is called the "middle class." They are composed of civil servants, lawyers, doctors, business owners, professors, etc. In modern society, middle-income people are the backbone and the most stable class in society. The increase in the income of the whole society is also driven by the expansion of the middle-income class. More low-income people entering the middle-income class means that they are the direct beneficiaries of reform and development, as well as their promoters. From the broadest perspective, the quantitative structure of the low-income, middle-income and high-income groups should not be a pyramid with the majority of the low-income people at the base but an olive-type structure with the majority of middle-income people in the centre. As the middle-income people account for the majority, the income gap of the entire society will be correspondingly reduced. The structure of middle-income people as the majority can drive the expansion and upgrading of consumer demand.

The increase in consumer demand is not only a matter of quantity but also an issue of consumption structure. Marx once pointed out the way to develop productivity by expanding consumption: "Firstly, quantitative expansion of existing consumption; secondly, creation of new needs by propagating existing ones in a wide circle; thirdly, production of new needs and discovery and creation of new use values."[8] The biggest difference in people's consumption between low-income and middle-income development is that of consumption structure. The basic content of consumption demand in the low-income stage is food and clothing, and their demand for material products is more intense. In the middle-income stage, people have reached the level of well-off status. Their demand for education, medical care and environmental protection has become a basic consumer demand. Meanwhile, quality requirements of housing, transportation and information are higher. Private automobiles, as well as housing and modern information products, have correspondingly become essential consumer products. In response to these new consumer habits, people's demand for public services, such as roads, transportation, internet, culture and education and medical services also arises. Satisfying these new and ever-increasing consumer demands will be the main driving force for economic growth in this period.

3.4.2 Narrowing the income gap

All countries face the challenge of equity and efficiency. It is difficult to have equality and efficiency concurrently, but we can take them both into account. The issue is to deal with the problem at different stages of development. In the stage of low-income development, economic development is generally driven by supply. At this time, to give prominence to efficiency, it is impossible to make equity the priority. After entering the middle-income stage, economic development is driven by demand, especially consumer demand. At this point, we must highlight equity and expand consumer demand through equitable distribution.

At present, the world's most commonly used indicator of equality of income distribution is the Gini coefficient, which is between zero and one. When the Gini coefficient is close to zero, income distribution reaches the absolute average. When the Gini coefficient is close to one, the distribution reaches absolute inequality. Based on the experiences of the economic development in some countries, many economists believe that the level of the Gini coefficient is related to the development level. Kuznets points out that the level of GNP per capita and the inequality of income distribution have developed in an inverted U-shape. This means income inequality (the Gini coefficient) grows ahead of the growth of GNP per capita. This level of inequality reaches the highest point when GNP per capita reaches a certain level, which then begins to decline.

Economists, who advocate efficiency as a priority, put forward the trickle-down theory when they emphasise growth and income distribution leaning toward the high-income class. The increase in economic growth rate and savings will "trickle down" income to the low-income groups, thus allowing them to share the fruits of growth.

At the beginning of the reform and opening era, China's Gini coefficient was at a low level for several reasons. First, the per capita income at this time was at a low level. Second, a long-term plan for the implementation of the equal distribution policy was in place. With the establishment of China's market economy system and the policy allowing some regions and people to get rich first, the Gini coefficient rose significantly with the increase of per capita income. In 2009, it reached its peak: 0.491. It dropped down gradually after 2012 to 0.467 in 2017. It was still higher than the level of 0.41 in the United States and 0.36 in the United Kingdom (Table 3.1).

In China today, one obvious issue is that tolerance of the income gap is related to the level of GNP per capita. With a low GNP per capita, even if the Gini coefficient is the same as that of the high-income countries, the inability to guarantee the basic livelihood of the low-income group may result in more serious social problems than those in the high-income countries (Table 3.2). During the economic transition period, farmers' income has declined relatively. Some urban

Table 3.1 Gini Coefficient in China

Year	Gini Coefficient
1981	0.239
1988	0.301
1995	0.340
2002	0.366
2003	0.479
2005	0.485
2007	0.484
2009	0.491
2011	0.477
2012	0.474

Source: *China Economic Information Network.*

Table 3.2 Correlation between Social Issues and Income Gap

GNP Per Capita	High	Low	Low
Income gap	Big	Big	Small
Social issues	Small	Big	Small

workers are unemployed or laid off, and their economic status has changed correspondingly. The ever-widening income gap has occurred not only across different regions but also across classes. Economic growth will be subject to opposition from the groups and classes that are in relative poverty. If the income gap is too wide and the basic needs of the lowest-income group for food and clothing cannot be satisfied when the GDP per capita is at a low level, there will inevitably arise social conflicts. At present, the Gini coefficient in China has reached or exceeded that of the United States and the United Kingdom. Under such circumstances, the GDP per capita (US$8,000) in China was significantly lower than that of the United States (US$50,000). This means that the basic needs of the low-income groups for food and clothing cannot be met. It is the root economic cause for serious social disorders, such as the appearance of robbers, gangsters and swindling at present.

Solving the equity or efficiency problem has a specific time sequence. If efficiency was the priority in the previous period, now is the time to balance equity and efficiency. Widening the gap is the driving force for efficiency, but if the gap expands too wide, especially when the opportunity is unequal, then the resulting social tension and complaints will inevitably generate resistance to the improvement of efficiency. Paying attention to social equity in this situation is a driving force for efficiency. The key to coordinating equity and efficiency is to correctly understand the meaning of equity. The emphasis on equity in income distribution is mainly reflected in three aspects:

- First is the fairness of the distribution process, including equal opportunity of market competition and the equal distribution of income in accordance with the same principle and standard. For example, income distribution for workers is based on the same labour standard, and for investors it is based on the share of capital input. The share of income distribution is equal to the proportion of its input, whether in labour, technology, capital, etc. It is consistent with the increase in efficiency. Fairness can promote the improvement of efficiency. The problem of unfair income distribution refers to the asymmetry between income share and input share. For example, if labourers do not receive their due share of income from their intellectual and technical investment, their efficiency will be seriously affected. Another example is that some people do not invest in productive factors but rely on their personal or political power. It is unfair to obtain higher income through wrongdoing because the results will affect efficiency and lead to social instability and friction. Therefore, the fairness of distribution at this stage refers to the equal opportunity to receive income and rights, which is consistent with efficiency. With equal opportunity, people will have more tolerance for the widening gap between the rich and the poor (unfair results), but they will find it difficult to tolerate unfairness.

- Second is the fairness of the distribution results. Distribution in accordance with the aforementioned fairness principle will inevitably lead to unfair results. The excessive pursuit of fair results will inevitably undermine the fairness principle of the distribution process. Therefore, the issue is not equalitarianism but rather the excessive income disparity from the development perspective. The basic requirement is that some people in areas who got rich should help the others to get rich. The government adopts certain income policies, such as progressive individual income tax, to regulate the income distribution so as to avoid excessive disparities in distribution that result in social instability. The basic consideration for balancing the consequences of unfairness is to increase the income of low-income people, thereby narrowing the income gap. Now the ever-widening income gap is occurring not only between different regions but also between classes. According to Kuznets' inverted U-shaped curve, the income gap tends to widen in the initial stage of advancing modernisation and begins to shrink at a certain stage. To develop an overall well-off society means that the widening income gap cannot wait to be resolved until the realisation of modernisation. It must be resolved in the process of building a well-off society.

- Third is fairness at the starting line. If knowledge, management and technology become more heavily weighted in the income distribution process, then the unfairness of the distribution at the start can never be overcome. Therefore, to overcome the unfairness of the outcome, we must first resolve the issue of fairness at the starting line. This is to provide people with equal opportunities to accumulate intellectual and human capital. The basic approach is to promote fair education, especially the popularisation of higher education, and increase investment in human capital for the low-income group.

3.4.3 The campaign on poverty alleviation

At present, China's low-income class is primarily composed of farmers, unemployed urban residents and laid-off workers. Farmers in this class, even with sufficient food and clothing, have a demand for basic industrial consumer goods that has not been fully met. The consumer demand of this group has the greatest elasticity of income. Each unit of increase in income is likely to generate larger consumer demand. Therefore, increasing people's income to stimulate consumer demand should focus on this low-income class. Since 1986, while allowing some people in some areas to get rich first, China has carried out a massive poverty alleviation campaign. By 2000, China had reduced the poverty-stricken population by an average of 6.39 million people per year. In the decade between 2001 and 2010, a total of 6.73 million were lifted out of poverty annually. However, by 2012, according to the poverty standard of rural households with a per capita net income of RMB2,300 per year, there were still 128 million poor people in China.

The "China Rural Poverty Alleviation and Development Program from 2011 to 2020" proposes that "the goal of poverty alleviation will be achieved by 2020. By then, the poverty-stricken population will be guaranteed opportunities to enjoy compulsory education, basic medical care and housing. This is referred to as 'two no-worries and three guarantees.'" According to this goal, China has established the current rural poverty standard of RMB2,300 per person annually based on 2010 price levels. The National Bureau of Statistics updates this standard annually based on the consumer price index of low-income rural residents. By 2014, the rural poverty standard was RMB2,800 per person annually. By the end of 2014, there were still more than 70 million rural people in China who remained in absolute poverty. The goal of abolishing poverty in the new era is to make sure that the rural poor can achieve poverty alleviation by 2020, and all poverty-stricken counties will be lifted out of poverty.

In October 2015, at the Fifth Plenary Session of CPC's Eighteenth Central Committee, President Xi Jinping made a statement in the "Note on the Proposal of the CPC Central Committee on Formulating the Thirteenth Five-Year Plan for National Socio-economic Development." According to President Xi, the goal of poverty alleviation and development in the 13th five-year plan is to steadily accomplish the mission by 2020 to satisfy the need of the rural poverty-stricken population in terms of food, clothing, compulsory education, basic medical care and housing security. Currently, the growth rate of per capita disposable income of farmers in poverty-stricken areas is higher than the national average, and the main indicators of basic public services are close to the national average. Through the implementation of the poverty alleviation project, the implementation of targeted poverty alleviation and reduction, we will achieve the goal of poverty alleviation for the 70.17 million rural poor people.

According to Xi Jinping, through poverty alleviation and corresponding methods and plans, by 2020, 30 million people can be lifted out of poverty by working by the manufacturing sector, 10 million can be lifted out of poverty by employment transfer and 10 million people can be lifted out of poverty by relocation. For the remaining 20 million poor people who have completely or partially lost their ability to work, their lives can be improved by including them in low-income insurance coverage.

China's poverty alleviation has made remarkable progress. The number of rural poor people declined from 98.99 million in 2012 to 43.35 million in 2016 with a cumulative decrease of 55.64 million and an average annual reduction of 13.91 million. The occurrence percentage of national rural poverty dropped from 10.2% in 2012 to 4.5% in 2016. Overall, during this period, it was 5.7%, representing an average 1.4% annual decline. In 2017, Jinggangshan City and Lankao County took the lead in poverty alleviation. Adding other poverty-alleviated counties, the number of impoverished counties decreased for the first time in history.

China has made a significant contribution to global poverty reduction. According to the current rural poverty standard, from 1978 to 2016, the number of rural poor people in China decreased by 730 million, while the poverty rate dropped from 97.5% to 4.5%. According to the international extreme poverty standard of US$1.90 per person per day, based on the latest data released by the World Bank, the number of poor people in China declined by 850 million from 1981 to 2013, accounting for 69.3% of the total global poverty reduction. The *Millennium Development Goals Report* released by the United Nations Development Programme in 2015 clearly stated that "China has played a central role in global poverty reduction." The new theory and practice of China's targeted poverty alleviation also provide a Chinese example for global poverty reduction.

Notes

1 Joseph E. Stiglitz, "China: Forging a Third Generation of Reforms," in *Prospects of China*, ed. Hu Angang (Hangzhou: Zhejiang People's Press, 2000), 151.

2 Karl Marx and Frederick Engels, *Karl Marx and Frederick Engels: Selected Works*, vol. 2, trans. Central Compilation and Translation Bureau (Beijing: People's Press, 1995), 94.

3 Robert Solow, "Economic Growth," in *Exploring the Journey of Wisdom: Interviews with Famous Economists from Harvard and MIT*, ed. Liao Li et al. (Beijing: Peking University Press, 2000), 202.

4 Karl Marx and Frederick Engels, *Collected Works of Karl Marx and Friedrich Engels*, vol. 46, Central Compilation and Translation Bureau (Beijing: People's Press, 1973), 225–26.

5 Karl Marx, *On Capital*, vol. 3, trans. Central Compilation and Translation Bureau (Beijing: People's Press, 2004), 273.

6 Marx, *On Capital*, 273.

7 Marx and Engels, *Collected Works*, vol. 46, 9.

8 Marx and Engels, *Collected Works*, 391–92.

4 The sustainability of economic development

Economic development must not only be sustained but also be sustainable. This involves the natural limits of economic growth. The scientific outlook on development requires that people live in harmony with nature and that development be coordinated with population, resources and the environment. The concept of ecological civilisation is reflected in all aspects of economic development. This is the meaning of sustainable development. It seeks a new path for civilisation (i.e. it cannot destroy the prospects for future generations to satisfy the welfare of the current generation).

4.1 The natural limits of economic growth

Economic growth is dependent on the supply of natural resources. Land provides economic growth with agricultural labour, food production and raw materials, while mineral resources fuel growth through energy production and raw materials. The environment is also an important natural resource. Clean ground, clean water and fresh air are not only good for health but also make possible economic growth beyond the limits set by environmental capacity.

4.1.1 The contradiction between supply and demand of natural resources

More than 100 years ago, Karl Marx quoted William Petty in *On Capital*: "Nature is the mother of wealth and the father of labour."[1] Engels took Petty one step further, concluding that labour and nature together are the source of all wealth. Nature provides materials for labour, and labour turns materials into wealth. It is evident that natural resources play an important role in creating national wealth. So-called natural resources under discussion here are meant in the broadest sense. Apart from the land and various natural resources, the term also includes the environment and ecology. The basis for sustained economic growth is that the elements of the growth can be continuously supplied.

There are many ways to classify natural resources. According to sustainable development research, resources can be divided into depletable and non-depleting resources. The former refers to resources that are used until they are exhausted. There are two kinds of depletable resources. One is a resource that may be depleted without human action, such as the oxidation of metals. The other is resource depletion owing to human action. It is the exhaustion of resources that raises new issues in economics. Existing economics is the effective allocation of resources in the face of limited resources. Today's economics is confronted with the exhaustion of resources. This raises the issue of the effective configuration of resources across generations.

Based on their respective features, special requirements may exist when renewable and non-renewable natural resources are analysed, in addition to the common requirements of saving and preventing waste. Renewable resources are not the same thing as a sustainable supply. If the ecological balance cannot be maintained and animal and plant habitats are destroyed, renewable resources may not be regenerated. Therefore, sustainable development for renewable resources must promote its sustainability, prevent ecological damage, the extinction of animals and so on. Non-renewable resources – i.e. resources that will eventually be exhausted – are the main factors constraining long-term economic development. According to the short-edge principle, non-renewable resources also restrict the extent to which renewable resources can be used in the long term.

During the course of human development, the relationship between man and nature has gone through the following stages. In the agricultural civilisation, man was completely dependent on nature. People accustomed to farming through the slash-and-burn method were totally reliant on natural conditions. In contrast, humans controlled nature after entering the stage of industrial civilisation. The most extreme version of this was China's slogan "making the mountains lower their heads and rivers change their courses." This led to a predictable result. Economic development not only reached its limits, but also human living conditions became non-sustainable.

During the Industrial Revolution, the development model was characterised by the ruthless plundering of natural resources, severe solid waste and liquid pollution and high carbon-intensive emissions. They led to unprecedented ecological disasters. Such impacts became so widespread that they led to the weakening or even destruction of the environment and to massive shortages of resources and global warming. In his time, Marx discovered that

> the abundance of natural resources tends to decrease correspondingly with the increase in productivity determined by social conditions. For example, we will understand just after considering the effects of the seasons that determine the majority of raw material production and the depletion of forests, coal mines, iron ore, etc.[2]

In response to the destruction of the balance of nature and the deterioration of the relationship between humans and nature caused by industrialisation, Engels argued convincingly, "We should not over enjoy our victory on the nature. For each such victory, nature will take revenge on us."[3] If human beings do not maintain their harmony with nature, nature will in turn endanger their own survival and development.

Primary industrialisation, urbanisation and then heavy industrialisation that occurred in the low-income stage will inevitably lead to resource depletion and unsustainable supply. The ecological destruction caused by industrial reliance on fossil fuels is manifested in the rapid depletion of natural resources, the destruction of ecological systems, the extinction of species, water pollution, air pollution and garbage accumulation. President Xi Jinping pointed out the problem in his writing:

> In the period of poor productivity and physical poverty, human society was able to continue for thousands of years because there was not much damage to the ecosystem. Although industrial civilization began barely 300 years ago, the enormous productivity of human society has created a western-style modernization of a few developed countries. It has threatened the survival of mankind and the continuation of the earth's biology.[4]

Based on a growing awareness of serious resource and environmental problems caused by industrial civilisation, people's understanding of the relationship between man and nature has entered a new phase. This is the phase in which man and nature will live in harmony. Its connotation is expounded by President Xi in his report to the 19th CPC National Congress:

> Man and nature are the communities of life. Human beings must respect nature, conform to nature, and protect nature. It is an irresistible rule that only by following the laws of nature can human beings effectively prevent detours in the exploitation and utilization of nature. Human damage to nature will ultimately hurt human beings themselves.

4.1.2 "The doomsday model"

In the early 1970s, the Club of Roman drafted a research report entitled *The Limits to Growth*. It used the system dynamics model to study the effect of five factors on human development: world population growth, food production, industrial development, resource consumption and environmental pollution. It also depicted a "doomsday model": if the current population growth rate and resource consumption continue because of food shortages, the depletion of resources and serious pollution, the world's population and industrial production capacity will undergo a sudden and uncontrollable collapse. More specifically, population growth and economic growth are constrained by food, non-renewable resources and pollution. The loss of land fertility caused by over-cultivation, reduced grain production and extremely depleted resources will eventually stop economic growth and lead to the so-called zero growth. Environmental pollution will eventually suffocate humans. According to "the doomsday model," technological advancement can only increase the growth of population and industry but cannot eliminate the ultimate limit of growth. This kind of growth limit theory is called neo-Malthusianism.

The publication of the report by the Club of Rome gave rise to widespread concern and controversy and was widely criticised. So the club commissioned relevant scholars to carry out the second and then the third research report.

The second report, entitled *Mankind at the Turning Point*, was written by Mihajlo Mesarovic of the United States and Eduard Pestel of Germany and their colleagues. It addressed the criticisms of the first report that considered the world as a whole. Mesarovic and Pestel divided the world into ten regions according to different levels of economic and cultural development and the distribution of globe-wide resources. Hence a "multi-level world system model" came into being. It shows that before the middle of the 21st century, different regions may have experienced economic collapses at different times because of different reasons. These regional breakdowns will affect the entire world. The greatest threat to growth is still the increase in population and the lack of an energy supply.

The third report, entitled *Reshaping the International Order*, was authored by Jan Tinbergen, the first Nobel Prize laureate in economics. It softened the tone of the arguments made in the first two reports. However, Tinbergen still believes that most of the land suitable for cultivation has been developed and population pressures remain. He considers energy to be the main resource problem. The way to ease the conflict is to use natural resources more effectively. Developed countries and poor nations must develop industries that are beneficial to them to expand international trade and exchange resources.

The basic starting point of all three Club of Rome reports is the scarcity, non-renewability and irreplaceability of natural resources. Faced with the threat of depletion of natural resources, population growth and economic expansion have natural boundaries (i.e. the limited availability of resources that can be mined but cannot be regenerated, the limited capacity of the environment to absorb pollution and the limited amount of arable land and food production per unit of arable land). These are the natural limits of economic growth.

Based on the actual experience of developed countries, many economists pointed out that the limits imposed by the aforementioned natural resources supply to growth can be broken. The reason is that the scarcity, non-renewability and irreplaceability of natural resources can be altered. Investment and technological advances can alleviate the scarcity of resources to some extent. With the advancement of science and technology, mankind can discover new resources in the natural world. With the aid of price mechanisms, relatively abundant resources can be used to replace relatively scarce resources. With investment and technological advancement, inferior land can become fertile, and the consumed land can, to a certain extent, return to its original conditions. The desert can become an oasis, and low-grade iron ore can be turned into pig iron.

In general, developed countries can rely on their abundant capital and advanced technology to overcome the limits of nature. For these countries, natural resources are relatively insignificant. In developing nations, however, the mitigation of scarcity of resources is limited by capital and technology. The less advanced a country is, the less capital is available, and the quantity and nature of the supply of natural resources become more important. As for now, economic growth in developing nations has to consider the natural limits set by the supply of natural resources, the effective and full use of resources and improvement of the supply conditions of natural resources.

It should be pointed out that the resources a country lacks can be obtained through international trade in the modern economy. This also depends on the export competitiveness of these countries, however. Many developing nations lack precisely such capacity.

4.2 The cost of development

For developing nations, the scarcity of natural resources, as well as their rigid impact on economic growth, is not only the result of their lack of capital and technology but also the strong demand for natural resources in this stage of economic development.

The process of economic development in developing nations is mainly the process of structural transformation: primary industrialisation, urbanisation and, finally, heavy industrialisation. This is a process that a country and a region have to go through when being transformed from a traditional society to a modern society and from poverty to wealth. However, no matter which aspect of the structural transformation leads to strong demand for resources, it can deplete those resources, thus forming the cost of development.

First is the industrialisation process. The process of transforming an agricultural society into an industrial one will not only create a strong demand for land resources but also a demand for mineral and water resources. During industrialisation, it is unavoidable that arable land is turned into industrial land because of the need to set up factories. Environmental impacts, such as water pollution and air pollution, caused by industrial production are the costs of development.

Second is the urbanisation process in which rural residents relocate to cities. With the corresponding development of urban facilities, as well as the expansion of the city scale, the construction of an urban-rural transportation network will inevitably require more and more arable land. Along with urbanisation, problems such as urban waste, wastewater and exhaust emissions will seriously damage the environment.

Third is the heavy industrialisation process. Heavy industrialisation is an important stage of the modernisation of national manufacturing. It is inevitable that heavy industrialisation will greatly increase the demand for mineral and energy sources, leading to an increase in the consumption of non-renewable resources.

For developing nations, rapid and wasteful consumption of natural resources are the result of two chief causes. First, in the early stages of economic development, developing nations tend to prioritise growth at any cost while ignoring sustainable development. They feel that what they lack the most are capital and technology and fail to realise the scarcity of natural resources. Therefore, in pursuit of economic growth, they do not take into account the cost of natural resource consumption. The abuse of natural resources inevitably follows. Second, although developed countries also increase heavy resource consumption when they go through industrialisation, they can plunder the natural resources of underdeveloped nations that still have agricultural economies. Moreover, in restructuring their economies today, they have transferred industries with high pollution and heavy consumption to developing nations. Such a practice has caused developing nations more crises as they are now entering the stage of industrialisation. This is why their problems, such as scarcity of resources and environmental and ecology pollutions, have become more prominent.

Developed countries now seem to pay more attention to sustainable development, but they treat the issue seriously only after they complete their industrialisation. In this sense, they should be responsible for the unsustainable development of developing nations. We live on the same planet. Therefore, developing nations are duty bound to sustainable development. As they enter the early stage of industrialisation, they must seek to secure a path to sustainable growth to reduce the cost of economic development.

China is now at the stage of industrialisation, urbanisation and modernisation. It is a process characterised by a significant transformation of the economic structure. It is evident that our economic growth has been driven by resource consumption. Structural transformation and economic development have created a huge demand for natural resources, which has further overstretched them. We now see several contradictions emerge.

First is the contradiction between the supply of and demand for land resources. Most developing nations in this stage of growth have encountered a potential crisis because they have to use arable land to build factories and construct infrastructure, such as roads. However, to ensure that the supply of agricultural products continuously grows, they have to control land use. Meanwhile, they need to develop technical means to increase the fertility of the land to compensate for the decrease in cultivatable land. Unfortunately, many developing nations have often overlooked this issue, thus creating a potentially severe crisis in land resources.

Second is the contradiction between the supply of and demand for mineral resources, including fossil fuels used as energy sources and metal and non-metallic minerals essential as raw materials. The course of growth in developed countries shows that industrialisation started with the rapid growth of mineral consumption. In the first 80 years of the 19th century, coal consumption in the United Kingdom increased by 15 times and iron consumption by 40 times. In the 48 years after the American Civil War, iron consumption increased by 27 times, copper ore by 47 times, aluminium ore by 32 times, coal by 38 times and crude oil by 98 times. Today, the industrialisation and urbanisation that most developing nations have experienced correspond exactly with this period of growth in the demand for mineral resources. Its important feature is that the growth rate of consumption of mineral products is faster than the economic growth rate. As reserves of the world's mineral resources, especially crude oil and coal, shrink and mining conditions deteriorate, the supply and demand dilemma will become increasingly serious.

While there is a rapidly growing demand for natural resources, developing nations are limited by their mineral reserves, exploration and mining capacity, as well as their ability to import mineral products. Growth in the supply of mineral products is slow, and the gap between supply and demand has become increasingly acute. The contradiction is more prominent in small countries at this stage. Compared with other countries, China's energy consumption per unit of GDP is significantly higher for several reasons. The proportion of industrial production in China's GDP is high, and energy-intensive industries account for a higher proportion. Another reason is China's low energy utilisation. This is a problem derived from lagging technology, a low level of professional collaboration and serious waste caused by institutional factors. According to the *World Resources Report* in 2000, a comparison of China's energy consumption and seven industrialised countries shows that the energy consumed to create one dollar of value in China is 4.3 times of that in the United States, 7.7 times in Germany, 7.7 times in France and 11.5 times in Japan. Overall, it is 5.9 times greater than the average of the seven industrialised countries.

Another important factor is the destruction and protection of environmental resources – the space in which we work and live. Using environmental resources comes at a cost. The capacity of the environment to absorb pollution is very limited. If the pollution cannot be absorbed, it will endanger human health and affect production. The deterioration of the environment has now become a huge obstacle to the progress of human civilisation. The main manifestations of environmental degradation are the greenhouse effect, which has caused global warming; damage to the ozone layer; acid rain pollution; water shortages; desertification of land; deforestation; species extinction; the spread of toxic chemicals, etc. According to a report published by the World Bank, 10 million hectares of forest are destroyed every year throughout the world, 20 million hectares of farmland are reduced because of the loss of soil. Twenty-five people are killed by severe water shortages and water pollution, and one-fifth of animal and plant species may be extinct in 20 years.

According to Professor Li Yining's analysis, environmental pollution is widespread. Whether through production or consumption, waste is inevitable. Clearly, no production and consumption can avoid waste discharge. What people can do is to control and manage environmental pollution. He also believes that pollution control is but one of the goals of human society. The reason why poverty is the enemy of environmental protection is that people are forced to abandon environmental protection just for the sake of survival.

4.2.1 The inverted environmental Kuznets curve

Environmental economics often uses the environmental Kuznets curve (EKC) to represent the inverse U relationship between the degree of environmental pollution and the stage of economic development (Figure 4.1). In the initial stage of economic development, environmental conditions are good because human activities are limited, and few environmental resources are used (Point A). As the economy continues to develop, people use more and more resources, but there is not much improvement in how resources are consumed. Thus human activity begins to have a greater effect on the environment. The environmental carrying capacity decreases and environmental pollution begins to surface and grow (Point B). When people realise this problem, they begin to pay attention to environmental protection and improving how resources are consumed to reduce the impact of human activities on the environment. Economic development also

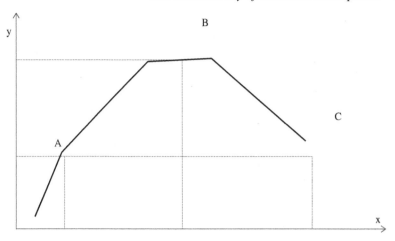

Figure 4.1 The Environmental Kuznets Inverted U-curve (x: Level of Economic Development; y: Degree of Environmental Pollution)

produces a strong ability to manage the environment. At this point, the degree of environmental pollution drops significantly. Technological progress outweighs the loss of resources. Environmental pollution begins to ease, and the environment gradually improves (Point C).

According to Figure 4.1, developed countries have now entered Point C, while China is in the middle between A and B, closer to B of the EKC. We have already begun to bear the consequences of environmental pollution and are increasingly aware of the importance of environmental protection. Meanwhile, the level of our economic development has reached a well-off stage. At this time, an important goal of modernisation is to improve the level of health. The main solution is to build a resource-saving and environment-friendly society and enter Point C.

China has experienced many years of extensive resource exploitation and simple reinvestment of economic development, resulting in more serious environmental problems, such as air pollution, soil erosion, land desertification, salinisation, water ecological imbalance, forest and grass vegetation destruction, sharp decline in biodiversity and deterioration of marine ecology. In the context of the greenhouse effect and global warming, these problems are particularly severe and prominent.

From the perspective of economic analysis, the limits of the growth will be manifested in the price increase determined by the supply and demand relationship. An insufficient supply of material resources will lead to an increase in their cost (i.e. an increase in prices), thereby creating an upward limit on economic growth. Environments such as air and water are non-competitive and non-exclusive. They are a kind of "public goods." The consumption by production and life is considered "free," so it is inevitable that abuse will occur. In the end, the use of air and water is not free. Nowadays, environmental pollution has caused huge losses in society. It has not only increased the cost as measured by the decline of health levels but also the environmental cost of economic activities, which exceeds the self-repairing ability of the environment. Therefore, it is no longer free. We also need to pay for the cost of environmental protection. In this way, higher and higher environmental costs will inevitably impose a limit on growth. In general, economic growth is incapable of paying the cost of necessary resources and environmental inputs, and economic growth will thus stop.

Faced with the limits of growth caused by resources and environmental pressures, China's modernisation must establish the concept of sustainable development and integrate ecological civilisation construction into all aspects of modernisation so as to ensure that modernisation is based on ecological civilisation. Advancing modernisation based on existing development requires a focussed solution to ecological and environmental problems. We have to address not only the symptoms but also the root problems. Only after the environment and ecology have been fundamentally improved will there be more space for economic growth and modernisation feasible.

4.3 Sustainable economic development

A study of economic development history reveals that most of the strategies and concrete measures adopted by developed countries in their pursuit of industrialisation and modernisation were predatory in nature. Today, in the context of the deteriorating global environment and resource supply, developing nations have begun to enter the stage of industrialisation and modernisation. What they have experienced thus far is exactly what developed countries encountered. Therefore, to achieve sustainable human-nature harmony, we must abandon the industrialisation model of developed countries and the modernisation path of pollution first, control after. Of course, the cost to developing nations is much greater than that of the developed countries.

4.3.1 The proposal for sustainable development

In general, humanity and nature are the most harmonious in the primitive state. This state does not merit our discussion, however. What we need to solve is how to maintain harmony between humans and nature with development, which is specifically reflected in the coordination of economic development with population, resources and the environment. This is called sustainable development.

Industrialisation has transformed agricultural civilisation. The modernisation of science, economics, politics and culture has reached a higher level in industrial civilisation. However, the rapid development of industrialisation and urbanisation has brought about a series of negative ecological effects. To achieve rapid growth, the overexploitation of resources, destruction of ecological balance and severe environmental pollution have resulted in the destruction of our living conditions. Although people's income levels have increased because of economic growth, their health has been significantly affected. This is obviously not a worthy development and is not sustainable.

In response to the world's resource and environmental crisis, discussions on "the limits of growth" began in the 1970s. In June 1972, the United Nations held the first-ever "UN Conference on Human Environment" in Stockholm. It resulted in the Declaration Concerning the Environment and Development and opened the door to people across the world to protect the environment. The idea of sustainable development came into being at the same time. In November 1983, the United Nations established the World Commission on Environment and Development. In 1987, the commission formally proposed the sustainable development model in a long report titled *Our Common Future*. The United Nations Conference on Environment and Development in 1992 approved the "Agenda of the 21st Century." It consolidated people's understanding of the theory of sustainable development in the contemporary era and officially proposed the concept of "environment friendly."

Sustainable development, according to the definition from the World Commission on Environment and Development, is "(human) beings have the ability to sustain development and ensure that they can meet current needs without endangering the ability of the next generation to develop."[5] The concept of sustainable development has actually opened the way to a new era of economic development (i.e. to provide for the welfare of people today without compromising the sustainable development path for the welfare of future generations). Sustainable development is a system with rich connotations.

First, sustainable development requires that population growth should be coordinated with resources and the environment. Rapid population growth will increase the burden on resources and delay a rise in living standards. Only with the population size and growth rate in tune with the changing production potential of the ecosystem can sustainable development be possible.

Next, sustainable development means meeting the basic needs of all people and providing everyone with an opportunity to live a better life. The outstanding issue at the present stage is the existence of a development gap between developed countries and developing countries. The level reached by developed countries has come at the expense of unfairly plundering the resources of developing nations and the resulting environmental degradation. The primary task for developing nations is thus to eliminate poverty through development. Because they face the most urgent goal of eliminating poverty, developing nations cannot afford to take the responsibility of protecting global resources and the environment. To meet their basic needs, it is not only necessary for developing nations to achieve a new stage of economic growth but also to ensure they obtain a reasonable share of the natural resources necessary for sustainable development. This requirement for sustainable development is also seen in the relationship between developed regions and underdeveloped regions in China.

Sustainable development requires intergenerational equity. We have used too fast our already excessively exploited environmental resources. If we continue to do so, the resources will disappear. Our descendants will suffer as a result, leaving future generations with no choice. Therefore, this kind of economic growth means the present is choosing to sacrifice the prospects of the future.

From the perspective of general economics, existing resources should be fully used and contribute to growth and achievement of "full employment." Even if we have to consider efficiency, we need to "employ" all these elements to use resources in the most effective way and to promote economic growth. At present, to live in harmony with nature, we must fully use non-renewable resources.

Sustainable development does not mean a stop in development but to take active measures in growth, adjust development strategies, reduce the demand for natural resources, increase investment in nature and improve the supply of natural resources.

Sustainable development of natural resources includes the protection and responsible exploitation of water resources, management and sustainable use of land resources, protection and control of forest resources, protection of marine resources, rational utilisation of mineral resources, development, utilisation and protection of grassland resources, etc. In reference to industry development, sustainable development mainly involves that of agriculture and rural areas, as well as the energy and raw material industries.

To realise the sustainable development of resources and the environment, it is necessary to change the mode of economic development. The most urgent priority is to change the traditional development mode, which pursues only the GDP growth and prefers industry to agriculture. The industry mode, especially the automobile industry, based on the use of fossil needs to be changed. New economic development methods in alignment with the requirements of sustainable development mean that we have to protect natural resources. Development should be based on renewable energy and resource reuse. The practice of putting development before treatment should be changed to placing equal importance on development and treatment and ultimately putting treatment before development.

Today, the sustainability of economic development has been emphasised. This is the inevitable result of the re-examination of the lessons learned after enjoying the brilliant achievements of industrialisation and modern civilisation while paying a heavy environmental price. The most essential innovation of the sustainable development theory is to change the previously conflicted relationship between man and nature to a harmonious one at present and transform the simple economic indicators of the past to the integrated and coordinated development of the economy, society and nature. The core issue of sustainable development is the contradiction between man and nature (i.e. the contradiction between the need for human survival and progress and the consumption of natural resources).

4.3.2 Ecological civilisation

Like other developing nations, China has adopted predatory growth methods in the early stages of industrialisation, especially in areas where industrialisation initially took place. The environmental damage that resulted from long-term overexploitation has been very serious (i.e. global warming, reduced biodiversity, acid rain pollution, desertification of land, marine pollution, water pollution, toxic chemical pollution, etc.). These problems must be resolved in the process of promoting modernisation.

The stage of ecological civilisation is the one in which people and nature live in harmony. As a development theory, it reflects the ability to respect, adapt to and protect nature. According to this notion, people not only refuse the barbaric and brutal plundering of nature but also actively improve and optimise the relationship between man and nature, thus forming an environment in which man and nature, as well as man and society live, in harmony, a virtuous cycle of all-around development and sustained prosperity. Human production and lifestyle ought to intervene in nature in the most appropriate and ultimately civilised way to gain the best result for both nature and humankind.

Ecological civilisation is also an expression of people's yearning for a good life. When economic development is at a low level, people only expect a basic supply of food and clothing, and they will therefore be tolerant of development methods that destroy the environment. The progress of science and technology has promoted the rapid development of the economy. It has greatly improved production, housing, medical treatment and entertainment. The latest technologies and products such as tablets and 3D printing have enriched people's lives. They have begun to enjoy the fruits of economic growth but also have to bear the consequences of environmental damages, such as global warming, acid rain, species-reducing ozone holes, sandstorms and haze. It is people who are paying the price for the economic development.

Having met our basic needs, we have gradually reached an affluent stage, longing for better education and health care as part of modernisation. What affects our health, however, is not just medical care but also the quality of the environment. We can no longer tolerate air, water and soil pollution that endanger health and life. In particular, our awareness of the need for environmental protection has been unprecedentedly heightened after the frequent haze attacks in cities in the north and east. Modernisation for ordinary people is not only wealth but also green mountains and clear waters. In fact, ecology and the environment are also wealth. Clean water, fresh air and a green environment are all valuable assets. Average Chinese need not only to acquire more material wealth and spiritual wealth through modernisation but also more ecological wealth.

The proposal for an ecological civilisation is not to abandon economic development to a kind of primitive ecological harmony but to solve ecological problems, resolve the current crisis, harmonise the relationship between man and nature and achieve rational development. In this sense, ecological civilisation is actually a matter of sustainable development.

The important feature of developed countries is the modernisation of the environment and ecology. Comparing the two indexes of comprehensive energy consumption per unit of GDP and carbon dioxide emissions per unit of GDP (Table 4.1), primary energy consumption in China in 2012 was 3.62 billion tonnes of standard coal, consuming 20% of the world's total energy. The energy consumption per unit GDP was 2.5 times that of the world average, 3.3 times that of the United States and 7 times that of Japan. We also can look at CO_2 emission intensity. Using U.S. dollars as a basis for comparison, China's million-dollar CO_2 emissions were 26.5 tonnes in 2008 – 3.4 times that of the industry average, 9.8 times that of Japan, 6.5 times that of Germany and 4.8 times that of the United States. The gap shows how much we have to do to catch up.

Ecological civilisation pays special attention to the environment that affects the sustainable development of human beings (i.e. ecological issues). The environment in which human beings live and develop includes the relationship

Table 4.1 Index of Energy Consumption and Carbon Emission in Five Countries

	United States	Japan	Germany	South Korea	United Kingdom
Unit GDP comprehensive energy consumption (tonnes of standard oil/US$10,000) in 2006	2.06	1.07	1.73	3.1	1.03
Unit GDP carbon dioxide emissions (tonnes/US$10,000) in 2007	4.1	1.9	2.4	4.8	2.9

between the biosphere and humans, as well as the things that people themselves create. The biosphere includes the earth, the earth's atmosphere and all the creatures on the planet. In this biosphere, people and the social economy become an inseparable part of the environment through the transfer of energy and material in different scales in time and space. Therefore, the development of natural resources by humankind and discarding of the waste have consequences. This environment is fundamental to our lives because a healthy ecological system is a precondition for human prosperity. After all, human beings did not create our planet. It evolved. Thus it is of utmost importance to reach a sustainable relationship with nature to ensure that humankind can continue to live on the earth. We have to understand the relationship between economy and ecosystem from this perspective.

As far as the strategy of building "a beautiful China" is concerned, developing an ecologically friendly, green and liveable homeland is exactly what it means. It requires putting the construction of ecological civilisation at its core and integrating it into the entire process of the economic development and political, cultural and social progress. Promoting ecological civilisation is not simply a matter of pollution control. We must also change the patterns of people's behaviour and the model of economic and social development to prevent the destruction of the environment. We must adhere to the basic national policy of resource conservation and environmental protection. We must also adhere to the principles of conservation, protection and natural recovery and focus on promoting green, recycling and low-carbon development to form a spatial and industrial structure. Meanwhile, we need to improve production methods and lifestyles to conserve resources and protect the environment. We should reverse the deterioration of the environment and create a good production and living environment for people. We will work hard to build beautiful China, realise the sustainable development of our nation and contribute to global ecological security.

4.3.3 Ecological wealth and green GDP

The concept of wealth refers to people's understanding of the value of wealth. The traditional concept of wealth is that of material wealth. In the early stage of economic development, people's understanding of wealth was limited to how it was used and attached to specific physical materials.

Moving from industrial civilisation to the era of ecological civilisation includes changing the concept of wealth. "Lucid waters and lush mountains are invaluable assets." Clean water, fresh air, biodiversity and a green environment are valuable ecological treasures. Such a view is an outcome of understanding the harmonious coexistence between man and nature. Economic development must not only seek material wealth but also ecological wealth. It is impossible to sacrifice ecological wealth for the pursuit of the material one. Based on the concept of ecological wealth, President Xi Jinping clearly stated that "firmly establishing the protection of the ecological environment means protecting the productivity and improving the ecological environment is the concept of developing productivity."[6] The green development concept in the new era means not only protecting and managing the environment but also solving environmental and ecological problems caused by past development and providing high-quality ecological products needed by the people for a better life.

It is necessary to establish the concept and direction of green GDP to make environmental protection and resource conservation become part of people's self-conscious behaviour. In the current national economic accounting system, the indicator of GDP does not truly reflect the costs of preventing environmental pollution, nor does it take into account the consumption and depreciation of natural resources and the cost of environmental degradation. Thereby it gives a misguided account of economic development, which leads directly to false prosperity at the expense of rapid deterioration of environmental resources.

The current widely adopted calculation of GDP does not take into account the effect on environmental destruction and resource consumption generated by economic growth. Consequently, tree cutting has produced GDP because of sales of wood, while tree planting has no value, as it costs time and resources. Such a policy leads to the blind exploitation and waste of resources, as well as pollution and destruction of the environment.

In response to the current GDP-calculation problem, some economists and international organisations have successively proposed ways to improve various indicators to measure GDP. The concept of "green accounting" proposed by the World Bank in the early 1980s and the concept of "green sustainable GNP income" subsequently put forward were quickly accepted. The two concepts have gradually become an important index of measuring modern development and alternatives to traditional macroeconomic accounting. "Green GNP" is defined as the level of income that must be guaranteed without reducing the existing capital level. Here capital includes artificial capital, such as factory buildings, machinery and transportation; human capital, such as knowledge and technology; and environmental capital, such as minerals, forests and grasslands.

First, assuming that the net national product equals the GNP minus the depreciation "Dm" of the artificial capital, in accordance with the definition of the green GNP, depreciation of the amounts of natural assets, such as forests, should also be subtracted. Use "Dn" as the depreciation of environmental capital and the value of the monetary loss of environmental degradation during the year as an indicator. Sustainable income (SI) or "green" GNP can be calculated by the formula

$$SI = GNP - Dm - Dn. \tag{4.1}$$

In Equation (4.1), the monetary loss of environmental degradation (Dn) will be shown in two forms: one is the original loss of the GNP calculations such as the disappearance of wildlife species and beautiful landscapes, while the other is the loss that has been included in the GNP but underestimated, such as crop yield reduction due to air pollution. From the perspective of consumption, sustainable consumption means sustainable income. This level of consumption is equal to the GNP minus the investment required to maintain all the capital, which includes natural resources and environmental capital.

In fact, the sustainable income defined by the aforementioned Equation (4.1) is not quite sufficient. Either GNP or GDP should also be minus (a) environmental restoration costs by pollution (R), (b) pollution prevention and treatment costs or prevention costs (A) and (c) losses owing to the non-optimal use of natural resources and exploitation (N). In theory, there are still some environmental damage costs that are difficult to reflect in environmental capital depreciation (Dn). It is the cost of environmental capacity and resource consumption before the pollution has exceeded the environment's recovery capacity. In this way, we can get a more representative formula for the sustainable income or "green GNP" on the basis of Equation (4.1):

$$SI = GNP - (R + A + N) - (Dm + Dn) \tag{4.2}$$

$$SI = GDP - (R + A + N) - (Dm + Dn) \tag{4.3}$$

The green GDP (i.e. the value of natural capital depletion and environmental damage) thus will be deducted from the total GDP. The cost for restoring environmental quality paid in the year will be deducted as well. The added value of natural resource assets should also be calculated.

Relevant to the green GDP index, the Third Plenary Session of the 18th CPC National Congress clearly put forward the proposal to improve assessment and evaluation of the system, to correct the bias in simply assessing officials' performance with economic growth rate and to increase the weight of the indexes of resource consumption, environmental damage and ecological benefits. Senior officials will be audited on natural resource assets when departing from their current positions. A life accountability system is to be established for the damages to the ecological environment.

4.4 The mechanism to realise sustainable development

In the view of development economics, the only economic judgement of a lack of land and other natural resources is not physical scarcity but cost. Developed countries can generally rely on their abundant capital and advanced technology to overcome the paralysis of nature. The mitigation of the scarcity of natural resources in developing countries is limited by capital and technology. The supply of natural resources is crucial. Severe scarcity of land and mineral and environmental resources imposes very strict natural limits on economic growth. Therefore, the important issue that China's economic development theory should cover is the study of not only ways to increase productivity for resources but also the mechanism for the economic use of resources, as well as ways to invest in resources to increase their supply capacity.

4.4.1 New industrialisation and the recycling economy

China currently stands at the industrialised stage. According to the requirements of sustainable development, it needs to take a new path to industrialisation. This is an industrialised road with good economic benefits, high technology content, low resource consumption, less environmental pollution and full utilisation of human resources advantages. Obviously, this is a new type because it differs from our original road to industrialisation. It is new also because it differs from the industrialisation patterns in Western developed countries.

The new road to industrialisation reflects the transformation of the economic growth model. Its most prominent feature is to change the traditional pursuit of output value and a preference for heavy industry over agriculture. We also need to change the industrial mode that relies on fossil fuels and is flooded with disposable goods, even though it greatly increased the standard of living in the 20th century. In dealing with the issue of development and environmental pollution control and treatment, we should change the practice of placing development ahead of treatment to placing equal importance on development and treatment, ultimately placing treatment ahead of development.

The development of the new industrialisation requires clear choices in resource consumption and environmental pollution. General industrialisation will experience high-consumption and high-pollution stages, such as heavy industrialisation whose general characteristics are the occupation of land resources, non-concentration, high resource consumption and serious environmental pollution. New industrialisation relies on the newest technology to cross this stage of high consumption and high pollution. In particular, the level of industrialisation has crossed the international frontier by pursuing IT applications. At the same time, it has achieved low material consumption and reduced pollution through its clean production with the substitution of and savings on material resources.

The development of the recycling economy is an important way to break down barriers to resource supply essential for growth. It is also an important aspect of achieving sustainable development. The "recycling economy" is both a scientific idea and an advanced economic model. It represents a tremendous transformation from the traditional economic model and can essentially eliminate the sharp conflict between economic growth and the environment.

The recycling economy is characterised by clean production, reuse of resources and efficient recycling of waste. The process of manufacturing products typically produces a large number of leftovers and side products. Part of them can be recycled. The recycling economy can thus minimise the damage to the environment by reducing pollution, maximising the use of resources, saving energy by improving efficiency and creating new value for enterprises by bringing down the social costs of economic development.

The recycling economy relates to various segments, such as production, consumption and recycling; covers fields such as manufacturing, agriculture and service industry; and involves both cities and rural areas. Therefore, promoting the recycling economy requires the adjustment of the entire national economy.

In the adjustment of the industrial economic structure, we must aim at improving the efficiency of resource use in order to reduce the intensity of pollutant discharge, optimise the industrial structure and eliminate outdated equipment, backward technologies and businesses that waste resources and pollute the environment. In the adjustment of the agricultural economic structure, we must vigorously develop organic agriculture, establish organic food and green food bases and drastically reduce the use of pesticides and chemical fertilisers. In the adjustment of the technological structure, the development of high technology focusses on the recycling economy, technology and ecological technology and energetic development of high and new technologies, such as energy savings, consumption reduction and pollution reduction.

4.4.2 The investment in natural resources

In microeconomics, the law of diminishing marginal returns of factors means that if the number of inputs remains the same, with only the input change of one factor, the growth in output resulting from the addition of one unit of variable quantity will gradually decrease with the increase in the input of such elements.

The most typical examples of the law of diminishing marginal returns are land and labour, as well as other essential resources in traditional agricultural production. In farming one mu (666.7 square metres) of land, if the number of labourers working it changes, total, average and marginal output will all subsequently change. Total output here refers to the entire output that can be gained after the input of all production factors. Average output is the result gained based on the average input per unit of the variable factors. It is equal to the total output divided by the total input of variable factors. Marginal output means the output increment that can be obtained by adding one unit of variable input. The aforementioned output changes with the variation in the number of input variables. In the beginning, the marginal output will increase as the variable input of labour increases. When the marginal output increases with the increase in the number of labour inputs, the total output also increases. When the marginal output increases to a certain amount, it begins to decrease. Although the total output will continue to increase for a while, it will gradually slow down. When the marginal output falls to zero, the total output will reach its maximum. As the labour factor continues to increase, the marginal production will become negative, and the total output will also decline.

The law of declining marginal returns tells us that the diminishing marginal returns of labour are not due to the use of less efficient labourers but to the excessive use of labour on a fixed amount of land. With more labour and less land, the role of the labour force cannot be efficiently managed. In the case of a fixed number of factors, the process of obtaining more production by increasing the number of variable factors has its limits. The combination ratio must have an appropriate balance between variable and fixed elements.

The only way to mitigate the trend of declining marginal returns is to invest in natural resources and technological advancement. Marx used the fertility of the land as an example to illustrate the way to change decreasing marginal income. The natural law of farming is that the natural fertility of the land can be used directly at the beginning with little or no investment. When farming reaches a certain level and the fertility of the land has been consumed, capital will become a determinant factor of farming.[7] The same applies to the development and use of other natural resources. The more the economy develops, the more important it is to invest in the supply of various economic development factors. Development economists believe in common that "(the) only judgment of the scarcity of natural resources is cost, not physical scarcity."[8]

Although technological advancement is well expected in overcoming the natural limits of economic growth, there is a problem of insufficient technology supply in developing nations at present. Therefore, scarcity and depletion of natural resources have a great effect on economic growth. Faced with this situation, developing nations need to increase their investment in natural resources and improve the quality and supply of natural resources.

In the face of the limits imposed on economic growth by natural resource supplies, achieving sustainable growth requires the use of capital and advanced technologies to overcome miserly nature. In other words, we must invest in nature before taking resources from nature. The more economic development, the more important it is to invest in natural resource supply conditions.

Faced with the environmental crisis caused by economic development, development economists have raised the question of whether development is desirable. It is obvious that economic growth and environmental protection must be taken into equal consideration. As a scarce resource, the environment itself is also an important factor in economic growth. Faced with the deteriorating environment, developing countries must attach great importance to the investment in environmental management. Only in this way can we expand the space for sustained economic growth.

Regarding land resources, industrialisation and urbanisation inevitably need land. The requirement for sustainable development is to make up for the amount of occupied land by improving the quality of land resources through investment in land. It is also possible to compensate for the amount of occupied land by developing new land resources, such as converting wasteland and tidal flats to arable land.

Investment in natural resources involves two aspects. On the one hand, new resources must be developed to replace non-renewable and scarce resources.

On the other hand, the conditions for maintaining healthy soil and other natural resources can be improved through the accumulation of funds and labour
to produce artificial fertility or increase the abundance and supply of superior
resources, thereby increasing the productivity of land and natural resources. In
general, this approach includes the following three aspects.

- First, mobilising all sectors of society to increase investment in natural
  resources. The allocation of government funds should undoubtedly increase
  the shares of investment in natural resources. We also need to mobilise
  the entire society to increase people's enthusiasm for investing in natural
  resources while diversifying investments. The stimulation methods are
  roughly as follows: (a) understanding that investment income (i.e. differential income) must be owned by investors, (b) ensuring that owners of land
  and other natural resources can use the resources they have invested in for
  a long period of time to increase their enthusiasm for investing in natural
  resources and accumulating labour and (c) adjusting the price system to
  increase the prices of agricultural and mineral products and energy. In the
  current price system, these products are priced too low to cover costs and
  expenses. When their prices are appropriately raised, they can improve their
  self-accumulation capacity.
- Second, adjusting the investment structure of fixed assets to channel more capital into technological transformation projects with a view to reducing the consumption of energy and raw materials. This will produce immediate results as
  energy intensity in China currently exceeds the level of developed countries.
  Our very low effective utilisation rate of energy is caused by technological
  problems. Therefore, those enterprises using more energy must upgrade their
  technology. We need to pay special attention to the technological transformation of the steel, petroleum refining, cement and chemical industries.
- Third, adjusting the natural resources investment structure and reducing the
  cost of its supply to increase efficiency. Developing nations need to reduce
  the cost of natural resources. This will ensure that their use will be no more
  than necessary, and they are being obtained at the lowest possible cost. The
  adjustment of the investment structure of natural resources includes three
  aspects: (1) investing in alternatives, as cheap alternatives could replace
  increasingly scarce and expensive resources; (2) prioritising all kinds of
  resource investment according to the degree of abundance of resources, the
  difficulty in mining and the needs of the national economy; and (c) highlighting investment in the protection of natural resources and providing incentives to increase it.

4.4.3 Institutional arrangements for internalisation of external effects

The small-scale issues that influence the unsustainable supply of natural resources
and clean air and water can be explained by the externality principle in microeconomics. Externality refers to the external effects arising from the economic

activities of an economic unit. There are positive, as well as negative, external effects. For example, establishing an enterprise in a certain area may generate positive external effects such as increasing employment. It may also produce negative effects, such as the emission of pollutants. Externalities that influence the unsustainable supply of resources and the environment refer to such negative effects. Externality must now be taken into consideration in the macro area. The economic activities of a region may bring external negative effects to the entire region. The economic activities of a country may also bring about global external negative effects.

The theory of externality shows that types of economic activity may have corresponding benefits and costs because of their positive and negative external effects. Some kinds of economic activity may collect fees from beneficiaries because of the positive external effects they generate, while others may have to pay compensation to the victims of the external negative effects they generate (i.e. the internalisation of the external costs). Therefore, the impact of externalities can be resolved through two approaches. One is the internalisation of external effects. The effects of production on external society are incorporated into the economic behaviour of producers, and the economic leverage or market mechanism is used to control the occurrence of the negative external effects effectively. The other is to control the occurrence of negative external impacts through government actions or legal means to encourage positive external economic effects on society.

In considering broader environmental issues, dealing with negative external effects is essentially the socialisation of private costs. Attracted by profit, producers generally do not process the waste generated during the production process. Waste treatment requires a certain amount of manpower and material resources, leading to an increase in the cost. Producers are thus reluctant to manage wastes – they want to place them in the external environment, causing economic losses to society (i.e. social costs). This allows producers to "save" their own costs of pollution control. Society, however, has to pay for it. This is the socialisation of private costs. Obviously, it is necessary to internalise the social/private. This means the producers themselves must bear the cost of pollution control, thereby reducing pollution and increasing social welfare to solve the problem of negative external effects of production. From the perspective of resource allocation, the internalisation of negative external impacts can make manufacturers allocate resources more rationally and effectively in recognition that their actions harm society. In this way, the integration of personal and social interests would reduce the waste of resources and environmental pollution. It will undoubtedly promote the sustainable use of resources and contribute to sustainable economic development.

In general, a reversal of the deterioration of the environment depends mainly on administrative and legal measures. The main method is to impose taxes on activities that lead to environmental degradation and make polluters pay. The taxation of automobile exhaust fumes will make it easier to adopt clean transport methods. The state can raise funds for environmental protection by making use of the policies and legal mechanisms, including requiring enterprises to directly cover costs of environmental protection.

The fact that an enterprise pays compensation for its external negative effects can certainly contain its behaviours. Nonetheless, it is impossible to completely eliminate its external negative effects. Emissions are unavoidable both in the production and consumption process. For the consumption of natural resources, as long as there is production, there must be labourers. It is inevitable to use land and consume energy and raw materials. Insisting that there be no environmental pollution and no use of land and other natural resources is tantamount to asking people not to work and consume. Therefore, in the face of external negative effects that cause an unsustainable supply of resources and environment, we need to make a series of institutional arrangements.

First is the adjustment of the price mechanism. It is necessary to establish a resource price adjustment mechanism that reflects the requirements of sustainable development. Prices reflect the scarcity of resources. Optimal resource allocation can only be achieved through the price adjustment mechanism. More specifically, this means (a) The market price of resources regulates the flow of resources to sectors with greater productivity. (b) The market price of resources forces users to analyse the costs and benefits of resources and use resources economically. (c) The resource price is a price ratio, and the prices of different resources are determined by the supply and demand of their respective markets. The prices of the scarcest resources are higher and vice versa. The user will substitute resources for various needs according to the price. They would use the scarcest resources in the most economical way so as to reasonably optimise the combination of resources. To overcome the limitations of the price mechanism, a Pigouvian tax can be coordinated with a licensing system.

Second is construction of a property rights system of resources. The property rights system is a basic social rule that stipulates the status of economic actors in the use of scarce resources. The norms must be followed by actors in their interactions with each other and by the costs they must pay if they do not comply with the norms. "The tragedy of the commons" has evidently reflected the drawbacks in the allocation of resources because common property rights are not clearly regulated. The exclusive property system emerged with changes in the use of resources and people's anticipated income, as well as the decline in the costs of defining and the implementation of property rights. The exclusive property system will solve the problems of overuse of public property and increase the efficiency of resource utilisation. When resources become relatively scarce, the establishment of an exclusive property system plays an important role in increasing social output and meeting human survival and development needs. Accordingly, where private property rights can be clearly defined, it should be done as thoroughly as possible so that natural resources are valued appropriately. For those natural resources that have to remain state-owned, we should try to avoid "the tragedy of the commons." It is necessary to perfect the national asset management system for natural resources and to shoulder the responsibility of ownership of natural resource assets.

Third is to optimise policies for sustainable development. We should include the following major goals in the design of sustainable development policies and systems:

a   promoting economic development;
b   improving the allocation of resources;
c   maintaining the sustainable use of natural resources, protecting the environ-
    ment and promoting harmony between man and nature in a virtuous cycle; and
d   coordinating economic and social development to establish a social security
    system of sustainable development.

Sustainable development policy should cover industrial and technological policies, regionally coordinated development, sustainable development of investment and finance, sustainable development of taxation and prices, international
trade and import and export policies, etc. The system of sustainable development involves the development of China's legal system, including the policies
and rules adjusting economic relations, guiding the development and protecting
social and economic environmental resources and various social relations that
will inevitably occur in the process of economic development and use, as well as
the protection of the environment.

Notes

1 Karl Marx, *On Capital*, vol.1, trans. Central Compilation and Translation Bureau
   (Beijing: People's Press, 2004), 57.
2 Marx, *On Capital*, vol. 3, 289.
3 Karl Marx and Friedrich Engels, *Collected Works of Marx and Engels*, vol. 3 (Beijing:
   People's Press, 2012), 695.
4 Xi Jinping, *Zhijiang Xinyu* (Hangzhou: Zhejiang People's Press, 2013), 119.
5 World Commission on Environment and Development, *Our Common Future*, trans.
   Wang Zhijia et al. (Changchun: Jilin People's Press, 1997), 10.
6 Xi Jinping, "Speech at the Sixth Collective Study Session of the CPC Politburo,"
   People's Daily, May 2013.
7 Marx, *On Capital*, vol. 3, 733, 762.
8 Charles P. Kindleberger, *Economic Development*, trans. Zhang Xin (Shanghai:
   Shanghai Translation Press, 1986), 90.

5 Economic growth and the drive for innovation

Steering China towards an innovation-driven economy means recognising innovation as a new driving force for economic development and making growth more dependent on scientific and technological advancement, improving the quality of labourers and management innovation. The goal of innovation-driven development is to improve the quality and efficiency of economic growth and cultivate the competitive advantages of technology, quality and brands. The innovation here involves a variety of factors: innovation in science and technology, institutional innovation and business model innovation. Amongst them, technological innovation is the core of the overall development.

5.1 The mode of innovation-driven economic growth

5.1.1 Innovation is the major driving force in economic development

China has long relied heavily on the input of production factors to promote economic growth. This is the characteristic of economic development at the low-income stage. When growth enters the middle-income stage, it must shift from relying primarily on material resources to innovation. The necessity can be illustrated as follows.

First, existing resource capacity alone, especially energy and land, cannot maintain sustainable economic growth. A new driving force must thus be found. The concept of innovation, first proposed by Joseph Schumpeter, is a new combination of factors formed by adopting intangible elements, such as knowledge, technology, corporate organisational systems and business models. The goal is to relocate existing tangible elements, such as capital, labour and material resources. Along with such a reallocation will come improved resource productivity, leading to savings and substitution of material resources. Apparently, innovation helps achieve economic growth by reducing investment in material resources.

Second, industrialisation in China has been accompanied by severe environmental pollution and the destruction of ecological balance. In addition, global high carbon emissions have led to climate anomalies, endangering human health and safety. From the perspective of improving sustainable development capacity, controlling environmental pollution, reducing carbon emissions and repairing damaged ecosystems do not represent an attempt to control and slow the industrialisation process but rather a process of relying on technological innovation to develop green technology, such as low-carbon technology and energy cleaning technology, to develop a circular economy and environmental protection industry. The wider adoption of innovative green technology achieves green and low-carbon production.

Third, although China ranks as the world's second-largest economy in terms of total GDP, its industrial structure remains at a low level, and it lacks global competitiveness and a strong ability to transform itself. According to Porter's competition theory, a country's competitiveness lies in its ability to innovate and upgrade its industries. Innovative industry drives the optimisation and upgrading of industrial structure. The new technological and industrial revolution is now burgeoning throughout the world. In the context of globalisation, information and networking, we must seize the opportunity to speed up our scientific and industrial revolution by relying on technological and industrial innovation to develop cutting-edge emerging industries, ultimately taking the lead in global economic and technological development.

Fourth, China's economy is large but not rich. Many products made in China are in the low-end value chain without core technology or brands. This creates a problem of high output with low income. To change the situation, we must transform the development mode, promote innovation to shift from made in China to create in China and rely on original, independent, innovative technologies to increase the brand value of Chinese products and services. In coastal areas, we used to rely heavily on the comparative advantages of labour, land, environment and other material resources to transition from an export-oriented economy to an open economy. The value of this comparative advantage, however, has been significantly attenuated, and the open economy is unable to enhance its international competitiveness. Therefore, it is necessary to shift from comparative advantage to competitive advantage to improve the quality and efficiency of the open economy. It is essential to rely on innovation as a core practice to create new advantages in export competition with enhanced technology, brand, quality and services.

Innovation includes technological, institutional and business model innovations, of which technological innovation is the most important. We thus can accurately understand the notion of shifting from development based on material resources to an innovation-driven model. It is commonly believed that the economic growth pattern is shifting to intensive growth. Intensive growth refers to the intensive use of material elements and the improvement of use efficiency. Although intensive growth includes the role of technological progress, it depends on material resources to promote economic growth. The innovation-driven growth model, however, does not simply address the problem of efficiency. More importantly, it creates new growth elements by integrating such intangible factors as knowledge capital, human capital and innovation-driven institutions. It is the application and diffusion of scientific and technological achievements in production and commerce. As a result, innovation-driven economic growth represents a higher level of growth than the intensive-growth mode.

The innovation-driven economy is proposed as a phase of economic development in relation to the resource-driven and investment-driven development of the past. Resource-driven development with comparative advantage is based on the low price of labour, land and other factors of production. In this stage, large-scale investment in production resources absolutely drives economic growth. In comparison, the investment-driven economy is mainly characterised by its scale. In this mode, technology is used in production equipment while technological advancement and capital accumulation are difficult to separate from each other. The investment-driven economy thus features both large-scale factor input and total factor productivity, while the innovation-driven economy uses innovation rather than these other elements as a major engine for growth.

5.1.2 Characteristics of innovation-driven economic development

The word "innovation" is frequently used in today's world, and it carries a wide range of connotations: cultural innovation, institutional innovation, management innovation, market innovation, technological innovation and scientific innovation. These are all essential to the current economic development. Innovation that drives economic growth, however, should mainly refer to scientific and technological innovation, while innovation in other areas forms an innovation-driven system around this core. Moreover, scientific and technological innovation as a mode of economic growth should be clearly defined as closely integrated with economic development.

Schumpeter, who applied the concept of innovation in economics, clearly stated that innovation is the reallocation of production factors within the following fields: product innovation, technological innovation, market innovation and institutional innovation. Later, when Freeman explained the concept of innovation, he summarised Schumpeter's work as the first attempt to apply new inventions, new products, new processes, new methods or new systems to economic development. This explanation emphasised original innovation and the application of innovative results.

The most common concept used in the past is technological innovation, while today the emphasis is on scientific and technological innovation. Under the impetus of new scientific and technological revolution, "knowledge and technological innovation are a prerequisite for any major economic growth. But in modern economic growth, the innovation frequency is obviously much faster, providing the basis for faster overall growth."[1] This statement emphasises that knowledge and technology innovation is a prerequisite for growth while the frequency of innovation is much faster in modern growth. The achievements of knowledge and technological innovation are largely original outcomes that rely on scientific discoveries and reflect the change of innovation sources. In the past, a large number of technological innovations were due to the accumulation of experience in production, technological improvements and development of new technologies within an enterprise. Even technological advancements driven by scientific discoveries would take decades or even hundreds of years to be applied to production.

The source of current technological advancement is scientific inventions. Since the emergence of the new economy in the second half of the twentieth century, it takes significantly less time, only a dozen years or even several years, for an invention to be applied to the assembly line and transformed into productivity. Now a scientific discovery-to-production application, especially industrial innovation, is almost simultaneous. It shows that the rapid transition to a new technology using the outcomes of the latest scientific discoveries can achieve a major technological leap. Examples include discoveries of new materials and breakthroughs in information technology and biotechnology that have been rapidly transformed into new technologies. This scientific and technological advancement model, based on innovation at the source of scientific discovery, reflects the convergence and integration of knowledge innovation and technological innovation. It is a revolutionary change along the technological advancement path. Therefore, China's "12th five-year plan" clearly defines scientific and technological advancement and innovation as a pillar to accelerate the economic development paradigm.

Innovation-driven development as a new development model means that China's technological advancement needs to change from an exogenous one to an endogenous one. The scientific and technological innovation in our country at present is largely exogenous. This is clearly reflected in the fact that most of the advanced innovative technologies are imported and imitated, and most advanced innovative industries are of the original equipment manufacturer type. In this model, the technological innovation essentially belongs to the diffusion of foreign innovation technology to China; the origin of the innovation is abroad. The innovative technology adopted is mature in foreign countries. The core technology does not belong to us. Therefore, the significance of this technological innovation lies in keeping up with the pace of international technological advancement, but it cannot move forward to the international frontier. The basic requirement for the innovation-driven model is that scientific and technological innovation is transformed from exogenous to endogenous with the following three implications.

First, we should rely on independent, original innovation and the reinvention of imported technology to create core technologies with independent intellectual property rights. There is a need to overcome the follow-up theory in developing nations. In the context of globalisation, informationisation and networking, China is able to stand at the same starting line for innovation with developed countries. When they are engaged in new energy, new materials and new biomedical medicines, we can conduct the same research. In this process, we can rely on innovation to achieve leapfrog development and take the lead in global science, technology and manufacturing.

Second, innovative knowledge and technology must be integrated in production factors. The traditional model attributes economic growth to material factors, such as the input of labour, capital and land; the role of technological advancement is the "remainder" of these factors. In this way, the role of technical elements is exogenous. Innovation drive refers to the reallocation of elements realised by aligning physical capital with innovative knowledge and technology, improving the quality of labourers and implementing management innovation. The endogenous growth is achieved by increasing innovation capacity through the input of new knowledge and technologies. The 18th CPC National Congress defines such an endogenous growth as "depending more on scientific and technological advancement, improvement of laborers' quality, and management innovation."

Third, we need to try hard to promote industrial innovation. National competitiveness today is increasingly manifested as industry competitiveness. Correspondingly, as a driving force of endogenous growth, innovation should be guided by industrial innovation to enhance national competitiveness. The optimisation and upgrading of our industrial structures should be driven by new innovative industries. Scientific and technological innovation are the foundation of industrial innovation. We need to foster innovative industries to seek competitive advantages and develop high-tech industries which can compete with developed countries to create endogenous competitiveness.

The innovation-driven economic development model can be summarised as follows: it can be further promoted based mainly on technological innovation achievements, knowledge and scientific and technological talents. The contribution rate of scientific and technological advancement to economic growth is an important criterion for business decisions and policy. In general, it has helped developed countries reach a 70% to 80% higher rate of growth. At present, the gap in this aspect is still very large between China and developed countries. It will be a long process for us to transform economic development to an innovation-driven development model, which should be viewed as a major goal to promote the transformation.

5.2   The basic elements of innovation-driven growth

5.2.1   New growth theory and the knowledge economy

The symbol of the so-called new economy that emerged in the West in the late 1980s and early 1990s was the rapid application of science and technology to various aspects of production and social life. The characteristics of the knowledge economy based on innovation are increasingly evident. This economic phenomenon has been summarised by a new growth theory. Scholars who have contributed to the creation and development of the new growth theory include Paul Romer, Robert Lucas and Dale W. Jorgenson.

New growth theory explains the source of technological advancement and economic growth from the perspective of endogenous technological advancement. It means that the advancement becomes an endogenous variable of the economic system, and the rate of technological advancement should be decided by the share of resources used for research and development in the economy. It identifies new production factors that affect income other than capital and labour – namely, knowledge and human capital.

Romer introduced knowledge as an independent factor in the growth model and held that knowledge accumulation is an important factor in modern economic growth. Knowledge not only has its own incremental effect but also penetrates production factors, such as capital and labour, making these and other factors of production generate incremental returns, thereby increasing the returns to the scale of the economy as a whole. Hence the Romer model is an incremental model of scale returns, and it has been proved by the practice of knowledge economy development in recent years.

Differences in investment in knowledge innovation between enterprises and countries ultimately show the differences in the rate and quality of economic growth. This difference could be changed through international trade. It can promote the dissemination of knowledge in the international community, reduce research and development costs in poor countries and indirectly achieve the purpose of increasing capital accumulation in developing nations. Developing nations can use the "late-mover advantage" created in the dissemination of knowledge and thus shorten the economic gap with developed countries more rapidly.

Knowledge that can promote technological advancement is a product of a company's investment decisions. To achieve technological advancement, companies must invest in the knowledge sector. Accordingly, Romer assumed there were three sectors in the economy: the research sector, the intermediary product sector and the consumer goods sector. Investment in the research sector is the most profitable. Total expenditures on research and development costs, as well as their proportions, are important indicators for the measurement of investment by the research sector.

According to Romer, knowledge acquired by the research sector can be protected by intellectual property laws, so knowledge is non-competitive and partially exclusive. This makes knowledge accumulation a product of a willing investment by companies. Knowledge differs from other products with its spillover effects. The knowledge produced by any manufacturer can increase the productivity of the entire society. Therefore, the marginal productivity of capital is not reduced by the fixation of a certain production factor, such as labour. This is the external positive effect of knowledge production, and it makes the social production rate of knowledge production higher than the manufacturer's private rate of return. Thus the government needs to intervene in the economy by investing in the knowledge sector to promote technological advancement, provide subsidies to producers of knowledge and carry out policies that can reward manufacturers' production knowledge.

Lucas's growth model also belongs to the new growth theory. Its primary proposition is that the accumulation of human capital is the source of economic growth. Human capital is endogenous. The accumulation of human capital in the form of education investment will also have an external positive effect of improving the productivity of the entire society. Productivity differences across different countries can be explained by differences in human capital accumulation. Lucas and other scholars held that the accumulation of specialised knowledge, skills and human capital can also generate incremental returns and increase other investment returns and total-scale returns. Human capital is the permanent driving force of modern economic growth.

The basic principles of new growth theory focus on the investment in research and development, as well as human capital. The former highlights knowledge creation, while the latter emphasises knowledge dissemination. Modern development theory divides capital into four types: (1) natural, (2) material, (3) intellectual and (4) human capitals. New growth theory shows that economic growth factors include not only tangible elements, such as capital, labour and land, but also intangible elements, such as intellectual and human capital. With the emergence of the new economy represented by information technology, the role of intangible elements in economic growth has become greater. Research on these intangible elements is of great significance for the Chinese economy.

The other expression of the new economy is the knowledge economy. The knowledge economy is a knowledge-based innovation economy. Relying on knowledge innovation, new knowledge and technologies continue to emerge, and the transformation from new knowledge to real productivity continues to accelerate.

An accurate understanding of the knowledge economy starts with an understanding of the function of science, which consists of two levels. The first is scientific discovery, which generates new knowledge. The second is scientific invention, which generates new technology. The knowledge created by scientific discovery serves as the basis for scientific invention. The two levels are combined, respectively, with the economy to form a technological and knowledge economy. In the era of the technological economy, with the combination of technology and economy, technological innovation is the decisive factor in production and economic growth. The current knowledge economy refers to the direct combination of the economy with knowledge created by science and the direct transformation of knowledge innovation to production and economic growth. The trend of modern society's development is that knowledge is increasingly becoming a more important economic factor than tangible material assets. The return on knowledge investment is much greater than other kinds of investment.

Universities and scientific research institutions are the sources of technological and knowledge innovation and innovative talents. Universities and research institutes no longer stay far away from economic construction but play an important role in it. As long as an effective mechanism for the integration of production, education and research is established, investment in universities and research institutes becomes more efficient than that in general production processes.

In the modern economy, knowledge can be encoded or digitised into software, trademarks, patents, brands and so on. These information products and assets make up what is known as knowledge capital. According to the analysis of Masahiko Aoki (2001), information capital is divided into two types: one is the inseparable information asset, in which the information processing skills are inseparable from the individual. It usually refers to human capital. The other is detachable information assets, such as software, digital content and inventions. They can also become information products. Their ownership can be separated from their producers for trading. Of course, the premise of trading these information products is to determine their ownership; otherwise, it is impossible to conduct transactions. The production of knowledge is the production of information. Knowledge innovation can generate innovative products or processes, which are valuable knowledge and information products themselves.

The aforementioned analysis shows that modern economic growth requires two aspects of capital accumulation related to the knowledge economy. One is to accumulate knowledge capital through knowledge innovation, and the other is to accumulate human capital through knowledge dissemination. In the modern economy, the gap between levels of development amongst countries, regions and enterprises is mainly reflected in the accumulation levels of these two types of capital. For the economic development of developing nations, the main point is to strengthen two abilities: the ability to create knowledge and the ability to combine knowledge directly with the economy. International information exchange and the acquisition of new knowledge are of crucial importance.

5.2.2 The accumulation of intellectual capital

According to the growth theory of Romeo and others, in the current era, production incorporates more than capital and labour. Knowledge is an independent factor that drives growth. Knowledge accumulation is the decisive factor for promoting modern economic growth. Investment and technology make each other more valuable. If human beings are to maintain long-term growth, they must devote themselves to the whole process of technological discovery and use considerable human and material resources for technological discovery rather than for production alone.

Knowledge can be divided into general knowledge and specialised knowledge. Each has a different role in promoting economic growth. General knowledge can increase economies of scale, while specialised knowledge can increase the incremental benefits of production. Combining the two could result in incremental benefits for knowledge, technology, human resources and capital. Once knowledge or information is obtained, it can be used repeatedly without paying additional costs, thus generating incremental marginal returns. For some companies, this incremental benefit is reflected in the return of intellectual property (monopoly profits), and the benefits of intellectual property can be reused in technological innovation to form a virtuous circle in which investment can promote knowledge accumulation and innovation. Knowledge innovation can promote the increase of scaled returns and the further expansion of knowledge investment. The economy thus maintains sustainable growth for a long period of time.

There are two main ways for a country to accumulate knowledge capital. One is based on the accomplishments of enterprises and is reflected in the form of technological innovation. Technological innovation is the creation of new products and technologies with the ultimate goal of applying new technologies to the production process. For a long time in the past, technological innovations usually arose from the accumulation of experience in production and the improvement of technology. In the modern era, however, technological innovations rely mainly on technology, as well as the research and development strength of an enterprise. In the new economic era, in just a few years, Microsoft has been able to surpass manufacturing companies, such as Ford and General Motors, which have been in business for more than a century. This "rags-to-riches" phenomenon has overturned the old pattern of technological innovation. Using the latest scientific discoveries to achieve a large technological leap, the creation of a new industry based on knowledge innovation can lead to a revolutionary change in the industrial structure.

The second way to accumulate knowledge capital is based on universities and scientific research institutes as incubators of new scientific discovery and knowledge innovation. New scientific discoveries have increasingly become the source of scientific and technological innovation, and the outcomes of original innovation are generally derived from the technology transfer of new scientific discoveries.

An impressive phenomenon of the knowledge economy lies in the fact that research and development make up a high proportion of overall expenditure. At present, research and development for enterprises in developed countries generally account for more than 5% of their sales revenue. Research and development in Organisation for Economic Co-operation and Development (OECD) countries generally account for more than 2.6% of GDP. This research and development cost is not only invested in enterprises; rather, most of it goes to universities and research institutes. As pointed out by the new growth theory, investing in scientific discovery is more valuable than investing in production.

For a long time, the subject of scientific research has depended solely on the interests of individual researchers. The U.S. Apollo programme represented an initial transition from this traditional orientation. Since then, research projects of scientists, including basic research, began to shift to national goals, mainly for military purposes. Major scientific discoveries were quickly applied to strategic military engineering and weaponry industries. With the end of the Cold War, the emphasis gradually shifted from a global military arms race to economic competition. The national strategy of the United States accordingly has turned from global military domination to economic hegemony. Correspondingly, the focus of its major scientific research has also shifted from military to economic purposes. The new American economy represented by digital and information technology discovery and application is the result of such transformation. Today, research interests across the world have been increasingly oriented towards national goals, with a trend towards serving economic purposes. Even research based on individual interests and hobbies is subject to national goals. The Chinese government's Major National Scientific Research Projects Programme embodies this spirit. This transformation demonstrates that the components of China's scientific research system, including universities, have become part of an innovation-based economic system.

Promoting the accumulation of knowledge capital in a country should be based on the following three aspects:

• First, it is important to establish a sound incentive mechanism for innovation, especially a strict intellectual property protection system. In general, sufficient market competition will create innovative pressure. The driving force for innovation is to rely on intellectual property rights protection and ensure that it obtains monopoly profits. Innovative knowledge and technology have the characteristics of public products. According to Stiglitz, "the marginal cost of others' sharing of the innovation benefits is nothing."[2] Specifically, the cost of innovation results is divided into the cost of innovation (information cost) and the cost of replication (diffusion cost). The former is significantly greater than the latter. The replication of innovation is almost without cost. Others obtain innovative benefits free from innovators, in which case the innovator goes uncompensated. In this circumstance, investment in research and development cannot receive timely returns, which, inevitably, seriously dampens innovators' enthusiasm. Therefore, the driving force of innovation relies on compensation for innovation costs. Monopoly profits to stimulate innovation is thereby proposed.

The institutional arrangement for protecting innovators' benefits is to make sure the manufacturers of innovative technologies have monopoly income rights (i.e. patents and full intellectual property rights). The promotion of new technologies can only be carried out through the purchase of intellectual property rights, such as invention patents. If someone replicates and adopts their innovations, they receive full benefits from the duplications and adopter, thus compensating their innovation costs. The monopoly of such innovative enterprises does not refer to the monopoly of a certain company of a specific industry and sector but to the monopoly of intellectual property rights, such as invention patents. This monopoly does not hinder innovation but becomes a driving force for innovation.

- Second, it is important to align innovation with national goals. The necessity for the government's active participation in innovation is based primarily on two different factors. On the one hand, innovation has spillover effects. Innovative knowledge and technology benefit not only innovators but society as well. This spillover effect shows that innovation pays not only personnel costs but also social costs. This social cost needs to be paid by the government as a social representative. On the other hand, innovative knowledge and technology embody the attributes of public goods. This public characteristic does not rely solely on government regulations to solve problems such as plagiarism and counterfeiting. More importantly, it is crucial to formulate national plans for major scientific and technological innovation and directly invest or guide investment in such innovation through public finance.

To study the national goal of technological innovation, we need to put forward the concept of national innovation capacity. Individual innovation in the market economy is the most powerful engine of innovation. In the modern economy, however, national competitiveness is mainly measured by national innovation capacity. This is not the sum of individual innovation capacity but the national integration capacity of technological innovation. Even in a developed market economy, the most successful major technological innovation programmes are typically planned and organised by the government. The USDA Agricultural Research Service, the Project Apollo and the Manhattan Project on nuclear weapons are all such examples. The most important technological advancements were made in government and government-funded laboratories. The same applies to major national scientific research projects that China has implemented, such as the "atomic and hydrogen bombs and satellite" project in the past and the aerospace and current moon landing programme. The important scientific breakthroughs made by the major national scientific research projects directly implemented by the state will drive scientific advancement throughout society. Because national competitiveness is reflected in a country's industrial innovation ability, especially in strategic emerging industries planned and determined by the state, major scientific and industrial innovation requires not only major financial support but also state funding and policy guidance for this long-term and risky form of technology investment.

- Finally, it is necessary to strengthen the sources of knowledge innovation. The focus of promoting technological advancement today is to develop high-tech research, shorten the international high-tech gap and take the leading position in international science, technology and industry. The fundamental research level of a country directly reflects its knowledge innovation level. At present, China's gap with international high technology is smaller than that of the high-tech industry. The gap between high tech in China and the advanced level found in universities and scientific research institutions around the world is not as wide as that in the high-tech industry. Silicon Valley in the United States is close to Stanford University. This is why it benefits from the latest innovation results. The technological innovation of enterprises has created a growing demand for research institutes to provide innovative achievements. Corporate innovation requires the acquisition of new knowledge from universities, but it also needs the latest international scientific knowledge from the same source. An analysis of the international mobility of scientific knowledge and new technology shows that the flow of new technology has encountered obstacles of intellectual property laws and even barriers to governmental protection. However, the flow of new scientific discoveries and knowledge between universities will not encounter such obstacles. The international mobility of science and knowledge is more fluid than technology. Relying on universities and using the latest international scientific discoveries for technological innovation, we can benefit from the latest scientific achievements in many areas in the world today.

5.3 Human capital accumulation

Labour's role in production is not homogeneous. Different qualities of labour have different effects on economic growth. Specifically, the labour force is the sum of two kinds of ability: non-technical manual work that anyone can engage in and technical work that needs education and training. The latter embodies the role of human capital. Human capital is the stock of human knowledge and technology. It is formed through human capital investment and reflected in people. The increase in knowledge and the skill set of workers gained through education has increasingly become an important source of modern economic growth.

Professor Theodore Schulz, Nobel Prize laureate in economics in 1979, first proposed human capital theory. He identified two trends in modern economic growth: First, national income, from the perspective of long-term change in the capital-income ratio, grows faster than capital. Second, national income grows faster than national resources. Both trends can be explained by the role of education and the resulting increase in the knowledge and skills of labourers. The improvement of labour productivity per unit is the same case. Improvements in machinery and equipment are of great significance for the improvement of labour productivity. It is undeniable, however, that the increase in the knowledge and technology skills in labour is also an important factor in an increase in labour productivity. Moreover, advanced equipment and technology require labourers with specific knowledge and skills. The American economist E. F. Denison found that 10% to 15% of the real GDP growth in the United States can be directly attributed to education. Jayvenson and Law, based on the results of research on agriculture in more than 30 countries, estimated that for each additional year of education received by each head of household, the average agriculture output will increase by nearly 2%. Research data from the World Bank indicate that in low-income countries, the output of farmers who received four years of education is 13% higher than that of the farmers who received little education. Even without inputs like high-yield seeds and chemical fertilisers, the former is 8% higher than the latter.

Lucas, a proponent of the new growth theory, explicitly states that human capital is the permanent driving force of modern economic growth. According to the new growth theory, the accumulation of human capital not only includes the improvement of the quality of the labour force but also the emergence of entrepreneurs with innovative qualities and improvement of the scientific and technological personnel involved in technological innovation.

For a long time, China's abundant labour resources and cheap prices were viewed as advantages for economic growth. It was believed that the lack of physical capital (machine equipment) was the main constraint on China's economic growth. Therefore, investment practice inevitably meant investment in fixed assets, such as machinery and equipment. Human capital investment and the introduction of foreign human capital were not taken seriously. Therefore, there has emerged a new imbalance in the supply of factors for economic growth. There is much labour, but the quality is not good enough; the skilled labour force is in short supply, and human capital is not in proportion to the stock of physical capital, resulting in low utilisation of machinery and equipment. The introduction of advanced equipment has a low absorption rate, resulting in a waste of material capital.

The modern practice of economic development demonstrates that knowledge and technology become the most valuable resources when they are compatible with advanced machinery and equipment. Scientific and technological advancement as the basis of modern economic growth includes an increase in labourers' knowledge and technological skills. Developing nations like China are lacking not only physical capital but also human capital. In the innovation-driven economy, technological entrepreneurs are lacking the most. Technological entrepreneurs possess not only the general qualities of entrepreneurs but also a scientific and technological vision.

In a broad sense, human capital involves physical fitness, cultural quality and professional skills. Therefore, investment in human capital takes many forms, including (1) expenses for education and training, (2) expenses for health care, (3) relocation costs for change of employment and (4) expenses for migrants and immigrants.

Education is a major part of human capital investment in terms of increasing human knowledge and technological skills. The primary reason behind the economic backwardness of developing nations is the general lack of education investment. Yet the return rates for education investment in these nations are the highest. According to the World Bank, in 1980, rates of return on education investment in 44 developing nations all exceeded by more than 10% the World Bank's standard minimum acceptable rate. The rate of return on primary education investment is 27% for low-income countries and 22% for medium-income countries, for secondary education 17% and 14% and for higher education 13% and 12%, respectively.

Since the founding of the PRC, the government has taken various measures to vigorously develop education and effectively guarantee people's rights to education, most notably through the implementation of its programme of nine-year compulsory education. Nonetheless, education remains a "bottleneck" that poses a hindrance to China's economic development. It can be illustrated as follows. First, the percentage of those who received a university education accounted for only 10.6% of the total population in 2012. This ratio was much lower than that of developed countries, such as the United States (31.2%) and Japan (14.3%). Second, although the prevalence of primary education in China is relatively high, progress is not consistent. In some regions, the rate of schooling is low, and the rate of dropouts is high, resulting in high rates of illiteracy and semi-literacy. Third, the in-service training of workers is insufficient, affecting the overall quality of workers. All these factors create gaps in the knowledge and skill set of workers who cannot adapt to different levels of technological progress. The problem lies in the lack of investment in education. In 2012, the government's budget for education accounted for only 15.4% of total financial expenditures. This was lower than the average level of 16.3% in developing countries. The education expenditure of the residents was even lower. In 2012, urban residents in China spent just 4.9% of their income on education. This was significantly lower than the 7% rate achieved by developed countries in the 1970s.

The subjective causes of insufficient investment in education are probably related to the characteristics of education investment. Education investment takes a long time to be effective. Investors are not necessarily the direct beneficiaries of their investment, so their initiative and enthusiasm are insufficient. It can thus be seen that the key to increasing investment in education is to systematically address the attribution of the benefits of investment and the long-term behaviour of investors. Since China institutionalised the reform and opening policy in 1978, its national income distribution pattern has undergone major changes. The share of state finance has decreased significantly, and the share of enterprises and residents' income has increased significantly. Correspondingly, the education investment pattern needs to change from a single government entity to multiple entities in which government, enterprises and residents make a joint investment. To mobilise people's voluntary investment in education, we must recognise their interests and show how their investment will benefit them. For education, students and their families now pay not only the direct costs, such as tuition fees, but also the opportunity costs of lost income during school years. Only when they see that they can get an adequate future return will people be interested and willing to invest in education.

Under current national income levels, even if all aspects of education investment are mobilised, it will still be insufficient. In particular, there is a shortage of quality education resources. To produce greater benefits from limited education funding, it is necessary to adjust and optimise the education structure so as to more effectively allocate educational resources. The education structure includes formal and vocational education. Formal education includes basic education at the elementary and intermediate levels and higher education at all levels. Experience shows that the educational structure should adapt to the per capita GNP and the need for technical training for labourers at each stage of development. The educational structure in the early stages of economic development should be a pyramid based on primary, secondary and vocational education. After reaching the level of the middle-income countries, the generalisation of higher education becomes a trend.

Migration and immigration are also important forms of human capital investment. If education is a long-term investment, then migration and immigration are short-term investments that can be rewarding in the interim.

In reality, the phenomenon of brain drain – the flow of highly educated and highly skilled labourers to developed countries – prevails in developing nations. While they must invest in a certain amount of immigration expenses, they acquire huge human capital as a result. Silicon Valley in the United States has risen by attracting talented, high-quality people from around the world, both entrepreneurial and high tech. Developing nations have paid for the cost of raising and educating people from elementary to tertiary levels. Unfortunately, because of the outflow of human capital to developed countries, they have not received dividends. The brain drain is clearly a loss of human capital for developing nations.

Of course, brain drain is not a complete loss to developing nations. The training of outflow talents in developed countries is also a process of human capital investment. If developing nations can adopt effective policies to persuade these talents to return, on a short-term or long-term basis, to serve their native countries and start businesses there, they can increase their total human capital. This is also an important way for a country to accumulate human capital. Thus it raises the issue of how to attract talent.

For developing nations, there will inevitably be a brain drain over a certain period of time, but there are also opportunities for bringing in overseas talent. Schultz pointed out this problem in developing nations when he proposed his human capital theory: traditional developing strategies often emphasise investment in physical capital. When they invest in the recruitment of overseas capital, they focus on housing, machinery and equipment rather than an increase of human capital. In reality, however, if human capital cannot go hand in hand with physical capital, it will become a constraint on economic growth. In the process of recruiting overseas capital, if we only increase physical capital, the capital absorption rate must be low. Therefore, effectively bringing in the knowledge and talent needed by advanced production technology helps attract the most valuable resources for development.

For the innovation-driven economy, recruiting talent can be viewed as the most effective human capital investment. The first factor here is remuneration. We need to correct the long-term dominant low-cost strategic theory. During the low-income development stage in the past, economic development relied mainly on the advantages of low labour costs. Now that we have entered the middle-income stage, high-level innovative talent is essential for innovation-driven development. Only high salaries can attract high-level talents to create new high-tech industries, thus creating our own competitive advantages. The second factor is the working environment. It is necessary to create a good industrial structure for talented employees to fully display their capabilities and build an institutional environment that is conducive to their continued growth.

5.4 National innovation system and collaborative innovation

5.4.1 Technological innovation road map and national innovation system

Innovation can be defined from a narrow or a broad perspective. Narrowly, it refers only to the application of a major scientific breakthrough. The usual explanation refers to the first business application of an invention, such as new products, processes, methods and institutional arrangements. Incubating a new technology is an example. In a broader sense, innovation covers the entire process of invention and innovation diffusion. It indicates that complete technological innovation includes both knowledge and technological innovation, as well as education's role in the diffusion of innovative knowledge.

The scientific and technological progress model based on innovation as the source of scientific discoveries reflects the convergence and integration of knowledge innovation (scientific discovery) and technological innovation. This consists of three components. The upstream components are scientific discovery and knowledge innovation, the incubation of that knowledge and discovery occurs in midstream and the resulting new technology is applied downstream. All three components work together to create technological advancement and innovation.

Today, the source of technological innovation is derived more from scientific invention. Scientific discoveries have increasingly become the sources of technological innovation. This combination includes different stages and different subjects. It raises the issue of the establishment of a technological innovation system that involves cooperation and interaction between the subjects in each link of research institutes, academia and industry. In summarising the characteristics of the era of the knowledge economy, OECD put forward the concept of a national innovation system: innovation needs to enable communication between different actors, including companies, laboratories, scientific institutes and consumers, while feedback is needed between scientific research, engineering implementation, product development, manufacturing and marketing. Therefore, innovation is the result of a large number of interactions between different actors. Taken as a whole, this constitutes a national innovation system.

A national innovation system thus consists of two systems: basic and cutting-edge technology research and research for the public good, undertaken primarily by research institutions. The technological innovation system, on the other hand, is market-oriented and integrates research institutions, academia and industry.

The knowledge innovation system is essentially a collection of institutions that specialise in the absorption, development, sharing, transfer and application of knowledge. The collection continuously absorbs existing knowledge and applies its own innovations to develop new scientific discoveries. The creation of knowledge and scientific research has increasingly become the source of technological innovation. Since the original technology is generally derived from scientific discovery, knowledge innovators must seek the top while keeping their feet on the ground. On the one hand, they should aim for cutting-edge scientific issues on the international frontier; on the other hand, they should aim for the practical issues associated with national economic development. Therefore, it is necessary to carry out the major national scientific research projects to break through the serious technological bottlenecks from a scientific perspective and provide a scientific basis for technological innovation. Thus the key to scientific and technological innovation is to improve the capacity for knowledge innovation. We can clarify the basic requirements for this capability by analysing why Nobel Prize-winning scientists are concentrated in several innovative countries. First, the basic strategic orientation of the country's development is to pursue original technological innovation. Next, we need a unique and dynamic national innovation system. In addition, world-class universities that foster and cultivate scientific elites are necessary. Finally, there must be sufficient investment in scientific research.[3]

For a long time, knowledge innovation lagged far behind economic development, while only technological innovation was closely linked to the economy. Today, the obvious trend is that the knowledge created by science is directly integrated into the economy to become an element of production and economic growth. Therefore, the decisive factor in determining economic growth has shifted from technology to knowledge. For example, new discoveries in research fields, such as materials, information, computer technology, clean energy and bioengineering, quickly create new industries and are directly transformed into productivity. In this silent revolution, economic development has relied closely on the innovation, dissemination and application of knowledge. The proportion of knowledge-intensive products has greatly increased. Knowledge-based industries have replaced traditional industries to play a dominant role. The efficiency of knowledge production and the conversion of knowledge into technology and products (i.e. knowledge productivity) replaces labour productivity as the main indicator of economic growth. In this sense, scientific research, including fundamental research, undertaken by universities and research institutes is no longer seen as far removed from the economy.

The long-term lack of a strong innovation capacity in China is mainly due to the significant gap between scientific research results and the adoption of new technology by enterprises. As long as the scientific discoveries made by research institutes are validated, rewarded and patented, their work is considered fulfilled. There is no direct connection between a company's self-developed new technology and a university's scientific research. Neither wants to reach out and devote much funding or energy to transforming scientific and technological achievements into productive forces. As a result, many of China's pioneering discoveries are laid aside and ignored, creating a serious waste of knowledge resources.

Universities as knowledge innovators have their own value to be realised through cooperative innovation with entrepreneurs because the value of scientific invention lies in practical application. The value of many major scientific discoveries remained unrecognised until the discoveries were applied. Only in the collaborative innovation of scientific researchers and enterprises can the value of scientific discovery be fully realised. Therefore, in the system of university-enterprise cooperative innovation, universities must not only establish their own position as knowledge innovators and achieve more important, original, innovative results that meet world-class standards. They must also take a step forward and innovate high-tech achievements with industrial value and actively participate in the process of putting them into practice to realise the full value of scientific discovery.

5.4.2 Collaborative innovation of industry, academia and research institutes

The theory of a national innovation system takes the interaction between enterprises, universities and national scientific and technological policies as its core. It considers, as the main source of innovation, the organisations that promote knowledge creation and diffusion, such as enterprises, research universities and government laboratories. According to this theory, scientific innovation cannot rely solely on enterprises. It requires collaboration between universities and enterprises, as well as scientists and entrepreneurs. The most important aspect of enhancing innovation capability is establishing a mechanism for effective convergence and coordination of knowledge and technological innovation systems. This is the collaborative innovation between industry, academia and research institutes. It means that a relatively low-cost innovation shortcut is to promote the integration of industry, academia and research institutes and rapidly industrialise and commercialise the high-tech achievements of universities and research institutes. Here we do not talk about establishing a research organisation in an enterprise, nor creating an enterprise in a university but starting a mechanism that integrates all of the actors – in other words, innovation between universities and enterprises through the collaboration of scientists and entrepreneurs.

For a long time, the emphasis on the relationship between industry, academia and research institutes centred on technology transfer. Knowledge innovation was limited to scientific research conducted by universities and academia, while industry adopted new technologies. This raised obstacles to the transfer of innovative technology from universities to enterprises. Collaborative innovation amongst industry, academia and research institutes has new specific intent: universities and enterprises create a joint platform. According to the scientific and technological innovation road map, the platform jointly used by industry, academia and research institutes is founded in the high-tech incubation stage. It allows knowledge and technology innovations to converge. On the one hand, the forerunner of technological innovation is the transformation of science to technology. On the other hand, knowledge innovation makes it possible to transform scientific knowledge into productivity. Market demand is connected to research and development supply to incubate and develop new technologies and products and even new enterprises that adapt to and guide the market.

Knowledge innovation by universities now has extended to the incubation stage. It is no longer limited to knowledge creation, which includes the conclusion of fundamental research projects, scholarly publications and applications for national patents. It goes one step farther to push scientific research results to practical application. To adapt to this trend, various incubators have emerged around universities in many regions. Scientists and faculty members in universities producing new ideas can take advantage of these incubators to test and develop them. If research and development (R&D) is successful, the incubated new technology and products flow into industrial parks and enterprises. Experience has shown that although this type of incubator often cannot transform new ideas into new technologies, and even fails in many cases, when the incubation is successful, innovations create obvious economic benefits. Even if the incubation fails, the cost of failure is low.

In the past, enterprises as technological innovators were limited to adopting new technologies. Now companies have extended the technological innovation to the incubation and application of scientific research provided by universities. In this way, they have become a nexus for incubating new technologies. On the one hand, such a practice provides investment in the incubation of new technologies. On the other hand, it guides the incubation of new technologies based on the needs of the market, ensuring that they have commercial and industrialisation value.

In the incubation stage, knowledge innovation and technological innovation have converged to create cooperation between entrepreneurs and scientists. Scientists conduct research in pursuit of academic leadership and breakthrough discoveries. Entrepreneurs, however, are more interested in commercial value and market prospects. By moving towards each other, the two parties integrate academic interest with commercial value to create high-tech products with good market prospects.

The system helps suppliers and purchasers of innovation achievements enter a cooperative system, and the three aspects of innovation (i.e. scientific discoveries and inventions, transfer of new inventions and adoption of new technologies), produce a new cooperative combination between universities and enterprises. In particular, the high-tech incubation process has become the interface of universities and enterprises and a platform for joint innovation between the two parties. On this platform, knowledge and market information inform each other, resulting in a learn-by-doing process that can effectively solve the problem of information asymmetry in the knowledge market.

The enterprise is a main player for technological innovation, and it is also the main player for collaborative innovation. While enterprises need to independently innovate technologies and products, they should not be restricted by this. They must move beyond the corporate scope to pay attention to the process of scientific discovery and translate scientific discoveries into production and technological innovation. The fruits of scientific discovery have increasingly become the direct source of technological innovation. Enterprises can no longer afford to limit themselves to their own R&D programmes for technological innovation. They need new technologies developed by universities and research institutes. While enterprises can acquire new technologies through technology trading, there are cost-effective considerations for the purchase of technology. Further, acquisition of new technologies has its own special requirements. Therefore, enterprises need to extend the process to the incubation and innovation stage of scientific research provided by universities. Its main role is as follows: on the one hand, the main work of technological innovation needs to be done through the enterprises; on the other hand, the incubated new technology must have commercial and industrialisation value. This is more important. Only an enterprise can determine the commercial value of potential products. In addition, incubating new technology is profitable so that investments can become funding resources for enterprises. It means enterprises ought to be responsible for the principal investment for both the construction of a collaborative innovation platform and the incubator.

In the market economy, the key to successful collaborative innovation is to establish an innovative profit distribution system for the mutual benefit of all parties involved. Cooperation between knowledge and technology innovation is not general project cooperation but long-term cooperation guided by industrial innovation. Therefore, it is possible to take a large technological leap and even lead a revolution in industrial structure. Moreover, the collaborative innovation platform built by scientists and entrepreneurs is an open one. The source of incubating new technologies is not limited to the achievements of scientific research by universities and scientists that have entered the platform. Scientists can also use innovations at home and abroad to provide ideas based on the needs of entrepreneurs, resulting in a steady stream of new technologies on the platform. The value of new discoveries in science lies in the collaborative R&D of scientists and entrepreneurs to innovate new technologies.

Collaborative innovation involves not only industries, academia and research institutes but also collaboration between technological and business model innovation. Successful innovation depends on leading technologies, as well as excellent business models. A new technological innovation needs a corresponding commercial model to promote it to the market and fully realise its value. In reality, there are many high-level innovations with expected commercial values, but they have not always reached their desired goals. Some even die on the vine. This is because they cannot find suitable business models to work with.

Collaborative innovation concerns not exactly a tripartite system of industries, academia and research institutes but is a function of industry development, talent cultivation and scientific research. On the one hand, universities contain "knowledge," which includes research institutes, and conduct scientific research. On the other hand, "production" is not limited to enterprises but also industrial development or industrial innovation. In addition to enterprises, there are various R&D institutes and venture capitalists. Therefore, the cooperation between industries, academia and research institutes is generally between universities and industries involving scientific research, talent cultivation and cooperative innovation in industry.

Collaborative innovation is inseparable from the government, which can organise and integrate the two systems of corporate technological innovation and university knowledge innovation. Integrated innovation is the collection, coordination and convergence of each link in the innovation system around certain innovation goals, resulting in collaborative innovation. The main method for a government to accomplish this end is to found university science parks and establish a collaborative innovation platform. It is in this sense that China's collaborative innovation needs to add to it the word "government" (i.e. the innovation of government, industries, academia and research institutes).

5.4.3 National innovation capacity construction

Scientific and technological innovation as the main driver of economic development is an important sign that China has become a country of innovation with a high concentration of key factors, including high-level innovation and entrepreneurial talents, scientific research and R&D institutes, venture capital and technological entrepreneurs. It should also see the efficient operation of innovation systems within the collaborative innovation platform. In addition, the favourable innovative environment includes the talent environment, supply environment, culture of innovation and institutional support. The result is that innovation activities are extremely dynamic, and innovation outcomes are continuous, while strategic emerging industries form clusters. Accordingly, we should pay attention to the following aspects:

- First is the input mechanism for innovation. Currently, the cost of R&D for innovative countries, such as OECD countries, generally accounts for more than 2.3% of GDP, while the R&D expenses of technology-innovative enterprises account for more than 5% of their total sales revenue. The gap between China and innovative countries is very wide. It also shows that the shift from a reliance on material resources to innovation means that innovation drive can only replace material resources, such as energy, land and environmental resources. It cannot replace capital investment. On the contrary, the government needs to increase investment in technological innovation and require resources to flow to the field of innovation. Not only does it require that enterprises become the main focus of innovation investment but also the government needs to increase its investment. Of course, the government and enterprises should divide their investment in innovation, with the former investing in knowledge innovation and the latter focussing on technological innovation. In the incubation of new technologies, however, both should actively invest to ensure the necessary incubation and R&D of new technologies. With more innovation investment in incubation and R&D, new technologies will steadily emerge. If we guarantee investment in these two areas, innovation-driven development is likely to take place.

    The core issue of the economic reform proposed by the 18th CPC National Congress is to handle appropriately the relationship between the government and the market. The same is true for the construction of an innovation system. We must respect market law and carry out the role of government better. With regard to the creation of an innovative investment system, there is a need for innovation in both markets and the government. Market innovation centres mainly on how to develop finance for science and technology. Analysis shows that an innovation-driven economy has its own requirements for finance. Commercial banks and financial institutions should thus provide financial services for science and technology. Such services promote a deep integration of scientific and technological innovation with financial innovation and provide essential funding to carry out the incubation of technological innovation and associated enterprises. Government innovation means the government needs to invest in innovation. Because innovation has spillover and public characteristics, the government must provide guidance and public welfare investment for independent innovation. At the same time, it needs to provide the necessary incentives and coercive measures for the adoption of innovation results, including preferential procurement of independent innovation products and services, etc. Of course, the government's investment cannot be a substitute for the dominant position of the enterprises' investment, let alone squeeze out the innovation input of the enterprises.

- Next is the construction of an innovative environment. It is vitally important in developing an innovation-driven economy. In the past, the development of an open economy in our coastal areas focussed on creating a "connections and levelling" environment to bring in foreign investment. For the innovation-driven economy, it is now necessary to introduce and accumulate innovation resources, including innovative talent, institutions, investment and achievements. The most important issue is bringing in innovative talent, especially high-level innovative and entrepreneurial talent. For this reason, the innovation and development environments are not exactly the same. It is important to provide high-level innovative and entrepreneurial talent with an ideal environment for living, conducting research and translating their discoveries into industry products. It involves the construction of infrastructure, such as internet and information channels, a cooperative innovative platform, a liveable environment for innovative and entrepreneurial talent, investment and financial resources and a culture of innovation. The public environment that stimulates innovation should strengthen market competition, which is necessary to increase the pressure for technological innovation of enterprises. The incentive for an innovative public service environment is equally important. Apart from the efficiency of the government's approval of projects and policy support, the most important thing is to provide a supportive legal system, especially intellectual property protection laws. A simple competition mechanism only solves the external pressure of innovation. It cannot produce continuous innovation-driving forces. While establishing the necessary competition mechanism, we should also allow innovators' monopolies to play a role to a certain degree. When enterprises with innovations monopolise their products for a certain period of time, they can gain full compensation for their innovation costs. The monopoly of intellectual property protection systems, such as patent applications, can solve the problem of "free ridership" of innovation results. It can also enhance the driving force of innovation.

In summary, the implementation of an innovation-driven development strategy is a systematic effort involving not only knowledge-based innovations but also technological innovations. It, in reality, involves a fundamental shift in the economic development paradigm and major reforms in the corresponding economic systems, combining both market forces and the government's active intervention. Different systems must work together to form a joint force to promote the efficient allocation and transformation of innovative resources so that the entire society can support innovation and development.

Notes

1 Simon S. Kuznets, "Modern Economic Growth," in *Comparative Modernization*, ed. Cyril E. Blake, trans. Yang Yu et al. (Shanghai: Shanghai Translation Press, 1996), 270.
2 Joseph E. Stiglitz, *Whither Socialism?*, trans. Han Liang and Yu Wenbo (Changchun: Jilin People's Press, 1998), 173.
3 Chen Qirong, "Nobel Prize in Natural Science and Innovative Countries," *Journal of Shanghai University*, no. 6 (2011): 10–18.

6 Industrialisation and upgrading industrial structure

Economic development reflects not only an increase in output but also the evolution of industrial structure. Development in developing nations is mainly restricted by their structural issues. This is why development economics, especially the structuralist school, tends to see restructuring as the central issue. China used to be an agricultural economy. When our GDP rose to second place in the world in 2010 with a per capita GDP ranking amongst the median-income economies, the agriculture ratio dropped to 10.1%, while the industry ratio grew to 46.8%. This was an indication that China had been transformed from an agricultural economy into an industrial one. In 2016, the proportion of added value in agriculture dropped to 8.6% while that of manufacturing was 39.8%. The service industry made up the rest. Promoting growth on such a basis requires further improvements in the level and quality of industrialisation through the transformation and upgrading of the industrial structure. At present, economic development relies on the modern service industry and emerging strategic industries, which will be the primary focus of China's economic development paradigm shift.

6.1 The evolutionary tendency of industrial structure

6.1.1 The content of industrial structure evolution

According to Karl Marx, industrial structure refers to the proportional relationship between the production of capital goods and the production of consumption goods. In statistical and comparative practices, it refers to the proportional relationship between the agriculture, industry and service sectors. It can also refer to the proportional relationship between traditional and emerging industries. The evolution of industrial structure depends on two factors: its balanced coordination and supererogation.

With regard to industrial structure coordination, one definition by Marx is that, at a certain rate of expanded reproduction or economic growth, the production of the two types of goods reaches a reasonable proportion. The overall needs for investment and consumption are reasonably met by these two types of goods. The other definition is the balance between the supply of all products, intermediary and terminal, from all industrial sectors and the society's demand for them. At a certain economic growth rate, the productive capacity of every industrial sector can thereby be fully exploited. In the meantime, there will be no localised spare or overused capacity.

The coordination of industrial structure is definitely dynamic, which is the coordination in the process of supererogation. The balance in industrial structure can be kept with no change in its level, but that is not the goal. The cause of China's current limitations on the supply side is not only its imbalance but also its long stagnation on a lower level. Industrial structure coordination must be integrated with its supererogation so that the balance between social productivity and satisfaction of social needs is retained on continuously rising levels. Industrial structure supererogation consistently breaks the balance of previous levels. New balance is achieved through coordination when the industrial structure attains a new level.

For developing nations, industrial development never aims just to keep the balance of the existing structure level. On a developing standard, industrial development is supposed to strongly push social productivity and satisfaction of social needs to new levels. With increasing social capital involved, the new levels cover the improvement of output capacity of all industrial sectors, development of emerging and developing sectors to meet the new social needs and decreasing or diminishing sunset industries. Apparently, industrial structure supererogation is meant to generate new production capacity and create and satisfy new social needs in a structural sense. In the light of American Nobel laureate in economics Kuznets's research methods, there are two indicators for industrial structure level: sector proportion of GDP and sector proportion of labour force. The empirical statistics provided by Kuznets (Table 6.1) reveal the trends of industrial structure supererogation as follows:

First, there is a supererogation trend of sector proportion of GDP. With per capita GDP growth, the percentage which the primary sector takes in GDP significantly drops. It is worth mentioning that the percentage drop does not mean a drop in gross agricultural product. That trend is the result of an increase in

Table 6.1 Industrial Structure on Different Development Levels, 1958

Per Capita GDP (US$)	Sector Proportion of GDP (%)			Number of Countries Investigated
	Primary	Secondary	Tertiary	
51.8	53.6	18.5	27.9	6
82.6	44.6	22.4	33.0	6
138	37.9	24.6	37.5	6
221	32.3	29.4	38.3	15
360	22.5	35.2	42.3	6
540	17.4	39.5	43.1	6
864	11.8	52.9	35.3	6
1382	9.2	50.2	40.6	6

Source: S. S. Kuznets, *Economic Growth of Nations: Total Output and Production Structure* (Shanghai: Commercial Press, 1985), 111.

Table 6.2 World Bank Data (%) of Industrial Structure of Selected Countries, 2014

Country	Per Capita GDP (US$)	Primary Sector	Secondary Sector	Tertiary Sector
United Kingdom	45,603	0.61	19.76	79.63
Germany	47,627	0.75	30.69	68.56
Japan	36,194	1.21	26.21	72.58
United States	54,629	1.45	20.50	78.05
South Korea	27,970	2.34	38.23	59.42

gross agricultural product and labour productivity. It can only be explained by the following trends. In addition, the size of the secondary (industrial) sector soars. An analysis of the internal structure of the industrial sector shows that the fastest-growing area is the manufacturing industry, which contributes half of the industrial sector. Next comes the construction industry, which results from an increasing demand for infrastructure in urbanisation and industrialisation, followed by transportation and communications. They are the most vigorous sectors of industrial development. Finally, the tertiary (service) sector expands as per capita GDP rises. The financial industry also develops considerably together with the socialisation of capital sources and movement brought about by socialisation and the commercialisation of production.

Second, there is a trend of labour-force sector GDP proportion. This is complementary to the GDP sector proportion. The change in the GDP affects demand for the labour force, leading to an employment structure change. As per capita GDP rises, the labour force flows from the primary to secondary sector. On the completion of industrialisation, it flows from the secondary to tertiary sector. The general trend is a gradual decrease in primary sector employment and a corresponding increase of secondary and tertiary sector employment. Compared with the sector proportion of GDP, however, it is noticeably different in time and speed. This is seen in the following two phases: (1) In the beginning stage of industrialisation, the proportion of labour force in the agricultural sector decreases far more slowly than that of its contribution to the gross product does. (2) After industrialisation, the proportion of the labour force in the tertiary sector increases faster than that of its contribution to the gross product. Nevertheless, the proportions of the labour force in each sector eventually tend to conform to those of production value.

In agricultural developing nations, industrial restructuring begins with industrialisation, a process that involves adjusting and upgrading the internal industrial structure. According to Hollis Chenery's analysis in his book *Industrialization and Growth: A Comparative Study*, the industrialisation of developed countries undergoes three phases. In its earliest phase, traditional structure based on agriculture gradually converts to industrialised structure based on a labour-intensive industry. It manufactures primary commodities, such as food, tobacco and mineral and building products. In the middle phase, also known as the heavy chemical industry phase, fast growth shifts from light industry to heavy industry when capital-intensive industry prevails. In the later phase, IT and biotechnology emerge and dominate. Meanwhile, the tertiary sector, especially emerging services such as finance, information, advertising, public utilities and consulting services, moves from steady growth to fast growth. This is a turning point to enter the modernised society. The tertiary sector starts to diversify as knowledge-intensive industries gain independence and dominance. Meanwhile, consumer desire shows diversity, plurality and pursuit of personalisation.[1]

Obviously, the secondary sector's share in industrial structure reflects its level at a certain period of time in a certain country or region. The trend of industrial structure supererogation is for the aforementioned share to drop in the earliest phase but grow in the middle and later phases. Industrial upgrading involves not only the introduction of competitive products to meet new market needs in existing industries but also the upgrading of the industrial structure itself. It includes a transformation from labour-intensive industries to technology-intensive ones, as emerging industries are introduced to meet new market needs.

Because of the fact that a large country has a huge population and a vast domestic market with massive and diverse needs, structural changes in large countries have the following characteristics. First, they can begin in the low-income stage. According to Chenery's analysis, in nations with a vast domestic market, the most rapid industrial structure change can take place earlier than in nations of other types. This is why China was able to initiate its industrialisation process with a relatively low per capita GDP level. Second, given the same per capita GDP level, the proportion of industrial product in the GDP of large countries is bigger than that of small countries. The accumulation rate in large countries is higher too. Third, as for international trade, compared to small countries, imports exceed net exports in large countries. The smaller a country is, the greater the effect international trade has on its structural transfer. For large countries, however, international trade accounts for less of their gross output. Therefore, expanding foreign trade contributes less to the transfer of their domestic production structure. Fourth, large countries encounter greater difficulties in the allocation and utilisation of production resources. All this determines the reasonable deviation between a large country's structure and Chenery's "standard structure." In his development model, a large country is defined as one with a population of 20 million or more, by which standard China is gigantic. Deviation between a gigantic country's structure and that of a large nation is also reasonable. It, of course, does not mean that we cannot adopt the "general structure of a large country" as a reference system in assessing China's current industrial structure. For the tendency of industrial structure change, Chenery published a group of empirical statistics on the standard structure and large-country structure (see Table 6.3). This is an important reference system for the industrial restructuring of all countries.

Table 6.3 Standard Structure and Large-Country Structure When Per Capita GDP Reaches US$1,000

	Primary Sector (%)	Overall Industrial Sector (%)				Service Sector (%)
		Total	Light Manufacturing	Heavy Manufacturing	Construction & Infrastructure	
Standard Structure	13.8	34.7	15.8	8.6	15.1	51.5
Large -Nation Structure	5.7	28.7	12.5	12.2	4	65.6

Source: Hollis Chenery, Sherman Robinson, and Moshe Syrquin. *Industrialization and Growth* (New York: Oxford University Press, 1986), 21.

6.1.2 The current situation of China's industrial structure

China's development kicked off from a semi-colonial and semi-feudal economic foundation. In the early years after the PRC was founded, the industrial foundation was a system of traditional agriculture with little modern industry, let alone an independent modern industrial system. With regard to industry, there were only handicrafts and traditional textile mills. National industrialisation was promoted mainly in urban areas in the early 1950s. When the project was said to have been essentially completed in 1956, the independent industrial system was limited to urban areas, accounting for less than 30% of the national industrial structure. It was the 1980s that witnessed large-scale industrialisation in China. It started with township enterprise development by promoting rural industrialisation and building various industrial parks and development zones with direct foreign investment. By 2011, the share of the primary sector had dropped to 10.1%, while the secondary sector's share had climbed to 46.8%, marking China's conversion from an agricultural country to an industrial one. Table 6.4 presents the three sectors' added-value proportions in the GDP of several representative years since 1978.

Table 6.4 The Three Sectors' Proportion in China's GDP in Selected Years

Year	Primary Sector (%)	Secondary Sector (%)	Tertiary Sector (%)	Per Capita GDP
1978	28.1	48.2	23.7	381
1982	33.39	44.77	21.85	298
2010	10.1	46.67	43.24	4,382
2013	9.41	43.67	46.92	7,081
2016	8.6	39.8	51.6	8,260
2017	7.9	40.5	51.6	8,836

As Table 6.4 shows, the pattern of three sectors' shifts over the past 40 years can be viewed in the following way. The primary sector's contribution to the national economy decreased from 50% in 1952 to 10% in 2013, with the downward trend slowing in recent years. The secondary sector's share in GDP increased before the reform era from 21% in 1952 to 47% in 1977. Since then, it remained between 43% and 47% until 2007. In this period, industrialisation experienced its fastest development. The growth rate almost equalled that of China's economy since the reform. Industrial output value soared, and its volume multiplied. Services in the tertiary sector grew steadily since the reform, especially after entering the 21st century when its contribution to GDP exceeded 40%. In 2013, the proportion rose to 46% and overtook the secondary sector for the first time.

Since the founding of the PRC and after more than 60 years of development, China's national economy has experienced its fast growth. The industrial structure has undergone tremendous changes and generally in the same direction with its supererogation. Nevertheless, its status is noticeably different from Chenery's standard structure typical of countries on similar economic development levels (Table 6.4). As Tables 6.2 and 6.3 show, it is apparent that China's industrial structure is still underdeveloped. The agricultural sector is larger, while the service sector is smaller than expected. This indicates the direction China's industrial structure upgrading should pursue.

In 2017, China's per capita GDP reached US$8,836. According to Chenery's criteria, the figure places China approximately in the mid-late period of the middle industrialisation phase. By comparing China's industrial structure in 2017 with Chenery's middle-income, large-country standard structure with a US$1,000 per capita GDP, we can identify the current status of China's industrial structure.

First, in 2017, China's primary sector accounted for 7.9% of its GDP, much higher than the 5.7% of the large-country standard and even more deviant from the developed-country standard. As for labour force share, according to official statistics, China's employment in agriculture accounted for 28%, compared to 3% or 4% in the developed countries. This 28% of the labour force contributed to only 7.9% of Chinese GDP. It illustrates the low labour productivity and slow technological advancement in China's primary sector.

Second, in 2017, China's secondary sector constituted 40.5% of its GDP, far higher than the 28.7% of the large-country standard.

Third, in 2017, China's tertiary sector constituted 51.6% of its GDP, lower than both the 65.6% of the large-country standard and the 70% of the high-income-country standard. China's underdeveloped service industry is characterised by not only its small proportion of GDP and its employment share of 36% but also its typical low-income-country underdevelopment of productive services. Wholesaling, retailing and catering have remained dominant. Newer services such as finance, insurance and social services are growing, but their proportion of this sector remains low. The same can be seen in scientific research, general technical services, education, literature and art, broadcasting, movies and television.

In summary, China's industrial structure does not align with the "standard structure" of a large country with similar per capita GDP. Rather than three components of one economy, the three sectors are more like a combination of three different societies – namely, middle-income-country industry, low-income-country agriculture and pre-industrial-society services. This status reflects the contradictions between the industrial structure, which has obvious low-income-country features, and the overall economy with its middle-income-country per capita GDP.

6.2 Modernisation of industrial structure

China has been experiencing rapid and remarkable industrialisation. Upon entering the 21st century, China transformed from an agricultural country into an industrial one and will launch the modernisation process after becoming a well-off society. Modernisation, first and foremost, means industrial modernisation. Through the analysis of the economic development process, modernisation, in countries with a dual structure of coexisting modern industry and underdeveloped agriculture, is typically initiated through industrialisation, urbanisation and transformation of traditional agriculture. In China, economic modernisation is featured with the simultaneous development of new industrialisation, information, urbanisation and agricultural modernisation.

6.2.1 Rapid growth of the service industry

It is an urgent necessity for China to develop a service industry as the focal point of the transformation and upgrading of its industrial structure.

First, in the mid-late period of industrialisation and urbanisation, services, especially modern services, generally grow rapidly. Service trade grows faster than product trade. Compared to manufacturing, services have greater development potential and appreciation space. People's demands for services in transportation, culture, education, medical care and information grow stronger after their ever-increasing demand for material products is met. The service industry provides more jobs, and most of its businesses are environmentally friendly. Moreover, it satisfies the increasingly diverse consumer demand and reflects the development level of a country. It deserves more attention and support.

Second, from the perspective of the industrial development sequence, manufacturing boosts services. Manufacturing on a higher level calls for corresponding services, which, in turn, bolster the former. Particularly, as manufacturing enters the phase of raised added value, more importance ought to be attached to developing productive services. According to the "smiling curve," the added value in the service sector is noticeably higher than that in the manufacturing industry. Emerging services, such as finance, information, advertising, public utilities and consulting services grow the fastest.

Third, investment-driven economic development has been replaced by consumption-driven growth that relies on the service industry. Differing from manufacturing, where locations for production and consumption or market can be separated, the service industry and its consumption are inseparable. A service network expands to wherever there is consumer demand, and wherever it reaches, demand, in turn, is generated. The most typical example is the reciprocal relationship between thriving information services and booming consumption.

The fourth factor is the present international background. Countries are usually categorised into the first, second and third worlds. The concept also applies to the nature of the economic structure, which divides countries into three types. The economy of the first type is driven by service and consumption, such as the United States, Japan, Britain and France, which are rich and powerful but face employment pressure. Manufacturing and export are leading industries in the second type, including China, which are characterised by an enormous economy of scale and high employment rates with low-income levels. The third is resource-rich countries. They can be further divided into two sub-types. Some are rich yet not powerful, like oil-exporting countries, while others are very poor. All three types have been seeking to transform ever since the 2008 financial crisis. The countries of the first type have been focussing on employment issues by developing manufacturing and expanding exports. The Obama administration, for instance, planned on doubling the value of exports in five years, as well as re-industrialisation. The countries of the third type have been inclined to develop manufacturing so as to reduce their dependency on the outside world. China has been largely affected by the industrial structure transformation in countries of both the first and third types. Re-industrialisation in developed countries and the development of manufacturing in resource-rich countries bring ever-increasing pressure on international competition and resource supply. For an economy driven mainly by manufacturing and export to solve the structural problem of "big but underdeveloped," as well as to cope with the pressure from the ongoing global economic transformation, it is practical to purposefully transform and upgrade the industrial structure by developing services.

As China makes a transition from the middle phase to the post-industrialisation phase, the service industry has developed rapidly. As statistics in Table 6.2 indicate, services in China have been growing much faster than the secondary sector since the beginning of the 21st century. Its contribution to GDP has been rapidly expanding and exceeded that of the secondary sector for the first time in 2013. It has become China's biggest industry. It is predicted that services will keep growing at that rate in the years to come, making up an increasingly large proportion of the national economy.

The ongoing urbanisation also boosts services considerably. Empirical analyses prove that services grow synchronously with urbanisation. Large- and medium-sized cities provide ideal conditions for the growth of modern services, such as culture, education, finance, insurance, real estate and information. They typically account for at least 70% of the economy of a global city. In a developed country, 60% of the GDP and jobs are generated by its urban-based service industry. The reason is that services in a city have a strong effect on its functions. They include marketing, information, finance, insurance, communications and so on. The urbanisation project in progress aims to enhance existing city functions and endow rural towns with urban facilities. With the expansion of urbanisation to rural areas, demographically and territorially, growing numbers of urban-based corporations and the service system can develop continuously.

The service industry itself calls for transformation and upgrading. Unlike traditional services, modern services were born and raised with more advanced technological and cultural genes to live up to the expectations of urban residents. There are two types of services, non-productive and productive. As they rapidly grow, their structures undergo constant optimisation and innovation, enabling new service types and content to provide the industry with more opportunities for development.

The development of consumer services is associated with the rise of people's consumption and a change in their consumption structure. As people's per capita income increases and the percentage of income spent on basic needs decreases, people's consumption of services keeps growing, which boosts sustained development of consumer services. Such consumer services as retail, catering, entertainment, tourism, sports, transportation, shipping, hospitality and housekeeping are labour intensive, closely related to people's living needs and easy to enter and exit. Hence, these services develop fast. Statistics show that health care, transportation, communications, entertainment, culture and education have been growing at tremendous rates and have become consumption hot spots. Tourism has also become a popular item in household spending. Income discrepancies amongst social groups result in widening gaps between consumption levels, whereby services for different classes are required. Therefore, consumer services can also have a higher class and added value.

Productive services are even more important for large manufacturing-driven economies. Service-led manufacturing is becoming a trend in the modern economy. Economic development has been increasingly boosted by modern services, such as finance, technology, culture, international business and information. Stronger development and higher quality of manufacturing call for highly developed services, such as finance, insurance, transportation, information, e-commerce and logistics, as well as standardised service agencies that specialise in law, accounting, consulting, engineering, designing, advertising and so on.

The service industry has also been upgrading technically, with traditional services challenged by digital businesses. Data from 2013 shows that e-commerce accounted for 20% to 30% of retail. The percentage went up to 50% for younger-generation consumers. Moreover, e-commerce has entered the financial field in the form of internet finance.

In the context of economic globalisation, developed countries not only transfer their manufacturing to developing nations but also modern services, such as finance, insurance, communications and network industry, which, in the latter, are relatively underdeveloped but are the most promising areas. Services provide a primary investment environment for introducing and developing international manufacturing. Because of their importance, developing nations must pay more attention to their services, especially modern services.

6.2.2 New type of industrialisation

The level of industrial structure is defined not only by the proportions of the three sectors but also, more importantly, by the internal structure of each industry. In a large manufacturing nation like China, innovation and upgrading are crucial. There are two directions to take: one is to use the latest technology to mobilise industrial innovation and develop key future-oriented industries; the other is to use high tech to transform traditional industries. For any economy, the key to industrial upgrading is to establish a modern industrial structure, especially for its pillar industry, which can generate more benefits and stronger competitiveness. The upgrading of industrial structure is based on increasing the proportion of emerging and technology-intensive industries through high-tech industrialisation.

In the past, manufacturing in China was able to develop for a long time because of a relatively unrestricted supply of resources, loose environmental regulations and, more importantly, steady demand from the overseas market. At present, however, this type of industrial structure is clearly less competitive. For one thing, pressure on resources and the environment imposes limits on manufacturing growth. For another, global crises and industrial transformation result in excess capacity in global markets where over-competition gives rise to protectionism, which frequently imposes various punitive restrictions on Chinese products.

China has become the world's leading manufacturer in terms of its total production volume. According to the standard international industrial categories, China is the leader in 7 of 22 categories and tops the world in more than 220 industrial products, including steel, cement and automobiles. At present, only two countries take up more than 10% of global trade volume. China accounts for 11.2% of the total export volume, while the United States accounts for 12.6%. China's leading position in export is guaranteed by its leading manufacturing capacities. This is how China has earned the name the "world factory." However, as China steps into the middle-income phase, its industrial structure poses a prominent issue.

First, its excess capacity is alarming. Caused by old-style, GDP-oriented development, the problem is especially serious in cement, steel, glass, nonferrous metals, chemical products, construction materials and other traditional manufacturing areas. According to a report released in early 2014 by the Research Institute of the State Statistics Bureau, in the second quarter of 2013, the capacity utilisation ratio for industrial enterprises was 78.6%. The capacity exceeded market demand, making a large quantity of products unsaleable. In addition, the costs of energy and raw materials kept soaring. As a result, the industrial structure generated high yield but low profits.

Second, China's manufacturing is at the lower end of the value chain with modest added value. Although our manufacturing output tops the world with some areas ranking either in first or second place, it is not so competitive internationally. The United States takes a lion's share in such high-tech areas as aircraft manufacturing, special industrial materials, medical equipment and biological technology, while China accounts for more in low-tech areas, such as textiles, clothing, chemical products and household appliances. As for products, there are more foreign brands than "China-created" items.

Third, China's energy consumption and pollution are high; hence, supplies of energy, other resources and environmental capacity are unsustainable and unprofitable. According to "Statistical Review of World Energy" (2017) released on June 13, 2017, China's primary energy consumption in 2016 topped an equivalent of 3.053 billion tonnes of oil. This was 23% of the world's oil consumption, much larger than China's share of the world's GDP (14.81%). As the statistics indicate, China's GDP did not account for a very large proportion of the global GDP, but it consumed a big percentage of coal and oil. At the current rate of energy consumption, China's GDP will not be able to reach that of the United States. Rather, China cannot sustain its present development pattern, even with global supplies of oil and coal.

Fourth, the issue of the industrial structure merits immediate attention. Products with excessive capacity are currently superfluous, while those incorporating high technology, performance and added value are in short supply. For instance, China is the world's leading steel manufacturer, but cold-rolled sheet steel is in short supply, with a self-sufficiency rate of only 65%. Further, the self-sufficiency rate for stainless steel is only about 15%. We have a surplus capacity for ethylene but an insufficient capacity for high-performance polyvinyl acetic, importing two million tonnes annually. The metallurgical industry is a buyers' market, but we rely on imports of many types of specialised steel. The same applies to other industries, such as construction materials and pharmaceuticals. Empirical analyses indicate that the strength of a buyer's market is in proportion with the level of the industry. The less technological content an industry has, the more overlapping competition; therefore, the stronger the buyers' market grows. Oversupply occurs with products and industries with less technological content; these industries are, apparently, easy to start but are unable to defeat competitors. In a buyers' market, the reason for a business encountering declining shares and even bankruptcy is typically its lack of technology. On the contrary, in an industry with high technological content, many competitors below the technological threshold are blocked out; hence, the buyers' market is weaker. Those businesses which adopt the most advanced technology earlier have a more competitive edge and are able to create a sellers' market for their products. Evidently, for businesses locked in an overwhelming buyers' market, the only way to get out is to use the most advanced technology.

After entering the middle-income phase, further industrialisation ought to focus on a newer mode, compared to both our past practice and that of developed countries. New industrialisation means higher technological content and profit with less resource consumption and environmental pollution. It also means the full use of human resources. Implementation of all of these factors means a modern industrial system can be established with optimised structure, advanced technology, a clean and safe environment and high added value to create more jobs.

The first priority is to raise the technological content in industry. Cutting-edge technologies can immediately bring a nation's industrialisation to the forefront of international competition. Consequently, substitution and saving reduce the consumption of material resources, and clean production reduces pollution. Increased technological content also generates higher added value. With the latest technological achievements applied to emerging and cutting-edge industries, we can establish a modern industrial system capable of independent innovation.

The second is to reduce energy use. China is undergoing a process of industrialisation. Its economic structure has been significantly transformed. This is characterised by resource-driven growth. This type of transformation and development imposes an enormous demand on natural resources, which are already in short supply. As the global environment and resource supply deteriorate, we must abandon Western patterns of industrialisation and modernisation to realise sustainable development. We need new patterns of economic development to replace overexploitation with repeated or recycled use of renewable resources. As for the balance between development and control over environmental pollution, it must switch from "development first" to "developing while protecting" and then to "protection first."

Third is to fully tap human resources. Labour is one element of economic growth. In China's modernisation process, one unavoidable problem is the oversupply of labour. It brings heavy pressure that curbs transformation and the upgrading of the industrial structure. China's modern structure thus has to diversify itself, seeking the coexistence of labour-intensive and technology-intensive industries. Nevertheless, even labour-intensive industries cannot be based solely on labour. At the current level of productivity, what really drives economic growth is not only labourers but also labourers with knowledge and access to technology. The overall contribution to economic growth depends upon the quality of labour. New industrialisation takes more advantage of the quality than the quantity of labour. Here the most valuable resources are knowledge and technology or the ability to work with advanced equipment. Human capital refers to labourers equipped with knowledge and technology. Clearly, investment in human capital and the improvement of labourers' quality are significant parts of new industrialisation.

Marx made an important observation that what differentiates one economic era from another was not their products but how the products were made and by what means they were produced. Consequently, he concluded that the economic era of feudalism was represented by the water mill while capitalism originated from the steam engine, which was a fruit of the First Industrial Revolution. The Second Industrial Revolution was marked by steel and electricity.

The technological revolution after World War II could be called the Third Industrial Revolution. It was based on the newest breakthroughs in natural science theories, including information technology, biotechnology, new materials and energy resources, as well as space and maritime technology. More recently, beginning in the early 1970s, another technological revolution occurred, represented by microelectronics, bioengineering and new materials. The economy today is driven by computer and internet technology. In a way, whether the internet is used has become a dividing line between modern and traditional industries and services. In recent years, mobile terminals have been integrated with internet access, which has been efficiently used in industries and services, thereby facilitating their modernisation.

Interestingly, in his popular book on the Third Industrial Revolution, American scholar Jeremy Rifkin uses energy sources to distinguish different industrial eras. He names the Second Industrial Revolution the "Fossil Energy Age." In the 21st century, the industrialised lifestyle can no longer be sustained by petroleum and other fossil fuels that have been gradually depleted. The technologies driven by fossil fuels are outdated. The industrial structure based on fossil fuels has turned sluggish. Even worse, carbon emissions from fossil fuel–based industrial activities threaten to destroy the ecosystems of the earth and climate, damaging human health. The Third Industrial Revolution has emerged as a response to the aforementioned problem. According to Rifkin's definition, it is based on renewable energy sources and integrates internet technology.

Many nations have taken or are taking active measures to address challenges arising from the emerging Third and Fourth Industrial Revolutions. According to relevant information, the United States has dedicated itself to the development of new energy sources, biomedicine, aerospace, aviation and a broadband network. Japan focusses on new energy sources, next-generation automobiles, low-carbon production, medical care and information technology. The European Union countries are devoted to green technology, low-carbon production and new-energy automobiles. Some developing nations, such as Brazil and Mexico, are also actively developing new energy sources and environmental protection technologies.

Therefore, the new technological and industrial revolution is characterised by innovative, knowledge-intensive and green-technology industries. The subsequently emerging strategic industries have a high level of integration of new technologies. They represent future directions for technological innovation and industrial development. China missed past industrial revolutions and opportunities. We cannot afford to miss the ongoing new technological revolution.

In this era of globalisation, information technology and networking, China's innovative industrialisation is on the same starting line with developed countries faced with the Third and Fourth Industrial/Technological Revolutions. We are developing the same industries that the United States, Japan and European countries are. Developed countries have recently shifted their focus from information to biomedicine, biotechnology and new energy sources, all of which are what China intends to develop.

According to the report of the 19th CPC National Congress, industrial modernisation is defined by the rapid development of advanced manufacturing. It includes the in-depth integration of the internet, big data, artificial intelligence and the real economy. It should also take the lead in promoting new growth and momentum in middle-to-high-end consumption; an innovation-driven, low-carbon and multi-layer economy; modern supply chains; and human capital services. In the meantime, we need to optimise and upgrade traditional industries. The goal is to lift China's industries to the middle-to-high end of the global value chain and create a number of world-class advanced manufacturing clusters.

Industrialisation has entered the information phase. In developed countries, such as the United States, information services and network technology have become the main driving force of economic development. Revolutionary changes are taking place in the technological base of the secondary sector and other industries. Many developing nations have also entered the age of industrialisation in different degrees. Their normal practice is to follow the footprints of developed countries (i.e. industrialisation before the information revolution). It turns out, however, that they cannot catch up and have lagged farther behind. Experiences from those successful countries indicate that we should employ the latest technologies of developed countries to achieve leapfrog development. Take industrialisation, for example. Heavy chemical industry is typically an unavoidable phase in development. It generates high consumption and pollution. Information technologies, however, enable us to skip such a phase.

As is stated in the "G20 Blueprint for Innovation and Growth" issued at the Hangzhou Summit, the information revolution at the world's frontier is going in two directions. One aims at manufacturing. Technology revolutions have brought new opportunities for middle- to long-term economic growth. Significant improvements are being made in internet technology, big data, cloud computing, artificial intelligence, robotics, additive manufacturing, new materials, augmented reality, nanotechnology, biotechnology and other emerging technologies. The other aims at the service industry. In the era of the internet economy, the term "digital economy" refers to a broader range of economic activities with digitised information and knowledge as key production elements, a modern information network as a main carrier and effective use of information and communication technologies as a driving force towards higher efficiency and an optimised economic structure.

Today's industrial innovation must be integrated with information technology, which pushes industrialisation towards leapfrog development. The information revolution is a historical process with fully used information technologies and resources, shared information and knowledge and improved quality of economic growth resulting in a transformed economy and society. It has evolved into the mobile internet. It represents not only the rapid development of the information industry but also the fast expansion and wide application of information technology in all sectors of the social economy, shared information resources and full use of human intelligence and social material resource potential. In the meantime, it gives rise to a major reform of economic and social structures. Therefore, the present society is also known as the information society.

The information revolution includes industrial innovation based on the latest information technology and high-tech industrialisation. In addition to the application of high technologies and an increase of high-tech content in existing industries, it is more important to support the development of some high-tech industries, such as microelectronics, information technology, bioengineering, new materials and so on. At present, the strategic emerging industries, such as the modern biotechnology and renewable energy that Rifkin mentioned, are inseparable from information and internet technology. The new technological revolution is based on network and information technologies.

The information revolution does not preclude traditional industries but integrates and transforms them. Through the wide application of information technology, many traditional industries have leaped into information society. Information technology has been widely applied and rapidly spread in such fields as research, development, design of industrial products, process control, business management and marketing. It raises automation, intelligence and management modernisation levels and, therefore, boosts structural adjustment, transforming and upgrading traditional industries. In China today, although products of many traditional industries are popular, they have high energy consumption and emission rates. Their only entrance into modern society is through an IT-based, green-technology transformation.

6.3 Strategies and mechanism for upgrading industrial structure

Modernisation of the industrial structure involves resource allocation amongst its different sectors. Industrial innovation relies on the allocation of innovative elements. In the socialist market economy, the mechanism for structural adjustment and innovation is the market mechanism that controls resource allocation. Meanwhile, the government must be functional.

6.3.1 Decisive factors for industrial structure transformation

The industrial structure level reflects the corresponding economic development phase. When China moved from the low-income to middle-income stage, its industrial structure upgraded. Likewise, the future transition from the middle-income to high-income stage requires further transformation and upgrading of the industrial structure.

In general, there are four factors for promoting industrial structure supererogation. First, the rise in GNP is the material foundation. It not only promotes industrial diversity but also provides funding for structural changes. Second, social needs are used to make adjustments in the industrial structure and influence the development scale of various industrial sectors, as well as their sequence and metabolism. Third, international trade is a contributor to changes in industrial structure. When a country's international trade strategies convert from comparative advantage to competitive advantage, the structural upgrading is significantly boosted in the sectors involved in the international division of labour. Fourth, technological innovation and the rapid popularisation of its achievements greatly accelerate industrial innovation.

In his book *Structural Changes and Development Policies*, Chenery summarised various decisive factors that consistently determined the mode of structural changes in all countries during certain historical periods as follows:

1   Growth of consumer demand in accordance with the increase of income (Engel function),
2   The need to accumulate output and human capital for an increase of higher per capita production,
3   Acquisition of the same technologies for all countries across the world and
4   The issue of entering the international market.

Factors determining discrepancies in structural change in different nations are as follows:

1   Differences in social targets and policy choices,
2   Differences in resource supplies,
3   Differences in territorial size,
4   Differences in external capital acquisition and
5   Diachronic changes of a given factor.

6.3.2 Market choice in industrial structure

Structural adjustment is a market function. It is viewed as an adjustment of resource allocation amongst all sectors as determined by the market. Given the free circulation of all elements, such as capital, labour force and technology, the market adjusts the industrial structure through the mechanism of independent choice and survival of the fittest. The government is not supposed to replace the market when the latter is functional. This is especially true because the market is capable of eliminating inferior production capacity and promoting innovation.

To some extent, market choice means market-demand choice. Social need structure consists of consumer need and investment need. The birth and size of an industry are dependent on the existence, scale and potential of the society's need. A discrepancy in the social need of different sectors' products directly affects their supply and the rate of their technological advance.

According to the Engel function, as income increases, the proportion devoted to food spending decreases. It indicates that the growth of consumer need does not simply mean growing numbers but progress in quality or structural change. When the per capita income level rises, demands for certain consumer goods may stagnate or even decrease. In comparison, the demands for other goods may surge rapidly. Major changes are bound to take place in consumption with economic growth. As income increases and the proportion spent on food consumption shrinks, so does the primary sector. Meanwhile, the secondary sector's share noticeably expands, as does the tertiary sector's (services).

As for investment need, the productivity of new industries is chiefly generated by massive investments. The three sectors differ in their ability to attract investments. In the process of industrialisation, the secondary sector (manufacturing) attracts most of the newly increased investment, which is an important reason for its rapidly rising importance in the process. In addition, for quite a long period of time, because of difference in capital structure, the tertiary sector (services) received far less investment than the secondary sector, while its development is more dependent on the increase of the labour involved. However, as industrialisation reaches a certain stage, with expanding markets and higher technological content for industrial products, the investment need for production-oriented modern services is generated. Thus productive services grow quickly.

In terms of capital, there is a stock structure and an incremental structure. Adjustment of the latter, or newly increased investments, is significant to the adjustment of industrial structure. At the current level of economic development, however, increasing investment alone cannot lead to the adjustment of industrial structure. The key here is the adjustment of stock structure. In reality, however, the fact is that divisions and barriers between various regions and industrial sectors block that adjustment. Empowered local interests would further strengthen barriers to the adjustment. As a result, those sectors that deserve development fail, while those that should go down rise. In his book *On Capital*, Marx defines full market competition as the free flow of capital and labour between different sectors. This market-regulating structure is a prerequisite condition of the adjustment of industrial structure. In an incomplete market system, with some regions and sectors hindering the free flow of elements to protect local interests, the circulation will fall into disorder or stagnation. Therefore, to guarantee the market's decisive function in structural adjustment, we must eliminate local protectionism. Market competition, especially its mechanism of survival of the fittest, must be strengthened.

In a sense, the market regulates industrial structure in proportion to price. Only if the product price and element price are both established in the market can the selection and regulation of structure be realised. In reality, however, prices are decided by both the market and the government. Consequently, market prices have been long contorted, while regulated capital flows are either too slow or too brief. In recent years, industrial structures of different regions have become identical. They all unconditionally compete, developing the same industries. That is partly caused by regional divisions and partly by indications of prices at present. The supply of underpriced basic industrial products, mainly coal, electricity and oil, does not meet the demand from inflated processing industries. To ensure the market's independent choice of industrial structure, we must establish a market pricing mechanism.

6.3.3 Government roles and industrial policies

For developing nations, the twin problems of traditional low-level industrial structure and incomplete market competition put the responsibility for adjustment on both the market and government. In addition to the necessary institutional environment for the market to allocate resources, the government needs to provide a clear orientation for adjustment and the upgrading of the industrial structure. Specifically, the government needs to determine and issue industrial policies periodically and provide a guide for investments. The government's industrial orientation consists primarily of the following four aspects.

The first aspect is to orient industry choice. As the economy grows, different sectors in the industrial structure have a different status. In each phase of development, the leading industries carry the whole structure to the next level. To lead the industry, a sector has to meet two requirements. One is rapid growth and considerable scale; the other is a broad and close connection with other sectors and strong "connective effects."

Regarding the first requirement, Japanese economist Shinohara Miyohei proposed two criteria when mapping Japanese industrial structure. One is "income elasticity," which directly affects the demand scale (i.e. the correlation between the increase of per capita national income and the increase or decrease in demand for certain products). The more elastic that correlation is, the bigger the market that sector owns. It makes high-income elasticity one requirement for a leading sector. The other is the "production rate," which directly affects supply capacity. Those with a faster ascending production rate or technological advance emerge as key industries.

The second requirement is composed of two conditions: a backward correlation with the sectors that supply it with intermediate products and a forward correlation with the sectors that receive its output as their intermediate products. Any leading sector must possess correlations of both types so that the whole industry can achieve strong network effects that enable all sectors to grow. Technically, backward correlation is more important. In addition, leading industries generate positive side effects. Their development triggers a series of dramatic changes in the local economic and cultural environments, with old urban centres transformed or new ones created. Led by those industries, urban infrastructure investment increases, banking and commerce sectors rapidly grow and so do construction and services.

All in all, the full play of the industry's leading role creates new technologies, materials, energy sources and industries, whereby economic activities are vitalised across a wider spectrum.

The second aspect is to incubate emerging industries with strategic importance in advance. These industries are the fruits of technological innovation and represent directions for future development. A nation's competitiveness is largely exhibited by its technologies and industries at the forefront of global competition, which are also known as strategic emerging industries. The environment in which they grow generally contains three types of demand. One is technological demand that calls for high-end science and technology, as well as unceasing innovation. Another is market demand. Their products need to be accepted in the market to realise their value. The problem is that this does not happen when they first enter the market. Moreover, they encounter resistance from existing products of the same kind. The third is financial demand. Factors like input, cost and scale affect financial and profit accounting. Problems that a new industry usually comes across in its earliest period are high costs and prices. They bring unbearable financial pressure and can crush the industry before it fully develops. Without government support, emerging strategic industries may be nipped in the bud.

Therefore, these industries need government support prior to entering the market. There are three methods: scientific planning, guided investment in incubation and post-incubation support. In addition to financial support, such as reduced taxes, other more important supportive measures include market support or consumption stimulation. In the meantime, plans must be made to avoid overlapping or scattered investments and to realise concentrated advantage. An industrial chain must be formed to link research, development, manufacturing and application so as to realise economies of scale. Evidently, incubation or support for emerging strategic industries should be incorporated in the industrial innovation initiative. After these industries grow to a certain scale, the government needs to withdraw support so that they face fair competition in the market. The government will then shift to support the next round of incubation of strategic emerging industries.

The third aspect is to introduce carefully selected advanced international industries. In an open economy, adjustment and upgrading cannot be separated from international markets. The international transfer of industries has become an important part of global capital flow. As a large manufacturing country, China has become the world's second-largest recipient of foreign direct investment. Of Fortune 500 corporations, more than 400 have invested in China. A large developing nation, China has set up clear goals for the handling of international manufacturing transfer: to build international manufacturing bases which are not just heaps of manufacturers and factories. The goal is to enhance the international competitiveness of China's manufacturing to promote domestic industrial upgrading. Important benefits and quality standards include added value proportion in exports, global proportion of high-tech and innovative products, international brand products made in China increased, enterprises with core technologies and energy consumption and environmental standards raised. These standards apply to both domestic and foreign enterprises. Hence, the introduction of advanced foreign industries is an important approach to establishing international manufacturing bases. Core technologies and enterprises equipped with high technologies are the targets. Whether that approach works on its own depends on local industrial levels. Advanced manufacturing is only attracted to the world-class industrial centres that possess high-level industries, high technological content, high opening rates and high added value.

Noticeably, developed countries tend to transfer sunset industries, not those positioned to be competitive in the future, to developing nations. This means if we rely solely on introducing foreign capital and industries, we cannot succeed in developing our own strategic industries. Hence there is another approach to building international manufacturing bases. This is independent research and development of high-tech industries or industrial upgrading based on independent intellectual properties. Our strategy to bring in foreign industries has to be based on such a way of thinking, shifting from directly introducing foreign industries to developing our own advanced international industries, especially those that are the outcome of advanced science and technologies, as well as human capital in the fields of science, technology and management.

Finally, adjusting and developing a strategy for upgrading the industrial structure needs spontaneous organisation and coordination. There are two ways to accomplish the work. One is to adopt a balanced strategy, meaning all industries develop simultaneously. The other is an unbalanced strategy, meaning developing industries non-synchronously. The latter can be a result of industrial transformation and upgrading, the rapid growth of leading industries and the emergence of strategic industries. In this case, where some sectors grow ahead of the rest, investors in the other sectors must respond actively and swiftly. It requires all investors in the industry chain to act as entrepreneurs, obtain accurate information from markets and stand up to the pressure of market competition. Otherwise, even the correct choice of leading industries cannot manufacture other essential influences to boost the development of other sectors to follow them. Enduring a long-term, unbalanced industrial structure, however, can result in the waste of resources and unsatisfied domestic demand. This is where the government should take action and spontaneously coordinate changes in the industrial structure. To coordinate these changes while continuing an unbalanced structure strategy, the government needs to tackle three issues. The first is to properly prioritise sectors for favoured development, making them the main recipients of resource allocation. The second is to enhance the radiation effects of these sectors to boost the development of others. The third is to adjust the structures of demand, as well as import and export according to the developing tendency of industrial structure so as to balance the unbalanced structure. When implementing an unbalanced development strategy, it is mainly the market mechanism that maintains the balance of the industrial structure. Therefore, the ongoing economic system needs to be reformed to vitalise businesses and to develop entrepreneurs whereby other industries can seek balanced development in a high-level industrial structure under the connective effect of leading industries.

Note

1 Hollis Chenery, *Industrialization and Growth: A Comparative Study*, trans. Wu Qi et al. (Shanghai: Joint Publishing Company, 1995), 98–9.

7 Urbanisation and agriculture modernisation

China used to be a developing nation with a dual economic structure. Sectors of modern industry with contemporary technology coexisted with traditional sectors of agriculture which relied on traditional methods. Therefore, the key issue for China's economic development is to modernise agriculture, transform our dual economy into a modern unitary economy and modernise the entire national economy. Since the reform and opening, China has promoted urbanisation and industrialisation in rural areas. As a result, the dual economic structure of China has changed significantly: the agricultural sector now accounts for only about 10% of the GDP, while the urbanisation rate has reached 58%. At this new historical turning point, China's economic development goal should serve the needs of *sannong* (i.e. agriculture/rural economy, rural residents and rural reconstruction). During this process, it is particularly important for industry and cities to back-nurture *sannong*.

7.1 The road map to changing China's dual economic structure

7.1.1 The dual structure theory

The dual structure theory was first put forward by Sir William Arthur Lewis, referring to the coexistence of the traditional and modern sectors, specifically in technology and production modes. In the dual structure economy, the agricultural sector relies on traditional technology, while the industrial sector adopts modern technology. The agriculture sector has a low level of marketisation, while the industrial sector has a higher level. The agricultural sector relies on a backward production mode, while the modern industrial sector uses an advanced production mode.

To change the dual economic structure, Lewis proposed an economic development model based on an unlimited supply of labour. According to this model, there exists an unlimited supply of labour in the traditional agricultural sector. On the one hand, labour is surplus in relation to arable land. As a result, the marginal productivity of agricultural labour is zero or negative. On the other hand, the minimum wage paid to agricultural labourers only allows them to maintain the lowest living standard. With comparatively higher labour productivity, as long as the industrial sector provides a slightly higher wage than agriculture, it can get a continuous supply of labour. As the industrial sector seeks to maximise profits and emphasises accumulation, it can expand its scope through the accumulation of profit reinvestment, thus enhancing the ability to absorb the surplus agricultural labour force. Therefore, the industrial sector can expand with the continuous supply of labour from the agricultural sector. When surplus labour enters the industrial sector, the labour productivity in the agricultural sector rises together with the salary level of farmers. When the labour force stops withdrawing from the agricultural sector, the economy comes to a "turning point" (i.e. the Lewis turning point in development economics). When the agricultural labour supply reduces to a certain level, it causes a labour shortage, leading to low agricultural output. Prices rise when agricultural products are short in supply. In addition, with the withdrawal of surplus labour, the wages of agricultural labourers may rise. It will in turn force the industrial sector to increase employees' salaries, and its accumulation ability will also reach a turning point. If the industrial sector still needs labour from the agricultural sector, it has to develop agricultural technology, improve the productivity of agricultural labour and increase the surplus of agricultural products.[1]

The Fei-Ranis model contributes to a theoretical innovation based on the Lewis model, making up for some of Lewis's fundamental defects. First, John C. H. Fei and Gustav Ranis redefined surplus labour. They put forward the concept of "recessive unemployment." It means the movement of surplus labour from the agricultural to the industrial sector includes not only zero marginal productivity but also below zero marginal productivity. In addition, the agricultural sector provides surplus labour, as well as surplus agricultural products. The transfer of the surplus labour force from agriculture to the industrial sector is impossible if there is no agricultural surplus. The agricultural surplus is of decisive significance to the expansion of the industrial sector and the flow of agricultural labour. Therefore, economic development needs balanced development of industry and agriculture. Duality is a dynamic concept. Its essential contents are technological innovation and non-agricultural capital accumulation. One of the development goals is to eliminate the surplus labour supply through the continuous relocation of the labour force. It requires investment and innovation in both the agricultural and industrial sectors to balance development until all of the recessive unemployed are driven out of the agricultural sector while marketisation is accomplished. At this point, wages will be equal to the marginal productivity of labour. This process is long and dynamic. It may last for several decades in less developed countries, along with their effort to grow in transition.[2]

7.1.2 Rural industrialisation and the transfer of agricultural surplus labour

In general, developed countries established their modern industrial sector only after their traditional agricultural sector had been transformed. However, in China's urbanisation in the 1950s, a considerable part of the industrial self-accumulation was based on agricultural income, deriving from the price scissors of the products from the industrial and agricultural sectors. Until the 1970s, a huge traditional agricultural sector with outdated technology coexisted with urban industry. In traditional agriculture, there is also the phenomenon of the infinite supply of labour revealed by Lewis. From 1952 to 1979, the labour force in China increased annually at the rate of 2%, far higher than the increase rate of available farmland. The growth of agricultural output mainly depended on the increase of the output per unit area. Nonetheless, restrained by the availability of farmland, the growth rate of agricultural production was very limited, while the marginal productivity of labour was lower than that of other low-income nations. Too much labour was crowded on small parcels planted with a single crop. It led to inefficient allocation of agricultural production factors. The unlimited supply of surplus labour was jammed into a limited amount of farmland, seriously hindering technological progress in agriculture. On the one hand, the farmland was not sufficient to accommodate the entire labour force. It reduced the marginal productivity of agricultural labourers to a state of zero or negative for a long time. On the other hand, too much labour crowded onto limited land excluded the entry of funds and technical elements, forming a low-efficiency factor substitution. In addition, to speed up the industrialisation, China actually kept implementing the policy of exploiting agriculture to provide the accumulation for industrialisation, transferring funds from agriculture to the industrial sector with the help of price scissors created by unfair exchange. Under this circumstance, a low-efficiency equilibrium structure was formed with the allocation of production factors in the agricultural sector. This was a balance between too much labour input and too little capital and technical input. To bring change to traditional agriculture, this equilibrium structure has to be broken to form a high-efficiency factor substitution. It depends on the flow of production factors in two areas. One is the flow of the surplus labour force out of the agricultural sector. The other is the flow of capital, technology and other production factors into the agricultural sector.

China has developed township enterprises in rural areas since the 1980s, initiating the transfer of agricultural surplus labour to the non-agricultural industry and the industrialisation of rural areas. Township enterprises were the non-agricultural businesses set up by farmers in rural villages and towns. It was a great invention by Chinese farmers and of profound significance in Chinese economic development.

First, township enterprises provided additional resources for China to launch a new round of industrialisation. Transferred to township enterprises for industrial production, surplus labour in agriculture actually replaced a part of the funding needed to develop non-agricultural businesses. Meanwhile, the labour force transferred from the agricultural sector with low marginal productivity to the non-agricultural sector with high marginal productivity increased the GDP. This, in fact, enhanced the self-accumulation of rural industrialisation.

Second, establishing township enterprises promoted rural industrialisation and absorbed surplus agricultural labour. It is a good way to transfer surplus labour from farming, forestry, animal husbandry and fisheries to township enterprises in rural areas. Such a practice not only reduces surplus rural labour but also increases agricultural output value.

Third, the development of township enterprises has led to structural changes in the rural industry and increased industrialisation in rural regions. For a long time,

Table 7.1 Total Output Value and Composition of Rural Society in Jiangsu Province (Unit %)

Year	Total Output Value of Rural Society	Animal Husbandry and Fishery	Industry	Construction	Transportation	Commercial Catering Industry
1978	100	57.55	33.93	3.16	1.39	3.97
1980	100	50.51	39.88	5.31	1.13	3.18
1985	100	37.20	49.70	7.83	2.51	2.76
1990	100	28.01	60.40	6.46	2.33	2.80
1995	100	15.96	72.89	4.72	2.17	4.25
2000	100	13.17	73.52	4.70	2.65	5.96
2003	100	9.34	76.09	5.03	2.59	6.96
2004	100	9.31	76.78	4.66	2.37	6.88
2005	100	8.00	77.95	4.65	2.34	7.07
2006	100	6.81	79.34	4.46	2.22	7.21
2007	100	6.17	80.50	4.15	2.03	7.16

Source: *Jiangsu Statistics Yearbook, 2008.*

the traditional structure of rural regions was based on the agricultural economy, especially on farming. The growth of rural enterprises has broken such a pattern. Township enterprises have become an important part of China's industrialisation and the main body of small and medium enterprises. In the study and plan of China's industrial structure, the rural industry has become an indispensable part that can greatly influence the development of the industrial structure in China.

Table 7.1 shows the evolution of the total output value and composition of rural society in Jiangsu province. The main driver of this evolution is the dramatic rise of township enterprises in Jiangsu.

7.2 New challenges to the transformation of dual structure

Rural industrialisation in China, characterised by the development of township enterprises, has raised the growth of industrialisation and urbanisation of rural regions. It has promoted the development of agriculture by industrialisation, improved conditions in rural regions by urbanisation and transformed villagers into town residents. The progress is remarkable. Rural residents are able to quickly move out of poverty and enter well-off society. Agricultural productivity has been increased rapidly, and living standards have improved dramatically in rural regions.

While we affirm the positive roles played by industrialisation and urbanisation in rural development, we should also understand the negative affect of absorbing agricultural factors. This is reflected in the following two phases.

The first phase was in rural industrialisation in the 1980s. China's rural industrialisation was launched in the context of national financial constraints and the low profit rate of urban industries. Such circumstances determined that the original capital accumulation or the initial capital of a large number of township enterprises must be taken from the agricultural sector. It means agriculture had to squeeze out surplus labour and funds for the development of township enterprises. These township enterprises also had a stronger and more direct capacity to absorb rural capital and resources. In other words, the capital, land and labour needed for industrialisation all came from agricultural production and farmers, who used their own and collective accumulation to provide the original accumulation for industrialisation. The land needed for the industrial development and urbanisation of small towns was acquired on site. Most capable rural residents also went to work for the township enterprises. In addition, rural residents built small towns themselves following the relative concentration of township enterprises.

The second phase was caused by the development of the open economy when China entered its overall industrialisation and urbanisation phase in the 1990s. Various development zones and industrial parks were established across the country. With the growing urbanisation of their regions, many rural residents left farmland and their hometowns for urban centres as migrant workers to find employment in factories. In fact, many urban enterprises could not operate without migrant workers. By 2011, the proportion of China's urban population grew to 52%, while the total amount of rural workers reached 253 million. Amongst them, 195 million dwelt in cities in the long term. They accounted for 23% of China's total urban population. In this process, a large amount of rural land was used for industrialisation and urbanisation. There was serious loss of agricultural land. More seriously, there was indiscriminate occupancy and use of farmland. Meanwhile, there were farmers who had lost their land without receiving full compensation. In particular, the enthusiasm for development zones and real estate investment brought a new "enclosure movement." Counties, towns and villages all sought to set up development and investment zones. A large amount of fertile land was occupied but then wasted because of the lack of investment programmes. The pollution produced by factories in the industrialised rural areas also destroyed rural ecology, resulting in water and soil pollution, causing serious damage to agricultural production, the development environment and living conditions of rural residents.

The aforementioned situation shows that the urban-rural dual structure in China today was not only a result of the difference in the technical level between the two areas but also the increasingly widening gap in the quality of development, development level and income level as both underwent rapid growth at the same time.

The widening gap between urban and rural areas in the process of industrialisation and urbanisation can be explained by the cumulative causation theory of development economics. With the inequality between regions

> influenced by economic and social forces, the accumulation and expansion of the favorable areas are made at the expense of other areas, resulting in the relative deterioration of the status of the latter and postponing their further development. This will lead to the further increase of inequality.[3]

This cumulative causation consists of two concepts: the expansion effect and the reflux effect. The expansion effect of industrial and urban areas has a favourable impact on the economic growth of agriculture and rural areas, spreading advanced production factors such as marketing, technology and information. On the contrary, the reflux effect of industrial and urban areas has a negative impact on the economic growth of agriculture, making factors such as labour and capital – especially human capital – flow from agriculture and rural areas to urban industry and cities. Therefore, the fundamental reason for the imbalance between urban and rural development is that the reflux effect is stronger than the expansion effect. It is evident that these factors are the main contribution from agriculture and rural areas to urban industry and cities, while income is the main means of back-feeding industry and cities to agriculture and rural areas.

By the end of 2017, there was a population of 813.47 million urban residents in China, accounting for 58.52% of the total population. New challenges emerge when the urbanisation rate reaches this level. First, the gap between urban and rural areas has not been narrowed but expanded. Second, the supply of urbanised labour is no longer as great as it used to be. Third, urban centres, especially large cities, have typically suffered "modern diseases," such as overcrowding, traffic congestion, environmental pollution and high housing costs. It puts severe pressure on the progress of urbanisation, making it less likely that conditions will improve. Fourth, in the agricultural sector, there is still a low-efficiency structure with too much labour and too little investment and technology. Therefore, to change the dual structure in China, in addition to moving surplus agricultural labour to non-agricultural industry, effective measures are needed to promote the flow of modern production methods to agriculture and rural areas so as to reform traditional agriculture and promote the development of the new socialist rural life. President Xi Jinping pointed out in a recent speech that even if the rate of urbanisation in China reaches more than 70% in the future, there will still be 400 or 500 million people living in rural regions. We should never let rural areas become wasted land, villages left behind and hometowns forgotten. Instead, we must promote urbanisation alongside agricultural modernisation and rural reconstruction.

In this context, changing the urban-rural duality has a new implication. We should treat *sannong* as our goal of modernisation, promote the integration of urban and rural development and establish a new relationship between industry and agriculture, as well as urban and rural areas. Industry should feed agriculture; cities should support rural areas. Workers and farmers benefit from each other and promote urban-rural integration.

7.3 The modernisation of agriculture

In the beginning stage of their economic growth, many developing nations generally pursued one-sided industrial growth, ignoring agricultural development. In their later development practice, however, these nations gradually found that favouring industrialisation would not help promote development. Moreover, it could not solve the problem of the food supply. Therefore, transforming traditional agriculture and promoting its modernisation become a major goal of development.

7.3.1 Reforming traditional agriculture

In development economics, apart from Lewis's theory of transferring surplus labour from the agricultural sector to deal with the dual structure, Theodore W. Schultz has made a different argument on how to reform traditional agriculture. The two economists with opposing views were both awarded the Nobel Prize in economics in 1979. Having transferred agricultural surplus labour to industry for many years, it is time for us to change our strategy for reforming traditional agriculture and promoting its modernisation.

In his book *Transforming Traditional Agriculture* published in 1964, Schultz argued that traditional agriculture did not contribute to economic growth, while modern agriculture could make a significant contribution to it. The key to changing the status of the dual structure is to transform traditional agriculture into a modern agriculture with high productivity.[4] The fundamental way to reform traditional agriculture is to introduce new production elements into the sector.

The problem for traditional agriculture is that it cannot bring in any new production factors nor create such a demand. The crux of the problem is not a lack of efficiency in the configuration of the factors nor the labour surplus in agriculture but barriers to the introduction of new production factors. According to Schultz's 1987 study, the transformation of traditional agriculture into modern agriculture needs investment in three areas: (1) material capital, (2) human capital and (3) high-yielding crops. The key issue here is to establish a system which can ensure adequate investment. To introduce new factors of production to agriculture, we have to do three things: (1) establish a system suitable to the reform of traditional agriculture, (2) create both supply and demand conditions for introducing modern production factors and (3) provide farmers with the necessary human resources.

There are two ways to reform traditional agriculture systematically. One is to rely on executive orders, while the other is to adopt a market approach based on economic stimulus. Schultz advocated the market approach (i.e. stimulating farmers with changes in prices of agricultural products and production factors, not executive orders). He believed – in both public and private ownership systems – that it was necessary to correctly handle relations between owners, economic data for making production decisions and the economic environment for making effective decisions.

In regard to input, the key to the transformation is to introduce new production factors through investment, including promoting and researching new agricultural technology and new crops. According to Schultz, there are two particularly important issues for introducing new production factors in agriculture. First, whether the new factors will succeed depends on how much risk and uncertainty will be involved. "How fast farmers can accept a new production factor depends on the profits they will make after a proper deduction of the risk and uncertainty."[5]

This is why in reality it is necessary to introduce and promote new technology and new crops before applying them to agricultural production. Second, we ought to invest in human capital for farmers, providing them with information and training about new production factors. The most important thing in agricultural modernisation is to increase farmers' knowledge and skills. The economic basis of rapid growth is not to promote farmers' diligence and frugality but help them obtain and effectively use some of the modern production factors. Therefore, Schultz's central argument is "treating human capital as the main source of the agricultural economic growth."[6]

The agricultural sector is the most unstable economic sector because it is heavily affected by unpredictable natural conditions. Based on this fact, Kuznets makes it clear that it is characteristic to see a decrease in the agricultural share in modern economic growth. In his empirical study, he finds that the regular decrease of agriculture in the total output value depends on two conditions. First, the productivity of agriculture increases, and the agricultural sector provides more surplus products. Second, when a nation enters its industrialisation stage, the demand for agricultural products decreases on the premise that the income elasticity of the demand for agricultural products is less than that in the past.[7] However, industrialisation in China was launched before the fundamental transformation of the traditional agricultural sector. At present, these two conditions for the decrease of the agricultural share have not yet been reached.

First, we have not yet entered the stage of an apparent decrease in the demand for agricultural products. China is a large country with more than one-fifth of the world's population but only 7% of the world's arable land. The pressure on China's agriculture is heavier than that of any other country. Meanwhile, the demand of industrial sectors for agricultural products has not decreased because they need agricultural products as raw materials to maintain rapid growth.

Second, the increase in agricultural labour productivity at present is mainly due to the effect of the transfer of surplus labour; the technical basis of agriculture has not changed. Moreover, in the process of promoting rural industrialisation, a structure of comparative advantages which is generated by the price scissors becomes explicit. It was hidden and irresistible to some extent in the past when the industrial and agricultural sectors were separated from each other. To deal with this structure, the direct countermeasure taken by farmers was to invest in township enterprises instead of agriculture, leading to a further weakening of the development of agricultural technology. It made it difficult for the agricultural sector to provide more surplus products, which would inevitably hinder rural industrialisation.

Rural reforms in China, especially the introduction of the household contract responsibility system, has essentially solved the problem of food and clothing supply. The transfer of surplus agricultural labour has raised the marginal productivity of agriculture. The challenges to agricultural development at present can be summarised in the following three areas:

- One is the low productivity of agricultural labour. According to the data issued by the *China Statistical Yearbook* in 2013, until 2012, agricultural added value, produced by 33.6% of the labour force, accounted for only 10.1% of the total GDP. The other 89.9% of the GDP was produced by

66.4% of the labour force. It means that the labour productivity ratio of the non-agricultural sector to the agricultural sector was roughly 4.5:1.

- The second is the low income of farmers. According to the data published by the National Bureau of Statistics, the per capita disposable income of urban households in 2012 was RMB24,564 (about US$3,830), but the per capita net income of rural households was only RMB7,917 (about US$1,234). The urban/rural ratio was about 3:1. Farmers' consumption capacity was also too low. By 2012, urban households made up 52.57% of the population and rural households 47.43%, a ratio of nearly 1:1. However, the average annual cash expenditure of urban residents was RMB16,674 (about US$2,600) as compared to only RMB3,742 (about US$583) for rural residents. The purchasing power ratio of urban to rural residents was about 4.5:1, a dramatic illustration that the backwardness of agricultural production and the low income of farmers are outstanding problems in China. Analysing the income structure of farmers in China in 2012 (Table 7.2), we find that the most serious problem is that the income from farming, the main source of farmers' income, is too low, although growth in non-agricultural income has increased it to some extent.

- Third, after entering the new era, agricultural products cannot meet the upgraded needs of the people for a better life. China is a large country with more than 21% of the world's population and only 7% of the world's arable land. Agriculture in China is under much heavier pressure than in any other country in the world. The Chinese have a growing desire for a better life, not only in quantity but also in quality of agricultural products. If the industrial sectors, which use agricultural products as raw materials, need to maintain a relatively rapid growth, then their demand for agricultural products will not soon decrease. All this indicates that the supply will remain insufficient compared to the demand. It is also impossible for China to rely on imports to satisfy the upgraded dietary needs of nearly 1.4 billion people. It is obvious that agricultural development has a direct effect on the modernisation process of China as a whole.

Table 7.2 Per Capita Net Income of Farmers in China, 2012

Source of Income	Amount (RMB)	Percentage (%)
Income of agricultural production and management	3,533	44.6
Net income of agriculture	2,107	
Wage income	3,448	43.6
Income from outside employment	2,290	
Transferred income	687	8.7
Property income	249	3.1
Total (excluding taxes)	7,917	100

Source: National Bureau of Statistics report on the sampling survey of 74,000 farmers in 31 provinces/autonomous cities.

7.3.2 Introducing new production factors to develop modern agriculture

China is a large country with a population of nearly 1.4 billion. If China is to grow strong, it must have advanced agriculture. Developing science and technology is the essential way to strengthen agriculture. Our food supply must be firmly held in our own hands – food primarily produced in China.

Agriculture serves as the basis for the development of other sectors of the national economy. As Marx said, "Labour productivity beyond the individual need is the foundation of all societies."[8] Agriculture plays a fundamental role in the economy because surplus labour from agriculture provides the foundation for the development of other industries.

Traditional agricultural development can be summarised with the "agricultural surplus" paradigm. Agricultural technological advancement and institutional adjustment are both aimed at increasing the agricultural surplus (surplus products and labour). The development of non-agricultural sectors is also supported by the agricultural surplus. Today, with the progress of society and culture, the paradigm of agricultural development has changed from "quantity" to "quality." This change is necessary because we now need to not only increase the agriculture surplus but also improve the current weak status of agriculture. The key to the development of agriculture is adopting modern science and technology, giving agricultural products higher added value. In terms of the demand for agricultural products, people used to consume only rice and wheat to satisfy their basic needs. Today, they need milk and safe and nutritious green produce. After people's living standard reaches a well-off level, they are more concerned about a healthy diet, food safety and hygiene. The aforementioned analysis of supply and demand shows that agricultural modernisation means agricultural development must embrace high quality, high efficiency and high added value. It involves optimising the variety of agricultural products, the improvement of quality and the extension of agricultural products from primary products to final products. The progress in these areas can be summarised as the quality paradigm of agricultural production. Accordingly, we need to build a modern agricultural industrial system, as well as a production and operation system. It is required to optimise and adjust the variety, factor input and industrial network and integration structures to promote the added value of agricultural products in the entire industrial chain. A high-quality and high-efficiency modern agricultural industry system needs to be put in place in which the variety and quality of agricultural products are compatible with the rapid upgrading of people's consumption.

In accordance with the paradigm shift to "the quality of agricultural products," innovation is essential to develop modern agriculture. In general, there are two aspects of scientific and technological innovation. One is biological innovation, which cultivates excellent varieties, improves the quality and increases the added value of agricultural products. The other is mechanisation, which increases agricultural surplus and saves labour. In a large country with a massive agricultural population like China, the application of mechanisation frees more labour to move out of farming. China has a strong capacity for agricultural mechanisation, but the pressure of employment makes it difficult to use machines to replace labour in farming. However, biological innovation is more important. It can improve the variety, quality and added value of agricultural products and is directly related to the sustainable development of the environment, representing the future direction of agricultural modernisation. Compared with mechanisation, however, China's biological innovation capability is seriously insufficient. For this reason, biotechnology has increasingly become the focus of agricultural innovation. It provides new technologies to cultivate superior varieties, improve the quality and increase the added value of agricultural products, promoting progress in all the aforementioned areas. It also provides green technology, which benefits sustainable development.

Investment in agricultural science and technology should include investment in research, development and the popularisation and application of agricultural science and technology. According to the "agricultural product quality" paradigm of modern agriculture, the technological factors that farmers need are fine varieties, advanced pesticides and fertilisers, modern agricultural machinery and improved planting and cultivation techniques. Therefore, it is important for the government to make this investment. The investment in science and technology, or its main part, should not be directly given to farmers. Instead, it should go to universities and research institutions to help them develop agricultural technology and innovation. This is the foundation for agricultural technology advancement.

Given its long and seasonal production cycle and vulnerability to natural conditions, it is risky to adopt new technology in agriculture. Farmers, as people who do business with small capital, tend to avoid technical risks. Therefore, there should be a process of promotion and demonstration of the new technology. The cost should not be borne by farmers. The government should subsidise farmers for adopting new technology, ensuring that they get a low price or even a free supply of technology and education. Meanwhile, we should encourage agricultural technology personnel to promote new technology and varieties in rural areas to help farmers solve technical problems.

7.3.3 Who should work on Farmland?

Agricultural problems are generally associated with low labour productivity. In China, however, our analysis should be based on specific conditions. Given that a large portion of the surplus labour force is flowing out of agriculture, the elderly and women make up a large percentage of the remaining labour force. Nonetheless, output has not declined, and agricultural added value has increased at an annual rate of about 5%. This shows that productivity measured by agricultural output is not low. Measured by income, however, the labour productivity is not high. This is probably consistent with the low human capital stock in agriculture. Therefore, to improve agricultural labour productivity, it is important to increase the income of farmers. The key premise of increasing farmers' income is to increase the stock of human capital in agriculture.

Modern farmers are the key to modern agricultural development. This raises the question of introducing the issue of human capital in agriculture. Non-agricultural sectors in China at present have a significantly positive effect on the increase of the agricultural surplus. But this also means agricultural human capital has moved to other sectors. The labour force left behind in rural areas is one with low human capital, consisting mainly of women, the elderly and the poorly educated.

The human capital requirement of the labour force is relevant to the level of agricultural development. When traditional technology was used in agriculture, the outflow of human capital did not affect the output, although it did, of course, affect income. In contrast, if we develop modern agriculture and promote technology, the knowledge and technical expertise of the labour force left behind in rural areas will not be good enough. Without adequate investment in human capital, it is impossible to modernise agricultural technology. Modern agriculture needs "the improvement of human capital presented in the form of educated and innovative farmers, qualified scientists and technicians, and visionary public administrators and entrepreneurs."[9]

It is generally believed that introducing the human capital factor in agriculture means investing in farmers by improving their educational levels. This is definitely correct. However, in the context of the labour mobility, since workers in agriculture are mainly composed of women, the elderly and the lower educated, it is far from sufficient to only invest in agriculture and raise the level of education for farmers who remain in agriculture. Development of modern agriculture needs a high-quality labour force with high human capital. It is necessary to bring in such a labour force from outside of rural areas. Therefore, the investment in agricultural human capital should focus on encouraging the labour force that has flowed out of agriculture to urban centres and non-agricultural sectors to return to agriculture. It is also important to encourage innovative and entrepreneurial talents, including college students, to enter the agricultural sector, thus forming a human capital structure aligned with modern agricultural technology.

It is investment that drives the input of modern factors in agriculture. An increase in the yield of agricultural input is the key to encourage the investment of modern production. For example, to invest in human capital in rural areas, we must first ensure equal income. If labourers cannot get equal income in rural areas and the comparative income of agriculture is too low, it is impossible to keep human capital in rural areas.

7.3.4 The innovation of the agricultural system

Analysis of the dual structure using development economics focusses not only on techniques but also on the system itself. Fei and Ranis pointed out that improvement of agricultural labour productivity depends not only on the acquisition of modern fertilisers and intellectual property but also on the market participation of the economic subjects and the commercialisation of the labour force and land assets. This is mainly because "the traditional agricultural population is scattered in space and far away from urban centers. They are neglected by forces of modernization."[10] They believed that in traditional agriculture, labour production and family life are combined in the form of the family farm system. Currency is rarely the medium of exchange, calculating scale or the standard of value. Money becomes important only when it is used as the total payment for the inflow or outflow of agricultural families and production sectors. The most significant change that modern input factors can introduce to increase agricultural productivity is an incentive effect. It is caused by greater market participation and farmers' greater engagement in trade. Market participation enables farmers to benefit from the input of modern factors through trade and incentive consumer goods, such as textiles.

Fei and Ranis analysed the relationship amongst commodities, finance and labour – the three markets related to the transfer of agricultural surplus labour. In the commodity market, by trading, owners of surplus agricultural products can obtain parts of industrial products or cash income. With the development and expansion of the financial market, the income would take the form of bank deposits, stocks and bonds. The financial market must provide the owners of all kinds of agricultural surpluses with acceptable financial assets that can convert their rural savings into productive industrial investment. Obviously, the two markets have to operate effectively to become an interconnected entity. The interdepartmental labour market enables farmers of low marginal productivity to be reallocated to the industrial sector with high marginal productivity. As for the farmers' participation in market activities, we can see that the reallocation of the labour force begins through the interdepartmental labour market and that farmers start to participate in the commodity and financial markets. Market forces determine the payments received by the agricultural labour force, and land is paid for according to its market value. The land, which is regarded as farmers' property, now enters the transaction as a commercial asset (i.e. being used for mortgages). In this situation, the competitive and commercialised principles of income distribution have also emerged.[11]

To raise farmers' income, government policy should be giving more, taking less and loosening controls, such as abolishing the agricultural tax and reducing farmers' financial burdens. This is only one aspect of increasing farmers' income. It is more important to promote systemic innovation in agriculture, revitalising the system and ensuring that farmers gain profits from it. The following are analyses of the marketisation of the agricultural system and the corresponding innovations based on the reality in China.

The first innovation is to rethink the land system and the scale at which land is managed. China began rural reform in 1978, implementing the household contract responsibility system. It was a significant reform which fully mobilised farmers' enthusiasm for land management. But more needs to be done.

First, it is necessary to establish a land management circulation system based on the separation of ownership and contractual and management rights of rural land. Under the premise of adhering to the collective ownership of land, the existing reform has been the creation of household contract responsibility management, which has fully mobilised farmers' enthusiasm for management and labour. However, further promotion of agricultural modernisation will inevitably conflict with farmers' small-scale operations of family-managed land. Marx once pointed out that small land ownership based on small production was only a necessary transitional stage for the development of agriculture itself. Its drawbacks include the fact that "the means of production are dispersed indefinitely, and producers themselves are separated indefinitely. There is a huge waste of manpower. Deterioration of production conditions and increasing cost of means of production are inevitable outcomes for small land ownership."[12] In terms of its relationship with modernisation, "small-scale land ownership by its nature excludes the development of social labor productivity, social forms of labor, social accumulation of capital, large-scale animal husbandry and the progressive application of science."[13] Although rural land in China belongs to the collectives, it is managed and contracted by families. The problem of ownership of small plots of land mentioned by Marx also appears in China today. Therefore, to promote agricultural modernisation, we must promote the large-scale management of land. Otherwise, the mechanisation of agriculture, the optimisation of agricultural structure and the large-scale application of modern science in agriculture are just empty talk. In practice, China has created the "separation of three rights," respectively, in land ownership, contractual and management rights. Allowing the transfer of land management rights to the dominant producers by market-oriented means, such as circulation and transfer of management rights, would represent an important step toward modernisation. This kind of institutional arrangement guarantees the leading position of the rural households in the new agricultural management system, provides protection for farmers' rights and expands their property income. Because farmers' assets are mainly in land, albeit land that they only have the right to use, and house property, this would require that the flow, transfer and expropriation of land and house property be fully compensated. Farmers obtain capital returns through trade and investment in land and attract modern factors of production to agriculture by conditionally making use of commercial assets.

Second, farmers' income from their assets should be guaranteed. Farmers' assets consist mainly of their right to use land and house property. Land needs investment, and farmers should benefit from it. It is necessary to attach great importance to land capital. Marx called the capital invested in land "land capital" and considered it a part of fixed capital. This means there are issues of loss and compensation, as well as that of income flowing from land capital. The income from land capital is "the interest paid for the capital invested in the land. For the investment, the land, as a tool of production, can be improved."[14] Land investment will be stimulated if those who invest in it can get a profit. To encourage land investment, we should set up a system stipulating that those who invest obtain the profit. Moreover, it is important to deal with the issue of extending the land lease period.

Only in circulation can land produce benefits. This requires full compensation for the flow, transfer and expropriation of land assets and house property. To this end, we need to promote the reform of the land system so that farmers can use commercialised land assets to draw modern production factors to agriculture. We should allow the transfer and the inheritance of the land usufruct according to law and allow farmers to use it in the form of subcontracting, leasing, sharing, etc. By circulating, the land will be concentrated in the hands of those who specialise in large-scale farming and gradually form the large family farms recommended by Schultz. These family farms would be guaranteed by the property right system and can adapt to market changes. They will help restructure traditional agriculture. Meanwhile, the rental, purchase and sale of land, buying shares and mortgaging of the usufruct can also promote the transfer of agricultural surplus labour and develop the process of urbanisation at the institutional level.

The second issue is the construction of the agricultural products market. In a market economy, an important way to increase agricultural yields is to ensure the market profit of agriculture so as to improve the farmers' ability to acquire modern factors. This involves the following two aspects:

- First, after withdrawing agricultural products from the planned market channel, we have yet to establish a sound agricultural product market to replace it. The result has been that farmers cannot find a market after they abandon planned acquisition and face great difficulty selling grain and cotton. Meanwhile, business sectors and individual vendors in the grain market have taken the opportunity to buy at a lower price. Consequently, although the market price of grain has risen considerably, farmers have not benefitted. Farming revenues cannot be further increased by raising the price of agricultural products. Instead, we need to reform the circulation system, establish and improve the market of the agricultural products, give full play to the effectiveness of the price reform and leave more profits to farmers. In particular, we should speed up construction of the wholesale agricultural market in order to improve the market network and resolve the difficulties in selling agricultural products. In view of the instability of agricultural production and the resulting price fluctuations, a large-scale wholesale market can be conditionally developed into a futures market to stabilise the supply and demand of agricultural products, prevent drastic fluctuations, avoid price risk and protect farmers.
- Next, we should speed up the establishment of competitive enterprises for the purchase and sale of agricultural products. A discussion of farmers' participation does not mean that every farmer should enter the market; rather, it means establishing a relationship between farmers and the market through marketing organisations. In the past, market management organisations were mainly small traders. This was suitable for the old dual-track system in which only a small number of agricultural products outside the contract would enter the market. Today, because all agricultural products have entered the market, the small trader system is inadequate. There must be large and competitive agricultural enterprises. In general, this kind of marketing organisation should have the following characteristics: (1) it must be a joint-stock cooperative enterprise with farmers as stockholders, and (2) it must be trans-regional, networked and open. If this kind of company becomes the main management body of the agricultural market, the comparative advantage of farmers will be increased in the process of improving the circulation of agricultural products.

Finally, it is important to promote the innovation of agricultural organisations. One reason for the comparatively low income of farmers is the lack of organisation in production and operation. Explaining this from the perspective of the negotiation theory, farmers' bargaining ability is weak because their production and operation are scattered, and they lack organisation. Improving the organisation of farmers can be achieved in the following three ways:

- First, we need to expand the division of rural labour to take advantage of specialised and market-based management. Agricultural income today is low mainly because agricultural products enter the market as primary products with low added value and low status. Apparently, only when the agricultural industry organisation moves its products from the primary to the intermediate, and even the final, level can we really increase agricultural income. It brings forward the requirement of agricultural industrialisation. Farmers can earn more only when they provide the market with processed agricultural products because these products have added value through processing. The social labour division also requires separating the pre-production, producing and post-production services from agriculture. These services should be undertaken by independent competitive business entities, establishing a new service industry for agriculture.

- Second, we need to promote the industrialisation of agricultural production. After industrialisation, the main changes in agriculture will be "the improvement of technology and education level, the development of commercialization, specialization and capitalization, as well as the increase of production efficiency, the expansion of agricultural scale and the decrease of farmers' numbers."[15] In view of the present situation in China, the industrialisation of agriculture involves technological transformation and market-oriented reform. By transforming technology, farmers will gradually alter traditional farming and change their working place from fields to factories. The basic characteristics of market-oriented agriculture are specialisation and professionalisation. Different regions should arrange their own agricultural production according to the requirements of the market and adjust their structure according to that market orientation.

- Third, we need to establish a new type of agricultural management body. Concentration and large-scale management of land involve cooperative operation. The cooperative economy is established on the basis of implementation of the contractual responsibility system because co-production actually involves the adjustment of property rights. With the means of production operated by farmers, there are both public (mainly collectively owned land) and private sectors. At the same time, there emerges an economic consortium. Farmers jointly invest and allocate their efforts according to the approved proportion of investment and labour.

After the transfer of land management rights and the concentration of land, a new type of business entity, such as family farms, also emerges. In addition, there are two other types of agricultural organisations. One is the various intermediary organisations that provide information, capital, processing, technology, sales and other services, especially to agricultural product sales organisations. Only if the selling organisations (cooperatives) in which farmers participate are in charge of selling products is it possible to ensure that farmers gain their desired benefits. The other aspect is to comply with the industrialisation of agriculture and establish a vertical and integrated organisation. The basic mode is a combination of companies and farmers. That is to say, relying on an agricultural basis, product processing enterprises or specialised wholesale markets play the leading part. Farmers can operate the production, processing, marketing, storage and transportation as a whole. To bring the modern enterprise system into rural areas, it is an important step to establish an agricultural-industrial-commercial complex. It will also become an important economic organisation in reforming traditional agriculture in the vast rural areas of China.

7.4 Integration of urban and rural areas and urbanisation

Traditional urbanisation is the resettlement and migration of villagers to urban areas, but villagers in China have created their own models of urbanisation. China's urbanisation rate reached 51.27% in 2011 and 57.35% in 2016. This means China has entered a new era and completed the initial urbanisation stage. Urbanisation in China in this phase has new meaning and goals. Because of the central position of towns in China's vast rural areas, they bear the responsibility of rural revitalisation and are centres of agricultural and rural modernisation. Therefore, urbanisation now needs to strengthen the functions of towns, such as industrial development, public services, employment absorption and population agglomeration. In this way, towns will be able to attract surrounding farmers, enabling them to enjoy the rights of urban residents and modernise farmers' lives. Agglomerating development elements in cities and towns can promote the modernisation of surrounding rural areas. If towns carry out the construction of infrastructure according to the requirements of modern cities, they will be able to push the modernisation of rural areas forward. To produce this kind of development capacity, towns need support from urban centres. It is necessary to "transform" the momentum of urban development into rural areas, effectively address rural underdevelopment and realise the integration of urban and rural growth. The 19th CPC National Congress established the plan to set up and improve the system, as well as the mechanism and policy governing urban-rural integration and development. It includes the establishment of a new type of relationship between workers and farmers, urban and rural areas. It includes agriculture promoted through industry, rural areas developed with the support of urban centres, workers and farmers benefitting each other and the integration of urban and rural areas.

7.4.1 Urban centres' feedback to rural areas

In general, it is agriculture and rural areas that have nurtured industrialisation and urbanisation in developing nations. As for China, there are two aspects of urbanisation: the transfer of population (i.e. farmers becoming urban residents) and regional urbanisation. Farmland has been transformed into urban land. Both aspects reflect rural support for urbanisation. When industrialisation and urbanisation have reached a certain level, industries and cities should provide feedback to agriculture and rural areas.

Industrialisation and urbanisation in China have already achieved comparatively high levels. It is time to demand overall industrial and urban feedback to
agriculture and rural areas. The feedback should concentrate on diffusing urban
development factors to rural areas and integrating urban development with that
of rural areas. There are two main characteristics:

- First, the content of the feedback should be factors instead of income. Introducing the factors of production – especially the advanced factors – is fundamental to changing the backwardness of agriculture and rural areas. To
  back-nurture agriculture and rural areas, it is necessary to form endogenous
  mechanisms or "hematopoiesis," which enables traditional agriculture to
  reform itself from within. The crux of poverty in rural areas lies in the lack of
  talented people. Income levels in rural areas are too low, which in turn leads
  to a lack of talented people, for they may move to cities, creating a vicious
  cycle of continuous rural poverty. The key to breaking the cycle is to establish the feedback mechanism of human capital, forming a continuous attraction to talented people. If high-quality human capital can flow to rural areas
  and agriculture, it can reform traditional agriculture and develop the rural
  economy. This brings forward the issue of the goal of feedback. Whether it
  is financial support or income distribution of rural economic organisations,
  it should serve the goal of expanding the number of middle-income rural
  residents. The rewards for human capital need to be increased at a number
  of levels to improve the incentive mechanism for the main thrust of rural
  construction.
- Second, the back-nurtured area has expanded from villages locally to that
  of entire regions. According to the practice of the Yangtze River Delta, the
  urban feedback to agriculture and rural areas has been greatly enhanced,
  entering the stage of overall feedback. The urbanisation that is being promoted now not only refers to the urbanisation of rural residents but also that
  of rural areas. Relocating the urban manufacturing industry to and establishing industrial zones in rural areas will turn rural areas into urban centres.
  At the same time, the expansion of cities will achieve the same result. This
  means small towns in rural areas can get the benefit of urban factors from
  nearby cities.

Integrating urban and rural development will transfer the factors that promote
urban development to rural areas and fundamentally change rural backwardness.
In the past, urbanisation has meant the migration of farmers to cities. However,
the integration of urban and rural development requires the outflow of urban
development factors and lifestyle to rural areas.

Modernisation of the relationship between urban and rural areas is embodied in
the integration of urban and rural development. While achieving integration with
development at the same level, the characteristics of both cities and rural areas
should be maintained. Such integration is not to weaken cities but to improve
rural areas, fusing the rural and urban economy, society, culture and many other
aspects. In fact, to integrate urban and rural areas is to narrow the gap between the

two. The gap is also that of economic and social development, which is reflected in such areas as the income gap, the gap in living conditions and the different economic systems of urban and rural areas. All these gaps should be narrowed in the long run. However, we can only deal with the solvable problems at different development stages. At the present stage, it is necessary to determine the necessary sequence to solve the problems. We should make a scientific decision on which should be given priority, narrowing the income gap or improving the living conditions of rural areas.

The income gap between urban and rural areas has to be narrowed. In reality, however, even if we take a series of measures to support agriculture, it is still hard to stop the further widening of the income gap. Urbanisation and industrialisation are unfolding quickly in China, but it remains difficult to enhance agricultural growth, which makes it very difficult to increase farming incomes. But the gap can be narrowed with real effort. Eliminating this gap and giving priority to the equalisation of living conditions for urban and rural residents can create the basic conditions for improving rural development, eventually reducing and overcoming the urban-rural income gap.

Studies of population flows show that when urbanisation reaches a certain level, migration is not only a result of seeking employment but also an attempt to improve living standards. Many qualified labourers have moved out of rural areas with their families. One reason is that they look for higher salaries. Another important factor is that they are pushed out by impoverished living standards in their villages. There are many serious problems in rural areas: poor road conditions, drinking water shortages, lack of cultural resources, severe pollution, insufficient social security services, problematic medical coverage and lack of schools. Obviously, the gap between urban and rural living conditions in China pushes rural residents to cities and directly impedes the flow of urban factors back to rural areas. If we can focus on improving rural living standards, we will make great progress in narrowing the gap between urban and rural areas. As long as we can equalise urban and rural living standards, villages and rural towns will not only retain rural human capital but also attract urban residents. The migration of urban residents to rural areas can develop new projects with their human capital and provide support for rural reconstruction.

To improve rural living conditions, we should reconstruct villages, building infrastructure and public facilities. Specifically, we should develop centralised supplies of water, power and gas in rural areas and provide them with transportation, telecommunications, TV and internet services. We should also establish schools and hospitals in rural areas.

Promoting rural modernisation should also take into account the scope and scale of the economy. In some pilot areas, there have emerged certain trends: the concentration of rural enterprises into industrial parks and population into small towns, the emergence of service industries in rural urban centres and large grain producers on farmland. This shows that the urbanisation of towns and villages is an effective way of integrating urban and rural areas.

Rural towns serve as connection zones between villages and cities. We must attach great importance to functioning such "connection zones" in the integration of urban and rural areas. In the past, the development of rural towns was to provide places for the resettlement of agricultural labour. Today, promoting the integration of urban and rural areas means turning towns into bases for rural modernisation. There is a vast amount of land in rural areas. Only by developing towns can we use it as a base for promoting rural industries and growing the surrounding villages, bringing prosperity and development to the vast rural regions. This is an important feature of the China path to rural modernisation. We can increase and spread the influence of urban centres in rural areas through towns. The basic measure is to promote the centralisation of towns to reach the scale economy. In addition, we need to establish facilities and services in rural areas based on city standards. If towns have the same function of cities, we can enhance rural modernisation in that region. In this sense, the urbanisation of towns is an important part of rural modernisation.

It is impossible to merge all the villages into towns in the vast rural landscape. However, if the villages are too small and scattered, it will be too costly to provide public facilities and goods for rural modernisation. It will also be difficult to achieve scale economy. The only feasible way is to centralise the villages. The advantages of such centralisation are that space in rural villages can be allocated more rationally so that more land will be available for construction and that centralisation promotes the creation of new communities, turning them into new towns. According to the experience of the southern Jiangsu region, the success of the process depends essentially on two factors. The first is that farmers can benefit from such concentration so that they voluntarily take part in the process. The second is to combine centralisation with improved rural living conditions. It is important to guide the centralisation of the construction and supply of infrastructure and public facilities based on scientific planning. In this way, the concentration of villages will not increase the burden of farmers. On the contrary, it can provide compensation for the relocation cost of the farmers. Consequently, farmers are likely to welcome the concentration of their villages. Further, they can be "urbanised" locally and enjoy city life after they resettle in the centralised villages.

The aforementioned integration of urban and rural development shows that currently, the focus of China's development has shifted from urban centres to rural areas, thus introducing urbanisation to villages. However, the urbanisation of rural areas also reveals the development level of cities. The higher a city's modernisation level, the stronger its capacity to reinvigorate rural towns will become.

7.4.2 The urbanisation of farmers

In contrast to urbanisation in the 1980s, which featured the construction of towns by farmers and their resettlement, urbanisation in China today should meet the following three conditions. It should attract industries and residents from large- and medium-sized cities to towns to promote urban modernisation. It should also attract residents of villages in surrounding areas to move to towns and thus enjoy the benefits of urbanisation. It should focus on the factors of development to promote agricultural modernisation in nearby areas.

Urbanisation in the 1980s was initiated by farmers. It was decentralised and failed to achieve the scale economy, leading to low-level duplication of construction and investment. Urbanisation today needs to be planned by the government. It should be conducted in a centralised way and planned in advance. In addition to basic urban functions, we need to pay special attention to the layout of towns and emphasise the requirements of centralising, accumulating and sustaining development.

The essential role of urbanisation is to transform farmers into urban residents. To some extent, urbanisation in China thus far has meant the migration of rural residents to cities. However, the problem is that those who stay on in rural areas have been marginalised, just like those villages located outside cities. Although it has been made clear that the first step is to transform those villagers who have migrated to cities into urban residents, this is far from sufficient. In a country with such a large rural population as China, it is impossible for cities at present to accommodate so many rural migrants. It is anticipated that the urbanisation rate in China in 2020 will exceed 60%. It means that from now on, an annual average of eight million rural residents will be urbanised. It is hard to imagine that so many villagers will resettle in cities. Therefore, the practical way to solve the problem is to ensure that villagers become urban residents without migration to cities. It means villagers can enjoy the same privileges as urban residents. Urban and rural residents should have the same equal political, economic and social status and live a similar lifestyle with equal access to the same public services.

The main barrier for villagers to become urban residents is the dual urban-rural system. In comparison to cities, the rural market economy is underdeveloped, with a large proportion remaining in a natural and semi-natural state. Markets of all kinds are heavily centralised in urban centres but not in rural areas. Farmers cannot enter the market of production factors on an equal basis with urban residents. The long-standing urban-rural household registration system divides people into urban and rural residents with separate residential status. Rural residents are thus made to appear conspicuously inferior to city dwellers. Therefore, a fundamental way to eliminate the urban-rural gap is to promote the economic integration of urban and rural areas and remove the dual system.

The first step is to raise the market economy of rural areas to that of urban centres. We need to expand the labour division in the rural economy to free rural society from the influence of the natural economy and its remnants so that rural areas can catch up with cities as soon as possible. In addition, we should break up the urban-rural division to balance the factors distributed to urban and rural areas. It is impossible to change the fact that the markets of production factors are concentrated in cities. Therefore, to establish an integrated factor market, we must create an environment in which all kinds of market entities, including rural markets, have equal access to the production factor market. We should also eliminate all institutional and policy barriers that block the free flow of factors between urban and rural areas and guarantee equal pay, land prices and market prices for products in cities and rural regions.

Second is to abolish the dual urban-rural household registration system so that urban and rural residents can move and settle freely without residential restrictions.

Farmers can live in cities, while urban residents can live in rural areas based on their own choices. Meanwhile, we should eliminate the discriminatory policies on farmers so that they can enjoy equal opportunities as urban residents. In terms of employment opportunities, college graduates who work in rural areas should be entitled to the same rights as their counterparts in cities. In terms of educational opportunities, farmers and their children should enjoy enrolment and selection rights equal to their urban counterparts. They should also enjoy equal health and medical care. All kinds of social security services should be provided not only to urban residents but also to villagers. Rural residents should have equal access to public goods as well.

Urbanisation of farmers needs the government to provide public services to eliminate the gap between urban and rural areas. Currently, many public services can only be enjoyed in the city. As a result, farmers have to resettle in cities to obtain the rights of urban residents. This would seriously overburden urban welfare services and add more social cost to the urbanisation of farmers. To solve this problem, we should provide villagers with urban opportunities and facilities, bring high-quality education and cultural and medical services to rural areas and increase the supply of public goods and facilities in rural towns. In this way, it will guarantee that farmers can enjoy all the rights of urban residents without living in cities, with a comparable lifestyle.

The level of equality in basic public services in urban and rural areas is affected by three factors: (1) the financial condition of local governments, (2) the ability of farmers' to pay for public services and (3) problems in the current ownership system.

First, it is necessary to ensure that farmers can pay for public services, such as culture, education, medical care and public transportation. These are not pure public goods. Both the government and users should bear part of the expense. The income gap will create differences in the ability of different groups to afford public services. Those who have higher incomes will enjoy more public goods. In comparison, those who have lower incomes (mainly farmers) will have fewer or even no opportunities to use public goods. This is why those who are unable to go to school or lack medical care because of poverty mostly live in rural areas. Therefore, accessing public goods and services requires not only the horizontal equity of pay-as-you-use but also the vertical fairness of paying according to capacity. With the support of public finance, low-income and poor families can also enjoy basic public services. To a certain extent, the free compulsory education currently promoted in rural areas can solve the problem of educating children from low-income families.

Second, we need to improve the revenues of different regions. Basic public services need financial support from local governments, but revenues of different regions are related to the level of local economic development. It means those regions that have higher levels of economic development in GDP will have more financial resources, a better supply of public goods and living conditions and vice versa. With current price levels, investment and development conditions, it is impossible to raise the rural living level to that of the urban centres. A low income results in poor living conditions, which causes a decrease of human capital. It will in turn lead to lower income levels. If we want to make the living conditions of rural residents equal to those of urban centres, at least at this stage, we need to change the ways of thinking and policies that determine the living standards of different areas based on the economic development level in GDP. For example, we can enhance the transfer payments so that people living in different regions can enjoy similar living conditions and public services.

Third, we should solve the problem of the ownership system. For a long time, the urban-rural division has been that of differences in urban-rural ownership systems. The state owns urban land, while rural land is held under collective ownership. Most urban residents are employees of the state-owned enterprises, while farmers are collective-employed or even self-employed. This means the state can invest directly in cities but not in rural areas. Cities can make overall plans for medical care, while rural areas can only provide cooperative medical service. Cities can establish social security funds with government support, but there are no such funds for villagers. With the development of market-oriented reform, both urban and rural areas have established the multi-ownership economy. The government is not just a representative of the state-owned economy but also that of all the people. Therefore, support to farmers from the government should not be restricted by the ownership system anymore. In particular, the social security funds supported by the government should also be provided to farmers. In this context, establishing an equal social security system in both urban and rural areas has become an important aspect of the urbanisation of farmers.

In conclusion, the modernisation of agriculture emphasises the quality of agricultural products based on scientific and technological progress. Rural modernisation stresses the improvement of rural life based on urban-rural integration and the urbanisation of farmers. Promoting the modernisation of *sannong* from this perspective requires external support and a new type of relationship between workers and farmers and between urban and rural areas. Industry should support agriculture, cities should help villages, workers and farmers should benefit from each other and urban and rural areas have to be integrated.

Notes

1 William Arthur Lewis, *Dual Economy*, trans. Shi Wei et al. (Beijing: Beijing College of Economics Press, 1989), 3–15.
2 John C.H. Fei and Gustav Ranis, *Growth and Development: From an Evolutionary Perspective*, trans. Hong Yinxing and Zheng Jianghuai (Beijing: Commercial Press, 2004), 2–5.
3 Anthony Philip Thirlwall, *Growth and Development: With Special Reference to Developing Economies*, trans. Jin Bei et al. (Beijing: Renmin University Press, 1992), 122.
4 Theodore William Schultz, *Transforming Traditional Agriculture*, trans. Liang Xiaomin (Beijing: Commercial Press, 1987), 5.
5 Schultz, *Transforming Traditional*, 26.
6 Schultz, *Transforming Traditional*, 132.
7 Simon S. Kuznets, *Modern Economic Growth: Rate, Structure, and Spread*, trans. Dai Rui and Yi Cheng (Beijing: Beijing College of Economics Press, 1989), 91–3.
8 Karl Marx, *On Capital*, vol.3, trans. Central Compilation and Translation Bureau (Beijing: People's Press, 2004), 888.
9 Yujiro Hayami and Vernon W. Ruttan, *Agricultural Development: An International Perspective*, trans. Guo Xibao et al. (Beijing: China Social Sciences Press, 2000),165.

10 Fei and Ranis, *Growth and Development*, 117.
11 Fei and Ranis, *Growth and Development*, "Translator's Preface", I-II.
12 Marx, *On Capital*, 912.
13 Marx, *On Capital*, 912.
14 Marx, *On Capital*, 698.
15 Everett M. Rogers and Rabel J. Burdge, *Social Change in Rural Societies*, trans. Wang Xiaoyi and Wang Dining (Hangzhou: Zhejiang People's Press, 1988), 35.

8   Regional economic development and coordination

Because of natural conditions and historical reasons, just as in other developing nations, a dual economic structure exists in different regions in China (i.e. the coexistence of economically developed and underdeveloped regions). Since the institutionalisation of the reform and opening policy, both developed and underdeveloped regions in China have made significant progress in economic growth. The development of coastal areas, however, has been faster, leading to greater regional gaps. Under such circumstances, ideal regional development in China should allow the regions that enjoy favourable development conditions to grow faster. Meanwhile, we should coordinate regional development with the aim of gradually achieving a common prosperity through a policy that features the first-riches helping the later-riches.

8.1 Background of the regional economic gap in China

A key goal of economic development is to accelerate the transformation of the regional economic structure from a dual to a single, unified model. In the course of economic growth, a regional gap is inevitable. Reasonable coordination of the regional economy must aim to eliminate such a gap as soon as possible while the efficiency of economic development is preserved. To meet such a requirement, market and government coordination must be implemented hand in hand to form two effective mechanisms that can manage the entire regional economy. Market coordination can provide efficient development while government coordination can contribute to equitable development. The widening of the regional economic gap can be attributed to the market, while the narrowing of the regional economic gap should be achieved with necessary support from the government.

8.1.1 China's regional economic gap

China has a vast territory of 9.6 million square kilometres. This, together with natural and historical conditions, results in a huge gap in the level of economic development between different economic regions. The gap, to be more specific, is caused by regional differences in geographic location, transportation conditions, quality of the labour force, scientific and technological levels, economic foundation, etc. As far as the larger geographical regions are concerned, China can be divided into eastern, middle and western economic zones. Even in the same province, the level of economic development is the same amongst different areas. For example, there are similarities between the southern and northern regions in Jiangsu province, eastern and western regions in Zhejiang and southern and northern regions in Guangdong.

With regard to the eastern, middle and western economic zones in China, the level of economic development is clearly reflected in descending order. The proportion of the modern industry in the eastern zones is higher than that of the middle and western zones, while its proportion of agriculture is comparatively lower amongst the three. As for the inner structure of industry, the eastern zone mainly produces technology-intensive manufactured goods. The western zone is clearly characterised by such basic industries as energy exploitation and raw materials processing. In addition, there exists a big gap between the western and the eastern zones in terms of the level of urbanisation, with the eastern zone enjoying a faster development rate.

The reform and opening-up that began in 1978 is a market-oriented policy that allows some regions to prosper before others. This in turn has gradually brought about the expansion of the regional economic gap. Although all of the regions have reaped the benefits from the reform and opening-up policy, the eastern coastal regions have obviously moved ahead much faster. The specific situations can be presented as follows. First, since the coastal regions took the lead in developing township enterprises, the development rate of rural industrialisation in the coastal regions is obviously faster than that of the middle and western regions. The interregional economic gap is primarily reflected in the gap between those regions that are industry-dominated and those that are financially dependent on agricultural production. Such a gap, in other words, can be reinterpreted as the gap between regions that enjoy a higher level of industrialisation and those that are comparatively underdeveloped owing to a lower level of non-agricultural economic activity. Second, thanks to geographical advantages, coastal areas are able to attract and make the most of a much larger amount of foreign capital to develop an export-oriented economy, which, accordingly, enables both the manufacturing and the service industries in the coastal areas to maintain a strong upward development trend.

A market-oriented reform causes a free flow of the factors of production in accordance with market signals. The factors of production that are efficiency-centred are more likely to flow to the developed regions in larger numbers. The inflow of foreign capital is channelled to the developed coastal regions by complying with market forces. The result brought about by this situation is expected to reinforce the theory of "cumulative causation" that was stated earlier. Specifically, the reflux effect should be stronger than the spillover effect, which can be manifested in the following two ways. The first is that the investment distribution is more likely to be in favour of coastal regions that enjoy better development capability. More fixed-asset investment from various central government ministries has been invested in eastern coastal developed regions. At the same time, the capital invested in the middle and western regions, as well as technical personnel, have both eventually flowed to the eastern developed regions. The positive effects caused by this situation enable the growth potential that eastern regions have enjoyed to be fully released. More significantly, the establishment of a new pattern of opening-up is advanced. As a result, the foundation of an all-round opening-up has been laid, and the condition of an all-round opening-up has been created as well. Compared with the eastern developed regions, the backwardness of the underdeveloped western regions related to the infrastructure of transportation, communications and water conservation is apparent. Moreover, the shortage of capital, the low level of science and technology and the low quality of the labour force all give rise to an invisible barrier that hinders economic development in the underdeveloped regions. Driven by the profits made in the market, such factors of production as capital, labour force and qualified personnel from the underdeveloped regions will flow to the developed regions that are profitable and enjoy a high return on investment.

What will be stated in the following sections are the theoretical explanations for the expansion of the regional economic gap so that an effective way to change the current regional dual economic structure can be found.

8.1.2 The industrial location theory

If we extend the German economist and sociologist Max Weber's industrial location theory to the macroscopic field, the selection of the industrial location will become an inevitable concern. Two key factors are the capital supply of a region and the expenses of production and transportation.

As far as funding is concerned, an industrial district is unlikely to be established without adequate investment. If there is no continuous supply of funds, a newly established industrial district will fall into decline, and the enterprises there would move to other areas. If we do not take into account the inflow of foreign investment, regional funding supplies will be determined only by each region's savings capacity and its residents' propensity to save money. This is a direct outcome of the level of economic development, cultural factors and traditional customs of the region. The per capita gross national income in underdeveloped regions is noticeably lower than that of the developed regions. The propensity to save in underdeveloped regions is, similarly, far weaker than that of developed regions. With the deepening of economic reform and the decline in the proportion of financial income collected by the central government, direct investment by the central government in underdeveloped regions will likely decline dramatically. Therefore, if government financial subsidies, as well as key investments, are ruled out, then the capital supply of developed regions is consequently greater than that of underdeveloped regions.

In terms of production and transportation expenses, the latter may be the most decisive factor. The optimal location for industry is generally the place that will generate the lowest transportation costs. More precisely, the cost mainly refers to the freight charges paid based on the distance between production sites and markets. The labour cost is the other significant factor. If the labour expenses of an industrial district account for a comparatively large proportion of the total cost of production, the lowest transportation expense is unlikely to ensure that the district enjoys the lowest cost of production. In this case, the ultimate selection of the optimal industrial location will change as long as a district with the lowest labour expenses is available. Moreover, centripetal forces are also a key factor. As a result of the growth and concentration of factories, centripetal forces will influence the selection of optimal industrial locations in addition to the scale economies and external economies that are brought to bear by these forces.

As for the level and capacity of economic growth, the interregional gap is reflected not only through key factors such as quantity but also the ability to attract outside investment. In an economic environment that is fully opening up to the outside world, both developed and underdeveloped regions are supposed to attract capital and technology from either other regions or even the outside world to boost development. If the investment environment of a region makes it possible for foreign capital to enjoy considerable profits, foreign capital is likely to be attracted to the region. Although reserves of natural resources in underdeveloped regions may be richer than those in developed regions, their capacity to attract outside investment is rather weak. There are a variety of reasons for this. Compared with developed regions, transportation and communication infrastructure in underdeveloped regions is barely satisfactory, transportation costs are high, the lack of qualified technical and management personnel is serious and a trend toward the equalisation of labour costs in both developed and underdeveloped regions have been widespread. Such an investment environment gives rise to much lower investment benefits. Therefore, underdeveloped regions are generally short of the capacity to attract capital from the outside.

Experience shows that the factors that have an influence on investors' ultimate selection of regional opportunities and, therefore, impact the regional industrial distribution gap can be summarised as follows. Of primary importance is whether a region has entered the stage of economic growth. If this is the case, the economic vitality, openness and growth rate, a sound legal system and economic security in a region are all significant elements that investors will take into consideration. A second aspect is the capacity of the market. Local purchasing power and market coverage both play a key role. The temporal distance to the overseas market is a particularly key element within an open economy. A third point is the importance attached to the agglomeration degree of economic energy. Specifically, the agglomeration degree of companies, service industries, foreign investment, the market and information are all essential concerns. The final issue is the nature of basic conditions – that is, the level of development in transportation, telecommunication networks and finance, as well as the level of urbanisation; the educational level of the labour force; the concentrative level of colleges, universities and scientific research institutions; the work efficiency and competence of the local government; and so forth. Each region is unlikely to enjoy all the aforementioned basic conditions.

8.1.3 The theory on urban functions

In general, urbanisation refers to an increase of the size of the urban population. Nevertheless, in terms of regional economic development, urbanisation should attach great significance to the improvement of urban functions that underlie the centre of the market where the flows of people, materials, information and capital are concentrated. In addition, cities play a role as the carriers of the service industry. All the key factors of production tend to be aggregated in cities. If a city enjoys more profound urban functions, it doubtlessly will generate a greater capacity to aggregate the key factors of production. François Perroux, the founder of "growth pole theory," regards cities as the growth pole of the regional development. As far as Perroux is concerned, regional differential effects are enhanced by the leading role played by cities. The geographically concentrated integrated industrial poles (i.e. cities) have changed the direct geographical environment. If such integrated industrial poles are powerful enough, they will change the entire economic structure. As the centre of the accumulation and aggregation of human and capital resources, integrated industrial poles accelerate the emergence of other centres that may accumulate and aggregate resources as well. When the two groups of centres are connected by the highways of materials, human capital and technology, extensive changes in the economic horizon and plans of both the producers and consumers will appear. Cities play the role of the growth pole that can promote regional development. Thus to a large extent, the development level of a region is determined by the number, scale and functions of its cities. A great number of cities and considerable urban scale will enable a region to attract the key factors of production more easily. Moreover, the growth pole of cities will function more effectively, and the development level of the region will be accordingly higher. A small number of cities and a limited urban scale, conversely, will limit the attraction of a region for the key factors of production. As a result, functions of the growth pole of cities will not be fully activated, and the development level of the region will accordingly hit a bottleneck.

Based on the aforementioned principles of urban functions, the regional economic gap can be accounted for by the gap in urbanisation levels. According to the relevant statistical data for 2008, the urbanisation rates amongst the eastern, middle and western regions in China are 55.9%, 40.9% and 41.5%, respectively. Such a statistical gap is due to supplies to cities in the eastern region being adequate. Such adequate supplies, nonetheless, are unlikely to be available to cities and towns in the middle and western regions. Another way to look at the issue is through the density of distribution of cities and towns. (The unit is the number of cities or towns/10,000 km². The national density of distribution is 0.69, while the regional densities amongst the eastern, middle, western and north-eastern regions are 2.50, 1.64, 0.25, and 1.14, respectively. The national density of the distribution of the designated towns is 20.91, while the regional densities amongst the eastern, middle, western and north-eastern regions are 68.02, 48.69, 10.35 and 19.45, respectively.

This data leads to the conclusion that the most fundamental interregional gap in levels of social and economic development lies in the gap of urbanisation. The developed economic conditions in the eastern region can be attributed to the larger number, greater scale and more powerful functions of cities. The smaller number, narrower scale and weaker functions of cities, accordingly, give rise to the underdeveloped economic situation of the middle and western regions. Owing to the severe shortage of both the number of and the supplies to their cities, the labour force migrating from rural areas are unable to become urbanised locally in the middle and western regions. Thus migration-urbanisation will be an inevitably hard journey for the labour force in these regions.

A more remarkable central role played by cities will exert a wider range of influence and generate a real impetus to overcome administrative barriers. The Yangtze River Delta Economic Zone (YRDEZ) can be taken as a typical example. The dominant reason YRDEZ can take the lead in terms of economic development is that it possesses a dense distribution of cities and a higher level of urbanisation. It has already become the largest metropolitan area in China and is upgrading itself into the sixth super metropolitan area in the world. The most influential metropolis in China, Shanghai, is located in YRDEZ. Such large- and medium-sized cities as Suzhou, Wuxi, Changzhou, Nanjing and Hangzhou are also located there. Thanks to the prominent central position of cities, both the market and the enterprises in YRDEZ are taking on an obvious city orientation, especially a central city-oriented tendency. Therefore, the most effective way to boost development in underdeveloped regions is to accelerate urbanisation so as to attract the key factors of production and aggregate the economic energy.

8.1.4 The cumulative causation theory

Gunnar Myrdal, a Swedish Nobel laureate in economics in 1974, applied the theory of "cumulative causation" to explain the causes of further widening of the economic gap between developed and underdeveloped areas in the process of modernisation. According to the neoclassical economic equilibrium theory, the mobility of factors may equalise their prices (i.e. wage rates, interest rates, etc.) amongst all regions, thus overcoming the regional imbalance. On the other hand, the theory of "cumulative causation" argues that when regional inequality exists,

> the role played by the economic power and the social power causes the accumulation and expansion of developed areas to be made at the cost of sacrificing other underdeveloped areas. A direct consequence is that the economic situation in the underdeveloped areas gets worse and further development in these areas is set back. As a result, the imbalanced economic development among different regions will be reinforced.[1]

This view suggests that the mobility of factors can by no means achieve a balanced distribution of the factors of production amongst different regions. The spatial distribution of factors of production, on the contrary, will become more imbalanced.

Myrdal applies the two concepts (i.e. expansion effect and reflux effect) to account for this cumulative causation theory. The expansion effect mainly refers to the positive effects produced by the economic development of one region on another. They are characterised by the spread of advanced factors of production, such as market, technology and information. The reflux effect can be defined as the negative effects produced by the economic development of one region on another. They feature the transfer of the labour force and capital from underdeveloped to developed regions, as well as the relocation of projects that may cause serious pollution from developed to underdeveloped regions. The regional development gap may be accounted for with an overwhelming impact of the reflux effect over the expansion effect.

Because of the existence of the cumulative causation, favourable factors of economic growth, such as capital, labour force and entrepreneurs, all tend to flow to developed regions. Moreover, commerce brings considerable profits to the developed regions. As a result, they are more likely to enjoy a faster pace of development. The speed of development in underdeveloped regions, however, is much slower owing to the loss of economic growth factors. For underdeveloped regions, the growth effect that is generated by using the latest technology is not as strong as the growth effect enjoyed by their developed counterparts. "Advanced technology does not necessarily bring expected benefits to underdeveloped newcomers. It is not uncommon at present that the output increased with the use of the advanced technology far exceeds the absorptive capacity of the domestic market."[2] Furthermore, a key issue with modern technologies is that an enormous amount of initial investment is needed given the fact that current technologies are dominantly capital intensive. "The investment of such a huge amount might have exceeded the weak and fragile financial strength in an underdeveloped region." This, therefore, constitutes a barrier for some underdeveloped regions to adopt advanced technology. In addition,

> if there are not effective regulating measures, the banking system will become an unfair means by which the deposits of the underdeveloped areas will be extracted and invested into the richer areas that then may enjoy guaranteed higher profits on capital.[3]

The mobility of the factors of production determined by the cumulative causation will have a negative impact on both developed and underdeveloped regions. A high concentration of people in the developed regions is likely to pose a potential threat to social security and pollute the environment. In underdeveloped regions, the loss of the labour force, especially young adults and those who have a special professional skill, is likely to stagnate development, aggravate poverty and even give rise to regional conflicts. Therefore, a wider regional development gap will seriously hinder sustainable economic development of not only the underdeveloped but also developed regions.

Market-oriented gradient transference has been ongoing since the implementation of the reform and opening-up policy. It has largely driven the overall economic development in the eastern region and enabled it to achieve greater development, further explore its markets and gain more raw materials. Consequently, enterprises in the eastern region will invest in the middle and western regions in an active manner. As a result, investment from the eastern region has become a powerful driving force to boost economic development in the middle and western regions in addition to the government funds. The labourers who have gone to the eastern region can take advantage of opportunities for human capital investment. Their remittances to their hometowns become a key financial channel for the middle and western regions to accumulate funds. For this reason, the economic growth rate of the middle and western regions also has been greater than they experienced prior to the 1980s. This has promoted the rapid growth of both the economic aggregate and the comprehensive national power of our country. Such a situation where industry – namely, the carrier of the new technology – continues to spread in underdeveloped areas can be described as the expansion effect from developed areas. This expansion effect, however, is rather limited because of the obvious shortage of a basic economic foundation, technology and skilled labourers in underdeveloped areas. The inadequacy of accumulated capital gives rise to a slow technological advance; the slow technological advance results in low labour productivity; low labour productivity produces low-income levels; low-income levels lead to the inadequacy of the supply of capital. Such a scenario creates a vicious circle that is holding back the development of the middle and western regions. As a result, the comprehensive utilisation and deep processing of various natural resources are unlikely to be accomplished in these regions. It prevents them from taking full advantage of their resource superiority. The impetus to promote regional development becomes increasingly weaker. The regional gap of economic development is further widened. The expansion effect from the developed to the underdeveloped areas is entirely unachievable.

8.1.5 Allowing some areas to get rich first

At present, the regional gradient related to economic and technological development levels exists objectively in China. Since there is a regional gap with regards to the ability to attract capital and technologies, we should recognise the existence of the gradient order. Economic development policies should be formulated based on acknowledging this reality and tendency. Policies should give active support to developed areas to introduce and master the world's leading technologies. The effective introduction and spread of modern technologies, then, can gradually be directed and promoted in the less developed or even underdeveloped areas. Just as Chairman Mao Zedong stated in his well-known speech "On the Ten Major Relationships," to even out the distribution of the development of industry, we must strive to promote industry in the interior. However, the coastal industrial base must be put to full use. If the desire to develop industry in the interior is genuine, "we must actively use and promote industry in the coastal regions."[4]

Because of the relation of the regional gap to the level of economic development, what priority different regions should place on their development has turned into a key research subject. As far as the national economic development strategy is concerned, a consistent policy should be applied to all the regions. Both the developed and underdeveloped regions should enjoy the same opportunities to attract foreign capital and advanced technologies. However, with regard to the reality of economic development, the process of gradient transference is a reality. This is determined by the regional gap involving output capacity and the investment environment.

As for the level and capacity of economic growth, the interregional gap is reflected not only in the stock of production factors but also in the ability of different regions to attract the output capacity of various input factors in different regions. Only if the local investment environment can ensure that external capital makes comparatively greater profits will external capital be invested locally. The quantity of natural resources in underdeveloped regions is likely to be larger than that in developed regions. Nonetheless, because of such problems as inferior transportation and communications systems, the high cost of transportation, a shortage of technical and managing employees, the ability of underdeveloped regions to attract external capital is still unsatisfactory. In addition, labour costs in underdeveloped regions are virtually the same as that of developed regions. Under such an investment environment, the investment benefit in underdeveloped regions is lower than that in developed regions. Consequently, the ability of underdeveloped regions to attract external capital is always weak and inadequate.

Since the reform and opening-up, China has implemented the policy of allowing some areas to get rich first. This indicates that the regional gap in development speed has been widely acknowledged. As an economic system that advocates the survival of the fittest, the market economy allows an imbalance of development speed. The interregional imbalance is determined by the regional technological gap. The regions that enjoy better conditions should be allowed to develop at a faster speed. Developed regions have a favourable technological base that can boost economic development, as well as the advantages related to the quality of their products and the resulting economic benefit. Therefore, the rate of economic growth in developed regions is understandably faster than that of other regions, as well as the national average. If developed regions slow their growth to that of other regions, they would ultimately gain nothing but the loss of precious opportunities and the sacrifice of the great productive forces they have enjoyed. The macroeconomic balance of a country is unlikely to be established on the basis of different regions growing at the same pace with the same balanced rate. In a market economy system, the regions that enjoy better economic benefits have achieved advanced development as production factors flow to them. As a result, the macroeconomic balance could only be achieved based on a faster growth rate and greater economic benefits. Even if the Chinese government implemented a macro-tightening policy, it would not halt the advanced development of the regions that enjoy better economic benefits.

In a market economy system, resources enjoy free mobility. The only factor that may restrict the speed of mobility is the market. As long as there are markets, both internal and external, a region can bring in or purchase capital, resources and technology, even if there were not any such regional factors in the past. Therefore, the major impetus contributing to the rapid development of a region is not rooted in the region itself. Instead, such an impetus comes from the national or even the international market. The increased mobility of resources primarily relies on the ability to attract external capital, technologies and resources rather than the local capacity to supply resources. Developed regions are able to attract external factors by means of various markets of factors and their price signals, as well as through the improvement of the investment environment.

Because of the aforementioned reasons, in spite of China's effective narrowing of the interregional economic and social gap thanks to "the West Development

Strategy," the gap remained severe until 2016. The provinces with GDP per capita surpassing RMB65,000 (around US$10,000) were all located in Eastern China in 2016. The GDP per capita of Tianjin, Beijing, Shanghai, Jiangsu, Zhejiang, Fujian, Inner Mongolia, Guangdong and Shandong was RMB115,613, RMB114,690, RMB113,731, RMB95,394, RMB83,923, RMB74,288, RMB74,204, RMB73,290 and RMB68,049, respectively. The provinces with GDP per capita less than RMB40,000 were all in middle and western China. The GDP per capita of Sichuan, Anhui, Guangxi, Tibet, Shanxi, Guizhou, Yunnan and Gansu are RMB39,835, RMB39,254, RMB38,042, RMB35,496, RMB35,285, RMB33,242, RMB31,358 and RMB27,508, respectively. This shows that the GDP per capita of Gansu was less than one-third of that of Jiangsu.

8.2 Coordination of the regional economy

The imbalance of regional economic development is an inevitable stage in a country's economic growth. Nevertheless, an excessive expansion of the regional gap will give rise to the unsustainable development of both the regional economy and the entire national economy. The modernisation of China is unlikely to be accomplished without the modernisation of underdeveloped regions. National economic development strategy should acknowledge the existence of such regional gaps and adopt effective strategies, policies and systems to narrow and, eventually, overcome them. Although the coordination mechanism to balance the regional economy will always depend on the market to some extent, the coordination and promotion efforts of the government actually play a major role in coping with the regional development gap.

8.2.1 The first-riches help the later-riches

Deng Xiaoping not only came up with the idea that some regions should be allowed to get rich first but also made it clear that coastal regions must be required to adhere to the line of "the first-riches help the late-riches" after the establishment of a moderately prosperous society. The negative effects on underdeveloped regions that result from the rapid growth of developed regions should not be ignored because factors of production, such as labour and capital, are transferred from slowly developing areas to fast-developing areas. In addition, developed areas tend to relocate the projects that cause serious pollution to underdeveloped areas. As a result, the regional gap is further expanded. The inadequacy of accumulated capital gives rise to a slow technological advance; this results in low labour productivity; low labour productivity brings about low-income levels; low-income levels lead to an inadequate supply of capital. Such a process forms a vicious circle that holds back development in the middle and western regions. With regard to the causes of such reflux effect, Myrdal conducted research that went far beyond fields such as funds transfer, population growth and resource shortages. He holds that inadequate development is mainly due to the roles played by market forces. The trade between developed and underdeveloped regions does not lead to the equality of productivity and income but to inequality. The reflux effect is produced not only by market regulation of the regional allocation of resources but also the inevitable cost at which the market economy system can be practiced. The underdeveloped regions have paid a high price for long-term economic stagnation simply to boost the growth of the developed regions. It is high time that developed regions repay such a great favour that their underdeveloped counterparts have done for them.

Unbalanced regional development inevitably means that "regional advancement" should be used to accelerate China's modernisation process. Deng proposed that common prosperity in China should be accomplished from one region to the next by allowing some regions to get rich first. Similarly, the process of development cannot be simultaneous in different regions. Practically, the comparatively underdeveloped regions are unable to meet the goal of the creation of a comprehensive well-off society. Therefore, they are unable to launch the modernisation process. In developed regions that have already reached the level of well-off society, it is necessary and timely to start the historical process of modernisation. As a result, the report of the 18th CPC National Congress declared clearly that developed regions should be encouraged to keep taking the lead in pursuing modernisation and to make greater contributions to nationwide reform and development.

In the past, economic ties were always a concern in relations between the eastern and western regions. A major cause of the widening of the regional development gap since the 1990s is a weaker interregional economic reliance. This is mainly an outcome of the following three changes. First, thanks to the economic opening to the outside world in coastal regions, they can obtain needed resources from the international market rather than from the western region, their previous source of supply. Second, because of economic structural adjustment in coastal regions, together with the development of advanced technology and the service industry, western region resources have become less appealing. Third, coastal regions have spared no effort to develop an export-oriented economy, which has reduced their reliance on the market in the western region. As a result, economic development in the eastern region is no longer reliant on the western region. In particular, the post-development advantages supposedly enjoyed by underdeveloped regions have not been as conspicuous as expected. For example, when manufactured goods in the western region enter the market, a considerable proportion of the market share has already been occupied by the enterprises from the eastern region. This means it costs the western region more to get their manufactured goods to market.

Joseph Stiglitz once reminded China not to simply count on the opening policy as the exclusive engine of economic development. The domestic economy can also serve as an engine for development. The traditional economic strategy that features an undue reliance on the overseas market demand has already revealed a number of drawbacks. First, export has encountered tough obstacles, which resulted in a striking decrease in export earnings. Second, the export-oriented economy only favours coastal cities. The inland provinces have not enjoyed similar benefits. Third, the sources of economic growth are of great significance for the economic development of underdeveloped regions. Based on this analysis,

Stiglitz concludes that China should take the necessary measures to make full use of its enormous domestic market as an engine for economic growth throughout the country.[5]

Currently, a considerable number of coastal areas have already reached the level of a well-off society. Consequently, their mission to offer support for the development in underdeveloped areas should be put on the agenda. Such a mission may also satisfy the needs of the coastal areas, as further growth of the gap between the eastern, middle and western regions will exert a negative influence on the sustainability of development in the east. Development in the middle and western regions is relatively low; thus, the growth of demand for processed goods in these regions is slow. This will definitely result in an obvious reduction in the domestic market demand for processed goods from the east. In addition, the middle and western regions are generally short of the necessary capacity to accelerate the technological transformation of enterprises, which results in a high cost of the products made of raw materials. The cost sometimes is even higher than the raw materials from overseas. Such high costs accordingly prompt the eastern region to import the raw materials from abroad. Furthermore, the slow upgrading of the industrial structure in the middle and western regions compels the coastal areas to continuously produce the medium- and low-grade goods to meet the needs of production and consumption patterns in these regions. This, however, delays the upgrading and replacement of manufactured products and accordingly exerts a negative influence on the optimisation of China's industrial structure. As for the middle and western regions, their roles as the market for manufactured goods and resource providers have been turned into the restraints that, to some extent, hold back the development in the developed eastern region. Consequently, the comparative advantage that our country should take from the regional division of labour will inevitably get lost.

Simply relying on the market adjustment mechanism is unlikely to eliminate or even narrow the regional gap of economic development. On the contrary, it will widen the gap. It means that the western region should not simply count on the gradient transference from developed regions to promote their growth. To rely on the role played by the market economy to narrow the regional gap of economic development is not practical either. The West Development Strategy determined by the Chinese central government, to some extent, means the development of the western region will be directly promoted by the central government.

8.2.2 Promoting the flow of production factors to underdeveloped regions

To promote economic development in light of the principles of the market economy, a further expansion of the regional economic gap is inevitable. The market economic system itself, however, may offer relevant methods or approaches that can adjust the gap. The key lies in the opening of an interregional market and the removal of the "fragment economy" that features self-protection. The following discussion offers an overall introduction on how to promote the modernisation of a dual economic structure under open conditions.

First, a reasonable division of labour amongst different regions should be maintained according to the principle of comparative advantage. On the basis of the division of labour, regional trade relations can be developed and expanded. Here the division of labour can be clarified with a dual-level interpretation. The first level divides labour in accordance with the comparative advantage on which different regions rely to offer products and labour, as well as the comparative gap concerning costs in different regions. Specifically, developed regions may prioritise the development of high-tech products since they enjoy a comparative advantage in technology. Underdeveloped regions, similarly, may give priority to the development of manufactured goods because they possess comparative advantage in the exploitation and utilisation of the natural resources. The second level of labour division is determined on the basis of the comparative adequacy of the supply of key production factors. Here the regions that enjoy a more abundant labour supply develop a labour-intensive industry, while the regions that possess a more plentiful supply of natural resources develop a natural resource-intensive industry. Similarly, the regions that have a more advanced technical force may develop a technology-intensive industry. An interregional commodity exchange based on such divisions of labour can promote economic prosperity amongst all regions.

Second, to bring about an interregional supply of capital, technology and human resources and implement economic and technological cooperation can promote an effective interregional flow and allocation of production factors. The relationship of the commodity exchange alone cannot create fundamental change in the interregional dual structure. Such a dual structure will continue to exist unless we can mount a nationwide reallocation of production factors, and thereby accomplish the modernisation of the dual economy. As a result, apart from the necessary plan and policy guidance from the central government regarding the flow of production factors, underdeveloped regions should spare no efforts to improve their investment environment. In particular, the transportation and communications infrastructure should be improved and investment in human capital emphasised. Moreover, preferential policies to attract scientific and technological talents should be adopted. Taking self-development into account, developed regions are expected to expand their economic and technological cooperation with underdeveloped regions and establish economic associations, as well as enterprise groups, so as to facilitate wider access to the energy sources, raw materials and market. This can also meet the needs of economic development in developed regions. The shareholding system, joint operation and joint venture are all key styles provided by the market economic system to facilitate the interregional reallocation of production factors.

Third, market mechanisms should be combined with government support. Regional coordination is supposed to make full use of the coordinating role played by the market mechanism. The middle and western regions are universally the places where abundant natural resources are found. The reproduction chain of the key industries in these regions is widely extended outside of the regions. Because of an imperfect market system that is unable to maintain a sound price mechanism, the sale of primary products at a low price and purchase of the finished products at a high price has placed economic development in middle and western regions in an unhealthy situation. To change this unfavourable pattern of labour division, some regions have blindly developed processing industries. It leads to the rise of an industrial structure convergence and breaks the economic and technological links between regions. As a result, it is unable to achieve sustainable regional development. Therefore, on the one hand, an integrated and unified price mechanism should be established; on the other hand, barriers erected by regional governments and departments should be eliminated. These necessary measures are expected to ensure the establishment of a standardised, institutionalised and legalised market order. Such a market order can create ideal conditions for conducting transactions on the basis of fairness. It is then that the advantages of different regions can be fulfilled in a real sense.

8.2.3 The growth pole and its expansion effect

As the founder of the "growth pole theory," the French economist François Perroux held that growth is unlikely to take place in all places at the same time. Growth will first take place at some growth points or growth poles and then be spread through various channels. In this way, growth will exert influence on the economy as a whole. Specifically, the momentum of growth will be concentrated in the leading sectors and industries that may possess potential innovation capability. Such sectors or industries, in most cases, tend to gather in major urban centres. These centres, accordingly, will form the growth poles that will create a spreading effect to the surrounding areas. Thanks to this spreading effect, the growth poles turn themselves into the regional centres of production, commerce, transportation and information. A powerful centripetal force will attract and gather more and more relevant sectors, industries and manufacturers that offer various services to the leading sectors and industries that enjoy the potential innovation capability. The momentum of growth will spread factors of production such as technology, capital, institutions and information to the surrounding areas and will consequently drive the development of the surrounding regions.[6] Obviously, compared with the development that features disparity transference, such spreading technology transfer powered by growth poles enjoys a faster speed and higher efficiency.

In terms of the modern economy, the formation of growth poles and economic centres is closely related to the formation of industrial clusters. These clusters refer to the concentration of enterprises that manufacture the same or relevant products in the same area or region. These types of clusters will continue to expand in both horizontal and longitudinal ways. They can be defined as the spatial aggregation of enterprises that either manufacture the same products or share the industrial correlation. In reality, this type of cluster is quite common. The leather shoe manufacturing cluster in Italy, the furniture manufacturing cluster in North Carolina, the electronics manufacturing cluster in California's Silicon Valley, the automaking cluster in the U.S. city of Detroit, the clothing industrial cluster in China's Zhejiang Province and so forth can all be regarded as typical examples of industrial clusters.

According to Myrdal's theory, the effective elimination of interregional economic imbalance can be achieved by weakening the reflux effects and strengthening the expansion effects. Growth poles serve as the centre of the regional economy and exert positive influence on the economic growth of the surrounding areas. The positive effects include the expansion of the market for products from other regions and the spread of advanced technologies to these regions. Accordingly, the priority of the development programme of a region must lie in the ultimate identification of the growth pole within the region. In the YRDEZ, for example, Shanghai should enjoy the status as the growth pole.

In reality, however, there have been no growth poles in underdeveloped regions. Hence, the establishment of growth poles should be given top priority because of their particular significance to economic development. The formation of the growth poles should follow the natural steps of development. The industries and enterprises that have a better capacity for innovation will generate considerable cohesion. In addition, such advantages as a reduction in cost and increase in returns that are brought about by geographic accessibility in various economic activities can greatly boost the regional economic growth. Therefore, a regional economic centre can gradually come into being. The gathering of capital, technological innovation, aggregation of industries and enterprises and improvement of the tertiary sector of the economy that includes the service of trade, finance and information can all be recognised as the key steps in the formation of a growth pole. So far, there have been two ways in which growth poles have been formed. One stresses the roles played by the market to attract and aggregate the factors of production; the other, however, highlights the roles played by the government in working out concrete plans and making key investments to foster their formation.

For developed regions, the establishment of growth poles should be fulfilled through the action of the market. The significance of the construction of the Pudong district in Shanghai, for example, is the creation of a growth pole that aims to transform and upgrade the district into the growth pole of the whole Yangtze River Delta. To establish and reinforce the growth pole by virtue of the market requires attaching importance to the handling of the mutual relations between aggregation and spread. What should be aggregated to the central area includes the factors of production, the leading sectors and the industries that enjoy the capability of innovation; what should be spread to the surrounding areas, however, is the development momentum of the central area through such channels as technology, institutions, factors of production, information and so forth. The precondition of the centripetal force is the ability to live up to the expectations of the surrounding regions in terms of a strong expansion effect in both hardware and software. Aggregation is unlikely to be achieved without spread; spread, similarly, is unrealistic if there is no aggregation. In other words, aggregation and spread are complementary to each other.

For underdeveloped regions, establishing the growth poles by means of the market will be time-consuming. Underdeveloped regions do not want and should not wait for such a long time. As a result, the government should get involved in the process. Based on the growth pole theory, the government's regional development programme should focus on development planning for specific areas instead of the whole region. The central government ought to concentrate capital investment, introduce technology and support the leading sectors in the specific areas of all regions so as to transform these areas into the growth poles that can drive regional development as a whole. A mechanism should be subsequently set up to achieve these goals. While the government focusses its coordinating role on the establishment of growth poles, the market will support the leading role played by growth poles in spreading development to the surrounding areas.

8.2.4 Modernisation of cities

With regard to the regional economy, cities undoubtedly serve as the growth poles within their regions. The leading role played by urban centres in regional economic and social development has become increasingly prominent. The more prominent the role played by cities is, the stronger the expansion effect it will have on the surrounding areas and the higher level of overall development a region will enjoy. Whether a city can fully play such a role depends on its development level and the aggregation of production factors and leading industries in that city.

In accordance with the growth pole theory, cities of various sizes in a region are likely to become the growth poles that may drive the economic development of surrounding areas. Southern Jiangsu, for instance, is one of the most rapidly developing regions in China and has already reached the basic level of modernisation. This noticeable achievement is mainly due to the existence of an integrated urban agglomeration into which the central cities, counties and towns are all incorporated. In the course of modernisation, we should continuously support and further strengthen the roles played by such urban agglomerations. According to the report by the 18th CPC National Congress, we should make scientific plans for the scale and layout of the urban agglomerations. We should also help small- and medium-sized cities and small towns to better develop industries, provide public services, create jobs and attract population. A modernised coordination of urban agglomerations must address the following three tasks. First, the status of central cities should be promoted to ensure that they are further upgraded into cosmopolitan cities and technologically innovative centres. Second, the functions of small- and medium-sized cities should be strengthened so as to enable them to attract industry and accommodate new residents from the central cities. Third, the construction of small rural towns should be stressed. They are the key nodes for achieving urban-rural integration and play a crucial role in boosting the modernisation of rural areas.

At present, in both the developed and underdeveloped regions, the promotion of the functions of growth poles primarily lies in the promotion of their modernisation level.

For quite some time, Chinese cities in general were defined as consumptive towns that had been transformed into productive cities. Productive cities were also referred to as industrial cities. At the first stage of industrialisation, the development of the urban industries played an indispensable historical role in promoting Chinese industrialisation. With the development of urban industry, however, such urban diseases as pollution and congestion brought about by the concentration of industry have become increasingly worse. When manufactured goods have easy access to markets, the problem of urban unemployment is exacerbated. As a result, a city with a higher level of industrialisation tends to be more underdeveloped. Furthermore, thanks to the development of rural industrialisation and small towns, the roles played by the cities have become less important than before.

Further analysis indicates that there are two more reasons for the low level of China's urban modernisation. During the planned economy period, the expenses of urban construction, expansion and reconstruction were all covered by the government budget. It meant that each additional urban resident would add to the government's cost and thus to the financial burden. During the period when the economic level in China was slow, the strict control over the development and construction of cities, especially the large urban centres, was necessary. To ensure that the limited funding was invested in production, the scale of the tertiary industry that stimulates consumption had to be curbed. This resulted in the backwardness and obsolescence of urban service facilities. With the deepening of reform and opening, the priority of urbanisation has now shifted from the construction of urban centres to that of small towns. As a result, the economic power that should have been concentrated in large cities has been spread to small towns.

To define the city in terms of modernisation, the "rectification of name" has become a key issue. In other words, the true features of a city should be restored. In the years when the development level was low, it was its role as an industrial centre that secured a city's role as the economic centre. At present, manufactured goods have gained easy access to markets. This means that the industrial centre has lost the functions of an economic centre. Only a market centre can serve as an economic centre. The experiences of developed countries show that cities have become centres of modernisation and birthplaces of science and technology, as well as culture and ideas, carriers of advanced productive forces and the modern market. Urbanisation, as a result, should become the driving force to realise rural modernisation in China. The promotion of urban modernisation will give impetus to technological innovation and the progress of civilisation and greatly boost the modernisation of society and the economy, as well as the spread of urban civilisation to increase regional modernisation.

With the aim of achieving urban modernisation, large- and medium-sized cities in China are currently mainly committed to seeking solutions to three major problems. The first deals with such "modern urban diseases" as traffic congestion, overcrowding, environmental pollution, etc. The second concerns the improvement of urban value. What should be stressed is not only the economic value but also the value of cultural and ecological factors in a city. The third is the optimisation of the central commercial activities of cities. The excessive concentration of key industries today (i.e. manufacturing and residential construction) give rise to such problems as overcrowding and a degraded environment. Moreover, the unit area of urban land that yields less profit and development space for modern and service industries is wasted. Thus it is difficult to raise the development level of most large- and medium-sized cities in China. Urbanisation has become the ideal solution to these problems. Specifically, many enterprises that are unable to pay expensive city rents and obsolete residential buildings should be relocated from cities to small towns to accommodate the financial institutions, business centres, corporate headquarters and public buildings that are capable of paying for the rent. This is an effective way to update urban functions. Accordingly, urbanisation is characterised by the enhancement of the functions of the towns in terms of industrial development, public service, job growth and population aggregation. In a word, towns should be significantly urbanised to accommodate urban industries and population.

Reinforcement of the functions of the urban market is closely related to the increase in the size of the urban service industry. To some extent, an industry-based city can only be upgraded into a city with strong economy. It is the service industries that can transform a city into a powerful business centre (see Table 8.1). The key issue of urbanisation is not simply the mobility and concentration of the population. The realisation of urbanisation relies on the improvement of urban functions that aims to transform industrial cities into trading centres, as well as service and consumptive cities. Therefore, urban modernisation means the recombination of urban industrial structure, spreading urban industry to the surrounding small cities and towns. In the meantime, the service industries in such fields as finance, trade, information, service, culture and education should be concentrated in the large- and medium-sized cities.

What businesses should a modernised city gather? The capacity of any city is limited. If cities are to serve as the growth pole in a region, they should gather the advanced factors of production and leading industries, such as manufacturing, R&D centres, corporate headquarters and marketing centres for service industries. Traditional factory-based cities should be transformed into corporate-based cities that can attract international banks, insurance companies, trade businesses, telecommunications companies and various high-tech R&D centres.

How large should the scale of a modernised city be? The modernisation of a city is by no means the same as the incessant expansion of the urban scale. Urban modernisation should apply stress to upgrading its implications and functions rather than a simple pursuit of scale. Past urbanisation was characterised by the expansion of urban scale, an outcome of the industrialisation stage in which

Table 8.1 Proportion of the Tertiary Industry in the Downtown Area of Selective Cities in China and Overseas

Cities	GDP Proportion of Tertiary Sector	Employment Proportion of Tertiary Sector
New York (1989)	80.00	86.70
Paris (1988)	72.70	77.90
Tokyo (1988)	72.50	70.00
Seoul (1989)	68.90	63.20
Hong Kong (2012)	93.00	88.50
Beijing (2012)	76.46	75.63
Shanghai (2012)	60.45	50.76
Guangzhou (2012)	63.58	53.88

the larger the scale, the greater the status a city enjoyed. Modern society, however, has entered the information stage. It is unnecessary to base the level of urban modernisation on scale. Therefore, the government widely resorts to land replacement to move a large number of traditional factories and residential buildings that are unable to pay the rent while occupying large spaces in urban centres. While helping traditional industries and urban residents move out of downtown areas, we should encourage corporate headquarters to move in. Meanwhile, we ought to provide more space for the construction of trading, financial and public services. All of these measures will greatly accelerate the upgrade of the functions of urban centres.

Modernisation emphasises greater convenience for the people. Therefore, urban modernisation aims to establish the optimal living environment, including science and education, a healthy environment and legal services. In light of such an aim, to establish urban modernisation, the country will first have to deal with the construction of an ideal urban and healthy environment. Modernised cities place importance on their ecological functions. As a result, environmental governance and comprehensive ecological improvement are of great significance to the promotion of urban value. The improvement of the environment will encourage the acceleration of the development of tourism. Second, the social construction of a city concerned with the modernisation of science and technology, medical and health services, education, culture and so forth should be stressed as far as urban modernisation is concerned. If cities are able to become not only centres of modernisation but also resources for advanced science and technology, as well as culture and ideas, the modernisation of society and the economy and the geographical spread of urban civilisation will be greatly boosted. It will also further increase the potential for regional modernisation. Third, the construction of the support system for urban facilities also plays a key role. The infrastructure of a modern city requires a high-quality system of finance, transportation, communication and water and energy supply, accelerated information networks and better housing, as well as a high-standard, multi-level modern market, strong market networks and optimised systems that can guarantee the normal operation of the market. Facilities that link a city to the surrounding regions are also amongst the basic conditions under which the functions of urban centres as growth poles should be reinforced.

8.2.5 The regional coordination in modernisation process

The efforts to realise modernisation in different regions should be in line with local conditions instead of a one-size-fits-all approach. China is a country with vast territory and a huge population. There are accordingly tremendous differences between resource reserves, geography, cultural traditions and industrial structure amongst regions. Therefore, the level of modernisation in different regions is wide-ranging. The comprehensive establishment of a well-off society and the goal of achieving the overall realisation of socialist modernisation in China requires that developed regions should be allowed to take the lead to start the process.

Globally, the countries that have achieved modernisation tend to exhibit different economic characteristics. For example, in some countries, the manufacturing industry makes up a larger proportion of GDP; in others, the service industry accounts for a greater proportion, and in others, it is agriculture that is responsible for a larger proportion of GDP. This clearly indicates that all the regions in China should carry forward socialist modernisation in light of local conditions. For different regions, unrealistic competition and uncreative imitation should be avoided. Instead, choosing a suitable path or creating an appropriate mode to realise modernisation in a practical and realistic manner is undoubtedly a wise choice. For different regions, the key points to construct modernisation are different as well. Indexes for our country to measure basic modernisation, such as the urbanisation rate and the proportion of service industry in GDP, are simply general indexes that probably should not be allocated to different regions on the basis of national averages. Meanwhile, it is unrealistic to require that all the regions reach the same level in their modernisation efforts. On the national level, for example, the proportion of agriculture in GDP should be lowered; the proportion of the service industry should accordingly be raised. For some particular regions, however, it is more appropriate to develop modern agriculture to reach the basic level of modernisation.

The process of modernisation is actually the process of regional economic integration. As a result, an overall plan that balances development amongst regions is necessary to realise modernisation. The spatial scale for the advancement of modernisation in different regions should not be limited to a city or a county. Even such megacities as Beijing and Shanghai are unlikely to accomplish modernisation by themselves. Modernisation should cover both the central and peripheral areas. The modernisation that simply benefits the central node while neglecting peripheral areas could not last long. The modernisation effort of the central cities is in need of coordination and distribution of responsibilities to the peripheral areas. It cannot only lower the cost but also generate agglomeration, as well as size effects. Similarly, the central cities may produce the radiation effect and the expansion effect, significantly driving the development of the peripheral areas. Both the central and peripheral areas can be upgraded into new urban centres, promoting the development of a larger area. Therefore, the process of modernisation can be recognised as one that may address regional fragmentation, carry forward regional economic integration and realise the coordinated development of regional economy.

8.3 The integration of the regional economy

China is a country with vast territory. As a result, an economic gap exists not simply amongst the eastern, middle and western regions. Even in the same region, relatively huge gaps can exist in two adjacent areas. Therefore, the regional economic coordination cannot simply focus on the coordination between China's east, middle and west at the national level. More efforts will be made to coordinate adjacent administrative regions where the gap in economic development levels actually exists. The synergetic strategy in Beijing-Tianjin-Hebei, the development strategy of the Yangtze River Economic Belt, and the development strategy of Guangdong-Hong Kong-Macao Greater Bay Area are all typical strategies that are being implemented by our country to carry out the integration of regional economies.

8.3.1   Reshaping economic geography

In 2009, the World Bank issued a report on global economic development entitled "Reshaping Economic Geography." The report studies the effects and functions of geographic factors in shaping regional development and details the roles played by geography in regional development policies. It pointed out that the global economy was primarily concentrated in large cities, developed regions and rich nations. This concentration of economic driving forces gives rise to the imbalance of development. The implementation of a balanced strategy of development, however, is likely to hinder the development of some wealthy regions. Can unbalanced economic growth coexist with or even complement common prosperity? The reply offered by the report is that the mainstream trend to improve the regional level of development and eliminate the regional economic gap is to reshape economic geography. It means to promote the integration of the regional economy amongst adjacent cities so as to create economic plates that can share internal economic connections and achieve mutual progress while optimising resource allocation on a greater scale and exploring the new development space.

Taking into account the latest research outcomes regarding economic geography and new trade theory, the report puts forward a new multidimensional analytical framework of economic geography. It generalises density, distance and division as the three basic features of economic geography, re-establishing the framework of theory and policy concerning urbanisation, regional development and integration.

First, density should be increased since it is the key step to achieve economic agglomeration. Density refers to the economic aggregate per unit area, reflecting the degree of economic concentration. A region that achieves a greater degree of economic concentration is likely to enjoy better development. There are four recombination approaches to industrial space that aim at improving the output density per unit area. The first features the promotion of the transfer of enterprises. The system advantages of the area extension resulting from the integration of the regional economy should be fully exploited to effectively realise the transfer of enterprises and industry. Then adequate space will be cleared to reshape economic geography. The second approach aims to boost the regional recombination of industries. The division of labour and dislocation of development are both sought at the regional level. During the course of the spread and recombination of the industries, some group companies may be established through merger and acquisition. The control of the market and the monopoly of advanced technology are the most effective methods to realise the value of agglomeration. The third approach is characterised by the agglomeration of the value chain. Enterprises or enterprise groups tend to take full advantage of the use of internal transactions to replace market transactions and evade market risks by exerting the influence of internalisation on the whole value chain of products. Nevertheless, great differences exist regarding the factor intensity and operation environment amongst different links in the value chain. The enterprises decide the division of labour, matching and agglomeration in light of the value chain with the aim of generating an efficient pattern of labour division both amongst the regions and urban and rural areas. The fourth approach focusses on the establishment of strategic industries. Innovative development is not simply equal to technological innovation. It is industrial innovation that should receive greater emphasis. In accordance with the positioning of a region amongst the global and regional divisions of labour, the suitable advanced technology that ought to be promoted intensively should be picked out first. Only if industries achieve a continuous spatial reorganisation with the enterprise groups and only if the regional economy enjoys a relatively strong renewability of industrial structure can the space utilisation efficiency, density and level of economic activities and value creation all be continuously improved.

Second, distance should be minimised to lower transportation costs. Distance here mainly refers to economic/temporal distance. More specifically, distance refers to the distance of commodities, service, labour service, information, etc., from the centre of economic agglomeration. It symbolises the speed of agglomeration, the degree of labour flow and the cost of logistics. Transportation and communications infrastructure are the concrete embodiment of distance. The majority of economic opportunities and value creation tend to concentrate in only a few urban centres, especially those areas with the most consumers. The development conditions in the surrounding areas are of vital importance. The prosperity of a region will benefit its surrounding areas. The benefits are even likely to be enjoyed by such areas that may not have a close geographic link but share the same close integrative system. Chile, a South American country that is geographically removed from global economic centres, is an example. Chile stands out from the surrounding region and leaps over the "middle-income trap," gaining access to the world market through an arrangement of a series of bilateral integration systems. Strengthening business links and shortening distances to developed areas in the surrounding regions are the most effective and feasible means by which the long-term convergence of living standards can be achieved. To shorten the interregional distance is to lower the transaction cost, facilitating enterprise mergers and the deepening of market division and to gain profits from both the economy of scale at the corporate level and the economy of scope from the specialised division of labour at the regional level. There are two ways to shorten the interregional economic distance. One is to improve the transportation infrastructure. Both the geographic separation between the sites of production and consumption and the relative rate between the scale economy and transportation costs of production play a decisive role in the division of labour based on specialisation and the geographic degree of the agglomeration of industries. During the past 20 years, a complete and efficient transportation system has successfully transformed developed regions into a huge market of agglomeration and division of labour based on specialisation. Some regions, however, are out of reach of such an efficient transportation network. Development as a whole is a feature of a modernised society. Thus the regions that do not have access to the transportation network should be given greater attention. The other is to raise the standards of information infrastructure. Information has already been widely recognised as the key factor to boost social development, as well as the foundation on which all significant decisions are made. A blocked information service and the high cost of information have become the common characteristics of all underdeveloped regions. The policies that aim to drive the integration of a regional economy should concentrate on information infrastructure, such as satellite television, the internet and professional search platforms, in order to facilitate market integration and promote the development of underdeveloped regions.

Third, divisions should be reduced to establish a single market. Division here refers to the limiting factors that hinder the international and interregional flow of commodities, capital, personnel and knowledge. Through the implementation of systems and policies to break regional divisions, the intercity, interregional and international division of labour and coordination based on specialisation can be accomplished. There are three ways to reduce regional division. The first is concerned with the regional functional orientation. An ideal orientation is far more important than the persistent pursuit of scale. An accurate functional orientation will give impetus to industrial division, avoid excessive competition and reduce regional division. In addition, a precise functional orientation will result in benefits at the regional scale by virtue of the specialisation of enterprises and the diversity at the regional level. The second approach aims at establishing an extensive information-sharing system. Regional divisions do not necessarily embody themselves in the form of administrative barriers. There are still such phenomena as the barriers between different sectors and regions, redundant construction and overlapping investment that have brought about the rise of development costs while lowering quality. Therefore, an extensive information-sharing system should be established to cover such fields as corporate credits and the testing of products. The third way deals with the promotion of urban integration. As the medium to connect various international economic activities, central cities serve as the centre of concentration for not only regional economic activities but also information, knowledge, technology and public goods. Efforts should be made to enable more regions to enjoy the benefits from the continuous increase of the economic density of the central cities.

The basic factors driving the integration of the regional economy stressed by the World Bank are an effective combination of policies concerned with institutional cooperation, sharing of infrastructure and special incentive methods. To be more specific, institutional cooperation is beneficial to intraregional coordination and the formation of a larger scale economy; the intraregional sharing of infrastructure can achieve the strategic connection between the region and the developed market, leading to lowered transportation costs. Coordinating intervention measures may promote the flow of factors and the convergence of living standards between developed areas and underdeveloped areas within a region. The success of countries that have achieved magnificent economic development shows that, while endeavouring to boost the concentration of production, the government may accelerate the convergence of living standards and thereby achieve common prosperity by implementing policies to support the transfer payment from the exchequer, the construction of infrastructure, the equalisation of public services and the necessary incentives.

8.3.2 The central and peripheral docking

In accordance with the theory of the spatial economy, the study of the concept of space in a regional economy should take into account both the centre and the periphery (i.e. the central cities and the peripheral countryside). The relations between centre and periphery do not simply refer to those between cities and rural areas in a region. The extent of such relations can be extended to refer to those between an urban centre and its surrounding areas in a large region. Cities may be regarded as the development pole or growth pole to drive the economic development of their peripheral areas. The central cities, however, may be treated as the development pole that can promote the development of the peripheral areas by driving the development of the whole region. To establish a close connection between the centre and periphery will be of great benefit to both.

In terms of the centre, its development is considerably reliant on the periphery since the periphery provides it with not only raw materials but also a market. The larger the periphery, the more remarkable the roles that the centre will play. More-over, as a result of the scale economy, there emerge increasingly serious problems in the course of the development of central areas, such as dense population, traffic jams, severe pollution and inadequate resources. Consequently, more and more production sectors, especially the manufacturing industry, will be moved out of central areas and relocated to peripheral areas. The sectors that will stay in the central areas are tertiary industries related to finance, trade and commerce, infor-mation, services and so forth. As the development poles for peripheral areas, these sectors will serve as the centre of the market, finance, information and ser-vices. Obviously, the integration of the central and peripheral economies will form a striking trend. In this case, evaluation of the economic strength of central areas will attach importance to how far and strong the influence of these areas can reach instead of how many industrial sectors can be concentrated in the central areas. In Asia, for example, several centres that possess greater competitiveness all rely on tremendous areas of backland to take the lead in economic develop-ment. South-east Asian countries are the backland of Singapore; the vast areas in South China are the backland of Hong Kong; Shanghai, similarly, takes the Yangtze River Delta as its backland.

As for the periphery, the centre is the development pole that plays a vital role. Central areas will spread capital, technology and information to peripheral areas, providing them with a development shortcut. The gradient of the inter-regional economic gap, to a certain degree, can be illustrated by the intensity of the expansion effect from the central to the peripheral areas. A World Bank report about the Chinese economy, for instance, accounts for the economic gap between the provinces of Jiangsu and Gansu based on their respective distance from Shanghai. As a result, the peripheral areas are supposed to actively seek the development poles that drive local growth, attract and accept the factors that are spread from the central areas, gain access to the market of the central areas and then go into the integrated economic system that is led by the central areas.

The docking between centre and periphery includes systemic and cultural connections. Here the docking roles played by the construction of transportation and communication infrastructure should be particularly stressed. Development economists tend to regard investment in transportation and communication as the initial investment to achieve the economic take-off. Even some areas that are geographically close to industrial centres can fall victim to backwardness simply because they are unable to capture the spread from central areas. Therefore, to emphasise the construction of modern transportation and communications facilities, shorten the temporal and spatial distance between centre and periphery and intensify the expansion effect of the growth poles should be the preconditions on which the development imbalance of both regional and interregional economy can be effectively coordinated.

An ideal docking between centre and periphery depends on the construction of a single market. The significance of the single market to regional economic development lies in the key part played by the integration of the regional market to accelerate the free flow of manufactured goods and factors of production nationwide. In this way, the decisive role played by the market in the allocation of resources will be strengthened to a higher degree and to a larger scale. The regional economic integration of the Yangtze River Delta, for instance, is exactly the equivalent of the market integration in that region.

The modernisation level of a single central city is obviously higher than that of its peripheral countryside. This, however, by no means suggests that the central city has already taken the lead to achieve basic modernisation. Modernisation of central cities requires adequate supplies of such factors as labour that are offered by peripheral areas so as to lower modernisation costs. The supplies and services in such fields as construction, transportation, housekeeping and so forth, for example, will all be offered by the peripheries to the centres at a low cost. If the central areas are isolated from low-cost peripheral supplies, then they will have to pay a much higher price. The centres should attract not only the factors of production from the peripheries but also spread the factors of production to them. In the course of regional modernisation, the limited realisation of business and living conditions that meet the standards of a "modernised society" in the central cities will induce both the population and production factors to concentrate there. With the improvement of the level of concentration, the price of such factors that cannot flow, such as land, will rise; the cost of living will also be on the rise. High housing prices are the typical examples. As a result, the low-level factors will step back and even retreat in the process of factor concentration; the high-level factors, on the contrary, will keep advancing. When the concentration reaches a high standard, the energy of modernisation from the central cities will be spread to peripheral areas, upgrading the original peripheries into potential centres. The low-level factors will then be transferred to marginal areas. The marginal factors that have been "baptised" by modernisation will in turn drive the modernisation of the peripheral areas.

In general, the regions that take the lead in promoting modernisation will have a spillover effect in peripheral areas. The modernisation momentum in southern Jiangsu will be transferred to central and northern Jiangsu in a gradient manner. The cities in central Jiangsu will be integrated into the modernisation process in southern Jiangsu by making full use of their locations. The concept of regional coordination mentioned here is not limited to this sort of natural and objective spillover. The active driving of modernisation from the pioneering regions into the regions that lag behind is of greater significance. In fact, the pioneering regions will definitely encounter two restrictions in the process of modernisation. The first comes from the limited endurance or tolerance of the environment; the second derives from the fact that the energy of economic development is restrained by regional capacity. Further economic development will inevitably worsen the two restrictions and then become the ultimate limit for growth. Therefore, the support given by the pioneering regions to the latecomer regions benefits the self-development of the pioneers. The production bases of manufacturing industries, for example, are moved out of a region while the headquarters, R&D centres, design centres and brands' intellectual property rights are still retained there. While the production bases of manufacturing industries are moved out, the space that has been cleared can be used to develop the service industry, especially the producer services that may extend manufacturing industries to a wider range and the service outsourcing. This may further strengthen and reinforce the central position of the pioneering regions in the process of modernisation.

8.3.3 The construction of a single market

As a key step to drive regional economic integration, regional coordination aims to break down the regional division and reshape the economic geography.

The economic background of regional market divisions is that China is a country with a vast territory; the interregional gap related to economic and social development is striking. Locality has turned into an economic unit. The level of local benefit, which is concerned with the employment rate, residents' income level and the supply capacity of public goods, is closely related to the economic development level of a region. In a sense, localities have been transformed into interest groups; local governments, accordingly, have virtually become the chief representatives of the local interest groups. The economic functions of local government are clearly reflected in the government protection of the local market, resulting in the division of the market. Therefore, a clear definition of the so-called market division is that local governments make use of the administrative functions to protect the local market. It has caused an interregional market division to come into being. The division of the market has two features. Market division aims at protecting the products and services of local enterprises by denying access to the products and services from other localities; local governments intentionally obstruct the entry of outside enterprises, discriminate against their personnel and employees and prevent them from sharing local interests.

The fundamental constraints on local benefits are the shortage of factor supply, as well as the inadequacy of the need for local products and services. The supply of goods outweighs demand. Accordingly, the market division is characterised by protection and monopoly. The exact features of this phenomenon can be summarised as follows: first, to compete actively for the inflow of enterprises, as well as foreign investment, and strictly limit the outflow of the enterprises; second, to compete actively for the inflow of the factors of production and strictly limit their outflow; third, to encourage the outflow of the local products and limit the inflow of the external products; and fourth, to limit competition, especially by offering special protection to the backward local enterprises, as well as local products that are inferior or outright fakes.

Similar to entry into the World Trade Organization, the integration of markets on an international scale depends entirely on the rules. The integration of markets amongst different regions should not only eliminate protective measures taken by local governments but also follow the regulations that the European Union has established to achieve market integration through a series of shared rules. There are five basic regulations. First, various sorts of markets should be open to each other; market transparency should be maintained. Second, the liberalisation of the capital market and financial services should be ensured. The free interregional flow of the capital should be promoted. Third, uniform technical standards should be set in place to eliminate trade barriers with regard to technical standards. Fourth, various certificates of technical qualifications should gain interregional recognition and acceptance. The free flow and employment of the labour force should be supported. Fifth, rules to normalise and regulate entrepreneurial businesses and enterprise operations should be made uniform to lay a solid foundation for interregional business flow and cooperation. The basic requirements of the aforementioned regulations are to establish a uniform interregional policy, lower the "high threshold" (i.e. high transaction costs) in the regions to which production factors will flow and create a single market that allows mutual access to products, the free flow of capital and production factors and the cross-region operation of enterprises. The establishment of a single market will produce such direct results as the reduction of transaction costs, expansion and reallocation of spaces for enterprises, improvement of the enterprise innovation and acquisition of scale economy, scope economy and technology spillover.

With these single-market requirements in mind, the promotion of regional economic integration is mainly concerned with the following three areas.

First, gaps between policies and institutions should be eliminated. For quite a long time, the opening and development of our country were mainly promoted through policies. Unequal policies, such as those for the special economic zones and the coastal open cities, were implemented for different regions and industries. At present, with the deepening of market-oriented reform, the central government tends to gradually abolish such unequal policies. The interregional gap of economic policies, nonetheless, is still rather noticeable. To attract outside enterprises and compete for factors of production, such as capital and skilled labour, many local governments will enact preferential policies in taxes, land use fees, treatment of talented employees and other aspects. These policies seem to lower the business costs for enterprises. The cost to the government, however, is dramatically increased – a total that exceeds the business cost savings realised by enterprises. What is worse, the so-called preferential policies made by local governments are likely to produce unexpected results. In reality, it is the local government instead of the market, for example, that selects and regulates the flow of the production factors and labour. In addition, production factor prices in such a process are not market prices. As a result, to eliminate such obstacles and establish a single market, the creation of unified policies is essential. This should include not only the policies made by the central government that apply to the local governments but also the policies the local governments themselves made to intervene in the market. While making the institutional arrangements, local governments at all levels should intensify mutual coordination and unify their mutual planning with an aim to improve integrated competitiveness. This will not only greatly lower implementation costs arising from the arrangement of each institution, as well as the friction costs amongst these institutional arrangements, but also generate scale and scope economies related to the arrangement and implementation of the institutions.

Second, shared infrastructure should be established. It is necessary to perfect the transportation infrastructure. Ports and airports are the key channels to connect to the outside market. An interconnected, convenient and shared transportation infrastructure of highways, harbours and airports can shorten the distance between developed and underdeveloped regions. In addition, basic facilities for information technology should be improved. The shortage and high cost of information transmission are common features of all poverty-stricken areas. Policies that aim to accelerate the integration of the regional economy should attach great importance to the construction of information infrastructure, such as satellite television, the internet and professional search platforms. The construction of infrastructure aims at not only increasing supply but also boosting the sharing of infrastructure through the construction of interregional information networks, promotion of the communication of information factors and sharing of information and credit system resources, such as electronic government affairs and electronic business. There are two prominent problems at present. On the one hand, there are localities that possess an infrastructure designed to make it tougher for outside enterprises to share. On the other hand, there are also localities that invested in infrastructure construction that should have been shared with another locality. Consequently, the use of the infrastructure of both localities is unable to reach the level of the scale economy. There are two countermeasures to solve this problem of a lack of integration. One argues that local governments should withdraw from the construction and management of key infrastructure projects. If such projects are operated and managed by enterprises instead of local governments, the issue of infrastructure sharing must be proposed and discussed. The other aims at making institutional changes to remove the market division of infrastructure. These systemic changes should enable infrastructure, such as ports, to be integrated and the interregional combination properly implemented.

Third, it is necessary to promote enterprise-centred regional cooperation. After the market plays a decisive role in the allocation of resources, the government's responsibility for regional coordination lies only in providing a modernised external environment for regional development. In comparison, enterprises can play a more significant role. The interregional flow of enterprises can also break the administrative segmentation of the market. Interregional cooperation amongst enterprises should be established on the basis of the industrial chain. The major form to carry forward integration is a combination of interregional distribution and interregional merger and acquisition by enterprises. This will produce cross-region property relations. In reality, the interregional distribution of enterprises refers to the interregional distribution of the headquarters and the production base or marketing systems. As a result, the free flow of production factors amongst enterprises can be realised on a larger scale, especially amongst different regions. The cross-regional flow and combination of production factors promote mutual access and the gradual integration of different regions, giving birth to a regional pattern of the professional division of labour, which is based on the efficient allocation of resources and the maximisation of overall interests. On the other hand, interregional cooperation amongst enterprises is supposed to be set up on the basis of the supply chain. A supply chain is the general cooperation between the upstream and downstream enterprises based on a large-scale division of labour that follows the entire supply chain composed of the raw materials, input, manufacture and sale of commercial goods. At present, on both the national and global levels, competition has been or is being transformed from competition amongst the enterprises located at different links in the same supply chain into a competition amongst different supply chains. Accordingly, the former competitive relationship has been changed into that of cooperation. On this basis, the cooperation amongst the supply chains from different parts of the same region will give a great impetus to the single market. In addition, modern circulation organisations should fully play their roles in unifying the market. Service businesses, such as the modern circulation organisations, can play a role in breaking up market division and creating a single market. While production and consumption can be divided from each other in manufacturing, they should not be divided in the service sector. The entry of the service industry into a locality means that the local market will be fully tapped. These service organisations include such financial institutions as banks and insurance companies, as well as supermarket chains. The interregional distribution and management of these service enterprises may boost the construction of the single market on a wider basis.

Notes

1 Anthony. P. Thirlwall, *Growth and Development*, trans. Jin Bei and Li Yang (Beijing: Renmin University Press, 1992), 122.
2 Gunnar Myrdal, *Asian Drama: An Inquiry into the Poverty of Nations*, trans. Tan Wenmu and Zhang Weidong (Beijing: Beijing College of Economics Press, 1992), 47–8.
3 Gunnar Myrdal, *Economic Theory and Underdeveloped Regions* (London: Duckworth Publishers, 1957), 28.
4 Mao Zedong, *Selected Works of Mao Zedong*, vol. 5 (Beijing: People's Press, 1977), 271.
5 Joseph E. Stiglitz, "The Blueprints for China's Third Generation of Reform," *The Economic Herald*, no. 5 (1999): 3.
6 François Perroux, "The Concept of Growth Poles," in *Selected Classical Essays in Development Economics*, ed. Guo Xibao (Beijing: China Economy Press, 1998), 335.

9 Investment-driven growth and financial development

Capital is an important determinant of economic growth, and it can play a decisive role in the economic take-off stage. In general, the current Chinese economy is in the stage of capital investment growth. In the process of seeking economic growth, China has increasingly experienced the "bottleneck" of inadequate funding. When the economy is overheated, there is a serious shortage of funds; when the economy cools down and the market is weak, the funds are also seriously insufficient. The accumulation and raising of capital have become major theoretical and practical issues in China's economic development.

9.1 An investment-driven economy

9.1.1 The first driving force of economic growth

The first or continuing driver of economic growth is investment. This is proven by the Harrod-Domar model, which was deduced by Harrod in the United Kingdom, as well as by Domar in the United States. The basic equation of the model is:

$$G = S / K.$$

G is the economic growth rate; S is the savings rate, while K stands for the capital-output ratio.

The Harrod-Domar model, on its own, studies economic growth in developed countries, but it also has important implications for developing nations.

- First, the model emphasises the role and significance of savings and investment in economic development. For developing nations that lack funds, raising savings and investment levels plays a significant role in promoting economic development.
- Second, the model objectively describes the relationship between capital-output ratios and economic growth rates. If returns on investment decline, the investment needed for each output unit will increase. If the investment increases, it will offset the increase in economic growth.

- Third, the model illustrates the role of investment in economic growth and ignores the enormous role that technological progress plays in the growth. This reflects the characteristics of the early stage of economic development.

When the economy is in an investment-driven stage, this model can be used to determine what kind of savings rate and capital-output ratio are needed to achieve a certain growth rate.

Walt W. Rostow's take-off theory points out that one of the three conditions for achieving an economic take-off is a sufficiently high investment rate. He held that an economic take-off can be achieved when productive investment increases from 5% of the net national output to more than 10%.

The big push theory put forward by Rosenstein-Rodan further pointed out the role of major investment in the economic growth of developing nations. This theory proposes that a "bit by bit" investment programme will not impact economic growth as much as is required. Only if the investment reaches a certain scale and a big push model is adopted will the goal of sustained growth be realised. It means the accumulation of funds must reach a sufficient scale. There exist three indivisibilities. First is the indivisibility of connections amongst various industrial sectors. The industrialisation scale must be large enough. Therefore, in the process of industrialisation, major investment is required to promote the industrialisation of various sectors at large. Second are the indivisibilities of investment. The precondition for economic development is a large amount of social and public investment, such as investment in power, transport and other basic construction programmes. Investment in infrastructure has long gestation periods and requires large amounts of capital. It must be invested in on a large scale and cannot produce production capacity without reaching that minimum scale. For instance, a port or a road cannot be left half-built; otherwise, it cannot be used. Similar programmes of the kind require large-scale investments. Third is the indivisibility of demand. Various industries are interdependent. If an investment is concentrated in only one sector or industry with no guaranteed domestic or international market demand, there will be a market bottleneck. To form a large market, we must have large-scale investment in all sectors. Developing countries usually have two characteristics. First, there is no perfect market information system dealing with key points, such as price, cost, interest rate or stock price. Therefore, potential investors cannot expect others' investments and should not hesitate to act because they cannot expect to know whether the market is large enough and worth investing in. Second, there is the lack of necessary infrastructure, which makes other investments uneconomical. This is an initial obstacle to launching economic growth. Without an overall boost of comprehensive investment, this obstacle cannot be overcome. Launching the economy of a country is a little like getting an airplane off the ground. There is a critical ground speed which must be reached before the craft can be airborne.

The previous theories illustrate the interrelationship of savings, capital and growth, which turns out to be far more complex and cannot be absolutely understood. Hirschman also points out that the Harrod-Dorma model should be treated differently in developed and underdeveloped countries. First, in advanced economies, savings and investment decisions are independent of one another to a substantial extent; income per capita is an important determinant of the supply of savings. Therefore, the equality between savings and investment is an equilibrium. In an underdeveloped economy, however, investment and savings decisions are largely interdependent. At the same time, additions to savings depend far more on the opening of investment opportunities and on the removal of various obstacles to investment activity than on increased income. Second, the capital-output ratio may on the whole be considered a technological coefficient in developed countries where during any period a variety of projects with some kind of balanced distribution of capital coefficients will emerge. This is far less certain in underdeveloped nations where "normal" productivity is often held back by shortages and bottlenecks. Therefore, Hirschman believes that a model based on the propensity to save and on capital-output ratio does not really tell us much about the key mechanisms through which economic progress gets under way and is carried forward in a backward environment.[1] The practice of economic growth in China also illustrates this model's limitations as follows:

- First, investment is not linear with economic growth. The increase in investment does not necessarily lead to an increase in production capacity, particularly in sectors with low output rates. Even if the production capacity increases, it does not necessarily increase output, which is the case for unused capacity. Moreover, savings is not linear with an increase in investment either. Savings do not necessarily lead to any incentive to invest domestically. Obviously, economic growth cannot simply depend on investment.
- Next, low income does not necessarily mean there would not be a high investment rate and high economic growth rate. For example, for many years, China has had a high accumulation rate, huge market purchasing power, a prosperous investment demand and a high economic growth rate. The explanation: high accumulation and low consumption policies are implemented in allocating national income, and the expansion of credit brought about the expansion of market demand, which promotes rapid economic growth for a time. However, such high accumulation and high growth without an effective supply will eventually lead to serious inflation. It in turn will require a mandatory "forced drop" of the economic growth rate.

In general, the level of accumulation in a country depends on the level of income. However, the level of income is not the only factor that determines the accumulation. The accumulation of funds in many developing nations is not entirely based on the level of economic development but on the system and policies in place. China once relied on centralised planning to keep up the funds and maintain a high rate of accumulation. It is very difficult to continue to raise the accumulation rate now, but it does not mean that there is no potential for accumulation. The key is to increase the benefits of accumulation.

The accumulative benefits mentioned here are not what people generally refer to as return on investment but rather the costs of accumulating each unit of funds – that is, the funds accumulated to pay for the accumulated costs of each unit. It involves a comparison between accumulated costs and accumulated funds. Fundraising is necessary to pay the price of such factors as the sacrifice of consumption, the cost of the accumulation process itself, the public's complaints and so on. Kalecki, a Polish economist, used a boycott coefficient to measure the public's response to increasing accumulation and reducing consumption. He then compared the returns of the economic growth resulting from accumulation with the short-term cost of sacrificing consumption to determine the boundaries of the effective benefits. If we use the concept of social marginal cost to express the cost of fundraising, then only when the marginal benefit of the funds is greater than the social marginal cost of fundraising does it become reasonable to increase the total amount of development funds through accumulation. Therefore, the choice of the accumulation rate, mode and mechanism is not arbitrary, and they should all be aligned with the goal of accumulating benefits.

The formation of the accumulation rate itself entails a certain kind of welfare evaluation criteria. In general, an increase in the accumulation rate means a reduction of the current share of consumption and an increase in the level of future consumption. The social welfare goal is to trade higher consumption levels in the future for the sacrifice of current consumption. In addition, the evaluation of cumulative benefits involves the issue of whether the costs paid for accumulation can be compensated. If the accumulation is too low and economic growth is slow, then the employment problem would become difficult to solve, making it impossible to satisfy people's current consumption. Although the accumulation rate is not high, the social cost is very high. If the accumulation rate is too high, despite the possible higher economic growth rate, the high-speed growth and low public consumption will cause the industrial structure to become unbalanced, and the consequent complaints and conflicts will not necessarily be compensated. In particular, the ups and downs of economic fluctuations caused by high accumulation cannot compensate for the huge losses caused to the entire national economy. This raises the question of seeking a modest and optimal accumulation rate according to the goal of accumulating benefits. It means seeking the kind of accumulation rate that can fully mobilise all available production resources and maximise the people's current and future consumption levels so as to ensure the sustained, healthy and rapid development of the national economy.

9.1.2 Investment demand and the gap of economic growth

Building on Keynes's belief in macroscopic equilibrium that savings are equal to investment, Harrod proposed the concept of balanced growth rate. It refers to the growth rate achieved when savings and investment are in equilibrium. The growth rate at this time has not only achieved the level of effective demand for full employment but also enabled the full use of the productive capacity. There is neither unemployment nor inflation in reality. The possibility of achieving such an equilibrium of the growth rate, in reality, is as narrow as the "knife blade."

Based on the macroscopic equilibrium that savings are equal to investment, to study the investment demand of developing nations and its macroeconomic impact requires consideration of two different scenarios:

- First, savings are larger than investment: saving > investment. This refers to insufficient investment demand. That is, investment is insufficient to mobilise the unused resources to achieve full employment. The shortage of funds here lies in excessive savings, which cannot be turned into investment.
- Second, savings are less than investment: saving < investment. This refers to the shortage of funds caused by insufficient savings, and the full conversion of savings into investment does not meet investment needs.

The second situation tends to be common in developing nations where there is always a strong investment demand. The first situation occurs mainly when stringent macroeconomic regulations intervene.

On the whole, developing nations will have strong funding needs as long as they enter the development rather than the stagnation stage. On the one hand, industrialisation requires the accumulation of sufficient funds for the development of manufacturing industries and related infrastructures. They need large amounts of capital and have long gestation periods. On the other hand, urbanisation needs to provide sufficient urban facilities for rural migrants to cities. To be the centre of modernisation, cities need to build modern facilities and develop modern service industries, all of which require sufficient capital investment. In addition, the course of high-tech industrialisation requires sufficient venture capital investment for the research and incubation on which scientific and technological enterprises depend.

In need of large amounts of capital, developing nations must strive to adopt effective mechanisms to mobilise people's savings to achieve rapid economic growth. For a long time, China's high accumulation rate has been based on the demographic dividend, the transfer of surplus agricultural labour and the long-running implementation of low-income policies. They all contribute to high accumulation on the basis of low per capita GDP. When China enters the middle-income stage of development and the socialist market economy system is fully implemented, the previous high-accumulation/high-savings mechanism will no longer exist. For this reason, it is necessary to seek new mechanisms for mobilising accumulation. What differs from the past is that we must make full use of market mechanisms to mobilise the voluntary accumulation of both enterprises and individuals.

With an open economy, the economic growth rate can be supported by not only domestic accumulation but also savings from overseas. In other words, the domestic funds gap can be closed by the introduction of foreign capital. Development economist Hollis B. Chenery and others used the "two-gap" model to illustrate the significance of developing nations' utilisation of foreign capital. The growth rate in developing nations generally is constrained by gaps in foreign exchange and savings. A savings gap is a situation where savings are insufficient to meet the investment demand. A foreign exchange gap means the current account deficit is greater than the value of a country's capital inflows. If the inflow of foreign capital is used well, it can balance the two gaps at the same time. For example, developing nations can accept foreign investment in the form of machinery or other equipment. These imports do not require corresponding exports to offset, nor does this investment require the use of domestic savings. For our country, establishing a mechanism for the effective introduction and utilisation of foreign capital will enable China's economy to grow faster without relying entirely on domestic savings.

The serious shortage of development funds in developing nations is not necessarily the result of an insufficient supply; rather, it is a product of systemic flaws that can be overcome by finance mechanisms. Under the modern credit system, when there is a difference or a gap between real accumulation and investment demand (i.e. savings are more than investments), banking credit can be used to fill the gap. Further, when bank deposits are less than loans, the gap between the two can be filled by issuing additional funds. People often think that banking credit has played an accumulating role here, causing an illusion where it seems that the shortage of funds is not caused by insufficient accumulation but by insufficient funds issued by banks. As a result, the pressure for funding shortages shifts from real accumulation to credit. Under the traditional system, budget constraints on fiscal and banking credit are "soft." It shows the phenomenon explained by Kornal:

> It is real investment that plays a primary role. The financial resources from which the real investment activity can be financed will automatically be created by monetary factors or changes in income distribution. But it is certainly true for a socialist economy that real investment is the primary factor while the availability of finance is a secondary phenomenon.[2]

Kornai is half right here. At a first glance, the availability of funds is derivative, but in the ultimate sense, investment needs cannot be separated from the real accumulation. When there is a gap between accumulation and investment, the increased supply of funds from fiscal deficits and banking credit can temporarily fill the gap of under-accumulation, but such post-compulsory accumulation cannot be said to be real accumulation. Only when additional money can boost incomes and be transformed into accumulation can we fill the gap with real accumulation. Otherwise, the inflationary pressure generated by the additional currency will interrupt the economic growth process. This is the reason China has experienced frequent economic ups and downs. When the economy is overheated, the investment demand cannot be met, which results in shortages of funds. Responding to the signal of a shortage of funds, currency is issued in large amounts. As a result, the expanded supply of funds exceeds the potential demand, and the supply of production factors and material resources becomes extremely tight; there appears a "bottleneck" in economic growth. When the economy contracts, the shortage of funds is caused by financial and credit constraints. What is tight now is the supply of unreal accumulation of funds provided by the banking credit. Its purpose is to forcefully balance the excessive investment demand with real accumulation. Against such a background, giving up "double tightening" should not be the solution to the shortage of funds but rather to make structural adjustments to the fund stock.

In fact, banking credit is not real accumulation. When there is a gap between savings and investment, banking credit temporarily fills the gap of insufficient savings, yet the gap still exists. Only when the increase of banking credit leads to an increase in profits, which in turn leads to an increase in savings, can the gap really be filled. This means accumulating funds by increasing banking credit. First, unused resources caused by insufficient funds can be mobilised by increasing banking credit. Second, most funds in a state of sluggishness caused by overstocked raw materials, finished products and arrears of funds can be mobilised by increasing banking credit. In both cases, banking credit can actually play a role in creating funds.

The essential difference between the use of credit to provide funds and the use of profits to provide funds is that the former has a direct effect on price and income distribution. Increased credit and money supply will directly cause prices to rise, creating inflationary pressures and causing redistribution of income. In the case of inflation caused by the increase in credit, if there is no increase in profits, there will be no increase in real capital accumulation. Inflation will then run out of control. In other words, although it is possible to accumulate some funds in the short term and achieve short-term prosperity, implementation of inflationary policies will pay a high price. Therefore, the accumulation of funds through increasing banking credit should be managed with caution. Development economists do not generally recommend this kind of policy.

Although we should remain cautious when issuing banking credit through the aforementioned method, it does not mean that banking credit should not play an active role in promoting the accumulation of funds. The financial system and economic development go hand in hand. A sound financial system can effectively mobilise social savings and put them into production, thus promoting economic growth and development. With economic development, the increase in people's income and demand for financial services have stimulated the development of the financial system. This virtuous cycle is undoubtedly of great importance to economic development in developing nations. In the past, China maintaining a high accumulation rate, mainly relying on the centralised financial distribution. In the future, in line with the establishment of a market economy system, traditional accumulation functions will be weakened, and the financial mechanism should be strengthened. This means it is time to reform and improve the financial mechanism and enhance its accumulation functions.

9.2 Deepening financial reform and development

The financial problems faced by developing nations not only involve capital accumulation but also face the issues of fund flow and allocation, as well as fund accommodation and operation. This is a financial issue. An important aspect of economic backwardness in developing nations is the backwardness of the financial system. To realise economic modernisation, financial modernisation must be dealt with first.

9.2.1   Development functions of finance

After China fully turned to a market economy, the market has come to play a decisive role in resource allocation. Faced with increasing numbers of decentralised social and economic activities, resource allocation will be mainly carried out through the financial mechanism. Correspondingly, finance will play a more and more significant role in social and economic activities.

Marx long noted in his *On Capital* that the modern market economy is a credit economy. All relations in the production process were based on credit. Finance plays roles as follows:

- First, credit and competition are leverages for capital accumulation.
- Second, the greater mobility of capital makes it easier for it to flow across geographic regions and amongst industries. The premise is that the development of the credit system has aggregated a large amount of scattered and available capital.
- Third, credit brings about the expansion of social production and markets and moves production across the world.
- Fourth, the credit system has strengthened the production process to the limit, thereby making the credit system a major lever for overproduction and excessive commercial speculation.
- Fifth, the development of speculation and credit has also opened up hundreds of sources of sudden wealth.

One situation is that "capital is transferred in the form of credit to the commander of the large industrial sectors." In another case, "large amounts of scattered small capital are forced to take the risky path: speculation, credit fraud, stock speculation and crisis."[3]

According to the analysis by Professor Robert C. Merton, a representative of American functional finance, the financial system performs six basic functions:

- First, it provides ways of clearing and settling payments to facilitate the exchange of goods, services and assets. An effective payment system is a necessary condition for social transactions. The advanced exchange systems can reduce social transaction costs and promote the development of social specialisation.
- Second, it provides a mechanism for financing. A financial system provides a mechanism for finance, including mobilising savings and providing liquidity. The main advantage of mobilising savings through financial markets and banking intermediaries is that they can diversify the risks of individual investments and provide relatively high returns for investors, as opposed to physical assets, such as durable consumer goods. The mobilisation of savings in the financial system can combine decentralised social resources,

thereby exerting the scale effect of resources. The liquidity services provided by the financial system have effectively solved the problem of capital sources for long-term investment, providing opportunities for long-term project investment and corporate equity financing. At the same time, it created channels for capital supply for technological progress and venture capital investment.

- Third, it provides ways for allocating resources. A financial system provides ways and a mechanism to transfer economic resources through time, across geographic regions and amongst industries. Modern society is full of uncertainty. It is difficult for individual investors to assess a company, a manager and market conditions. The strength of a financial system lies in providing investors with intermediary services and providing a mechanism to share risks with investors. It can thus make the investment allocation of social capital more efficient. At the same time, the financial system provides various mechanisms for pooling funds and investing in large-scale and indivisible investment projects. It also divides large-scale investment projects into small shares so that small and medium investors can participate as investors.
- Fourth, it provides ways for managing risks. It is possible for the financial system to price and trade the uncertainty or risks of medium- and long-term capital investment, forming a risk-sharing mechanism. Because of the lack of information and transaction costs, the financial system and institutions can play a part in trading, diversifying and transferring risks. If there is no mechanism for trading, transferring and offsetting social risks, the social economy cannot proceed smoothly.
- Fifth, it provides incentives. A financial system provides incentives when one party to a financial transaction has information the other does not have or when one party is an agent of another. In such a case, the incentives provided by the financial system are stocks or stock options. By allowing enterprise managers and employees to hold enterprise stocks or stock options and connecting the two sides' interests, managers and employees can do their best to improve the performance of their enterprise. Because they hold the same stocks, there are no conflicting interests for one party to serve as an agent of the other.
- Sixth, it helps to gain information. A financial system not only provides information on the prices of various investment products and factors that affect these prices for investors, but also information on the costs of different financing methods. Additionally, management can obtain information on whether the financial transactions are normal and follow rules and regulations. It thus helps different participants in the financial system make their decisions.

To sum up, the aforementioned functions of finance are particularly important to economic development in developing nations. These functions fill the gap between savings and investment, stimulate economic development and further promotes the accumulation of social capital. Combined savings are effectively allocated amongst various investment projects, thereby improving the efficiency of investment. With the precondition that the total amount of funds has been set up, the more active the financial activities are, the more efficient the use of funds will be because competition will ensure that funds flow to industries and regions with low investment risk, a short payback period and high profitability. Moreover, a well-functioning financial system can play a role in transferring and distributing risks. All economic activities have certain risks. A well-functioning financial system will provide a variety of financial instruments with different degrees of risk. The result is that risks are minimised. Of course, financial institutions are also powerless when there are risks caused by natural disasters or the worldwide economic recession.

In reality, the backwardness of developing nations' economies is largely a result of financial backwardness. To develop and improve the financial system is a primary strategy in the transformation and growth of developing nations towards modernisation.

9.2.2 Progressing from financial repression to financial development

A backward financial system in nations in the early stage of their development is reflected in a low currency degree (i.e. the proportion of currency transactions used in GNP is small), insufficient markets, particularly underdeveloped capital markets and insufficient financial institutions. It is also the government that regulates interest rates and exchange rates. Underdeveloped financial institutions and other institutional obstacles have limited financial accumulation and use of monetary policies. The reason is the systemic intervention syndrome. In the course of economic development, developing nations often fail to give full attention to the role of market mechanisms and carry out excessive administrative intervention in all areas of economic activities. This type of intervention in the financial sector is characterised by strict controls on funds, mandatory regulations and control of interest rates, especially deposit rates, and exchange rates which are kept below market equilibrium levels. The low interest rates suppress savings, and the low exchange rates (overvalued local currency values) suppress exports, which ultimately inhibit economic development and form what is known as "financial repression."

The interest and exchange rates stipulated by the governments of developing nations cannot truly reflect market supply and demand. They increase the cost of bank loans, severely curb the role of financial intermediaries and seriously dampen the enthusiasm for saving. The flow of funds is not subject to relative prices such as interest rates. When selecting possible investments, people do not base their decisions on the trade-offs between different investment profit margins and social returns but on subjective and contingent factors. In the face of low interest rates, people have a strong demand for funds while there is a serious shortage of funds. Under such circumstances, loans can only take the form of allocations, such as rationing, which inevitably leads to unfair distribution of funds and lack of efficiency. In addition, unemployment in developing nations is partly due to the repression of financial activities. Insufficient savings cannot provide sufficient employment for the labour force. Further, low interest rates are compounded with relatively high minimum wage levels. Against the background of a shortage of funds and an abundant labour force, employers are more willing to use funds, thus worsening already serious unemployment and underemployment.

If developing nations want to achieve economic growth, they can only succeed through thorough financial reforms. This means developing nations must abandon their excessive administrative interventions in the financial system and financial markets, free the control of interest and exchange rates and allow them to fully reflect the supply and demand of funds and foreign currency. Developing nations must make full use of market mechanisms, thereby enabling the financial system, especially the banking system, to attract large amounts of savings at an appropriate interest rate. Meanwhile, it should also meet the demand for funds from various sectors of the national economy at an appropriate interest rate. It will thus expand the financial system itself and promote economic growth through the intermediary role of that system. This is the famous concept of "financial deepening."[4]

There are two criteria for measuring financial deepening: one is to use quantity as a measure. This means that financial deepening is examined from the perspective of the stock, the flow of financial assets, the number and size of financial institutions, the type and quantity of financial assets and the price of financial assets. As Edward S. Show points out, "Financial deepening is the faster growth of financial assets relative to real wealth." Ronald Ian McKinnon uses the M2/GNP model to measure the level of financial deepening to assess the real effect of a country's strategy to eliminate financial repression. With regard to the real effect of the strategy, Goldsmith mainly uses financial correlation rate indicators – namely, the ratio of financial assets to GNP – to show the degree of financial development. These quantitative indicators reflect the scale of financial development in a country. Another is using quality as a measure. It examines whether financial mechanisms are complete and mature, the setting of financial institutions is optimised, financial assets are complete and financial markets are advanced. To put it simply, there are two major standards in measuring financial deepening at an appropriate interest rate: quality and efficiency standards. Without taking these two criteria into consideration, the expansion of the financial industry and the increase in financial assets will not necessarily mean that financial deepening has reached a considerable level.

In general, the aforementioned standards for financial deepening have been met, but the achievements in financial reform are basically confined to extension and quantity. They need to be further developed in terms of connotative financial operating mechanisms and efficiency.

9.2.3 Financial modernisation

Despite the fact that the financial system of developing nations is lagging behind that of the developed countries, the financial deepening proposed by McKinnon and Shaw in the 1970s cannot remain in the context of economic globalisation. The modern economy is expressed in credit and capital securitisation, which constitutes the major components of developing modern finance. Through the lens of financial functions, Jiang Wang, a professor at MIT, proposed the idea of reforming China's financial system. Although banks mainly provide a payment system and credit, with the development of financial technology and the widespread use of credit cards, they play an increasingly less important role. With regard to providing credit, banks also play a role in pooling the savings of households into a profitable return on a kind of short-term and highly liquid investment. Long-term and highly liquid investments can be made through investment banks and securities markets.[5] The development of various types of mutual funds aims to provide people with a clear risk and return mechanism. Avoiding taking risks, they can invest their money in money market funds that invest in short-term treasury bonds. If they want to take risks for greater returns, they can invest more in stocks or stock-based funds. In developed countries, people now increasingly invest in mutual funds, treasury bonds, pension funds, insurance policies and stocks. The role of the bank is significantly weakened. Based on the general concepts for the development of modern finance, financial deepening in China has not really been completed and should be further promoted from the perspective of financial modernisation.

- First, it is necessary to deepen the financial system. At present, several major banks in China have become specialised state-controlled commercial banks through listings and other means, as well as leading banks in the world. Meanwhile, a number of other commercial banks and financial institutions have been developed. The existing financial repression problems are as follows. Banks generally lack the capacity for financial innovation, but that is precisely what the modern economy needs most. Different ownership enterprises cannot have access to financing sources equally. Non-state-owned enterprises are subject to significant loan discrimination.[6] The financial system is responsible for these situations. For one thing, there is an obvious monopoly of large banks; for another, the state has very strict administrative control over banks. To get rid of such financial repression for the good of China's economic development, we must meet the requirements of the market economy and reform the financial system. It is necessary to develop financial institutions with all kinds of ownership and, in particular, to allow qualified private enterprises to own banks and other financial institutions. It is also necessary to separate policy banks from market-operating banks and to promote the commercialisation of specialised banks through strict budget constraints and enterprise-oriented management. On this basis, a financial market with commercial banks as the main body will be cultivated and developed.
- Second, it is necessary to deepen bank interest rates. Government control of bank interest rates distorts the regulatory function of interest rates. When the official interest rate is lower than the equilibrium interest rate, the balance will lead to a series of misconceptions about the accumulation and flow of funds. (1) When bank financing becomes the main channel for funds, the official low interest rate encourages the use of funds but not savings, thus artificially creating financial constraint. (2) The balance, caused by the situation when the official interest rate is lower than the equilibrium interest rate, will create a "rent phenomenon" for the bank to "seek rent" when lending

at the official interest rate, resulting in corruption. (3) When official interest rates are low, a bank is not profitable, and large amounts of funds flowing out of the bank are priced at the official interest rate, causing the external circulation of funds (shadow banks). This not only raises financing costs but also causes the flow of funds to run out of control. The way to change this situation is to liberalise the administrative control of interest rates and accelerate the marketisation of bank interest rates so as to accurately reflect and regulate the supply and demand for funds. Of course, the liberalisation of interest rates must be synchronised with the development of financial markets.

- Third, it is necessary to deepen financial markets. Compatible with direct and indirect finance, a country's financial system includes both banks and financial markets. Since China has long focussed on banks, the financial market is highly immature. This is shown as follows. (1) The amount of funds entering the financial market is very small, which hinders the circulation of funds. (2) Financial instruments (assets) circulated in the financial market are monotonous and not standardised, especially the stocks, bonds and insurance policies that can be used for long-term investment; the total available for investment is small, and the proportion of financial assets that can be traded in the secondary market is even smaller. (3) Financial markets are lacking in specifications and are overly segmented. (4) Bank assets have limited liability structure. They are concentrated on loans and the loans are limited to credit loans. Because of excessive governmental intervention, corporate budget constraints are too soft, and bank loans often fail to generate returns, resulting in a large number of bad debts and dead accounts. Corporate bankruptcies are often the bankruptcy of banks. All this indicates that the degree of marketisation of China's financial assets as a whole has been low and lagged behind the marketisation of other factors, resulting in a lack of effective market regulation in the accumulation, flow, accommodation and allocation of funds. Financial markets are important for providing platforms and mechanisms for direct financing so that the financial risks that may arise are directly borne by investors, unlike banks where the risks are borne by society. Therefore, it is important to accelerate the construction of financial markets in order to realise financial deepening. To reach such goals, we need to accelerate the commercialisation of specialised banks, expand direct finance and establish and cultivate money market short-term funds and capital market long-term funds. We also need to develop a variety of financial instruments and expand the variety and quantity of financial assets circulated in the markets. In addition, it is necessary to break the segmentation of the financial market and establish an open and single financial market. Finally, we should establish the necessary competition norms and ensure orderly competition in financial markets.
- Fourth, it is necessary to deepen the insurance market. Modern economics not only views finance as a mechanism for allocating resources but also as a risk allocation mechanism. Financial instruments are instruments with different levels of risk. Choosing financial instruments is taking risks, such as

entering a bank to select different savings accounts or loans of different terms or entering the capital market to select different stocks. Finance also provides insurance tools which require financial innovation. Robert Shiller, a 2013 Nobel Prize Laureate in economics, puts forward six modern insurances in his book *The New Financial Order*. They include livelihood insurance related to the livelihood risks of clients, covering unemployment and real estate insurance related to real estate value. They also include macro-markets insurance related to macroeconomic fluctuation risks, income-linked loan insurance related to risks of future income changes, inequity insurance related to risks of future income inequality, intergenerational social security insurance related to risks of intergenerational income inequity (sustainable development) and international agreement insurance related to risks of national economy.[7] According to Shiller's definition, the above six types of insurance are varied. Some are commercial insurance provided by the financial system, some rely on the financial market while others rely on governmental protection. They can also be called lock-in risks or spread risks. Shiller's ideas for a new financial order are worth studying and considering. First, the real world is full of risks. In relying on existing insurance mechanisms, there are many risks that cannot be resolved and dispersed. Thus Shiller proposed the idea of establishing an insurance-centred financial order. Economic security is a primary precondition. In addition, long-term economic risks are actually borne by individuals and families. The poor and the elderly cannot control these risks, however. Shiller's new financial order gives a priority to providing insurance for these disadvantaged groups and "bringing the advantages enjoyed by the clients of the Wall Street to the customers of Wal-Mart." It means that the focus of solving inequality issues is on low- and middle-income groups. While income inequality is normal, how to provide insurance for low-income groups is the key.

9.3 Venture capital and financial technology

Financial technology advancement and innovation are important supports for accelerating the transformation of economic development modes. In terms of innovation investment mechanisms, government investment alone is not enough. Social investment must be mobilised to promote the combination of science and technology with finance and to cultivate and develop venture capital investment. At present, financial technology needs to be cultivated in China, which requires a series of institutional arrangements.

9.3.1 Scientific and technological innovation and financial technology

Eventually, economic growth shifts from the input of material resources to the innovation-driven development. While it can save material inputs, such as material resources and environmental resources, it cannot save capital investment. Scientific and technological innovation requires sufficient capital investment, as well as a deep cooperation of science, technology and finance to cultivate and develop financial technology.

The core of the innovation-driven economic development is innovation in science and technology, which has obvious uncertainties. There are two distinguishing characteristics of innovation investment. The first is a long gestation period. For instance, the invention of a biomedicine has to go through a long period of time from scientific discovery to clinical use, during which continuous investment is still needed. Second is the uncertainty of return on investment. Whether new ideas can be developed into new technologies is always a matter of great uncertainty; there are also great uncertainties about whether new technologies and their products will be accepted by the market. Uncertainty in innovation results in investment risks. Because of worry about risks, people are often discouraged from investing in innovation, which leads to insufficient investment in innovation. This is the crux of the challenge: finance is difficult to find to explore the frontiers of scientific and technological innovation.

Financial technology has its own fields and functions. It is an activity in which financial capital uses scientific and technological innovation to incubate new technologies and technology enterprises and then promote financial activities oriented towards high-tech industrialisation. By analysing the innovation-driven economy's demand for finance and financial innovation, commercial banks and financial institutions become the main participants in financial technology. This constitutes an important aspect of financial innovation.

Drawing on the history of financial innovation, finance is continuously innovating together with the development of science, technology and the economy. Every science-technology and industrial revolution will drive financial innovation and lead to explosive growth in financial wealth. In the era of industrialisation, the combination of bank and industrial capital produces financial capital. In the information age, finance is also combined with information to produce electronic banking and electronic money. At present, the combination of finance, science and technology to create financial technology is a product of the ongoing technological and industrial revolution. Technological innovation not only generates industrial wealth but also brings about financial wealth. When finance participates in scientific and technological innovation actively, it will be able to share the latest developments, profit from them and accumulate financial wealth. For example, the NASDAQ stock market established in America in 1971 is derived from the rise of the information and services industry. Therefore, it is inevitable to combine financial capital, science and technology to promote financial technology.

In general, technological innovation is based on the technological progress of enterprises, which are the main source of innovation and investment. The funds needed for an enterprise's innovation can be fully covered by the company's entry into the market. The innovation discussed earlier is that of scientific and technological innovation based on new scientific discoveries. It involves multiple aspects like production, education and research. From the creation of new ideas to the incubation of new technologies and the application of production to the market, investment is required for every phase. This means that innovation investment cannot be solved by a single entity; multiple investment entities need to be mobilised, particularly in the early stages of innovation.

Risk-return comparisons at various stages of investment can be made by using the approaches of information economics. In terms of risk level, the closer the stage of innovation investment is to the market, the more complete the information and the less risky. The farther away from the market, the less complete the information, the worse the risk. As far as the potential returns on investment are concerned, the closer to the market, the more intense the competition and the smaller the potential earnings are. The farther away from the market, the less intense the competition and the greater the potential revenue. To sum up, the risks and returns of innovation investment at all stages of the process of scientific and technological innovation are equal.

If we further classify the potential returns associated with innovation investment as social and individual returns, the earlier the stage of innovation investment is, the clearer the social returns are. It is difficult for individual investors to benefit from the returns associated with innovation in the earlier stages. This is the common wisdom about the spillover effect of innovation achievements. The later the stage of investment in innovation is, the clearer the individual returns of innovation achievements are. It means innovation returns can be beneficial to individual investors in the later stages. The individual investors mentioned here include enterprise investors. The analysis of general investment behaviours shows that cutting-edge science and technology innovation is the stage of knowledge innovation and the source of scientific and technological innovation. Investment at this stage draws attention to general health and happiness. Undoubtedly, fiscal capital from the government constitutes the investment entity in these earliest stages. In the later stages of innovation, when the products of innovation enter the market, financial capital will be actively invested, and market-oriented and individual investment income will play a clear role. However, the stage when new ideas and discoveries that are hatched into new technologies requires the largest amount of funds is precisely the stage when capital investment is seriously insufficient. The reason is that at this stage of innovation, on the one hand, innovation returns begin to benefit individual investors, so the government can no longer make major investments. On the other hand, this stage is far from the market and has high risks. Individual investors have risk aversion and are therefore reluctant to invest. This stage of scientific and technological innovation is a stage that requires financial technology. It needs to guide sufficient financial capital investment in the earlier stages of innovation, especially that of the incubation of new technologies.

When financial technology enters the early stages of scientific and technological innovation, different measures will be taken to promote financial innovation. When new technologies and new products are being incubated, there can be many projects based on a certain scientific discovery that are scattered over a variety of fields. The success rate is low. In those fields where the application of the new knowledge is successful, profits are very high. So-called angel investment is the term applied to the venture capital that backs this process. The term "angel" refers to the first investors who provide money for innovative start-ups before the birth of new technologies and products. Although the funding from angel investors is small, it plays a key role in promoting technological innovation and start-ups. Many new technologies and products benefit from angel investors. This can be viewed as a form of financial technology. However, because innovation projects are often scattered across many fields, it is not sufficient to rely simply on angel investors for funding. This raises the question of how to provide aggregated business incubators. The main task is to provide an optimised incubation environment and conditions for the transformation of high-tech industries and innovation by science and technology enterprises. Because business incubators are shared by and benefit society, incubator investment requires the government to provide some funding or governmental support. At the same time, programmes aimed at incubating new technology are market-oriented and their investment income is also market-oriented. Thus enterprises are welcome to participate in incubator investment, which also requires the involvement of financial technology.

To apply innovative achievements to technological entrepreneurship means new technologies and products freshly financed by incubators are used in the entrepreneurial stage. Enterprises at this time either apply new breakthroughs to production or adopt new technologies to produce new products. What is needed at this time is investment in entrepreneurship. Entrepreneurship is generally supported by venture capital companies. As Knight pointed out,

> In the modern economy, the separation between the establishment of new enterprises and the operation of the enterprise afterwards is very clear. The purpose of some investors in establishing an enterprise is to get profit from the normal operations of the enterprise. More people expect to make profits from the sale of newly established enterprises, and then use the capital for new venture capital activities.

In the modern economy, although there is uncertainty in venture capital, "a large and increasing number of individuals and public enterprises have not spared their efforts on the establishment of new enterprises."[8] In reality, many manufacturers also expand the future market for their own products and gain future returns. They incubate new technology with innovative investment. Although the entrepreneurs are aware of the risks involved in such investments, it is closely related to the long-term development of their enterprises. In this case, enterprises may rationally guide innovative behaviours and can constantly adjust the means of achieving the goals to minimise the uncertainty. As long as a project is successful in the end, there will be huge profits.

The innovation stage of high-tech industrialisation is the stage when new products gradually grow into emerging industries. At this time, market information is sufficient, except for financial technology, and the common financial market begins to intervene. Venture capital can gradually withdraw when innovative technologies enter the market. Meanwhile, bank credit financing becomes the main source of investment. If the previous stage of innovation is generally based on producers and innovators as the objects of credit, the objects of credit at this stage should shift to consumers. By then, the main obstacle to the industrialisation of innovative products and the expansion of their market is the lack of consumers, just as with new forms of energy and new energy vehicles. Despite the fact that they are high-tech products, they will not be accepted by the markets if there are no consumers. Consequently, their value of innovation cannot be appreciated by the public.

9.3.2 Institutional arrangements for developing financial technology

Financial technology has two components. One is direct financial technology provided by venture capitalists, which involves equity financing, as well as the corresponding equity trading market. The other is indirect financial technology, which involves credit provided by banks. In real economic operations, the two parts are not completely separate. Those venture capitalists adopting equity financing to participate in innovation and investment also rely on indirect financial technology supported by banks. Therefore, to develop financial technology and raise sufficient funds for innovation, it is necessary to encourage finance capital to enter the frontier of innovative science and technology and support venture capital investment, as well as direct investment in scientific and technological innovation. For the development of financial technology, it is also necessary to promote existing banking and non-banking financial institutions to invest financial capital into scientific and technological innovation. It is important to make the necessary institutional arrangements to cultivate, guide and stimulate existing financial organisations and capital based on their characteristics.

Normally, financial technology's entry into the incubation of new technology is largely attributed to venture capital investors. There are currently two types of venture investors. One is production enterprises that directly incubate new technologies in order to promote their own development and gain returns from their innovative projects. The other is the type of professional venture capitalists who provide venture capital for innovation and entrepreneurship, aiming not to pursue shareholders' equity gains but to pursue equity transfer income. They also anticipate withdrawal with profits from the sales of newly established enterprises and the use of this capital for new venture investment activities. These venture investors largely contribute to the innovative orientation of the modern economy. Both types of venture capital investors are in need of support provided by financial technology credit.

Venture investment in financial technology innovation also needs to deal with the issue of the sources of funding. This depends more on external funding, in addition to the venture capital. There are mainly two issues here:

- First, it is important for banks to provide sufficient funds. Indeed, there are risks for banking credit entering the early stages of innovation. There is no reason to blame commercial banks which tend to be risk averse. In reality, unless encouraged by government policies, financial institutions always adopt principles based on market orientation, pursue profits and pay attention to liquidity, even when they enter the field of scientific and technological innovation. The earlier stage of more innovative technology, where financial technology enters, tends to deviate more from these basic financial principles. The institutions set up for this purpose thus need to take into account both goals. By doing so, they can help more science and technology projects to receive financial support and reduce risk without affecting the liquidity of the funds. Therefore, it is necessary to provide corresponding credit guarantees and insurance. Just like the establishment of an SME financing guarantee company to encourage banks to finance SMEs, it is also necessary to provide guarantees and insurance for financial technology that enters the early stages of technological innovation. Since innovative technology produces spillovers and publicity, financing guarantees for financial technology can come not just from private companies (enterprises) but also venture investment guarantee companies led by the government.

- Second, it is important for various kinds of innovation and venture capital investors to provide funds. Internally, the sources of venture capital funds include the following three types: (1) government risk funds; (2) financial intermediary institutions in the capital markets, such as securities companies, investment banks, insurance companies and venture capital funds formed by various fund organisations; and (3) specialised venture capital companies established by profit-making companies with solid growth to invest in venture capital. Some funds, such as savings and pension funds, may not necessarily enter the banking system. They may be involved in the venture capital field in capital markets. Even small amounts of investment by individuals can be aggregated as a source of venture funds. Although the government will play a leading role in the formation of various venture funds to promote innovation and entrepreneurship, this investment cannot be directly managed by the government. It should be handled by commercialised companies with returns, as well as timely exit channels. In particular, it is important to emphasise that venture capital experts play a decisive role. Venture capital projects and risk capital operations should be selected by professionals. In this way, venture capital funds may optimise their portfolios and diversify risk amongst different stages of the process, including the seed stage, start-up stage and maturity stage.

Since investment in scientific and technological innovation involves venture funds, it requires that the financial system play a role in transferring and distributing risks. People are often cautious when making decisions and afraid to take risks, thus losing many opportunities. The financial system can manage risks through insurance, hedging and diversification, thereby encouraging investors to take risks. It is important to encourage entrepreneurship and entrepreneurial spirit at this stage. The basic institutional arrangement should provide a complete exit mechanism for venture capital so that the funds invested in scientific and technological innovation can be withdrawn in a timely manner when new technologies and enterprises are established so as to ensure the continuity of venture capital investment. In particular, if technology enterprises that invest in venture capital were listed at its early stage (or transferred their shares), it would not only make it possible for them to withdraw and pay the funds off in time upon the completion of their tasks but also attract the financial support needed to realise the success of technological enterprises. This requires opening up equity trading markets. At present, China has opened up the Growth Enterprise Market (GEM, the second board market), but if we rely solely on the existing GEM, we cannot meet the needs of innovative economic development. Building equity trading markets in the regions with active innovation activities can create a platform for trading in unlisted enterprises or enterprises that cannot be listed, thus providing a more convenient exit channel for venture capital and entrepreneurship investors, as well as mechanisms to avoid risks.

Developers of financial technology should pay attention to the government's guiding investment. As Roberts said, "When the community is moving into new areas, venture capital is very important. Some countries use government venture capital, i.e. the government establishes a risk investment mechanism to compensate for private venture capital institutions."[9] The government identifies programmes that are in line with national goals and combines government investment with financial technology to provide support. This can enhance the investors' confidence in providing needed financial capital. It is inherent in the government's function that it should make long-term investments and provide financial support from the seed stage on.

9.4 Financial risks and prevention

Financial deepening and modernisation in developing nations are an important aspect of the current financial globalisation. A global financial crisis could spread to developing nations through financial channels. Meanwhile, with the growing prominence of the role of finance in the domestic economy, the accompanying financial risks may also be systemic and global. Therefore, developing nations must face the task of preventing financial risks at the macroeconomic level.

9.4.1 Theoretical hypothesis of financial risk

Marx pointed out long ago in *On Capital* that there was potential crisis in currency's circulation and payment. The circulation of products happens across time, space and individual restrictions. The excessive amount of paper money in circulation not only runs the risk of losing creditability but also sparking inflation. The currency payment may form a chain of claims and debts. When this chain is disrupted, there is a monetary payment crisis. Marx made it clear that the crisis happens on the condition that "there must be a whole series of relations,"[10] and "this currency crisis will only happen if the payment chain and the artificial compensation system for offsetting payments are fully developed."[11] According to Marx, we can seek institutional factors that lead to a financial crisis from such aspects as an "artificial system" and "a whole series of relations." This series of relations can be called market economy relations. It is the credit economy that best describes the modern characteristics of the market economy. Credit in the economy is essentially the financial economy. Financial issues are also issues of an overall macroeconomy. "Once the social nature of labor is manifested in the currency of commodities and thus appears as something beyond actual production, an independent currency crisis or a currency crisis resulting from a sharp crisis in reality is inevitable."[12] Marx at that time noted, "The development of speculation and credit has also opened up hundreds of sources of sudden wealth."[13] This sudden wealth results from various kinds of credit speculation behaviours. This can be viewed as a subjective factor causing various modern financial crises.

Based on the financial crisis that occurred successively in Mexico, South-east Asia, Brazil, Russia and other developing nations and regions in the 1990s, modern development economists made it clear that "[Financial] liberalization offers clear economic gains, but it carries risks as well."[14] According to these scholars, the financial risks of developing nations come mainly from the following. (1) After liberalising their financial markets, many developing nations lack adequate institutional and regulatory frameworks for money, foreign exchange and capital markets. (2) Along with opening to foreign capital, there is a shift from official to private sources of capital, as well as from government to private entities as the main recipients of foreign capital. The lack of transparency and unavailability of data often tend to mask the true state of financial markets. (3) At the national level, poor risk control, lax enforcement, weak prudential rules, inadequate supervision and government-directed lending practices all lead to a lower quality of investments. In light of the earlier situation, they believe that moving forward, financial liberalisation will require taking action to effectively control financial risks as follows: "It will take stronger regulatory mechanisms, better supervisory standards, greater transparency of financial transactions, better risk-control mechanisms for preventing liquidity crises, and better risk-sharing mechanisms between creditors and borrowers in dealing with existing debt overhangs."

The shift of developing nations from a centrally planned economy to a market economy should promote financial deepening. In the 1990s, McKinnon first proposed the theory of financial deepening in developing nations and put forward the order theory of marketisation in these nations. He believed that "stabilizing the domestic price level without resorting to direct price controls and keeping deposit (and thus lending) rates of interest sustainably positive in real terms while limiting variance in the real exchange rate are crucial for successful economic development."[15]

9.4.2 The virtual economy leading to financial risks

As mentioned earlier, there are many factors that lead to financial risks. We point out here in particular the impact of the virtual economy, which caused the recent financial crisis. As Marx noted, a virtual economy is caused by three factors:

- First, virtual capital in the form of credit that includes commercial credit and bank credit. Commercial credit aims to make it possible to expand the economy beyond the limit of existing capital. Marx's analysis showed that it is impossible for businesses to use their own capital to buy and sell national products, but it was possible with commercial credit in a mechanism as follows. The purchase and sale of goods take the form of bills of exchange, and bills of exchange are bonds with a certain payment period. Such a bill of exchange will circulate as a means of payment until it expires or before the date of payment. The circulation of such commercial bills replaces that of money. At this time, "the real credit currency is not based on currency circulation, whether it is metal currency or national banknotes, but on the basis of circulation of bills."[16] Through the creation of this circulation method, virtual capital is produced. Bank credit can also expand the economy, allowing the same currency to act as deposit tools or loan capital. Bank credit can take different forms, such as bills of exchange, checks, banknotes, loans in the forms of interest-bearing securities, national securities, various mortgaged stocks, overdrafts of deposits or discounting of undue bills of exchange. The repeated use of the same currency generates virtual capital. This kind of virtual capital produced in the course of credit circulation shows as credit expansion in reality.

• Second, virtual capital in the form of income capitalisation. As Marx put it,

> The formation of a virtual capital is called capitalization. Every periodic income is capitalized by calculating it on the basis of the average rate of interest, as an income which would be realized by a capital loaned at this rate of interest.

Income of bonds, stocks and other securities can be capitalised at the interest rate and thus can become virtual capital. The capital raised by these securities participates in the operation of the enterprise and forms the basis of the real economy. However, circulation with ownership actually represents the right to claim future earnings, so these securities can circulate in the markets as in the case of real estate investments. The circulation of securities and real estate, stocks, bonds and real estate prices is specially operated: "On the one hand, their market value fluctuates with the amount and reliability of the proceeds to which they afford legal title." On the other hand, their "market value is in part speculative since it is determined not only by the actual income, but also by the anticipated income, which is calculated in advance." The change of interest rates, the number of securities entering the market, speculative propensities, false information, market manipulation and other factors all can cause the market value's deviation from its real capital value. The stock market is in fact a speculative market; hence, excessive speculation will lead to a bubble economy.

• Third, virtual capital expressed in the form of financial derivatives. Marx found that stocks, bonds and other types of virtual capital can increase dramatically. In this way,

> in all countries based on capitalist production, there exists in this form an enormous quantity of so-called interest-bearing capital, or moneyed capital. And by accumulation of money capital nothing more, in the main, is connoted than an accumulation of these claims on production, an accumulation of the market price, the illusory capital value of these claims.[17]

This mechanism to multiply monetary capital creates a strong temptation to create virtual capital. Financial innovations afterwards can be based on the creation of virtual capital. While revising the third volume of *On Capital*, Frederick Engels found that there were financial companies in the market that simply bought certain kinds of interest-bearing securities: "This doubling and trebling of capital has developed considerably, for instance, through financial trusts."[18] These financial firms simply invest in securities rather than in the real economy, further inflating the virtual capital. It makes the market value of virtual capital increasingly divorced from real capital.

Marx's theories about the creation of virtual capital and its potential financial risks explain the series of financial crises that have occurred since the 1990s. The virtual economy is a speculative economy based on virtual capital. It differs from the real economy which bank credit serves directly. A virtual economy emerges when credit is used on speculation. When an enterprise raises funds by issuing shares, it is not part of the virtual economy, but when it uses stocks for speculation in the stock market, it is part of the virtual economy. Similarly, purchasing housing for speculation is part of the virtual economy but not if it is used as a personal residence. Again, using foreign exchange for speculation is an expression of the virtual economy but not if it is used for import and export businesses. The modern economy cannot avoid the virtual economy, but excessive speculation in the virtual economy can lead to systemic financial risks. In reality, the phenomenon of the virtual economy developing rapidly while the real economy encounters difficulty should be taken seriously. This is because it will spur enterprises to invest in the virtual economy rather than the real economy; similarly, it will lead banks to invest in speculative activities in the virtual economy. It is important to bear in mind that the economy is supported by the real economy, and it is the virtual economy that serves the real economy. If the real economy does not develop while the virtual economy flourishes, the bubble could burst at any time.

Banks and markets mainly constitute the financial system. The financial system has different models in different countries. Japan is dominated by banks while the United States is based on capital markets. Americans attribute Japan's bubble economy to its lack of advanced capital markets. But U.S. capital markets soon got involved in financial events like the Enron scandal, the dot-com bubble and especially the subprime mortgage crisis in 2007, which triggered a global financial crisis. This indicates that there are potential systemic risks involving every entity in either the capital market or amongst banks.

- First, out-of-control bank credit could lead to an economic bubble. Unrestricted lending offered by financial institutions beyond the support of the real economy will inevitably lead to crisis. This was best reflected in Japan's bubble economy in the late 1980s. At that time, the so-called low-cost expansion and debt operation led to the emergence of a credit bubble. Unrestricted loans and capital could not be returned, resulting in unsustainable credit. Eventually, when the bubble burst, Japan experienced a decade-long economic recession.

- Second, excessive speculation in the virtual capital markets could lead to a bubble economy. The South-East Asian financial crisis in 1997 was basically caused by excessive speculation in securities and real estate. In 2001, companies such as Enron and WorldCom in the United States falsified and manipulated their stock price, leading to America's credit crisis.

- Third, excessive innovation in financial derivatives will also lead to a bubble economy. Since the 1990s, with the development of informatisation, the speed of financial innovation in Western countries led by the United States has been greatly accelerated, creating a series of financial derivatives, such as financial futures, stock indexes and options. The varieties of virtual capital have also greatly increased. According to relevant data, the virtual capital traded in various types of capital markets every day is tens of times that of real capital. Financial derivatives are speculative instruments in a sense. Derivatives trading means the transfer of risks. The immediate cause of the subprime crisis in the United States in 1997 was excessive financial innovation and excessive creation of derivatives. It essentially virtualised the real economy.

- Fourth, the virtual capitalisation of bank capital structure has accelerated the spread of financial crises across the world. Marx pointed out in his time that

> the greater portion of banker's capital is, therefore, purely fictitious and consists of claims (bills of exchange), government securities (which represent spent capital) and stocks (drafts on future revenue)...the money-value of the capital represented by this paper is itself fictitious.[19]

It also explains why the subprime mortgage crisis in the United States quickly spread to banks, causing major banks, such as Citibank, to come perilously close to bankruptcy. Banks' capital structure is dominated by virtual capital, and their excessive speculation in virtual economy cannot avoid flowing to risks. As a result, a crisis in the entire financial world will inevitably arise.

The financial crisis that occurred in the United States in 2007 quickly spread all over the world, even to countries with a healthy economy. This started with the trend of financial globalisation. Financial globalisation is defined as follows: convertibility and globalisation of currency, globalisation of financial markets (monetary and capital markets), virtual economy globalisation, the free flow of capital and global payments produced by the globalisation of trade. Since the United States is a country with financial strength, its financial crisis is bound to spread rapidly to the rest of the world through the channels of financial globalisation. Therefore, the more vulnerable developing nations in the financial system should build an effective financial firewall.

9.4.3 Effective prevention of financial risks

From the end of the 20th century to the first decade of this century, several major financial crises broke out in both developed and developing nations. Every financial crisis caused a global crisis. This shows that in the process of financial modernisation, it is necessary to establish a system to guard against systemic risks.

It should not only prevent the systemic risks to banks but also that of capital markets.

The frequent outbreak of financial crises reveals the failure of neo-liberalism that believes implicitly in self-regulation of the market and proves that relying on this mechanism cannot solve macroeconomic problems and recession. Effective government intervention should be involved inevitably.

- First, the scope of the macroeconomy expands to the general level of asset prices in the capital market. Macroeconomic theory in the past analysed the aggregate equilibrium problem through the real economy's three major markets (commodity, job and money markets). Governmental intervention theory is also mainly limited to the balance between total supply and demand in the real economy. The aggregate indicators that the government needs to adjust are mainly the general price level in the commodity market, the general employment level in the job market and the general interest rate level in the money market. Even the financial issues involved essentially analyse the money supply and money demand in the money market; the analysis is limited to its impact on the general level of commodity prices and that of employment. However, the economic crisis now taking place is basically in the virtual economy. The aggregate indicators affecting the macroeconomic equilibrium are not only the general price level in the commodity market and the general employment level in the job market but also the general level of interest rates in the money market, and even the general asset price level in the capital market. The general asset price level in the capital market not only has relatively independent determinants but also independently affects the macroeconomic equilibrium. Excessive speculation causes inflation in asset prices, forming a bubble without the support of the real economy; hence, inflation follows. Once the bubble is broken, asset prices shrink sharply, and deflation and recession follow. Therefore, the capital market and the virtual economy must be examined in the macroeconomic context, while the asset price level must become an indicator of macro-regulation.
- Second, the virtual economy has become the focus of governmental regulation and supervision. The market failures in earlier years, such as externalities and monopolies, all happened in the real economy. This is why government intervention used to focus on the real economy. Economic crises of recent years, however, were triggered by virtual economy issues, such as dishonesty and excessive speculation. These problems cannot be solved by the self-regulation of the market only, but contrarily, they would become worse because of the operation of market mechanisms. The excessive speculation causes the deviation of virtual capital from real capital. Dishonesty could encompass several forms. For instance, there are securities and derivative financial instruments in circulation which hold

> an enormous quantity of money representing a plain swindle, which reaches the light of day and collapses; furthermore, there are unsuccessful speculations with the capital of other people; finally, there is

commodity-capital which has depreciated or is completely unsaleable, or returns that can never more be realized again.[20]

The problems pointed out by Marx more than 100 years ago are common in the modern virtual economy. For a long time, the virtual economy can be said to have been a blind spot for financial regulation. As early as in 2002, the Enron scandal in the United States and its bankruptcy led to the collapse of the stock market, indicating that many problems in the virtual economy can be attributed to a lack of credibility and moral corruption. The credibility mechanism of the capital market cannot rely solely on self-discipline. It must emphasise heteronomy. Heteronomy requires the government to intervene and strengthen legal constraints and supervision. It prompted the passage of the Sarbanes-Oxley Act in the United States. Its main provisions include developing more rigorous standards for accounting audit systems, monitoring the behaviour of various entities in the market and strengthening the penalties for dishonesty in capital markets. Its passage coincided with the declining competitiveness of the American financial system based on the United States' belief in liberalism and market self-regulation. These beliefs contributed to the decision of the United States to relax its financial regulations and issue the Financial Services Regulatory Relief Act in 2006. In 2007, the U.S. subprime mortgage crisis broke out, triggering the global financial crisis in 2008. In a sense, it was a punishment for the deregulation of the United States. The outbreak of the global financial crisis in 2008 forced the U.S. government to issue the Financial Regulatory Reform – A New Foundation: Building Financial Supervision and Regulation. This bill established the central position of the government in the handling of the crisis, which meant that the government took the responsibility for implementing full regulation and strove to solve the problems of coordination and equilibrium between financial regulatory agencies. The uncontrollable and excessive practices of American financial innovation demonstrate that the focus of financial regulation should be to regulate the creation of financial derivatives. The innovation of financial derivatives has an obvious leverage effect on the creation of virtual capital. This is also a leverage effect on the deviation of the virtual economy from the real economy. Therefore, the state must specifically regulate the creation of financial derivatives so that they are strictly controlled within the scope of the real economy as the support.

- Third, in essence, dealing with the relationship between the virtual economy and the real one is to aim at the development of the latter. In fact, the virtual economy is created on the basis of the real economy, serving its interests. However, in reality, excessive speculation in the virtual economy has caused a serious deviation from the real economy, resulting in the frustration of the real economy and subsequent economic recession. Therefore, the government's supervision and policy orientation must be to curb excessive speculation in the virtual economy and support the development of the real economy. Upon the arrival of a crisis, both the virtual economy and real economy will be in need of assistance. The government will undoubtedly have to focus on saving the real economy to protect growth and employment from deteriorating. It is only after the real economy is saved that the virtual economy can recover, not the other way around.

• Finally, it is necessary to emphasise that China's financial development will undoubtedly follow the path of marketisation, but market-oriented reforms cannot take the path of neo-liberalism, while the government-regulating market must be strengthened. Financial innovation can only be carried out gradually, and the operation of financial institutions must be standardised.

Notes

1 Albert O. Hirschman, *Strategy of Economic Development*, trans. Cao Zhenghai and Pan Zhaodong (Beijing: Economic Science Press, 1991), 28.
2 János Kornai, *Economics of Shortage*, vol. 2, trans. Gao Hongye (Beijing: Economic Science Press, 1986), 526.
3 Karl Marx, *On Capital* (Beijing: People's Press, 2004), vol.1, 651; vol.3, 544, 555, 585.
4 Ronald Ian McKinnon, *Money and Capital in Economic Development*, trans. Lu Cong (Shanghai: Joint Publishing Company, 1988), 76–7; Edward S. Show, *Financial Deepening in Economic Development*, trans. Wang Wei et al. (Beijing: China Social Sciences Press, 1989), 6–11.
5 Liao Li, Wang Ren and Chen Lu, eds., *Exploring the Journey of Wisdom: Interviews with Famous Economists from Harvard and MIT* (Beijing: Peking University Press, 2000), 151, 153.
6 "In LDCs, there exists a large fringe of smaller firms, farms or investing households (small artisans) without access to credit from the formal banking sector. The costs of serving such small-scale loans are just too high per dollar lent." Ronald I. McKinnon, *The Order of Economic Liberization*, trans. Zhou Tingyu (Shanghai: Joint Publishing House, 1997), 35.
7 Robert J. Schiller, *The New Financial Order: Risk in the 21st Century*, trans. Guo Yan and Hu Bo (Beijing: Renmin University Press, 2004), 4–5.
8 Frank Hyneman Knight, *Risk, Uncertainty and Profit*, trans. Wang Yu and Wang Wenyu (Beijing: Renmin University Press, 2005), 187.
9 Edward Roberts, "Venture Investment and Operation Mechanisms," in *Exploring the Journey of Wisdom: Interviews with Famous Economists from Harvard and MIT*, eds. Liao Li, Wang Ren and Chen Lu, 241–64 (Beijing: Peking University Press, 2000), 247.
10 Marx, *On Capital*, vol. 1, 136.
11 Marx, *On Capital*, vol. 1, 162.
12 Marx, *On Capital*, vol.1, 585.
13 Marx, *On Capital*, vol.1, 685.
14 Gerald M. Meier and Joseph E. Stiglitz, eds., *Frontiers of Development Economics: The Future in Perspective* (Beijing: China Financial and Economic Press, 2003), 124.
15 McKinnon, *Money and Capital*, 43.
16 McKinnon, *Money and Capital*, 451.
17 McKinnon, *Money and Capital*, 531.
18 McKinnon, *Money and Capital*, 533.
19 McKinnon, *Money and Capital*, 532.
20 McKinnon, *Money and Capital*, 555.

10 Economic globalisation and the open economy

Since the implementation of reform and opening-up policies, China has made great achievements in its economy, ranging from opening-up to the outside world to establishing an export-oriented economy. The economic development has also benefitted from the export-oriented economy. In the early stage of the opening-up economy in developing nations, it is generally passive. Developing nations mostly make use of international capital to offset the insufficiency of domestic savings and gain foreign exchange from the international market. China's economy has now reached the level of middle-income countries. The total import and export volume ranks first in the world while the foreign exchange reserve has amounted to nearly US$ 4 trillion. The opening-up economy based on this requires further transformation. For one thing, the target needs to be aligned, i.e. transforming to an active opening up so as to seek stronger international competitiveness. For the other, the opening-up strategy also needs to be readjusted from seeking the quantity to seeking the efficiency and lowering cost.

10.1 The open economy under economic globalisation

With the initiation of China's opening-up policy in the early 1980s, China's economy developed from an export-oriented economy to an open one. The open economy has become the major driving force for development in China, especially in the coastal areas. It uses international resources and markets with open systems and policies. At present, China has made clear the expansion of domestic demand as a strategic basis for the economic development. However, this does not mean that economic growth no longer needs external demand or opening to the outside world. Rather, it is more about raising the level of an open economy.

10.1.1 Economic globalisation and its effects

The concept of economic globalisation began to spread widely in the late 1980s. According to the International Monetary Fund (IMF),

> Economic globalisation refers to the increase of the form and scale of the international trade in goods and services and capital flow as well as the

increasing interdependence between the countries of the world economy facilitated by the technology widely and quickly spread.

According to the OECD, economies, markets, technologies and communications are increasingly going global. This includes the globalisation of production and trade. In the process of economic globalisation, the economic relations between countries in the world have been strengthened and become interdependent. The domestic economic rules in various countries have become consistent, and the international economic coordination mechanism has been strengthened. It is certain that the information technology revolution represented by the internet has played a critical role in promoting economic globalisation.

In fact, before the concept of economic globalisation was put forward, there was a concept of the world economy and the corresponding international division of labour. In terms of economic relations between the developed and developing countries, there is a centre (core)-periphery (edge) theory. This theory divides the world economy into two levels: the developed countries are the countries in the development centre, while the underdeveloped countries are the countries in the development periphery. The relationship with the development centre is involved in the development of the developing nations.

William Arthur Lewis (1915–1991), in his book *Growth and Fluctuations* published in 1978, analysed the relationship between the centre and the periphery in greater detail. He sees the industrial sector as the "engine of growth" in the core countries: "Our first concern is the response of the peripheral countries to the growth engines of the core countries."[1] The engine function of the core countries is that their technology, resources and market play an important role in the development of the peripheral countries. Specifically, they offer more productive and more up-to-date technologies, resources – particularly capital and manpower – and their own markets. There are two options for the response of the peripheral countries: one is to directly copy the industrial revolution of the core countries, and the other is to create conditions for the industrial revolution through trade with the core countries. However, the response of distinct peripheral countries is dissimilar, resulting in the difference in the development of peripheral countries.

The centre and periphery theory by Raúl Prebisch (1901–1986) has concluded that the free trade between the central and the peripheral countries is favourable to the core countries. This is mainly because the difference of the industrial structure in the two categories of countries. The industrial structure of the core countries is diversified and homogeneous. On the one hand, modern technology extends all over the whole economy. On the other hand, the production sector covers a wide range of areas, including capital, intermediate goods and final consumer goods. The industrial structure in the peripheral countries is single and heterogeneous. Therefore, these countries cannot achieve the same production and technological progress as the core countries. The labour productivity of their primary product export sectors is lower than that of the manufacturing sectors in the core countries. Its average income increase is also slower than that in the core countries.

To sum up, the former world economic theory and the corresponding centre-periphery theory mainly focus on two aspects. First, the economic relationship between the developing and developed countries is more about trade relations. Second, in the economic relations between the developed and developing countries, while the developing nations may obtain some benefits, the developed countries obtain greater benefits, thus further widening the gap between the developed and developing countries.

In the context of economic globalisation, international economic relations have undergone major changes. Just as Joseph E. Stiglitz and Gerald M. Meier articulated,

> Globalization means closer integration of the world economy, which is a combined result of the increasing flow of trade, ideas, and capital as well as the emergence of the international production networks generated through the investment activities by the multinationals.[2]

According to his analysis, the effect of economic globalisation on developing countries is highlighted in the following aspects:

- First, the significant growth in trade is an important aspect of globalisation. Developing nations are involved in international trade not just for gaining foreign exchange. In particular, they rely on their own advantage to participate in the international division of labour. In the context of globalisation, more and more developing nations are participating in transnational production like their industrial counterparts and arranging their business activities from a global perspective.
- Second, the international capital flow is becoming an important driving force for development. In the past, developing nations needed abundant capital to achieve industrialisation, modernisation and urbanisation. Domestic savings were insufficient, so the savings shortfall was offset by the introduction of foreign investment. In the context of globalisation, the industrial countries in the leading position in the financial markets of an economy are integrated into the global financial system, making the allocation of capital on an unprecedented scale in these economies, which in turn flows to the developing economies. This is to say, the inflow of foreign capital to the developing nations is actually the allocation of the global finance market. With the allocation of financial globalisation, the international flow of production factors has become the mainstream. The international capital that flows to the developing nations may exceed its capacity to make up for the shortfall in domestic savings, and the capital in the developing nations may also be integrated into the global financial system.
- Third, economic globalisation is largely the globalisation of international economic operation rules and regulations, represented by WTO rules and the free-trade zones. WTO is an international coordinator of the trade policy of the contracting parties. It includes the principle of a series of rules designed to promote trade liberalisation. It includes principles of no discrimination, most-favoured nation treatment, national treatment, tariff concession, mutual benefit, general elimination of quantitative restrictions, transparency and no

dumping. By joining WTO or establishing free-trade zones and other routes, all countries align themselves with the international economic operation rules and overcome various types of protectionism, thus leading to the reform of the domestic economic system.

The impact of the aforementioned economic globalisation is quite different from that of the centre-periphery theory. Although economic globalisation is still dominated by the developed countries, which still obtain larger interests and benefits in the economic globalisation, the benefits obtained in the process of globalisation are comparatively greater than in the past. It is even equal to the benefits obtained by the developed countries for those developing nations that enter the stage of economic growth and actively integrate themselves into the global economy. China has harvested considerable benefits of globalisation as China's policy of reform and opening- up coincided with the trend of economic globalisation.

10.1.2 *The formation and development of an open economy in China*

For a country whose economy has been stagnant for a long time, its economic development needs to be driven largely by external forces. Economically, it is to develop an export-oriented economy to enter the international market and to fully absorb and use the international economic growth factors.

*   First is the development driven by foreign investment. Developing nations are faced with two major pressures on economic growth. One is the lack of domestic savings. In China and other developing nations, the GDP per capita is low, and savings ability is weak, leading to a serious shortage of capital supply. Absorbing foreign investment with the export-oriented economy can support a higher investment rate and economic growth. The second is the market. One disadvantage for the less-developed nations is that the overseas market has been occupied by the leading countries, and the development of the export-oriented economy can effectively break this restriction. The introduction of foreign direct investment (FDI) brings not only technology but also projects and export channels. It can help those countries enter the international market.
*   Second, it is the external force of the system transition. The unrelenting pressure of international competition will become the external impetus to reform the economic system and strengthen the competition mechanism. After being integrated into the international market, domestic price changes have not only international standards but also external adjustment leverages. After being integrated into the international market, China will have more commercial exchanges with the well-developed international commercial market and enter the international financial market to participate in many financing activities. There will be more labour exporting, and technology will be introduced from the international technology market. In the international labour market, management and technical personnel will be brought in. After being integrated with the international market, the international practice will

be transferred to the domestic market, the disadvantages of the traditional management system will surface, and the domestic practices that hinder the reform of the economic system will be eliminated.

China's open economy is based on the development of the export-oriented economy. In the context of economic globalisation, the implication of an open economy is to develop China's economy with international resources and the international market.

There are open indexes to measure the level of openness of an economy. According to the characteristics of economic globalisation, a country's openness should be divided into two aspects.

On the one hand, in terms of the flow of elements, the introduction and utilisation of foreign trade is an important carrier to absorb international resources, especially knowledge and technology. The successful use of foreign capital will also have a double economic effect. One is the ability to augment exports. Projects built with foreign capital can increase exports directly. The second is to raise the level of savings. The use of foreign capital to promote economic development can raise the income level and promote the overall savings (total accumulation) level of the whole national economy. Therefore, openness in this regard should be continually cultivated, and the flow of capital, technology and personnel be freer, and the way of attracting and using foreign resources be more flexible.

On the other hand, in terms of international trade, China's dependence on international trade as a major country is different from that of small countries. Small countries have a very high dependence on international trade. The development of small economies depends on product exports. Small countries can only accelerate economic growth if the dependence on foreign trade increases. For large countries, the dependence on foreign trade is less than that of small countries. The reason is that the domestic market and resource conditions in large countries allow them to develop specialisation and larger economies of scale.[3] China's economy is not only a huge economy. It is a colossal economy compared with many small countries, and the domestic market capacity is very large. Therefore, China cannot be as completely open as a small country can be. The one-sided pursuit of openness and the abandonment of the big domestic market will incur great cost. Admittedly, foreign trade is the engine for economic growth. China cannot do anything without the openness of the economy. It is necessary in some areas to develop an export-oriented economy, where there is a higher open degree that drives the modernisation of the economy.

First, the flow of international elements and the forms of international capital flows are diversified. It can be divided into three categories: FDI, indirect investment and flexible investment. FDI is mainly the output of industrial capital.

Indirect investment refers to the investment through loans, which is the output of loan capital, including private bank loans, international financial organisation loans, government loans, etc. Flexible investment refers to such capital export methods as stock investment, securities investment and compensation trade. Foreign aid is also a form of foreign investment. China's science, technology, and industry lag behind the developed countries, especially lacking in capital, technology and other factors. It is necessary to introduce technology through the introduction of foreign capital so as to improve the level of science and technology and industry in China. The significance of FDI is not only to bring capital but also technology and management, as well as advanced industries. Therefore, attracting FDI has gradually become the focus of introducing foreign capital. In 2011, FDI in China reached US$116 billion, ranking second in the world. China has become the world's second-largest FDI recipient (second only to the United States) and has ranked first for 19 consecutive years in developing countries. So far, FDI accounts for more than 70% of the total foreign investment.[4] FDI has also brought to China the international market. It has contributed to the substantial increase in China's exports.

There is a price to be paid for using foreign capital, which means paying interest or leaving a certain amount of profits to foreign capital. As Vladimir Lenin said, "We are going to make a certain 'contribution' to the world capitalism and to some extent to 'buy' from them. Yet we immediately find a certain way to consolidate the Soviet government and improve governance."[5] The effective utilisation of foreign capital by socialist countries can enhance their economic strength and accelerate the socialist economic development. Foreign capital not only introduces the capital resources needed for development but also introduces management, entrepreneurship and advanced production technology, as well as the production craftsmanship needed by the developing countries. The direct investment by the transnational corporations in the developing nations has the nature of a package. Money is an important part of the package because transnational corporations have the powerful capacity for raising money. In the package, there are other elements that are more difficult to get for developing nations. They are not only necessary to the industrialisation process but also for developing nations to catch up with an increasingly complex and rapidly changing international community.

These elements include advanced technology, management, other well-trained specialised personnel and extensive ready-to-use links with the international market. While the positive role played by foreign investment is recognised, it is necessary to point out the limits of its positive role based on the actual situation in the developing countries. The growth rate in the developing nations is not directly proportionate to the percentage of the foreign capital in its GDP. Developing nations may lack the ability to absorb foreign capital, such as a shortage of skilled personnel, infrastructure, administrative capacity, flexible economic systems and a stable political environment. Without these important complementary elements, higher investment rates do not necessarily lead to higher economic growth rates. Even if these complementary elements are equipped, the introduction of the foreign investment may not increase investment and export accordingly. Instead, it may lead to the increase in consumption and reduction in export because foreign savings have replaced domestic savings.

To effectively absorb and use foreign capital, developing nations need to create a favourable investment environment in the political, legal and economic fields. At the same time, to safeguard national sovereignty and interests, any political conditions and conditions that may damage their rights and interests must not be accepted. The investment projects should be viewed from the macroeconomic perspective.

As for the country's trade, the usual foreign trade dependence relies only on the trade of goods. Here service trade is also included. In terms of the total import and export volume, China's foreign trade dependence increased from 9.8% in 1978 to 47% in 2012 (Tables 10.1 and 10.2). Combined with the total import and export of services, China's foreign trade dependence reaches 52.7%.

By analysing the structure of China's foreign trade dependence (see Tables 10.1 and 10.2), we can find that the export orientation of the trade in goods is higher than that of the service trade. In terms of goods, the proportion of the total export volume in GDP has risen from 4.6% in 1978 to 24.9% in 2012, while the total import volume in GDP increased from 5.2% to 22.1%. The total export volume ranks first in the world, accounting for 11.2% of the world market. The total import volume is the second-largest in the world, accounting for 9.8% of the market share. In terms of service trade, the export volume ranks fifth in the world, accounting for 3.1% of the market. The import volume ranks third in the

Table 10.1 China's Export Structure in 2012

	Export			Import		
	GDP Proportion	Share of World Market	World Ranking	GDP Proportion	Share of World Market	World Ranking
Goods	24.9%	11.2%	1	22.1%	9.8%	2
Service	2.3%	3.1%	5	3.4%	9.7%	3

Source: *China Statistical Yearbook*, 2013.

Table 10.2 The Proportions of the Total Export Volume in GDP in Countries and Regions in the World

Year Countries (Region)	1982	1985	1990	1995	2000	2012
USA	6.9	5.4	7.1	10.1	10.8	10.3
Germany	26.9	29.5	27.3	25.1	33.8	43.9
Japan	12.7	13.1	9.8	10.8	11.5	13.3
UK	19.9	22.0	18.9	26.8	27.6	19.7
France	17.5	19.3	18.1	23.7	29.1	21.6
Indonesia	23.6	21.3	24.0	22.3	44.1	22.7
South Korea	29.3	32.6	26.6	28.3	43.8	47.4
Hong Kong	68.4	90.0	115.1	132.9	146.7	166.9
Singapore	136.1	128.9	149.6	162.5	177.4	155.7

Source: IMF, World Bank.

world, accounting for 9.7% of the world's market. Further analysis also finds that the world rankings and percentage of world market share in service trade are both higher than its export. Evidently, China has great market potential in terms of service trade.

The benefits of an open economy are proven and obvious. The introduction of foreign capital, technology, management, and other factors combined with the labour force and land elements have promoted rapid economic growth in China.

Foreign investment also brings with it the advanced foreign industries, promotes the industrial structure in China and shortens the gap of industrial development between China and the international level. Some regions with a high level of open economy in China are, therefore, called "the factory of the world." China has become a major manufacturing country in the world, and the open economy has made significant contributions in this regard.

10.1.3 *Import substitution and export substitution*

In fact, all developing nations will go through a stage in which they export primary products for foreign exchange at the beginning of entering the world economy. Two strategic options will emerge based on this general conclusion. One is the import substitution strategy. Its goal is to lead the foreign trade by industrialisation, which is to focus on industrialisation to substitute importation. The other is the export substitution strategy, which is to replace the strategy of primary products exportation.

The import substitution concept has two meanings. First, it means to use domestic products to replace the original imported products. Second, the foreign exchange gained from the export of the primary products is not for imported consumer goods but imported investment products. Therefore, the import substitution strategy also encourages export, and the main products for export are primary products. This is to say, the export of the primary products is not inconsistent with the substitution of the import industry.

The typical import substitution strategy first determines which product has immense domestic market demand according to past import statistics. Through the establishment of tariff barriers on those products, the government can then impose higher tariffs or stipulate the import quota and protect the production of the domestic manufacturers of these products. It is also possible to attract foreign capital to bypass the tariff barriers of the country and build factories in the country by offering a variety of incentives to encourage investment. Compared with the international market, the initial production cost of the import substitution products may be high. However, it is estimated that the growing industry will be gradually maturing, economies of scale will become evident and production cost will be decreasing and will start to have the ability to compete in the international market. The balance of payments will be improved due to restrictions on imports and the strengthening of exports.

Substitution costs are different at different import substitution stages. In the process of replacing non-durable consumer goods (such as clothing and footwear) with domestic products, countries in the early stage of industrialisation are better suited to produce these products, so there is no need for such protection. Therefore, the production of these products has a large scale, and the replacement cost will not be very high. The second stage of import substitution is the replacement of durable consumer goods.

Such sectors are essentially capital-intensive, and import prices are high. The cost of protection is needed, and the substitution costs are high.

Many of the current import substitutes in China are products of the replacement of durable consumer goods, and the achievement of the import substitution strategy is often disappointing because of the high cost of substitution. Most disappointing of all, inefficient imports of substitution industries have been a hindrance to the process of industrialisation. We hoped that the import substitution industrial sector could stimulate and accelerate the development of industrialisation through the interaction between the import substitution sector and other economic sectors. However, because of the high investment cost of the products produced by the import substitution industrial sector, which can be used as a potential antecedent connecting industry, the core technologies and key technologies still need to be provided abroad. Therefore, the added value of the substitution industry is low, and it hinders the industrial modernisation process.

After the economic development reaches a certain stage, the export substitution strategy naturally draws attention when faced with the high cost of import substitution. Export substitution is not a general expansion of exports. The export substitution strategy emphasises the replacement of primary products with finished products as the main export commodities. The implementation of this strategy requires the implementation of tariffs and exchange rate policies that encourage the export of manufactured goods, which is to change the trade protection policies adopted in the substitution of imports. Therefore, it is a major adjustment of the foreign trade strategy and foreign trade policy to replace import substitution with export substitution. According to the cost-efficiency analysis, the outward efficiency of the export substitution strategy is obviously higher than that of the import substitution strategy. The implementation of the export substitution strategy will help the alleviation of foreign exchange restrictions in developing nations. Export substitution can go beyond domestic market restrictions, use international markets and, thus, continuously obtain the efficiency brought by economies of scale, learning effects and international competition. Export substitution has a greater appeal to foreign investment. In terms of providing more employment opportunities and improving income distribution, export substitution can be more effective than import substitution.

The governments of the developing nations have adopted the strategy of import substitution, which aims to promote industrialisation. However, the process of industrialisation is relatively fast in those countries and regions that have adopted export substitution strategies. The development in South Korea and Taiwan has proven the aforementioned point. Therefore, the strategy of implementing export substitution is, in general, not contradictory to the goal of industrialisation and modernisation.

However, China is a large country, which is different from other small countries. China's industrialisation and modernisation cannot be built solely on the basis of labour-intensive export industries. While implementing the export substitution strategy, China should pay more attention to the import substitution of certain infant industries. The country also needs to protect the industries properly until they can implement export substitution.

John C. H. Fei (1923–1996) and Gustav Ranis (1929–2013) divided the export substitution into two stages. The first stage is to replace the primary products with labour-intensive manufactured goods. Labour-intensive, non-durable industrial products export means "the less developed countries found, for the first time in the life cycle, a way to fully use their surplus labour."[6] The second is to substitute the labour-intensive export stage. At this stage, export is characterised by diversification and flexibility. Further export substitution is the "technology-driven phase."[7] This is a high-level open strategy. At present, the export level of different regions in China is diversified. The export products include primary product exports, labour-intensive manufactured goods and technology-oriented exports. In general, China is yet in the labour-intensive export substitution for primary product export stage. Only some developed areas have started to enter the replacement stage of the technology-intensive export products.

It must be pointed out that both import and export substitutions are opening strategies practiced in developing nations prior to the emergence of the global economy. After the rise of economic globalisation and with the implementation of the WTO rules, the two strategies in developing nations have been downplayed. The primary concern in all countries is to form an open economy to integrate into the global economy.

10.2 From comparative advantage to competitive advantage

After China became the world's second-largest economy and reached the middle-income level country, transformation and upgrading of the open economy became an urgent need. The key is to transform the theoretical framework on China's participating in the international division of labour and international competition to maximise the benefits in global trade. This is the transition from the theory of comparative advantage to that of competitive advantage.

10.2.1 The comparative advantage theory

In general, most international exchange is necessary due to the international division of labour. Such a division enables countries to specialise in the production that is most suitable for them. Through international trade, both parties gain more benefits.

The earliest theory of the comparative advantage is that of comparative cost put forth by David Ricardo (1772–1823), the leader of the classical school in the 19th century. There exist differences in productivity or cost in the production of different products in different countries. Their respective divisions of national production have comparative advantageous products (i.e. cost of labour productivity is higher or lower). While the cost of products in a country, usually in an underdeveloped nation, has a relative advantage in these products over other countries, usually the developed countries, it does not have a relative advantage in the same products.

The factor endowments theory, also known as the H-O model, put forward by Eli Heckscher (1879–1952) in 1919 and Bertil Ohlin (1899–1979) in 1933, is of the greatest influence on modern international trade. The theory holds that the resource endowment of each country is different. In some countries, labour resources are abundant; in other countries, natural resources or capital resources are abundant. Each country produces the product that uses the most abundant factor of production in their land. Through international trade, each country obtains the biggest benefit.

The basic argument of the comparative advantage theory is that the developed countries have the advantage of capital and technology, while the developing nations have abundant labour and natural resources. Hence the former produce and export capital- and technology-intensive products, while the latter focus on labour- and natural-resource-intensive products. Each side can obtain benefits from international trade. According to this theory, China, as a large developing nation compared with the capital from developed countries, is in a disadvantaged position in its technology and industry. It only has a comparative advantage in labour and natural resources, especially land and environment. China's opening to the outside world is, therefore, advanced by this comparative advantage. In terms of the trade structure, China is committed to the products that are labour and resource intensive, and high energy consuming and high emission producing. As for the introduction and use of international resources, cheap labour and land resources are the conditions for the introduction of foreign capital. Foreign investment enterprises in China are mainly labour- and resource-intensive sectors at the cost of environmental resources.

Admittedly, this open strategy was successful in the early stage of development. Otherwise, it would be impossible for China to enter the global economy, and it would be impossible to take advantage of the international resources and international markets to achieve leap-forward development in a relatively short time. The challenge is that this open strategy based on the comparative advantage is not long-lasting because of the external factors in the international market and internal factors in China's own development.

10.2.2 *The unsustainability of China's trade structure with comparative advantage*

At present, China's international division of labour and export structure can be explained by the traditional comparative advantage theory. Such a structure of China's initial resource endowment mainly refers to the direct export of resource-intensive products or labour-intensive products. For example, textiles, clothing, leather goods and light industrial goods accounted for about 30% of the total exports in 1998. With China's economic growth and the widening of the open economy, China's trade structure has begun to upgrade. On the one hand, exports have shifted to industrial goods. In 2013, the proportion of industrial goods rose to 95.1%, and the export volume reached US$1.95 trillion, a rise of 437.8 times, as compared with that in 1978. On the other hand, mechanical and electronic products are the main industrial products. In 2012, the export of mechanical and electrical products amounted to US$1.18 trillion, accounting for 57.6% of the total export volume, making it rank in the first category of the export commodities in China. In particular, the proportion of high-tech mechanical and electronic products with high technical content, deep processing and high added value increased from 4.9% in 1977 to 58.7%, which is higher than the overall level of mechanical and electrical products. However, the current export structure still depends on the comparative advantage of resource endowment. The main form depends on processing industrial goods for export trade.

Unlike general trade,[8] the so-called processing trade refers to the import of raw materials and components from abroad. After being processed in the country, the products are re-exported. In this way, the country earns the added value. Up to now, processing trade accounts for 50% of China's foreign trade. According to the analysis of the industrial structure, about 80% of transportation equipment, electrical machinery, electronic products and instrumentation, as well as more than two-thirds of leather and mechanical products, are exported through processing trade.

In addition, most of the exports of metallurgy, clothing and paper products are processing trade. This processing trade is actually using China's labour, land and environmental resources.

The international trade structure of processing trade has basically realised the substitution of labour-intensive industry for primary product. This kind of substitution can fully develop the advantage of abundant labour resources in China, and it will also help increase employment opportunities, thus alleviating heavy employment pressure. More importantly, the technology spillover effect of the processing trade provides learning opportunities for Chinese enterprises. However, the export benefit of the trade structure based on processing trade is not high.

Processing trade is the introduction of international resources to take advantage of the low wage labour and cheap natural resources, especially land and environment in China. Even for the production and export of high-tech products, foreign investment enterprises in China mainly focus on labour- and resource-intensive sectors. The key technology is not in China but provided from abroad. Chinese enterprises only provide additional labour value. Strictly speaking, it still belongs to the export of labour-intensive products. Therefore, although the quantity of China's export products is large, the added value is not high. It is estimated that 70% of the export earnings from the processing trade are paid to imports. Many of the exports appear to be high-tech products, such as computers, but China is basically using labour to process the assembly. In particular, in recent years, there has been a wave of "wage increases," and in addition to China's implementation of more guaranteed labour rights, the "sweatshop wage system" of some foreign-funded enterprises cannot be sustained. Under such conditions, it is difficult to build an open economy on the basis of low labour costs and abundant labour force. The export at the cost of environmental resources cannot last in China for a long time. This means that the basis of the open economy needs to be improved and changed from cheap labour and natural resources using independent technology innovation to replace imported products so as to enlarge additional value. On this basis, the proportion of general trade accounting for more than the proportion of processing trade means the improvement of export efficiency.

The 2008 worldwide financial crisis seriously hit export demand. In particular, the international market demand of labour-intensive products fell sharply, and it promoted the transformation of industrial structure in Western developed countries.

With regard to the re-industrialisation process in the United States, labour-intensive industries also received attention in addition to the development of new industries. To solve the employment issue, even developed countries with comparative advantages in technology and capital should develop labour-intensive industries and provide job opportunities. On the one hand, they block foreign labour-intensive products with all sorts of barriers. On the other hand, they rely on the capital and technology advantages in labour-intensive industries to dominate the products in the competition of labour-intensive exports from developing nations. Therefore, the international market environment and trade conditions of our labour-intensive products are worse. This makes China's export strategy of labour as a comparative advantage unsustainable in the long run.

The decline in international demand reflects the fact that overcapacity does exist in a significant number of exports around the world. This means that even if the world economy recovers, many exports may still have no market. At the same time, international trade frictions are increasingly frequent, reflecting the rise of protectionism in various countries. Thus the challenge to China is not only the low export earnings of labour-intensive products but also the resistance to protectionism. Faced with these frictions, China's export products need to be upgraded. Only by increasing the technological content of exports can China reduce the frictions in international trade.

It is important to note that the supply of labour, land and other resources cannot be unlimited after more than 30 years of rapid development. The price increase was inevitable. Along with the improvement of people's living standards and the improvement of health requirements, the ecological and environmental constraints on development projects are also stricter. This means that compared with other developing nations, China's comparative advantage in labour and natural resources is fading away. As proof, many foreign companies using Chinese labour, land and environment have begun to move to other countries.

As far as China's own development is concerned, the global share of China's manufacturing exports is not commensurate with the added value of China's exports. As the world's second-largest economy, China is faced with the historic task of striving to be a great world economic power. The primary task is to rise from a large manufacturing country to a powerful manufacturing country. At this time, China's participation in the global economy cannot only seek to compare the trade interests but also bridge the economic and technological gap with the developed countries as soon as possible.

While the comparative advantage can expand exports, it will freeze the gap between China and the developed countries. Only by seeking competitive advantage can China bridge the gap with developed countries.

From the current status of the international trade mentioned earlier, it is clear that the economic globalisation process is also the end of the comparative advantage of products based on labour and resources.

- First of all, with the development of economic globalisation, the factors of production and resources can flow globally. With the new wave of technological revolution, resources and labour can be replaced by capital and technology. All this shows that the comparative advantage of natural resources and labour resources that most developing nations process in the international competition is no longer obvious.

- Second, the products produced by using the relatively abundant resources in a country are not necessarily competitive in international competition. The reason is that there may be several developing nations in the world that provide the same labour-intensive products, such as clothing, shoes and hats, based on their resource advantages. In addition, the same labour-intensive products are produced in different countries, and the national competitiveness is quite different. Some countries have higher quality or well-known brands because of their high technology or high capital investment. This is actually the substitution of capital and technology for labour. Faced with the competition, many of China's products with a comparative resource advantage have no international competitive advantage.

- Third, labour-intensive products are not necessarily low cost. It is possible for developing nations to export mainly labour-intensive products because there exist some differences in each country's element capital. Under such conditions, the wage/rent ratio in those developing nations with abundant labour force remains low. The challenge is that with economic globalisation, the tendency of equal price inevitably exists in the element price, including labour price, in different countries. For example, wages in China's coastal regions, especially in the highly open economy, have increased rapidly in recent years. This means that the labour cost of labour-intensive products shows a tendency to increase. It makes the comparative advantage of abundant resources start to have a downward trend, the result of which further reduces international competitiveness of labour-intensive products.[9]

The aforementioned discussion shows that the effect of the existing open economy model based on the use of natural resources and labour in China is diminishing. This open economy model is unsustainable and thus needs transformation and upgrading. This is to change the export-oriented structure, which has been characterised by the comparative advantage of labour and resource intensified economy, to modify the strategy which emphasises export quantity, not export benefit, and to enhance the science and technology used in the foreign-invested enterprises in China.

10.2.3 Implications of the transformation from comparative advantage to competitive advantage

It has been widely accepted that international trade is the engine for development in developing nations. It is now necessary to study in what aspect international trade plays an engine role and is most beneficial to developing nations. According to Hollis B. Chenery's analysis, a country's foreign trade strategy is associated with the country's industrial structure of comparative advantage. The adjustment of a country's foreign trade strategy is associated with the change of the comparative advantage in the country's industrial structure. That is to say, only international trade can promote the optimisation and upgrading of the domestic industrial structure, and this kind of driving function is most needed.

In the past, all countries focussed on the comparative advantages of products because of the enormous trade barriers. With the advance of economic globalisation, this comparative advantage has significantly attenuated in the developing countries. Economic globalisation includes the globalisation of free trade, investment and finance. It means that the domestic market is internationalised, and the international competition is localised. The entry of foreign capital means that a country's unique labour resources and natural resources can be used by foreign capital. In this way, the resource advantage in a country is not as obvious as it used to be under the conditions of globalisation. Moreover, the so-called international competition is not entirely the competition of domestic products in the past. It may be the competition of foreign brands made in China and foreign brands made in foreign countries. The competition between foreign brands using domestic resources is also likely to appear in the domestic market.

What is competitive advantage? According to Michael E. Porter (1947–), the differences between the theory of competitive advantage and comparative advantage theory are illustrated in three aspects. First, under the condition of today's economic globalisation, competitive advantage theory sees countries as economic units. Competitive advantage points more to the open strategy at the national level. Second, the theory of competitive advantage emphasises the creation of new competitive advantages based on quality, characteristics and new product innovation. Therefore, "the new national competitive advantage theory must put technological advancement and innovation as a focus of thinking."[10] Third, competitive advantage theory emphasises competition with the superiors, meaning whether "a country's industry has the competitive advantages to compete with the world-class competitors."[11] It also means that this country will make competition with the world-class competitors a goal to promote science and technology and industry innovation so as to form the national competitive advantages. The definition of competitive advantage becomes the theoretical guidance from comparative advantage to competitive advantage.

The competitive advantage in international competition is prominent in the industrial advantage. It has long been considered that the international division of labour is only a division of labour between technology-intensive, capital-intensive and labour-intensive industries. Now, there are new types of international divisions of labour. One type is the international division of labour in three industries. Some countries are agricultural countries, some are industrial ones while others focus on services. The other type is the division of labour in every part of the chain in industries. For example, some high-tech products are manufactured in many countries, with high added value of research and development in some countries and low added value manufacturing in others.

In the new international division of labour pattern, China has to seek an industrial competitive advantage. In addition to making more efforts to develop the modern service industry, China needs to implement two types of replacements. The first is to replace the export of products with low technology content and low added value to the export of products with high-tech content and high added value. Exports not only need to enter their supermarkets but also their high-end markets. The second is to replace the manufacturing role in the international division of labour in the industrial chain with research and development. It will not only increase the added value but also reduce the occupation of land resources, save energy and reduce emissions.

The third is to rely on innovation to foster competitive advantage, transforming from an average manufacturing country to a strong manufacturing country. Its indicators are the global share of high-tech products and innovative products, the number of products as international brands "invented in China" and the number of Chinese multinationals with core high technology, and so on.

Turning to competitive advantage is actually an upgrade of comparative advantage. If the advantage of abundant labour resources should be that of international competition, there must be a transformation process. The switching point is to combine high technology, including high technology introduced from abroad, with abundant labour resources, thus producing a real comparative advantage. When considering the foreign factors of production and domestic factors of production, foreign capital and advanced foreign technology can be combined with China's abundant and cheap labour so as to produce competitive products in the international market. At this time, the comparative advantage is that China's high-tech products have the advantage of price competition because of China's lower labour cost than that in other countries.

10.3 International free flow of development elements

In developing nations, the opening to the outside world is usually "sell for purchase," in order to obtain foreign exchange to import products. After entering the middle-income stage, opening to the outside world is about to turn to "purchase for sell," which is to buy production factors to expand the export. For these developing nations, to enhance their international competitiveness, more development elements have been gained in the international free flow of factors.

10.3.1 The globalisation context of using international development elements

It has been argued that international trade is the engine for growth. This may be true amongst the developing nations in their early stages of development. When William Arthur Lewis (1915–1991) pointed out the role of international trade, he compared the developed and developing countries and found that "[i]f the engine of growth is the export of industrial products of more developed countries and the primary products of less developed nations, the engine of former runs slightly faster than that the latter."[12] This means that in the international division of labour, developed countries are the exporters of manufactured goods, and developing nations are the exporters of primary products. The exports of the latter depend on the growth rate of the former. Thus the latter is dependent on the former. Developed countries have always been in an advantageous position. Moreover, in international trade, the trade conditions for the exchange of primary products and manufactured goods have deteriorated.

Obviously, the way for developing nations to change the structure of the present international trade is to improve their own industrial structure and enhance their international competitiveness. The condition is to obtain sufficient international development elements in the opening up of the economy. The current economic globalisation offers such opportunities and conditions.

International economic relations include not only the international circulation of commodities but also the international flow of factors of production, including the flow of capital, technology and labour. China's economic development should not only fully use domestic resources but also fully absorb and use international resources. The international circulation of economic resources can be carried out in the form of foreign trade and through the output and input form of production capital. Immigration is also an important method.

An important feature of economic globalisation is that resources and factors of production can flow internationally. A country's endowment of resources supply condition can be changed with the aid of new technology revolution achievement; it can also change and optimise itself by gaining international factors of production by way of opening up. In the past, China's opening-up focussed on expanding exports to gain foreign exchange to expand the purchase of imported goods. Large-scale exports and abundant foreign exchange are not automatically translated into positive economic development. Modernisation cannot be bought by such a vast country as China. The driving force of China's economic development is the international competitiveness of its own industries. Therefore, China continues to develop an open economy, and its ultimate goal is to establish the modern foundation through the introduction and adoption of new technology and revolution achievement to transform traditional industries, to optimise industry organisation and to improve the factors of production conditions. This is the focus of the introduction and use of international resources.

Technology and knowledge have no boundaries. According to Simon Smith Kuznets (1901–1985), the development and utilisation of technology and social knowledge in the world is a sign of the rapid growth of production and the entry of developing countries into the stage of modern growth. In his view, the economic growth of any individual country, regardless of the source of its resources, has a foreign basis, reflecting the dependence of a country's economic growth on the world's intellectual stock. All countries now rely on the use of the world's knowledge stock to enter the stage of modern growth. The economic gap between developing nations and developed countries can be illustrated in their exploitation and utilisation of the world's stock of knowledge and technology. The later the country enters the modern growth stage and the greater the unused technology and social knowledge that exists, the bigger the economic disadvantage is compared with developed countries.

If later-developing nations, such as China, want to enter the modern stage of growth, they must fully develop the world's stock of knowledge and technology for their own good and enhance their efficiency.

According to Kuznets, the countries which enter the stage of modern economic growth at a later time have a later-mover advantage. The later they enter the stage, the more technical resources and choices are available.[13] Because of different national conditions, however, the choice of a country depends not only on the time that it enters the stage of modern growth but also on such characteristics in the country as area, natural resources, historical tradition and so on.

There are many ways to develop and use the world's knowledge and technology stocks. They may be from foreign investment or talents. It is particularly important to point out the introduction of talents. The process of well-educated, skilled talents from the developing nations moving to the developed world is known as "brain drain." On the one hand, this is a kind of a loss of human capital. On the other hand, through human capital investment, talents moving into the developed countries can become carriers of the world's stock of knowledge and technology after they learn new technologies and introduce them at home. It is also the most efficient way. Therefore, in the international competition for talents, China need not rely on blocking international talent flow to keep the talents at home. Instead, China should actively encourage and channel the international flow of talents. China needs to attract talents with advanced foreign technology in the competition. The key is that the popularisation of education is the basic condition for taking advantage of the international development elements. According to Kuznets, regardless of the physical location, modern economic growth refers to increased use and sharing beyond traditional knowledge. Using and sharing new knowledge does not mean that the country becomes subordinate to others. It means that a country's economic growth is increasingly affected by the new knowledge in other countries. Therefore, there are two ways for developing nations to share the world's stock of knowledge and technology. One is to attach great importance to education to cultivate a large number of workers capable of absorbing and learning and developing modern science and technology. The other is to increase the proportion of human resources devoted to the development of scientific and technological knowledge.

10.3.2 The transformation of an open economy to obtain innovation factors

Since the outbreak of the world financial crisis in 2008, the global economy has entered a rebalancing stage. Developed economies have been stagnant for a long time and emerging economies have risen from the underdeveloped countries. Developing countries have significantly weakened their economic dependence on the developed nations, especially since China has become the world's second-largest economy and entered the development stage of middle-income countries. In this context, the strategy of China's opening to the outside needs adjustment. Its international division of labour and competitive positioning will enable China to ascend in the global industry chains. The specific goals are to improve the added value of manufacturing exports and create new advantages of trade in services. The key to opening-up is to follow the trend of international free movement of elements and relax investment access and overseas investment.

The export-oriented development strategy is to arrange industry, trade structure and international competition strategy according to the needs of export. It naturally leads to dependence on the international market. This strategy is carried out in the initial stage of economic development, which is seriously lagging behind developed countries in terms of domestic economic development capacity and international competitiveness. When the country's economic development capacity is improved, the export orientation and low level of export will significantly weaken its role in economic growth. At this time, it is necessary to upgrade the domestic industrial structure, especially to develop the same emerging industries as other developed countries and master the world's advanced science and technology and industry. The essence of the development strategy that contains these contents is the development of an innovative economy. It relies on talents, technology and management innovation factors. The goal is to develop core technologies and key technologies with independent intellectual property rights, focussing on industrial innovation and reflecting the endogenous and innovation-driven growth. The growth engine has turned to innovation, not to the closed economy but to the open economy. Of course, it plays a role within the main engine of the innovative economy. Admittedly, if the open economy needs to continue to play the engine role of economic growth, it also needs transformation and upgrade, which is to develop an open economy based on innovation.

The open economy is innovation-oriented. On the one hand, the export substitution means the export of green high-tech products replace the export of labour-intensive and resource-intensive products by means of innovation, which is to improve the technological content of export products. In particular, energy and environmental exports, such as high energy consumption and high polluting exports, are reduced. Therefore, it is especially important to expand the international market with strategic emerging industrial products and services. On the other hand, import replacement should be adopted. In the past, import substitution referred to the replacement of imported products with domestic products. Here import replacement means replacing the imported general consumer goods with imported advanced equipment in order to enhance their level of science and technology and innovation so as to form their own competitive advantage and support the export of high-tech products. Although turning to entrepreneurship-oriented exports can significantly reduce the total exports over a period of time, it is changing from the simple pursuit of quantity to the pursuit of efficiency and quality, so the added value of exports will be higher.

The competitive advantage needs to be cultivated. The orientation of China's open economic transformation and upgrading is to introduce innovative resources to foster industrial advantages. Today's international economy is dominated by the flow of economic factors. In the past, China used international resources by introducing foreign investment. The reason is that such elements as technology and management always follow capital. Turning to innovation now means turning to talents. The reason is that various innovative elements follow the talents. Most high-end innovation elements, especially high-end talents, are in the developed countries. China needs to use the open economy to introduce high-end technology and managerial talents from the developed countries.

The innovation-oriented open economy will also require transformation and upgrading by FDI. The foreign-invested enterprises in the past not only used domestic labour and environmental resources of manufacturing in China through "the three types of processing plus compensation trades" but also brought the mature technology and industry, not the advanced technology and industry. Now with innovation as the guide, there should be stricter requirements for foreign capital and technology. On the one hand, it is required that their high and new technology research and development be introduced to improve local manufacturing added value. On the other hand, the industry should be an internationally advanced one. Encouraging foreign investment in China's indigenous innovation and development technology has become an important guide to attracting foreign investment.

First, China will raise the level of foreign investment and encourage foreign enterprises to develop and innovate technologies. Innovation is without borders. An innovative economy is not only the innovation of local enterprises but also the continuous innovation of foreign enterprises in China. When China loses the advantages in labour costs and land prices, it needs to strengthen the advantage of human capital and innovation environment, encourage the entry of foreign capital enterprise and research and development centres of science and technology and embrace foreign investment in the value chain of the high-end link and research and development link. In this way, it is not only the cheap labour and the unfettered environment resources that foreign capital makes use of when they enter China but also high-quality human capital and innovation environments. International direct investment has also entered the stage of transformation and upgrading. In other words, more and more high-tech foreign capital is replacing the foreign capital of general technology, and foreign capital is likely to set the world's leading technology and industrial base in China.

The second is to expand the sectors for foreign investment to enter. International direct investment focusses on the expansion of manufacturing and modern services. The reason is that an innovative economy needs the support of international resources not only in manufacturing technology but also in modern service industry management and service support, involving finance, insurance, transportation, information services, outsourcing services, e-commerce, modern logistics, etc. Service outsourcing is an important way to use China's superior intellectual labour force. Some service outsourcing enterprises and employees from China have learned and improved their innovation ability in the outsourcing service.

The third is that China will expand financial openness. Making use of international resources does not only mean the use of FDI but also needs to attract and use the international financial capital through the financial industry opening to the outside world, shifting from attracting industry capital to attracting financial capital. It includes attracting international financial institutions and companies to enter China, encouraging Chinese enterprises to get listed on the overseas capital markets to raise funds, gradually removing restrictions for foreign investors to enter the Chinese capital market. In particular, China should attract international venture capital firms to participate in China's scientific and technological innovation and technological entrepreneurship.

10.3.3 Improving the investment environment for foreign investment

According to Yu Zongxian (1930–), former president of the Central Economic Research Institute in Taiwan, there are nine requirements to attract foreign investment and improve its efficiency. First is social stability. This is related to government administrative efficiency and economic situation in society. Second is political stability. This is related to investment safety.

To cultivate an excellent investment environment, China must first have a modern financial system. Fourth is the rationalisation of the tax burden. There should not be too many tax items, and the tax rate should be low to attract foreign investment. Regarding transportation systems, the domestic and external transportation systems are unimpeded, which is itself a reduction in production cost, and it can improve competitiveness in both domestic and international markets. There also needs to be a complete power system. Typically, there should be a complete water and electricity facility to enable construction and production of a plant. In addition, it is important to have a sufficient labour force. In particular, the quality of the labour force should meet the demand of enterprises. It is equally important to have harmonious labour-capital relations. Finally, the increase in administrative efficiency is significant. In addition to these general requirements, there are two other considerations for foreign investors. One is the degree of freedom to enter and exit the country. If foreign exchange controls are tight and money can only be invested and cannot be withdrawn, foreign investors will lose interest in investment. The other is the difference in interest at home and abroad. If foreign interest rates are high and domestic interest rates are low, the capital will flow abroad.[14]

There are three types of export-oriented economic zones in various countries and regions of the world:

1   The free-trade area. This includes the free-trade zone, duty-free zone and free-trade port. The traditional free-trade area (FTA) is a regional economic and trade group, including the agreement country (region), established under the agreement between several countries. It refers to a number of countries and regions or economies giving each other preferential trade policies, such as zero tariff. The AFTA (Association of Southeast Asian Nations Free Trade Area) belongs to this category. The China (Shanghai) Free-Trade Zone (FTZ) was established in 2013 according to China's laws and regulations in its territory, taking the policy of "outside the customs and within the boundary."

The trade rules of the Shanghai FTZ are set up by China alone, which is different from those of many countries in the traditional FTA. The administration of pre-established national treatment plus a negative list is implemented.

Policies and measures for reform and opening up in FTZ should be tried. It includes expanding the opening-up of the investment areas and opening-up in finance, shipping, commerce, culture and other services. China should also create a negative list management model and gradually form a foreign investment management system with international standards. It will reform the method of overseas investment management and support various forms of overseas investment by various types of investors in the pilot area. It will promote a shift in the way trade is developed. We will actively cultivate new forms and functions of trade and promote the transformation and upgrading of trade. China will also deepen trials of international trade settlement centres, encourage enterprises to coordinate international and domestic trade and realise the integration of domestic and foreign trade. It will upgrade the international shipping service level, deepen opening and innovation in the financial sector and establish a foreign exchange management system compatible with the pilot FTZ to facilitate cross-border financing. Finally, China will promote the all-round opening of financial services to qualified private capital and foreign financial institutions and encourage product innovation in financial markets.

2   Export processing zone. The export processing zone is a kind of FTZ. Developing nations establish an export processing zone to improve the export exchange capacity and accelerate industrialisation. The zone is generally established in the areas currently weak in industrial infrastructure, but strong with an existing transportation network, and thus influences the economic development of the peripheral regions. Export processing zones are characterised by the fact that the supply of raw materials is from foreign countries, and the market is also in foreign countries. Export processing zones carry out special policies and flexible measures to create a good environment to attract foreign investment and export processing industry development. Tax relief is implemented on imported raw materials, machinery and equipment, and an export tax is implemented on processed goods. In the beginning, the export processing zones in developing nations mainly aimed at solving problems, such as insufficient funds, backward technology and insufficient employment in the region. By introducing foreign capital to run some labour-intensive industries, some processing zones have now turned to capital-intensive and technology-intensive industries.

3   Scientific industrial park. The scientific industrial park is also called science park or technology city. This is a high-level, export-oriented economic zone. Its goals are to concentrate on the development of new industries and advanced technology and focus on high-tech research institutions and higher education institutions, scientific research activities, engineering technology development and industrial production, forming a complex of "science and technology-production." The park has industrial infrastructure and service facilities specialising in cutting-edge technology, providing good working conditions and living conditions for experts and technicians. The Silicon Valley, built in northern California, covering an area of 768 km^2, is a scientific and industrial park. Taiwan and South Korea have also established such export-oriented science industrial parks.

In addition to the three types of export-oriented economic zones, there are various types of specialised export-oriented economic zones, such as tourism development zones and agricultural development zones. The export processing zones also have their own characteristics, some of which are electronic export processing zones, while others are garment export processing zones and so on.

All kinds of development zones built across China, such as economic and technological development zones, high-tech zones and industrial parks, are the product of an open economy and the platform and carrier for developing an open economy. At that time, the basic objective of the development zone was to introduce foreign industries and foreign investment enterprises. The attraction of the development zone to foreign capital lies in the ideal infrastructure in the development zone, as well as incentives in land use fees and taxes. Practice has proved that China's development zone as an open economy carrier is successful. The development of foreign trade in the development zone has produced an obvious development effect: it has become the most open region in all regions and has formed a cluster of local emerging industries.

The innovation-oriented open economy requires the transformation and upgrading of various development zones. The existing development zones are basically built according to the model of the world factory. Essentially, the conditions offered by the development zone are cheap land and labour resources, as well as the relatively loose environment resource capacity constraints. Now in many areas, especially the first opened areas, more and more of the aforementioned conditions no longer exist. In particular, the use of cheap migrant workers is approaching the limit. In fact, foreign capital attracted by cheap labour and natural resources is often foreign capital with low technology or without any high technology in China. Coupled with the outbreak of the world financial crisis, foreign capital is far less abundant than previously. These new issues pose challenges to existing development zone models.

From the practice of developing various development zones all over China, the development zone is an industrial agglomeration of advanced production factors and a growth point for economy development in various regions. Development zones can be used not only for open economies but also for innovative economies. In particular, they have an open function, which will play a greater role if transformed into the innovative function.

The basic direction of transformation and upgrading of the development zone is from the introduction of foreign resources and the main carrier of the foreign industry to a leading area of the development of the creative economy. The function transformation of the development zone requires changes in the evaluation standard of the development zone. In the past, the main evaluation criteria on the development zone were how much foreign capital was introduced and how much GDP was produced. The important aspect of the transformation of the development zone in southern Jiangsu is the transformation from a world factory to the incubation base of research and development, making the industrial park a high-tech incubator. Accordingly, the evaluation of the development zone should shift focus to the research and development institutions of universities involved as well as technologies and products created.

According to the requirements of the leading innovative economy development area, all kinds of development zones need construction in the following several aspects. One is that many of the existing development zones in the manufacturing industry agglomeration are also the main producers of emissions. China needs to promote low-carbon construction in accordance with the requirements of ecological civilisation. The second is that the existing development zones are basically the manufacturing industry base, which is a factory district and cannot attract high-end innovation talents. Therefore, it is necessary to promote the urbanisation of the development zone. These zones should provide and gather not only the production elements but also the urban elements. Some development zones can also be transformed from manufacturing centres to service industry centres to realise the coordinated development of the manufacturing and service industries. The third is that the existing development zones should shift focus from the introduction of foreign capital to that of innovation resources. They should take the initiative to attract resources from colleges, universities and scientific research institutions and actively introduce the world-renowned enterprises and their research and development centres of science, technology and venture capitals to turn the development zones into university science parks and high-end talent centres. In summary, China should combine opening-up and innovation in the economic development zones and form high-tech manufacturing centres, high-tech research and development centres and modern service industry centres.

In China, such conditions as technology, industrial base, geographical position, economic centres, raw material supply and transportation vary in each region, so it is impossible for each region to use the same pattern to develop an open economy. Every region needs to take advantage of its own foundation to build an open economic model with its own characteristics. With its unique function and influence, it should have its own advantages in the introduction of advanced technology, capital and export structure. If all kinds of characteristics are integrated, the overall effect of the open economy would be increased greatly.

Notes

1 William Arthur Lewis, *Growth and Fluctuations*, trans. Liang Xiaomin (Beijing: Huaxia Press, 1987), 4.
2 Gerald M. Meier and Joseph E. Stiglitz, *Frontiers of Development Economics: The Future in Perspective*, trans. an Anonymous Group (Beijing: Chinese Financial and Economic Press, 2003), 168.
3 Simon Smith Kuznets, *Modern Economic Growth*, trans. Dai Rui and Yi Cheng (Beijing: College of Economics Press, 1989), 265.
4 Department of Trade and External Economic Relations Statistics, National Bureau of Statistics, "The Leap-forward Development Realized by Opening to Outside World," August 21, 2012, http://www.stats.gov.cn/ztjc/ztfx/kxfzcjhh/201208/t20120821_72840.html.
5 Vladimir Lenin, *The Complete Works of Vladimir Lenin*, vol. 32, trans. Central Compilation and Translation Bureau (Beijing: People's Press, 1985), 338.
6 John C. H. Fei and Gustav Ranis, *Growth and Development from an Evolutionary Perspective*, trans. Hong Yinxing and Zheng Jianghuai (Beijing: Commercial Press, 2004), 462–64.

7 Fei and Ranis, Growth and Development, 2004, 462–64.
8 "General trade" refers to the import or unilateral export trade of enterprises with the right to import and export in China; the goods imported and exported in general trade mode are general trade goods. In short, general trade means is to purchase raw materials, process them domestically and then export the products.
9 Hong Yinxing, "The Comparative Advantage and the Competitive Advantage under Economic Globalization," *Economic Perspectives*, 12 (2002), 6, 10.
10 Michael E. Porter, *The Competitive Advantage of Nations*, trans. Li Mingxuan and Qiu Rumei (Taipei: Commonwealth Publishing Ltd., 1996), 30.
11 Porter, *The Competitive Advantage of Nations*, 37.
12 William Arthur Lewis, "The Slowing Down of the Engine of Growth," in *The Selected Papers on Modern Foreign Economics*, vol. 8, ed. Central Research Society for Foreign Economics (Beijing: Commercial Press, 1997), 251.
13 Kuznets, *Modern Economic Growth*, 253.
14 Yu Zongxian, *The Revelation of the Development in Taiwan* (Taipei: Sanmin Book Co. Ltd., 1980), 46–51.

11 The institutional drive for economic development

Institutional factors are the keys to economic development. Whether various factors of economic development can effectively function and economic development can be built on the basis of profits and efficiency depends on the state's institutional arrangements. China's transition to a socialist market economy, whether motivated by the desire to allow the market to decide resource allocation or to help the government better function, will be determined by institutional arrangements. Institutional arrangements are interrelated with both macroeconomic control systems and market systems, as well as resource allocation and distribution.

11.1 Institutional transformation and economic development

11.1.1 The inseparability of development and institutions

General development theories consider institutions to be pre-determined and do not examine them as a development factor. However, institutional factors cannot be ignored while studying economic development in those developing nations which are transitioning from a planned to a market economy. To a certain extent, these nations will not be able to enter the economic growth stage if they cannot solve their institutional problems properly.

Studying the relationship between an institution and development is not a matter of whether there should be an institution, but how to ensure that the institution is right (i.e. to establish a system for the healthy development of the economy). This involves economic efficiency, people's well-being and macro-stability.

According to Walt W. Rostow, one of the three characteristics for an economic take-off is "the existence or quick emergence of a political, social and institutional framework which exploits the impulses to expansion in the modern sector and the potential external economic effects of the take-off, giving growth an on-going character."[1] Kuznets's definition of modern economic growth also includes institutional adjustments: "A country's economic growth may be defined as a long-term rise in the capacity to supply increasingly diverse economic goods to its population, this growing capacity based on advancing technology and the institutional and ideological adjustment that it demands."[2] It is evident that institutional arrangements play a crucial role in economic growth and economic take-off. When a country enters the stage of economic growth, it needs institutional arrangements. China is a case in point. It implemented its reform and opening policy in 1978 and established a socialist market economic system, which promoted China's rapid economic growth. Practice has proved that reform is the emancipation of productivity.

Institutions, according to Douglass C. North, Nobel Prize laureate in economics, are the humanly devised constraints that structure political, economic and social interactions. They consist of both formal rules (constitutions, laws and property rights) and informal constraints (sanctions, taboos, customs, traditions and codes of conduct). "It is a mixture of principles, regulations, and specific mandatory rules that determine economic performance."[3] In his account of economic history, North pointed out that there are three cornerstones of institutional change: (1) the property system (2) a country that guarantees a certain property system and (3) an ideology which is the basis of common social values and moral standards. In reality, institutional changes are based on these three systems.

From the development perspective, the function of an institution is primarily efficiency-related. A country's economic resources (capital, labour, technology, land and other natural resources) are limited. Resource allocation refers to the allocation of resources in various production sectors. It solves the problem of what to produce, how much to produce and how to produce. It also refers to the combination of various factors in the process of economic growth. All factors, such as capital, labour, technology and natural resources, have their own respective supply and demand relations. Resource allocation should determine how to allocate the scarcest resources to the places where they are most needed and produce the most profits. The allocation of resources is always arranged by a certain system, and different systems have different ways of allocating resources. The combination of the efficiency of resource allocation and the minimum cost of resources has become the standard criterion when choosing systems. Using markets to allocate resources in the market economy system is the most effective in the world today. Thus there is a tendency for most countries to transform their economic systems to a market economy.

In reality, there are costs for every institution which are called "the costs of running the economic system" by Kenneth Arrow, a Nobel laureate in economics. Comparing these costs becomes the basis for choosing an economic system. In a certain sense, the transaction cost discovered by Ronald Coase is an institutional cost in terms of the allocation of resources because the cost of a market economy is lower than the cost of a planned one. Therefore, we tend to choose a market economy. However, in the framework of a large market economy system, there is still a process for institutional choice and adjustment. As Stiglitz warned, "Many underdeveloped market-based economies are extremely poor, although these countries are willing to pay the price for economic transition. It is worth mentioning that there are many forms of a market economy."[4]

In the actual operation of an economy, the choice and adjustment of institutions are ubiquitous. For example, transaction costs exist in market transactions between enterprises. Transaction costs can be overcome through mergers and acquisitions amongst related enterprises, through replacing the market with enterprises and through transforming the external division of labour and transactions amongst enterprises into management within the enterprise. Of course, after the replacement of enterprises by the market, if management costs of the enterprises are lower than the original transaction costs, such an institutional alternative is unworthy.

Economic development requires performance. Efficiency-related institutional arrangements are not only a matter of choosing an institution but also the creation of incentives to promote efficiency. Only when the institution provides effective incentives can technological progress and capital accumulation continue. Its necessity is related to the existence of incomplete information systems and incomplete competition. At the same time, no matter if economic development is under the management of the country or enterprises, there exists a series of principal-agent relationships. The supervision in this process is often inefficient. To avoid opportunistic behaviours, such as adverse selection and moral hazard, a series of incentive mechanisms should be established to overcome these behaviours and achieve the goal of efficient economic development.

11.1.2 Path dependence of institutional change

To study institutional change and reform, we should pay attention to the importance of the initial choice of a path during transition. North pointed out, similar to technological change, increasing returns and self-reinforcing mechanisms also exist in institutional change. Once such a mechanism commits to a certain path, the path's direction will be reinforced as development progresses. Therefore, "people's past choices determine their possible choices in the present." Following this established route, institutional change may enter a virtuous cycle and optimise quickly. It may also travel along the wrong path and become locked into an inefficient state. Once in a locked state, it is very difficult to escape. To change such a situation, exogenous variables should be introduced through external effects.

The path dependence of institutional change theory is illustrated by the southern Jiangsu model and the Wenzhou model at the beginning stage of China's reform and opening period. Marketisation can have different development modes in different regions. In China's early stage of marketisation, most township enterprises in Wenzhou were household enterprises. There was no collective input, for there was no "collective economy." This is why the Wenzhou model has a high percentage of private enterprises. When southern Jiangsu began to develop township enterprises, however, it had collective economy, in contrast to the Wenzhou model. The use of collective accumulation to develop township enterprises is quick and easy to scale up. Therefore, the southern Jiangsu model relied heavily on the collective economy. The variability of the environmental conditions determines the variability of the development mode. In their later development, both the southern Jiangsu and Wenzhou models underwent important changes in many ways. From the late 1980s to the early 1990s, economic development in southern Jiangsu entered a new historical stage, developing many new features that marked a significant departure from the past. The most important were an export-oriented economy, enterprise restructuring and urbanisation. These shifts further changed the economic environment in southern Jiangsu and at the same time greatly enriched the content of the southern Jiangsu model. The traditional model, with the township collective economy as its basis, has gradually been abandoned by southern Jiangsu. This is the innovation of the southern Jiangsu model.

The path dependence theory also indicates that the focus of an economic transition is building new systems. In other words, the transition is more about building new systems than breaking down old ones. According to Asahi Kazuhiko, an economic system is based on historical, social, technological and economic environments. The existing system will determine the path of reform, create path dependence and cause the reform path to deviate from its goal. To prevent such a deviation, it is necessary to change the various environmental variables upon which the path depends. When the external conditions on which the system depends change, the society will modify the institutional arrangements according to the new conditions. This way, their preferences can be consistent with these new institutional arrangements and reap the benefits of institutional changes.

11.1.3 Coordination between reform and development

The reform of an economic system is a powerful driving force for development. But whether the reform direction and the chosen path are correct, and the steps of reform are appropriate will have a direct impact on the effectiveness of development. According to the "order of economic liberalisation" theory proposed by Ronald McKinnon, it is of crucial importance for prioritising fiscal, monetary and foreign exchange policies in the marketisation process. The government cannot, and probably should not, implement all the marketisation measures at the same time. On the contrary, there is an "optimal" order for the marketisation of the economy. It may differ amongst countries undertaking market reforms because of their different starting points. We should be cautious about the economic system chaos resulting from the wrong order.[5] Many countries that have shifted from a planned to a market economy have generally experienced such problems as economic fluctuations, inflation, deflation, unemployment and corruption. This shows the importance of coordination between reform and development.

The so-called Washington Consensus holds that there are three pillars for the transition: (1) price liberalisation, (2) privatisation and (3) macroeconomic stabilisation. It argues that transition should be a big bang, a radical shock to the system, and that all-important reforms should be carried out simultaneously without prioritised order. The countries that adopted the Washington Consensus are Russia and other former members of the Soviet Union. Their focus was on privatisation, essentially adopting the big bang "shock therapy" strategy. Countries adopting this approach experienced significantly higher inflation and lower economic growth – even negative growth – for many years.

China has adopted gradualism as its economic transition strategy. Experience has demonstrated that a gradual economic transition will not only cause no damage to productivity but also promote economic growth because of less friction and the smooth advancement of marketisation. China's gradual approach has led to a high growth rate (approximately 10%) during the transitional period, which is much higher than Russia and other Eastern European nations, with much lower inflation. By the early 1990s, China's marketisation level actually surpassed that of Russia and Eastern European nations that had applied shock therapy. In this new historical starting point, China's marketisation requires higher goals and more coordinated reforms and development at a higher market level.

At a seminar organised by the World Bank on the second-generation transition in early 1995, Michael Bruno, chief economist of the World Bank, put forward three insights into the second-generation transition: (1) the interdependence between stabilisation, liberalisation and economic growth; (2) the restructuring of enterprises; and (3) the rule of law, which concerns the issue of anti-corruption. These three observations represent challenges to China's current reform and development.

The first observation is to establish a mechanism to ensure stable economic growth. Almost all nations undertaking economic transitions suffer from macroeconomic problems, such as severe inflation. Other destabilising factors may include deflation and the potential coexistence of economic stagnation and inflation. In reality, some countries in transition have seen economic stagnation or recession, while economic stagnation and inflation even coexist in certain countries. Nonetheless, China's gradual reforms cause less institutional friction. Therefore, China can avoid damages to productivity and maintain continuous economic growth during the transitional phase. While the planned and market systems coexist, however, we cannot overlook the tenacious behaviour (influenced by the old system) of focussing on growth in productivity at the expense of efficiency. This will result in economic over-heating or over-cooling. Markets are then likely to see either inflation or underemployment. Economic instability in countries experiencing economic transition thus might include inflation, economic stagnation, recession or combined inflation and stagnation. Challenged by severe inflation and economic stagnation in transition countries, economists have offered various solutions for stability and growth.

The second observation is the structural realignment of enterprises, which concerns two issues. One is property rights reform for state-owned enterprises (SOEs). Realignment inevitably touches on changes in the ownership structure of SOEs and other types of enterprises. The goal is to establish a modern enterprise system by carrying out reforms of SOEs and transforming them into corporate enterprises with diversified equity. The reforms have proven that the shareholding system can serve as a major form of public ownership. Except for some small- and medium-sized enterprises restructured into private enterprises, a large number of SOEs in China have been transformed into diversified-equity corporate enterprises by absorbing private or other corporate capital. Realignment also requires the trading of property rights amongst enterprises by mergers, acquisitions and restructuring. As the state-owned economy makes adjustments, private enterprises also enter a new development phase. In many areas, the growth of private companies no longer focusses on increasing in number but on expanding in scale and advancing their competitiveness. In addition, various policy barriers have to be removed to give private enterprises more market access. The two objectives can be entirely realised by merging, acquiring or restructuring SOEs. In conclusion, these two aspects aim at improving the ownership structure of the enterprises to enhance their competitiveness.

The third observation is to implement the rule of law to govern the market economy and prevent corruption. For countries in transition, corruption is another source of instability, as it may delay the reform process by reducing political credibility and weakening confidence in government. In fact, corruption did exist widely under the previous planned economic system. For example, obstructions in the free flow of goods and services provided incentives for "rent-seeking" through the allocation of scarce goods and services. With the ending of the planned economic system, rules of a legitimate free market would become common practice, while illegal "rent-seeking" and other forms of corruption would be reduced. It has not become reality, however, and corruption has become a common problem in countries in transition. This is mainly because governments continue to control the "purse strings," which gives rise to potential "rent-seeking" and other forms of insider trading. Marketisation will eventually reduce corruption because the government will decrease its interventions in the economy. Corruption will not decline simply as a result of less government intervention, however. People may try to create new paths for "rent-seeking" under the new system. For this reason, combating corruption calls not only for reducing government intervention in the economy but also for building a corresponding legal system. Transitional countries should establish legal standards and at the same time restrict government intervention to reduce the possibility for "rent-seeking."

The basic framework of China's socialist market economic system includes the establishment of the following conditions: (1) an ownership structure in which public ownership dominates while coexisting with diverse forms of ownership; (2) a modern enterprise system with clear property rights, the separation of government and enterprises and clearly defined rights and responsibilities with scientific management as its main content; (3) a macro-indirect regulation and control system; (4) a unified and open market system; (5) a system of income distribution which "gives priority to efficiency and attaches importance to equality"; and (6) diversified social security systems. These six aspects of the basic framework constitute the foundation of the operation of a modern market economy.

11.2 The decisive role played by markets in the allocation of resources

The institutional premise in almost all development economics is the market economy. In the meantime, "there is no reliable market price system in developing nations, the supply of entrepreneurs is limited and major structural changes are needed."[6] This means the establishment of a sound market economy. China's economic reform was market-oriented at the very beginning. In 1992, the 14th CPC National Congress explicitly proposed the establishment of a socialist market economic system and confirmed that the market played a fundamental role in resource allocation under the state's macroeconomic control. The Third Plenary

Session of the 18th CPC Central Committee in 2013 made it clear that the core issue of economic reform is to handle the relationship between the government and the market, leaving it to the market to play a decisive role and the government to play a better role in the allocation of resources. This is a major breakthrough in socialist market economy theory.

11.2.1 Allocation of resources decided by the market

Economics not only studies efficiency goals but also, more importantly, the mechanism that achieves efficiency goals. Both Marxist economics and its Western peers argue that in the market economy, only the market mechanism can achieve the effective allocation of resources. Marx explains that the standard for the effective distribution of social labour in various sectors is that the total amount of labour spent in each sector should be socially necessary. "Competition, the fluctuations of market prices which correspond to the fluctuations of demand and supply, tend to continually reduce this scale of the total quantity of labor devoted to each kind of commodity."[7] Western economics illustrates this as the law of welfare economics. Every competitive economy has Pareto efficiency, and every resource allocation with Pareto efficiency can be achieved through the market mechanism. The market determines the allocation of resources competitively in accordance with the principle of efficiency. It leads to a flow of resources to regions, sectors and enterprises of high efficiency. China's economic development has passed the stage which relies on resources input. Given an unsustainable supply of resources, we have entered the stage to ask for resources based on efficiency. Thus it is even more urgent to let the market determine the allocation of resources.

The basic implication of market-based resources allocation is to distribute resources according to market rules, prices and competition so as to maximise profits and optimise efficiency. There are two major functions of market-based resource allocation. One is the selection mechanism for the survival of the fittest, while the other is a system of clear rewards and punishments. The reality is that the market decides what to produce, how to produce it and for whom to produce.

The idea that the market decides what to produce refers to production depending on consumers' monetary choices. The market should play a decisive role. It requires not only producers (enterprises) to operate and make decisions independently but also requires consumers' independence and freedom to choose. Only if producers create according to consumer demand can they supply products that are really needed by society. Correspondingly, it is necessary to abolish all kinds of government approval of what the enterprise produces.

The idea that the market decides how to produce refers to the enterprises' independent decisions about their own production, management methods, technological improvements and choices. In a fully competitive market environment, producers will choose the most advanced technology, the most scientific mode of operation, the cheapest production methods. The more competitive the market is, the more efficient the allocation of resources. The corresponding institutional arrangements are intended to break down all kinds of protection and monopoly and adhere to the principles of the survival of the fittest while producers assume the business risks.

The idea that the market determines for whom to produce refers to the distribution of production results amongst the owners of production elements. It depends on the supply and demand of various production factors in the market. The resources that the market allocates include labour, capital, technology, management and natural resources. All resources have supply and demand relations and their corresponding prices, which may or may not be complementary to each other. Thus an important aspect of resource allocation efficiency arises: the scarcest resources should be used in those places where they are most needed and can produce the best economic result. The most abundant resources should be used to the fullest extent. This adjustment goal is determined by the prices, which are determined by the supply and demand of the market for each factor. The factor users compare the costs and profits of each input element based on their prices, which are formed by the production factors, and use these at the lowest cost. The factor suppliers adjust their own supply according to the prices they are able to get on the market. The corresponding institutional arrangement is that all kinds of production factors enter the market and let it determine their prices, which will accurately reflect the scarcity of various factors of production and regulate the supply and demand. The corresponding institutional arrangement is that all factors of production enter the market.

The idea that the market determines the allocation of resources highlights the autonomy of the market. This kind of autonomy is not only reflected in the market's role in resource allocation but also in the market regulations that signal that the market price is formed without any undue interference from the government. On the formation of the price in the market, Marxist economics has a clear explanation. Only when the price is formed in a competitive market can we form a price system that accurately reflects market supply and demand and the law of value. All prices formed by the market should be allowed to stand, and the government should not intervene in any improper way. The market price signal is more accurate, and the market regulation range is more extensive. Moreover, the formation of market prices refers not only to commodity prices but also to the price system of various production factors. Interest and exchange rates should be formed on the market, reflecting the market's supply and demand of various factors and autonomously adjusting the supply and demand of these factors. Market determination of the allocation of resources can only be realised by all-round deepened reform.

11.2.2 Cultivating dynamic market players

The micro-foundation of a market economy is the dynamic market players. The previous enterprise structure in China was public-owned enterprises and dominated by SOEs. It was the micro-foundation of a planned economy. Now China has turned to the market economy. We must cultivate the dynamic market player. To do so, we must carry out ownership reform, first through the structural adjustment of the ownership system and development of various forms of the non-public ownership economy; second, by reforming the property rights system and state ownership; and third by establishing a modern enterprise system.

Although marketisation does not equal privatisation, the source of market vitality lies in the development of a private economy. The reason is that there can be real competition between public and private economies. As a competitive partner for public ownership, private ownership can stimulate market vitality if it can be developed as an important part of the market economy.

The initial stage of China's development of diversified non-state-owned economies was the spontaneous use of resources that were unused by the planned economy, which accounted for a considerable amount at that time of the development of a diversified economy of ownership, while the country provided a relaxed policy environment. Therefore, the development of non-state-owned economies was unhindered, and the development speed is rather rapid. The fastest-growing part of China's non-state-owned economy is the private economy. The private ownership economy includes the individual economy, private economy and foreign-invested economy.

The deepening of market reform inevitably touches upon the state-owned economy itself. Compared to economies with other ownership, the overall efficiency of the state-owned economy is low because it is largely related to the all-inclusive layout of SOEs. First, SOEs had entered some sectors in which they did not need to get involved and did not enjoy competitive advantages. Second, a large amount of state capital was invested in enterprises of low efficiency. Third, because of structural weakness, some sectors in which state capital was invested were in oversupply. Finally, with the speeding up of market-oriented reform together with changes in national income distribution, it was increasingly difficult to support the huge scale of state-owned entities with state capital. Under these circumstances, many sectors require the participation of non-SOEs. All these factors reveal the necessity of regulating the arrangement of SOEs.

Considering the overall effectiveness of the state-owned economy, SOEs do not need to dominate all industries. Instead, they should be concentrated in industries in which they can play a leadership role. SOEs should maintain their control of the lifeline of the national economy in such areas as railroads, aviation, harbours, postal services, telecommunications and finance. They should also play an active role in basic industries that are crucial for development yet are the weak links of the national economy, such as energy and raw materials. Of course, their concentration in these sectors should go hand in hand with the contraction of state-owned entities in other fields. In the general competitive sector that does not involve the lifeline of the national economy, the state does not need to maintain a dominant position and there should not be institutional restrictions on the withdrawal of state-owned capital. According to the efficiency principle, state-owned capital should gradually withdraw from low-efficiency enterprises and long-term industry in which there is no need and no advantage for state-owned capital. This will help to improve the overall efficiency of state-owned capital. As a result, there have been many forms of "denationalisation" in which a considerable number of SOEs have been transformed into private enterprises.

In the general competitive field, there are also many SOEs that have good credit, brands and profits. There is no need to withdraw all state-owned capital from these fields. Here are the three issues to be considered: First, the basic economic system in the primary stage of socialism requires diversified ownership with public ownership as the foundation. How can state-owned capital proliferate if it has been withdrawn from highly efficient enterprises in the general competitive field? The profit of state-owned capital in high-efficiency enterprises is an important support for the dominant position of public ownership. In particular, the existence of SOEs with good credit, brand and profits is the embodiment of public ownership as the dominant model. Second, not all of the existing SOEs are so-called rubbish, as some people have said. Many advanced production factors, such as advanced equipment and human capital, are concentrated in SOEs. The problem is that the existing property rights system hinders its competitiveness. Therefore, the attitude toward SOEs is not to give up and let them go bankrupt but to release their competitiveness through new property rights arrangements. Third, not all improvements in the efficiency of enterprises should be based on the premise of privatisation. As long as competition is intensified on the basis of clear property rights, the institutional environment for improving efficiency can be solved.

First, SOEs must continually dominate in those areas that are crucial to the lifeline of the national economy. This does not mean state-owned capital cannot "withdraw" from these areas. The monopoly and state-controlled sectors, including the natural monopoly industries, are characterised by inefficiency and poor service quality. In these areas, the supply is often unable to meet the demand. Their behaviours cannot always reflect the people-oriented principle. Therefore, marketisation reform cannot avoid the monopoly sectors where state-owned capital enters, except those concerning national security. The paths are as follows: first, even in the natural monopoly sectors there exist competitive aspects. Allowing non-state capital to enter these areas is entirely possible. Second, even in the national economic lifeline sectors controlled by the state-owned economy, total state ownership is not necessary. It is feasible to grant some equity to non-public capital through a joint stock system under the stipulation that state-owned capital holds the controlling share.

Marketisation reform has formed three major dynamic economies: (1) the private economy, (2) foreign economy and (3) listed companies. The importance of these three dynamic economies lies in their inclusion of a private property economy. Therefore, the direction of state-owned economic reform is in line with the three vital economies. The specific approaches include, first, SOEs that absorb private equity. Listed companies absorb private equity on the market, with company employees holding shares and enterprise managers holding shares and other stakes. The entry of private investments into SOEs can not only provide them with more channels for expanding capital but also allow them to be restructured because they include private property rights. Second, SOEs and private enterprises are integrated with an ownership structure that includes the private-owned and the state-owned absorbing each other's equity. In this mutual shareholding process, there is no need to pursue state-owned capital holding the controlling share.

In the early stage of reform, the common development structure of public-owned and non-public economic sectors was limited to the external relations of enterprises (i.e. the development of non-public enterprises outside the public-owned enterprises). After public-owned enterprises establish various types of mixed-ownership enterprises through the absorption of private equity, they form a framework in which public ownership is the mainstay of the same enterprise, and various types of ownership are developed together. Practice has proved that this kind of mixed-ownership enterprise has obvious competitive advantages. In reality, mixed-ownership enterprises, such as China-foreign joint ventures, joint stock enterprises and cooperative stock enterprises, embody the common development of the socialist and non-socialist components within the same enterprise.

Public ownership used to be achieved through state-owned and collective enterprises. It is now clear that the public-owned economy refers not only to public-owned enterprises but also to state-owned and collective capital. Correspondingly, public ownership can take many forms, especially various types of mixed-ownership enterprises that include private property rights. They can also become forms of public ownership. Mixed-ownership enterprises that contain private capital are more dynamic than purely state-owned and collective enterprises.

The most typical form of mixed-ownership enterprise is the shareholding system. SOEs also rely on the shareholding system for their restructuring through the absorption of various non-public property rights. It is in this sense that the shareholding system will become the main form of public ownership. The joint stock system is a form of property rights organisation. It can accommodate diversified investment and form diversified equity. The basic approach to the market-oriented reform of SOEs is to introduce private property rights into enterprises and even allow private capital to hold a controlling share. On this basis, the governance structure can be rebuilt. The various ways in which SOEs absorb private equity are, in fact, aspects of the withdrawal of state-owned capital. It can be expected that in the future, adjustment and consolidation of the ownership structure of enterprises, mutual participation of various types of public capital and various types of non-public capital, mergers and acquisitions amongst enterprises and changes in the controlling shareholders in the enterprise will be the norm in the market.

The establishment of a mixed-ownership system, such as a joint stock system, is an important step in enhancing the vitality of businesses. It definitely does not mean a joint stock system alone can achieve all the expected results. To sustain the vitality of enterprises, a modern enterprise system should be established. It consists of three aspects: first, the establishment of a modern ownership system with clear ownership, clear powers and responsibilities, strict protection and smooth circulation; second, the establishment of a corporate governance structure that is coordinated and effectively balanced; and third, the establishment of a professional enterprise management system.

Vitality comes from competition. Competition is not limited to private companies. The competition between public-owned (mostly state-controlled) and non-public enterprises may be more effective. In particular, modern competition is not only about efficiency but also social responsibility and social credit.

The competitive effect in this area is reflected in different ownership. In this competition, SOEs, including state-controlled enterprises, are more concerned with social responsibility, and private enterprises are more concerned with economic responsibility. The competition involves mutual learning so that both economic responsibility and social responsibility can be achieved in competition.

11.2.3 Establishing a unified, open and orderly competitive market system

The market determines the allocation of resources through mechanisms that include market prices, competition and rules. The effectiveness of resource allocation depends on whether the market mechanism is complete. Just as Xi Jinping, the CPC general secretary said, China's market economy was transformed from the planned economy. The market system is not complete when difficulties still exist in allocating resources efficiently. This requires building an effective market for resource allocation.

The first task is to establish an effective competitive market in lieu of the imperfectly competitive markets. The classic description of the market economy by Marx was that the market "acknowledges no authority other than that of competition."[8] According to the definition of neoclassical economics, the effective allocation of resources by the market must be based on a perfectly competitive market. The classic assumption of a perfectly competitive market is that any commodity, at any time, any place or any natural state (any risk state) is in a perfectly competitive market, while a large number of manufacturers pursuing maximum profit (or value) and rational consumers pursuing maximum utility interact and influence each other. This perfect market model has several basic requirements: (1) all commodities enter the market; (2) the market is perfectly competitive; (3) market participants (manufacturers and consumers) are rationally pursuing maximum utility.[9]

In reality, such a perfectly competitive market does not exist, especially with the evolution of the capitalist system from free competition to the monopoly stage. Many large monopolies, such as trusts and cartels, emerge one after another, making it impossible for the theory based on perfect competition to match exactly with reality. Samuelson said, "Once a perfect competition is abandoned, the principle inferring that laissez-faire is likely to cause the invisible hand to satisfy the need in the most efficient way will no longer exist."[10] This shows that the system of competition is a way of organising economic activities, and perfect competition is the ultimate peak and will never be fully realised. We can gradually get close to perfect competition, but we can never reach it. The solution to the problem lies in maintaining "effective competition."[11] To maintain effective competition under imperfect competition is actually to maintain the effectiveness of competition in the allocation of resources.

The creation of an "effective competition" market is to create a fully competitive market environment. Corresponding to a completely competitive market, imperfectly competitive markets refer to markets in which individuals or a small number of firms have market shares that control the market. The general economic theory has pointed out that a monopoly seriously weakens the vitality of the market, thus reducing the efficiency of resource allocation. The monopoly prices, monopoly income and the quality of service of the monopoly sector are essentially institutional issues. The three forms of imperfectly competitive markets are monopolies, oligarchic markets and monopolistic competition markets. The existence of these three forms of monopoly can be said to be the normal state of the real market. The modern market economy cannot be built on a decentralised atomic enterprise. The complete monopoly enjoyed by the natural monopoly industry itself has economies of scale. From decentralised production to concentrated large-scale production, even the emergence of oligopolistic markets is the result of market economy development.

In the monopolistic competition market, many producers provide differentiated products in response to the different preferences of consumers to create their own monopoly in the market. This is the result of competition from which society can also benefit. To avoid the destruction of both sides, competing companies must seek to cooperate with each other on their own initiative when they are in neck-to-neck competition. They can either sign a contract to share the market, or they can unite as one company. The monopoly formed in a certain range will reduce the competition and save social resources. This also reflects the efficiency of resource allocation.

In this sense, the formation of monopolies by mergers between enterprises is not generally opposed in the modern market economy. The main reason that the United States allowed Boeing to merge with other major companies, such as McDonnell Douglas, is for market size. In the past, there was a theory that a monopoly exists if there are only one or two companies in a region or a market. This kind of monopoly should be broken. The problem now is that the size of the market has expanded, and companies subsequently face both national and global markets instead of the local or regional market. Furthermore, to encourage innovation, intellectual property rights, such as patents, must maintain monopoly income rights within a certain period of time. Otherwise, there will be no incentive for innovation. Based on the understanding of monopoly in the modern market economy, creating a competitive effective market environment mainly involves the following institutional arrangements:

- First, the barriers of free entry into a certain industry have to be limited to the minimum. In particular, there should be no administrative barriers, and the resulting competition can contribute to technological advancement within the industry.
- Second, the complete monopoly formed in the non-natural monopoly industries should be broken. Monopolies should be strictly limited to the "natural monopoly" industries, such as water, oil, natural gas, electricity and transportation. For example, China has split the grid company into northern and southern companies and telecommunications into China Mobile, China Telecom and China Unicom. Consumers can benefit from the competition amongst companies. According to the theory of government regulation, not all-natural monopoly sectors need government regulation. Both the forward and backward links of a network-type natural monopoly can be

used as a competitive area, and their prices should be liberalised and determined by the market. The scope of government pricing should be limited to important public utilities, public welfare services and network-type natural monopolies.

- Third, the focus of anti-monopolists is on behaviour, not structure. That is to say, it does not oppose the monopoly formed by the merger of enterprises in a certain market. But it firmly opposes monopolistic behaviour, such as high prices, collusion and tying. These behaviours are obviously contrary to the direction of the market mechanism adjustment. The suing of the Microsoft Corporation for its behaviour according to the anti-monopoly law is one such case.

Currently, in China, the government's administrative restrictions on competition should be broken. Protection by the local government or supervising administrative sectors of backward companies and preferential government policies for certain enterprises in certain regions are the main reasons for the unfair competition. Only by removing these competing administrative restrictions can an effective competitive environment be created.

The second is to establish a well-organised and well-regulated market faced with high competition costs.

China's marketisation reform has been going on for more than 30 years. The competitive environment has already taken shape, and the economic efficiency of enterprises should have significantly improved. However, in reality, the economic benefits of enterprises have not increased but declined. A careful analysis finds that competition has indeed played a significant role in promoting the improvement of production efficiency, and production costs have indeed been greatly reduced. The problem is that there is competition but no cooperation amongst enterprises. Disorderly competition, excessive competition, vicious competition and excessive competition all increase costs. With the intensified competition amongst enterprises, the competitive costs of enterprises have greatly increased. Inflated competition costs have seriously eroded the benefits of the business. In this situation, people may wonder whether competition is worthwhile. Competition, as a means to increase efficiency, has its own costs. Therefore, it is also necessary to analyse the cost and utility of competition. If competition costs are too high and are even higher than the efficiency of competition, this competition is not worthy.

The modern market economic theory finds that the market economy as a resource allocation method has its own cost. Transaction costs include the search for markets, the information cost in finding real prices, the cost of negotiations and the costs of signing and monitoring contracts. Because of its uncertainties and incompleteness, there are costs to accessing information which may cause unfair trade behaviours, such as reciprocity, monopolisation free ridership and fraud. The decentralised market economy has also produced huge advertising and competitive costs. The costs of transactions and the unreliability of trading partners are high enough to cause people to lose confidence in decentralisation.

In the market economy, there is a mechanism to reduce the cost of competition. This is cooperation. The combination of competition and cooperation can reduce competition costs, thus amplifying the effectiveness of competition. According to Adam Smith, the function of the invisible hand of the market is organisation and coordination. Specifically, market regulation affects competitors who are pursuing their own interests. The function of market regulation is to coordinate the activities of different competitors and establish a certain cooperative relationship amongst these competitors to achieve the goal of perfect resource allocation amongst them.

Milton Friedman, a Nobel Prize laureate in economics, further pointed out, "The price system enables people to cooperate peacefully in one phase of their life so that each one goes about his own business in respect of everything else."[12] John Hicks, another Nobel Prize laureate in economics, pointed out in the preface of his book *Prospect of Economics* (1977) that the modern market economy is distinctly different from the market economy described by Walras and Marshall. It is mainly reflected in two aspects. First, the market is no longer an "atomic market." Because of the concentration of production and capital, monopolistic companies control the market, and the internal planning of monopolistic companies will drive the planning of the markets it controls. Second, unorganised markets have been replaced by organised markets. In Hicks's analytical framework, whether the market is organised is reflected in the price system. Obviously, the market economy has both competitive and cooperative economies. The market economic system that we are talking about today must not only emphasise competition but also establish a compatible relationship between competition and cooperation. In view of the current market situation in China, building a modern market and improving the market mechanism mainly involves the following aspects:

- First, it is necessary to establish fair, open and transparent market rules. Games all have their rules. Market transactions are no exception. Establishing market rules means regulating market order. It is an important way to improve the effect of market regulation and reduce market operating costs. The reason that the market mechanism can effectively allocate resources lies in its principle of adhering to market fairness, which includes equal rights, equal opportunities, fair trade and fair rules. In this fair and competitive market, companies are free to enter or exit the market, consumers are free to choose, production factors are free to flow and trade can be conducted on an equal basis. The market can achieve its efficiency goals by allocating resources in such a fair and competitive market environment.

The unfairness of the current market competition in China is apparent in three aspects. First, different ownership economies are treated unequally, and the non-public economy is subject to various forms of discrimination. Second, there are market monopolies, some of which belong to the administrative monopoly rooted in the planned economy. Enterprises that are in a monopolistic position can manipulate the market and gain monopoly profits. The third is the various preferential policies introduced by the state and local governments. There is discrimination when there are preferences. These policies do not treat enterprises equally, and they create unfair competition opportunities and weaken the regulatory effect of the market mechanism.

Building a fair market for competition highlights the need to build a legal business environment. Market regulation includes three key aspects. First is regulating market access and implementing unified market access and exit system. All kinds of market entities can enter fields as long as they have not violated rules and regulations. The second is regulating pricing practices. Unleashing prices does not mean that pricing can be arbitrary. The monopolistic, dumping and excessive profit-seeking behaviours in pricing should all be restricted to avoid major price fluctuations. The third is regulating competitive behaviour. Unfair competitive behaviour, such as fraud, collusion and false advertising may all result in excessively high competitive costs and transaction costs, which could lead to inefficiency.

Institutional arrangements for regulating competition must cover two areas.

- First, there must be strict rules to protect fair and open market competition. Second, market transparency should be increased, and manufacturers should be encouraged to adopt a voluntary code of competitive behaviour. The openness and transparency of the market require the establishment of a market information disclosure system. If market information is incomplete, the party with exclusive access to information can monopolise and manipulate the market so that market transactions do not achieve a win-win situation. For society, it is necessary to force market participants to disclose information through certain institutional arrangements. The government also needs to establish a market information disclosure system to provide market participants with information such as overcapacity, technical standards and market demand, thereby reducing information costs.
- Second, we need to build a unified and open market. A unified market has three characteristics. First, it ensures the free flow of production factors, enterprises and products and services. Second, all market participants have equal opportunities to enter all kinds of markets and obtain production factors. Third, all regional markets should operate under unified market rules and regulations. China moved directly from a natural economy to a planned economy and now is in transition to a market economy. Strictly speaking, China has yet to form a unified market. In addition, the reform of fiscal and taxation systems and regional development policies have strengthened local interests during the course of reform. Local protectionist market barriers produced in the reform have hindered the effective allocation of resources.

At present, the construction of a unified and open market in China requires three actions. The first is to break down regional barriers. Local governments usually use their administrative powers to protect uncompetitive local products and enterprises. Their protection enables weak enterprises and products to stay in the market. This leads to inefficient resource allocation and makes it impossible for the perfect allocation of resources. The second is to break down administrative monopolies and regional barriers to ensure the free flow of commodities and production factors nationwide so that all market entities can conduct market transactions on an equal basis. The third is to break down urban and rural market segmentation and build a unified urban-rural market. The main solutions to these challenges are to upgrade the level of rural marketisation, improve the mechanism for the formation of agricultural product prices in the market and build a unified market for urban and rural factors.

• Third, it is necessary to optimise the market system, which is the mechanism for ensuring effective resource allocation. This requires that capital, land, labour, technology and other factors of production must enter the market. Only when these factors enter and move freely in the market system can there be a real market-driven, resource-allocation system. Only when the supply and demand for each element in the market determine their prices and the remuneration of owners of various production factors are adjusted can resources be effectively allocated. Since the market economy is a credit economy and resources are allocated through credit channels, it is particularly important to improve the financial market system.

Marx pointed out in *On Capital* that the requirement for a fully competitive market was that capital has greater activity and is easier to move from one sector or place to another. The premise of this condition is that in addition to complete commercial freedom within society, "[the] development of a credit system has pooled a large number of scattered and disposable sources of capital in society." The improvement of the financial market system at this stage, as pointed out at the Third Plenary Session of the 18th CPC Central Committee, involves four aspects. First, various forms of the ownership economy have equal access to financial resources. Qualified private capital is allowed to establish small- and medium-sized banks and other financial institutions in accordance with the law. The second aspect is to improve the regulatory signals of the financial market. The goal is to marketise interest rates so that they can reflect the supply and demand and adjust them accordingly in the capital market. The third aspect is to encourage financial innovation and enrich financial market levels and products. The fourth aspect is the use of the financial market as a channel for opening up to the outside world and connecting the domestic market with the international market.

There are also costs for China to shift from a planned economy to a market economy. Excessive transaction costs will make it too expensive to implement a market economic system. Therefore, the establishment of a socialist market economic system in China should aim at reducing transaction costs. From the very beginning, we must pay attention to the construction of a legal system and other institutional arrangements. China should not only reduce the cost of system construction but also lower transaction costs in the established market economy system.

11.3 The proactive promotion of economic development by government

"Good government is one of the scarcest resources in developing countries."[13] For a developing nation like China, which is still in the primary stage of socialism, development remains its top priority. Promoting development should be an important function of the government, and letting the market determine resource allocation can improve development efficiency. Under this premise, governments at all levels must also undertake the tasks necessary to promote development, including the integration of urban and rural development, urbanisation, fostering an innovation-driven economy, economic restructuring, environmental protections, an open economy and so on. All of these government measures need to work effectively with the market's decision-making mechanism for resource allocation.

11.3.1 Understanding government functions from the perspective of development economics

Whether a government should play a role in a country's transition to a market economy has been the subject of a long-standing debate. The theory recommended to developing nations by the earliest development economists upholds their liberal tradition. They argue that the role of the government should be limited to specific cases of market failure. The first role is to help overcome the problem of wide income disparities caused by the market system through redistribution. The second role is to deliver public products that cannot be provided by the market system, such as national defence, public security and education. The third role is to solve the external problems that may arise from the market system, such as environmental pollution, through laws and other means. The fourth role is to stabilise the macroeconomy and maintain healthy economic growth. The fifth role is to maintain market competition through anti-monopoly laws and other means.

For a long time, scholars of development economics have considered government and the market as two sides of an either-or-not resource allocation mechanism. The traditional economic theory believes that the only proper role for government is to define and enforce property rights and provide public products. Government intervention may be inefficient, unnecessary or hinder productivity if it strays out of this area.

A new generation of development economists has found that "most success stories in economic growth involve high levels of government intervention."[14] They argue that the government and the market are not entirely opposed to each other but can be supplementary. They even constitute an essential factor in the economic system. Government intervention still functions extensively in

> dealing with the market failures (incomplete information, incomplete markets, turbulent externalities, increasing returns to scale, multiple equilibriums and path dependence), providing public goods to satisfy the need for

education, health, reducing poverty, and improving income distribution, providing physical and social infrastructure, and protecting the natural environment.[15]

Seen in this light, the government is not merely an alternative mechanism to address market failures; it can also increase the development capacities of private sectors. Therefore, the interdependence between the government and the market is formed. This is what the World Bank report pointed out: "No planning agency can calculate and manage the relative shortage of all goods and services, and no government dares to trust the free market without certainty."[16]

This new understanding of government promotion of development is also verified by the success of East Asian economic development. The World Bank published its report *The East Asian Miracle: Economic Growth and Public Policy* in September 1993. It attributes the different forms of economic achievement in the countries and regions of East Asia to government. The governments in these countries have successfully managed the problem of rent-seeking and promoted a market policy framework. Meanwhile, they solved the problems of coordination on such issues as export-oriented policies, rapid deepening reform of financial markets, accumulation of human capital through human investment and introduction of advanced technologies. "East Asia showed that countries could generate a very high rate of voluntary savings without high levels of inequality."[17]

The government's function in the aforementioned areas is based on market failures in developed countries. The market background in developing nations is different. Even for the nations that have adopted market economies since their independence, their degree of market development lags far behind that of the developed countries. At the same time, these nations are also faced with urgent economic development tasks. Their economic development cannot wait for the natural development of the economy; thus, government promotion is needed. It means the scope and extent of the government intervention in a developing nation's economy has a special role. According to the World Bank, the scope of the government's role includes macroeconomic stability, substantial investment in human resources, a stable and reliable financial system, reduction of price distortions and opening up international technology.

11.3.2 *The promotion of economic development by government*

The United States is often cited as an example of neo-liberalism that does not require government intervention in the economy. However, the actual situation is that in developing nations, such as China, government intervention is still needed because of the following two reasons:

- First, market players need support. In the United States, the overall size of enterprises is sufficiently large. The output value of a large company is even larger than that of a developing nation. Naturally, there is a liberal theory which argues that government intervention is not needed. In developing nations, such as China, the overall size of companies is small, and their competitiveness is weak. It will take a long time for such companies to grow up to compete with those in developed countries. Therefore, it is necessary for the government in developing nations to support the growth of their enterprises.

• Next, the market needs government cultivation. The market economy has been developed for hundreds of years in developed countries. Both the market system and its organisation have become increasingly mature. But the market economy in China has a very short history. It is incomplete in structure and in functionality. In reality, factor markets in China are disorganised, while market signals are neither sensitive nor accurate, failing to reflect the real costs of commodities. The market is also distorted by segmentation, barriers to the free flow of information and government controls of prices and interest rates. Consequently, prices and interest rates cannot reflect scarcity and opportunity costs, and consumers cannot equally access information about products and markets. The flow of production factors is hindered, and prices cannot be used as a basis for evaluating and selecting investments. Therefore, the market allocation of resources is not so effective. Under such circumstances, government intervention should promote the authenticity of prices, the availability of information and the liquidity of resources, thereby promoting the development of the market. The government must take effective measures to cultivate the market and adopt a variety of attractive methods to develop the market economy. Of course, these government actions will gradually decrease with the development of the economy and the market.

After launching their modern economic growth, developing nations are generally faced with major development issues. In particular, they must catch up with developed countries and achieve leap-forward development. The mechanism for promoting development, in addition to giving full play to the market's mechanism of resource allocation, should also give full play to the government's promotional role. It mainly involves the following two roles:

• First is the adjustment, transformation and upgrading of the economic structure, primarily the industrial and urban-rural structures. The economy in developed countries is essentially a problem of growth rather than that of development. Therefore, structural adjustments can be fully delivered to the market. In developing nations, however, the main problem of the economy is development. The major constraint to development is the economic structure. The structure problem is not only that it is unbalanced. What is worse is the low level of development, overcapacity and widening disparity between urban and rural areas. To solve these structural problems, the market mechanisms of the survival of the fittest and free choice should be given full play. Using these mechanisms to regulate industrial structure can effectively eliminate backward and surplus production capacity.

For large developing nations, such as China, however, the adjustment of the economic structure cannot solely rely on the market. It is impossible for the market alone to overcome structural conflicts in the short term. The transformation and upgrading of the industrial structure need the guidance of the country's industrial policies. Support of the development of leading industries and high-tech industries should be an important part of government policy. The forward-looking strategic cultivation of emerging industries requires government's guiding investment. Industry subsidising agriculture and cities lending help to rural regions also are areas that need government promotion.

- Next is innovation-driven economic development. In general, market competition can stimulate innovation, while technological innovation needs a market orientation. The role of the market in these two areas should be brought into full play, but it is not enough to rely on the market to drive modern technological innovation. There are two reasons why this is the case. First, innovative knowledge and technology have an overflow effect, and society can benefit from it. Second, what the market allocates is existing resources, but innovation factors require non-material resources, and new elements have to be created. Therefore, the government needs to intervene and stimulate innovation. This includes the following elements: (1) the country implements major scientific innovation plans; (2) the state must integrate two innovation systems, i.e. technological and knowledge innovations; (3) the state must provide guiding investment to incubate new technologies; and (4) the state should establish an incentive system and mechanism for innovations. Finally, the government must invest in intellectual capital and human capital for aggregating innovative elements.

- Third, openness must be promoted to the outside world. Economic development in developing nations cannot be separated from the global economy. Developing nations need to make full use of international resources and markets to catch up with developed countries. These measures include developing international markets, introducing foreign capital and advanced technologies and implementing innovation-driven development strategies. These need to be carried out after a country implements its opening-up strategy. Whether it is export-oriented or import substitution, joining the WTO or establishing free-trade zones or adjusting the exchange rate or the internationalisation of the RMB, it must rely on the government's open policy and implementation.

11.3.3 The government need to follow market laws

The market plays a decisive role in the allocation of resources, and an important benchmark for the role played by the government is that it must abide by the market order. Inappropriate government operations and the abuse of power will lead to market disorder and disrupt its resource allocation function. Bureaucracy, rent-seeking and administrative monopoly can be seen as some main examples of government failure. In addition, "the policy makers' personal understanding may also result in government failure."[18] To address these problems, government must be connected with the market mechanism, and its allocation of public resources should be combined with the market's allocation of resources. The basic requirements are as follows:

- First, it is necessary to clarify the boundaries between the government and the market. Based on the rules, both must fully and effectively play their own roles. As the World Bank pointed out in its *World Development Report: The Challenge of Development* (1991), high-speed growth is inseparable from effective but carefully reduced government intervention. The government should not only reduce interventions in sectors that are effective under market mechanisms, such as production, but also increase its role in those sectors where market mechanisms cannot function. The market should also be used to the maximum extent where the government plays a role. In terms of adjusting the industrial structure, the government needs to take resolute actions to change the structure of production and trade. In general, the government's attempts to allocate resources are generally unsuccessful in improving economic efficiency. Directing resource allocations in foreign trade, financial markets and labour markets will cause resources to flow into sectors with low productivity and lead to widespread rent-seeking behaviours.

  Therefore, there should be a clear mandate for the government to regulate industrial structure. The pro-market school represented by the World Bank limits the function of the government to four areas: (1) human resources investment, (2) enhancing international competitiveness, (3) opening to international trade and (4) providing public goods. Beyond these areas, government intervention may cause more harm than good. The basic function of the government in this regard is to provide a stable macroeconomic environment, high-quality human capital and a high degree of integration with the world economy to ensure intense competition amongst enterprises.

- Second, the government cannot function in isolation. It needs to work with the market mechanism. The infant industry theory of developing nations emphasises that to cope with economic globalisation, it is necessary to protect the enterprises in infant industries. But the World Bank, in introducing the experience of successful East Asian countries, discovered that the applicability of the theory was limited. It pointed out that many infant industries never grew up, and protection could not guarantee the realisation of the commitment to learning and economies of scale. As a result, the effectiveness of industrial policies was rather poor and could not change the pattern of industrial structure and productivity changes. Therefore, industrial policies need to be combined with the market mechanism of "the survival of the fittest." The basis for the promotion of industrial growth comes from learning, technological improvement or catching up with the world's advanced experience. Externalities related to learning have been an important reason for the failure of developing economic markets. The actual external effects occur when an enterprise obtains knowledge about production from other companies without any cost. The role of the government is to promote learning based on the protection of intellectual property and to link learning with capital and technology-intensive industries.

- Third, the government should create an attractive external environment for market activities. For example, in the coordination of regional development, the main players are still market-oriented enterprises. The market's determination of resource allocation inevitably results in the flow of resources to regions, sectors and enterprises of high efficiency. The government should not seek to intervene in this flow of resources. Under such conditions, it can use its own financial and public resources for monetary transfer in accordance with the principle of equity. It can also promote the equalisation of basic public services or carry out major infrastructure construction to attract enterprises from developed regions for underdeveloped regions and ultimately create external conditions for urban development factors to go into rural regions.

- Finally, the government can function through the market. It is the responsibility of the government to protect the environment, but the government cannot do it alone. It can adopt the method of purchasing services, allowing enterprises to participate in environmental protection. The government can also use market methods, such as sewage charges and emissions trading, to control emissions.

Notes

1 Walt W. Rostow, *The Stages of Economic Growth*, trans. He Liping (Chengdu: Sichuan People's Press, 1988), 30.
2 Simon S. Kuznets, "Modern Economic Growth: Findings and Reflections," in *Nobel Economics Prize Laureates' Lectures, 1969–1981*, ed. Wang Hongchang (Beijing: China Social Sciences Press, 1986), 97.
3 Gerald M. Meier and Joseph E. Stiglitz, *Frontiers of Development Economics: The Future in Perspective*, trans. an Anonymous Group (Beijing: China Financial and Economic Press, 2004), 19.
4 Joseph E. Stiglitz, *Whither Socialism?*, trans. Zhou Liqun, Han Liang and Yu Wenbo (Changchun: Jilin People's Press, 1999), 3.
5 Ronald Ian McKinnon, *The Order of Economic Liberalization: Financial Control in the Transition to a Market Economy*, trans. Zhou Tingyu (Shanghai: Joint Publishing Company, 1997), 5.
6 Meier and Stiglitz, *Frontiers of Development Economics*, 10.
7 Karl Marx, *On Capital*, vol.1, trans. Central Compilation and Translation Bureau (Beijing: People's Press, 2004), 214.
8 Marx, *On Capital*, vol.1, 412.
9 Stiglitz, *Whither Socialism?*, 5.
10 Paul Samuelson, *Economics*, vol.1, trans. Gao Hongye (Beijing: Commercial Press, 1979), 190.
11 Samuelson, *Economics*, vol.1, 70.
12 Milton Friedman, *Free to Choose: A Personal Statement*, trans. Hu Ji, Xi Xueyuan and An Qiang (Beijing: Commercial Press, 1982), 18.
13 Meier and Stiglitz, *Frontiers of Development Economics*, 338.
14 Meier and Stiglitz, *Frontiers of Development Economics*, 296.
15 Meier and Stiglitz, *Frontiers of Development Economics*, 24.

16 Warren Baum, *Investing in Development: Lessons of World Bank Experience*, trans. Wang Furang and Yan Zelong (Beijing: China Financial and Economic Press, 1987), 24.
17 Baum, *Investing in Development*, 308.
18 Hamid Hosseini, "Uncertainty and Perceptual Problems Causing Government Failures in Underdeveloped Nations," *Comparative Economic and Social Systems*, no. 2 (2004): 34–8.

Afterword

My research on the theory of economic development began in late 1987 when I worked at Nanjing University after receiving my doctoral degree from Renmin University. In 1990, I co-authored with Lin Jinding a book titled *General Theory of Development Economics*, published by Jiangsu People's Press. I wrote in its postscript,

> When we wrote this book, we had a strong desire to combine Western development economics rooted overseas with China's reality to establish development economics with Chinese characteristics. Limited by our current knowledge and understanding of the rules of China's economic development, however, we are fully aware that our ability does not match our ambition.

Therefore, despite our best efforts, that book only served as an introduction to the integration of development economics with China's reality. Four years later, I wrote a monograph on the development of China's economy. Titled *Economic Development under the Conditions of Market Economy*, the book was published by Higher Education Press in 1998 and awarded the second prize for outstanding achievement in the humanities and social sciences by the Ministry of Education.

Six years later, I made substantial revisions to the book with the consent of Higher Education Press. In 2005, a revised edition, titled *Development Economics and China's Economic Development*, was published by Higher Education Press. The book was recommended by the Academic Degrees Committee of the State Council as a national textbook for graduate studies in economics. Since then, China's economic development has undergone earth-shaking changes. In particular, the Scientific Outlook on Development has been put forward; the transformation of the innovative economic development mode has been promoted, and China has become the world's second-largest economy and entered the middle-income stage of development. These changes call for an innovative new approach to Chinese economic development theory.

For this reason, since 2010, I have published a number of articles on Chinese economic development theory at the dawn of a new historical starting point. They include "Innovative Thinking after Becoming a World Economic Power" in *Theoretical Horizon*, 5 (2010); "Development Theory Innovation in a New Stage of Economic Development" in *Academic Monthly*, 4 (2011); "China's Development

Economics Needs to Keep Pace with the Times" in *Economic Perspectives*, 11 (2012); and "Innovation in Development Stages and Economic Development Theory" in *Administration Reform*, 9 (2013). Based on these articles, I started writing this book. The most important difference between this book and previous textbooks on development economics is that this work reflects the fact that we have begun a new stage of development. It is necessary to provide a theoretical summary of the China path – the road China has followed over the last 40 years from a low-income nation to that of a middle-income nation. It is also necessary to put forth a theoretical study on the path that China must follow to further develop from a middle-income nation to a high-income country in the coming years.

When the book was selected by the translation programmes sponsored by the National Social Sciences Fund in 2017, I made revisions, including the addition of my new research findings based on the main contents of the 19th CPC National Congress. Professor Sun Ninghua, my former doctoral student, helped me finish writing the book.

Yinxing Hong
Nanjing University
Summer, 2020

Bibliography

Atkinson, Anthony B., and Joseph Stiglitz. *Lectures on Public Economics*. Translated by Cai Jiangnan, Xu Bin and Zou Huaming. Shanghai: Sanlian Publishing House, 1992.

Baum, Warren. *Investing in Development: Lessons of World Bank Experience*. Translated by Wang Furang and Yan Zelong. Beijing: China Financial and Economic Press, 1987.

Chen, Qirong. "Nobel Prize in Natural Science and Innovative Countries." *Journal of Shanghai University* no. 6 (2011): 1–21.

Chenery, Hollis. *Industrialization and Growth: A Comparative Study*. Translated by Wu Qi and Wang Songbao. Shanghai: Joint Publishing Company, 1995.

Deng, Xiaoping. *Selected Works of Deng Xiaoping*. Beijing: People's Press.

Department of Trade and External Economic Relations Statistics, National Bureau of Statistics. "*The Leap-forward Development Realized by Opening to Outside World.*" Beijing: China Information News, August 22, 2012. http://www.stats.gov.cn/ztjc/ztfx/kxfzcjhh/201208/t20120821_72840.html.

Durlauf, Steven N., and Lawrence E. Blume, eds. *New Palgrave Dictionary of Economics*. Vol. 2. New York: Palgrave Macmillan, 2008.

Fei, John C.H., and Gustav Ranis. *Growth and Development from an Evolutionary Perspective*. Translated by Hong Yinxing and Zheng Jianghuai. Oxford: Basil Blackwell, 1997.

Friedman, Milton. *Free to Choose: A Personal Statement*. Translated by Hu Ji, Xi Xueyuan and An Qiang. Beijing: Commercial Press, 1982.

Hayami, Yujiro, and Vernon W. Ruttan. *Agricultural Development: An International Perspective*. Translated by Guo Xibao and Zhang Jinming. Beijing: China Social Sciences Press, 2000.

Hirschman, Albert O. *Strategy of Economic Development*. Translated by Cao Zhenghai and Pan Zhaodong. Beijing: Economic Science Press, 1991.

Hong, Yinxing. *The China Path to Economic Transition and Development*. Translated by Xiao-huang Yin. Berlin/New York/Singapore: Springer, 2016.

Hong, Yinxing. "The Comparative Advantage and the Competitive Advantage under Economic Globalization." *Economic Perspectives* no. 12 (2002): 6–10.

Hosseini, Hamid. "Uncertainty and Perceptual Problems Causing Government Failures in Underdeveloped Nations." *Comparative Economic and Social Systems* no. 2 (2004): 34–38.

Johnson, D. Gale. *Agricultural Issues in Economic Development*. Translated by Lin Yifu. Beijing: Commercial Press, 2004.

Knight, Frank H. *Risk, Uncertainty and Profit*. Translated by Wang Yu and Wang Wenyu. Beijing: Renmin University Press, 2005.

Kindleberger, Charles P. *Economic Development*. Translated by Zhang Xin. Shanghai: Shanghai Translation Press, 1986.

Kornai, János. *Economics of Shortage*. Vol. 2. Translated by Gao Hongye. Beijing: Economic Science Press, 1986.

Kuznets, Simon S. *Modern Economic Growth: Rate, Structure, and Spread*. Translated by Dai Rui and Yi Cheng. Beijing: Beijing College of Economics Press, 1989.

———. "Modern Economic Growth." In *Comparative Modernization*, edited by Cyril E. Black and translated by Yang Yu and Chen Zuzhou, 270–290. Shanghai: Shanghai Translation Press, 1996.

———. "Modern Economic Growth: Findings and Reflections." In *Selected Lectures of Nobel Prize Laureates in Economics, 1969–1981*, edited and translated by Wang Hongchang, 95–101. Beijing: China Social Sciences Press, 1986.

Lenin, Vladimir. *The Collected Works of Vladimir Lenin*. Vol.3. Translated by Central Compilation and Translation Bureau. Beijing: People's Press, 1985.

Lewis, William Arthur. *Growth and Fluctuations*. Translated by Liang Xiaomin. Beijing: Huaxia Press, 1987.

———. *Dual Economy*. Translated by Shi Wei. Beijing: Beijing College of Economics Press, 1989.

———. "The Slowing Down of the Engine of Growth." In *The Selected Papers on Modern Foreign Economics*, edited by Central Research Society for Foreign Economics. Vol. 8. Beijing: Commercial Press, 1997.

Liao, Li, Wang Ren and Chen Lu, eds. *Exploring the Journey of Wisdom: Interviews with Famous Economists from Harvard and MIT*. Beijing: Peking University Press, 2000.

Mankiw, Nicholas Gregory. *Principles of Economics*. Translated by Liao Xiaomin. Beijing: Joint Publishing Company, 1999.

Mao, Zedong. *Selected Works of Mao Zedong*. Vol. 5. Beijing: People's Press, 1977.

Marx, Karl. *A Contribution to the Critique of Political Economy: Introduction*. Beijing: Foreign Language Press, 1976.

———. *On Capital*. Translated by Central Compilation and Translation Bureau. Beijing: People's Press, 2004.

Marx, Karl and Friedrich Engels. *Collected Works of Karl Marx and Frederick Engels*. Vol. 46. Translated by Central Compilation and Translation Bureau. Beijing: People's Press, 1973.

Marx, Karl. *Karl Marx and Frederick Engels: Selected Works*. Vol. 2. Translated by Central Compilation and Translation Bureau. Beijing: People's Press, 1995.

———. *Collected Works of Marx and Engels*. Vol. 3. Translated by Central Compilation and Translation Bureau. Beijing: People's Press, 2012.

McKinnon, Ronald Ian. *Money and Capital in Economic Development*. Translated by Lu Cong. Shanghai: Joint Publishing Company, 1988.

———. *The Order of Economic Liberalization: Financial Control in the Transition to a Market Economy*. 2nd ed. Translated Zhou Tingyu. Shanghai: Joint Publishing House, 1997

Meier, Gerald M. and Joseph E. Stiglitz, eds. *Frontiers of Development Economics: The Future in Perspective*. Translated by An Anonymous Group. Beijing: China Financial and Economic Press, 2003.

Myles, Gareth D. *Public Economics*. Translated by Kuang Xiaoping. Beijing, China Renmin University Press, 2001.

Myrdal, Gunnar. *Economic Theory and Underdeveloped Regions*. London: Duckworth Publishers, 1957.

———. *Asian Drama: An Inquiry into the Poverty of Nations*. Translated by Tan Wenmu and Zhang Weidong. Beijing: Beijing College of Economics Press, 1992.

North, Douglass C. *Structure and Change in Economic History*. Translated by Chen Yu and Luo Haping. Shanghai: Shanghai People's Press, 1994.

Oman, Charles P. and Ganeshan Wignaraja. *Postwar Evolution of Development Thinking*. New York: Palgrave Macmillan, 1991.

Perroux, François. "The Concept of Growth Poles." In *Selected Classical Essays in Development Economics*. Edited by Guo Xibao. Beijing: China Economy Press, 1998.

Porter, Michael E. *Competitive Advantage of Nations*. Translated by Li Mingxuan and Qiu Rumei. Taipei: Commonwealth Publishing, 1996.

———. *On Competition*. Translated by Liu Ning, Gao Dengdi and Li Mingxuan. Beijing: Critic Press, 2003.

Roberts, Edward. "Venture Investment and Operation Mechanisms." In *Exploring the Journey of Wisdom: Interviews with Famous Economists from Harvard and MIT*, edited by Liao Li, Wang Ren and Chen Lu, 241–264. Beijing: Peking University Press, 2000.

Rogers, Everett M. and Rabel J. Burdge. *Social Change in Rural Societies*. Translated by Wang Xiaoyi and Wang Dining. Hangzhou: Zhejiang People's Press, 1988.

Rostow, Walt W. *The Stages of Economic Growth*. Translated by He Liping. Chengdu: Sichuan People's Press, 1988.

Samuelson, Paul. *Economics*. Translated by Gao Hongye. Beijing: Commercial Press, 1979.

Schiller, Robert J. *The New Financial Order: Risk in the 21st Century*. Translated by Guo Yan and Hu Bo. Beijing: Renmin University Press, 2004.

Schultz, Theodore W. *Transforming Traditional Agriculture*. Translated by Liang Xiaomin. Beijing: Commercial Press, 1987.

Shapiro, Carl, and Hal Varian. *Information Rules*. Translated by Zhang Fan. Beijing: Renmin University Press, 2000.

Schumpeter, Joseph. *The Theory of Economic Development*. Piscataway: Transaction Publishers, 1982.

Show, Edward S. *Financial Deepening in Economic Development*. Translated by Wang Wei, Mao Xiaowei and Mu Huaipeng. Beijing: China Social Sciences Press, 1989.

Solow, Robert. "Economic Growth." In *Exploring the Journey of Wisdom*, edited by Liao Li, Wang Ren and Chen Lu., 195–212. Beijing: Peking University Press, 2000.

Stiglitz, Joseph. *Whither Socialism?* Translated by Zhou Liqun, Han Liang and Yu Wenbo. Changchun: Jilin People's Press, 1998.

———. "The Blueprints for China's Third Generation of Reform." *The Economic Herald*, no. 5 (1999): 3–5.

———. "China: Forging a Third Generation of Reforms." In *Prospects of China*, edited by Hu Angang, 151–165. Hangzhou: Zhejiang People's Press, 2000.

Stretton, Hugh, and Lionel Orchard. *Public Goods, Public Business, and Public Options*. Translated by Fei Zhaohui. Beijing: Economic Science Press, 2000.

Thirlwall, Anthony P. *Growth and Development: With Special Reference to Developing Economies*. Translated by Jin Bei and Li Yang. Beijing: Renmin University Press, 1992.

Todaro, Michael P., and Stephen C. Smith. *Development Economics*. NJ: Pearson Education Inc., 2005.

World Commission on Environment and Development. *Our Common Future*. Translated by Wang Zhijia and Ke Jinliang. Changchun: Jilin People's Press, 1997.

Xi, Jinping, *Zhijiang Xinyu*. Hangzhou: Zhejiang People's Press, 2013a.

———. Speech at the Meeting of the Political Bureau of the Communist Party of China. *People's Daily*, July 29, 2013b.

———. *Speech at the Sixth Collective Study Session of the CPC Politburo*. Beijing: People's Daily, May 2013.

Yu, Zongxian. *The Revelation of the Development in Taiwan*. Taipei: Sanmin Book Co. Ltd., 1980.

Index